Sappho Goes to Law School

D1082495

BETWEEN MEN ~ BETWEEN WOMEN
Lesbian and Gay Studies
Lillian Faderman and Larry Gross, Editors

Nonfiction

Lesbian (Out)Law: Survival Under the Rule of Law
    (Firebrand, 1992)
Gay Men, Lesbians, and the Law (Chelsea House, 1996)

Fiction

Eye of a Hurricane (Firebrand, 1989)
Cecile (Firebrand, 1991)
Another Mother (St. Martin's, 1995)
A/K/A (St. Martin's, 1997)

Sappho Goes to Law School

FRAGMENTS IN LESBIAN LEGAL THEORY

Ruthann Robson

Columbia University Press

NEW YORK

Columbia University Press
New York   Chichester, West Sussex
Copyright © 1998 Ruthann Robson

Library of Congress Cataloging-in-Publication Data
Robson, Ruthann
    Sappho goes to law school: fragments in lesbian legal
theory / Ruthann Robson.
        p.   cm.
    Includes index.
    ISBN 0-231-10560-6 (cloth) —ISBN 0-231-10461-4
(pbk.)
    1. Feminits jurisprudence. 2. Lesbians—Legal status,
laws, etc. *. Title.
    K349.R63 1998
346.7301'3—dc21   97-52686

    CIP
Casebound editions of Columbia University Press books
are printed on permanent and durable acid-free paper.

Printed in the United States of America

c 10 9 8 7 6 5 4 3 2 1
p 10 9 8 7 6 5 4 3 2 1

Contents

Acknowledgments

My education in lesbianism, law, and theory, has been an ongoing process to which numerous people have contributed.

Many of these pieces have been presented as talks in a variety of fora, and I am grateful to the students and faculty who have invited me and have participated in discussions, especially at California Western University School of Law, John Marshall School of Law, Massey University (NZ/Aotearoa), Queen's University (Canada), Radcliffe/Harvard Colleges, State University of New York at Buffalo (SUNY) School of Law, Tulane Law School; University of British Columbia Faculty of Law (Canada), University of Chicago School of Law, University of Colorado School of Law, University of Connecticut School of Law, University of Oklahoma, University of Pennsylvania School of Law, University of Puget Sound Law School (now Seattle University School of Law), University of Melbourne (Australia), University of Southern California, University of Sydney (Australia), University of Toronto School of Law (Canada), University of Victoria Faculty of Law (Canada), Waikato University (NZ/Aotearoa), Washburn University, and Yale Law School.

I am also grateful to the organizers and participants at numerous conferences, especially American Association of Law Librarians Conference, Australiasia Law Teachers Conference, CLAGS conferences and colloquia, Constructing Change Conference, Critical Legal Studies Conferences, Feminism and Legal Theory Conferences at Columbia Law School, Lavender Law Conferences, LeGal: Lesbian and Gay Law Association of New York Conferences, Lesbian, Gay, Bisexual Studies Conferences,

Modern Language Assiociation Conferences; and National Women Studies' Association Conferences.

Earlier and substantially different versions of the some of these essays have appeared in the *Australian Feminist Law Journal*, *Flinders Journal of Law Reform*, *Hastings Law Journal*, *Journal of Law and Sexuality*, *New Zealand Yearbook of Jurisprudence*, *SIGNS*, *The St. Thomas Law Review*, the *Southern California Journal of Law and Women's Studies*, the *Texas Women's Law Journal*, the *University of Connecticut Law Review*, as well as in the following books, *Feminist Bibliography*, *Legal Inversions*, *Lesbian Erotics*, *Queerly Classed*, *A Queer World*.

I have had the privilege of engaging in many conversations about the subjects of this work with a wide range of people. These conversations have occurred at conferences, on e-mail, or over dinners, and a few have been in the context of formal if ephemeral reading groups, such as the postmodern project (1993), the Tompkins Square Queer Social Theory Group (1994–1995), or the informal reading group at the University of California, Berkeley. Further, many works by other writers have also constituted a kind of public conversation, which has been invaluable, and I have had the privilege of being able to continue some of these conversations in person. While I cannot include everyone who has been important, I must mention Penelope Andrews, Elvia Arriola, Jane Caputi, Claudia Card, Ruth Colker, Mary Dunlap, Jeffrey Escoffier, Joshua Gamson, Didi Herman, Sharon Hom, Joan Howarth, Karla Jay, Joyce McConnell, Vivien Ng, Lisa Orsaba, Dianne Otto, Nancy Polikoff, Julie Shapiro, Carl Stychin, Kellye Teste, and Margot Young.

Also vital have been numerous students at the City University of New York (CUNY) School of Law. Students who have enrolled in classes on feminist legal theory and sexuality and the law have taught me much, especially about ranges of sexualities. Working with students who have gone on to publish their own legal scholarship, including Margaret McIntyre and Colleen Sullivan, as well as Darren Rosenblum, has sharpened my own approaches.

I am especially indebted to the students who have worked as my research assistants, at times without any compensation and always without sufficient compensation, including Selene D'Alessio, William Flynn, Denise Holzka, Jana Jacobson, Charlie McCarron, Vickie Neilson, Lisa Sbrana, Maria Schopp, Larry Sharpe, Leslie Thrope, Julian Kahuna White, and Maria Willett. Thanks to them all.

Last, for their faith in this book as well as for their concrete and critical contributions, I am deeply appreciative to S. E. Valentine and Victoria Brownworth as well as to my editor, Ann Miller, and copy-editor, Susan Pensak, and to the anonymous reviewers for Columbia University Press.

Introduction: The Appeal of Sappho

If Sappho were alive today, she would be attending law school. Or so I sometimes think, especially at the beginning of a semester when I half-expect to see her walking into a classroom. She might be wearing flowing robes and have garlands of flowers in her hair, although I suspect she will be wearing jeans and a leather jacket. No matter. I assume I will recognize her. For how could I not?

There are some who think she would be in graduate school, in writing or literature or education. And perhaps she was, before she came to law school. But given today's market for lyric poets and teachers she is probably drawn to a career in law, which despite the downsizing of corporate law firms still has room for public interest attorneys. Sitting on a rock, surrounded by spring flowers, Sappho may have reasoned that a legal education would allow her to do some social good and thus decided in favor of law school. Despite her aristocratic background, I imagine that Sappho would be very interested in impoverished communities and social justice. And surely her experiences on Lesbos would make her interested in postcolonial jurisprudence. Undoubtedly, she would enroll in a feminist legal theory course, for she has always been concerned about the legal status of women, having endured such discrimination herself throughout the centuries. She might also be interested in the rumblings she hears about queer legal theory and lesbian jurisprudence and sexual orientation and the law, for she would know she is a lesbian.

Like other fantasies of Sappho, this one is partial and personal, but perhaps no more than most. As all recent Sappho scholars have agreed, our knowledge of Sappho is largely fantastical. The surviving Sapphic lyrics are fragmentary, save one, and preserved through quotation in other sources or in an ancient refuse pile. Moreover, the fragments themselves are heavily interpreted, being not only fragments but composed in a language sufficiently ancient to eschew punctuation or breaks between words. And even if we had access to accurate fragments, the nature of poetry is such that it is always naive to assume an unproblematic relation between the poem and the poet.[1]

Nevertheless, a notion persists linking lesbian sexuality and Sappho, the very term *lesbian* having been derived from the isle of Lesbos, home of Sappho. This notion rests, in part, upon surviving fragments as well as upon the statements of ancient commentators. In our own time it is generally agreed that to call Sappho a "lesbian" is anachronistic, a rather interesting irony given the derivation of the word. Historically, Sappho's reputed sexuality has been variously accepted, condemned, denied, and reclaimed, but the very persistence of the linkage between Sappho and what we understand as lesbianism for more than two and a half millennia—accepting the dating of Sappho in 600 B.C.—seems phenomenal.

Contemporary reconstructions of Sappho emphasize her one extant poem, "Hymn to Aphrodite," as well as the fragments of various songs, and extoll her reputation as the "tenth muse" of Greek arts.[2] It is generally agreed that she was from an aristocratic family on Lesbos, an island closer to Turkey than to Greece, and may have abandoned the island during a period of political turmoil. For most of her adult life on the island, however, she is believed to have run a school for girls, who may have been more important to her than her "family." Some of her surviving pieces name a daughter, although there is controversy whether the term *daughter* is being used metaphorically or not. The legend that Sappho threw herself from the White Rocks of Leukas out of unrequited love for a man named Phaon is generally discredited, as is her reputation, largely Roman, as an ugly courtesan.[3]

Despite the attempts at fact, Sappho remains nothing short of an enigma. Monique Wittig and Sande Zweig, in their book *Lesbian Peoples: Material for a Dictionary*,[4] supply an entry for Sappho that is an empty page. The blankness is provocative, for the space is a rebuke to anything we think we know about Sappho. Yet it is also an invitation, for there is an entry, after all—a page entitled Sappho—although there is not a page entitled "Socrates" or "Plato."

Arguably, Socrates and Plato would feel welcome in contemporary

United States law schools, which pride themselves, probably erroneously, in employing the "Socratic method" of teaching. Sappho reputedly taught in the context of *thiasoi*, dedicated to the muses and artistic pursuits and a rival institution to Plato's more intellectual academy. Invoking Sappho rather than Socrates in the context of legal theorizing requires wondering about a legal pedagogy and theorizing that prided itself on a Sapphic rather than Socratic methodology. How could that change the ways in which we understand, practice, and apply law? What if we adopted the Sapphic lyric as a mode of communication and understanding rather than Socratic argumentation?

Invoking Sappho as a law student also requires some attention to the concrete, if mythical, Sappho. What if she did choose to attend law school? This Sappho is perhaps a woman of color or perhaps not. She is perhaps bisexual or perhaps not. She is perhaps a mother or perhaps not. Perhaps a prostitute or perhaps not. She calls herself a lesbian. Or perhaps not.

The existence of lesbian legal theory is as problematic as Sappho. The essays that follow are explorations of some of those problems. Some consider the complexities of lesbian identity itself and others consider the ways in which legal doctrines and theories posit lesbianism, often to the detriment of persons who call themselves lesbians. These essays also attempt to unravel the relationships between feminism, postmodernism, and lesbianism in terms of legal theorizing. Several essays also analyze the constructs of family and relationships in lesbian legal contexts, especially as enforced by state power. Finally, interwoven throughout the essays are many of my own experiences as a dyke law professor at a progressive law school.

Whatever the topic, however, the essays each have as their purpose the development of a lesbian legal theory that would welcome any Sappho who might choose to enter the legal arena as the historical Sappho is said to have entered sacred women's spaces on Lesbos. I believe we have a responsibility to make the world of law an inviting one to Sappho, whoever she might be. Moreover, if Sappho does not choose to attend law school, the responsibility is even greater, for the task is then to ensure that the law protects and nourishes Sappho rather than silencing, distorting, and appropriating her talents.

Sappho Goes to Law School

I

The Specter of a Lesbian Supreme Court Justice:

Problems of Identity

"To start with, we need a lesbian on the Supreme Court."

It was the last summer of the Reagan-Bush regime, although the demise of that era was far from certain. I was being interviewed by a gay and lesbian magazine for a feature article about the Supreme Court. I was staying in Provincetown, a place renowned for its lesbian/gay culture, surrounded by lesbians of every ilk. While lesbians appear in periodicals, on the streets, and in legal theories, not one lesbian has appeared as a United States Supreme Court Justice, ever. So, when the interviewer asked me a general question about changing the United States Supreme Court, I replied that we should start with the appointment of a lesbian.

My proposal, glib as a Provincetown summer, implies that lesbianism would be a relevant quality of a United States Supreme Court Justice. More explicitly, it presupposes that a lesbian United States Supreme Court Justice would, by virtue of her lesbianism, possess certain judicial philosophies and political positions. For example, she would not be a strict constructionist who relied upon the original framers of the Constitution as her touchstones. As a lesbian, she would be aware that none of the original framers were lesbians, or even women; she would not be bound by worldviews that excluded her and her lovers. Further, as a lesbian she would believe that *Bowers v. Hardwick* was wrongly decided, since she would believe her own sexuality deserved constitutional protection. Also as a lesbian, although perhaps more tenuously related, she would uphold privacy doctrine generally, including abortion rights for all women; she would give an expansive reading to the equal protection clause of the fourteenth amendment, not only to include lesbians as lesbians, but to include all lesbians, even if the categories at issue were racial, religious, bodily, gendered, sexual, or cultural; she would declare capital punishment unconstitutional under the eighth amendment; she would resurrect the rights of criminal defendants; she would understand the importance of free speech, but it would not be her shibboleth in this nation of disparate access to speech. Given the current composition of the United States Supreme Court, she would be writing an excessive number of dissenting opinions.

All of the presumptions informing my wish for a lesbian on the high court raise an issue that has troubled lesbian and political theory, the issue of identity politics. Any invocation of identity, political or otherwise, provokes postmodernist apprehension, an apprehension that has been particularly potent with respect to sexual identities. As a sexual identity, lesbian identity evokes other postmodernist-influenced issues. Particularly problematic are lesbian identity's imperceptibility until claimed or avowed and lesbian identity's uncertain classification as an identity status or a sexual act. Thus it has become increasingly necessary to interrogate the predicaments posed by identity politics, including postmodernist questionings of identity and the identity/activity dichotomy. Nevertheless, I continue to believe in the desirability of a lesbian Supreme Court Justice.

Identity Politics?

My suggestion that a lesbian should serve as a Justice on the United States Supreme Court seems to rest on the discredited foundation of identity politics. Identity politics posits a relationship between one's identity, in this case, identity as a lesbian, and one's politics, in this case progressive politics. The underlying assumption of identity politics is that given a social structure that is cognizant of group identities (such as sexuality, gender, and race), one's identities will shape one's experiences, which in turn will influence one's thinking, including one's politics. This, in and of itself, seems hardly arguable, unless one wants to argue that experience and thought are totally disconnected. Much more arguable is the more insidious assumption that identities and politics are consistently related in a particular pattern; the conventional configuration is that one's experience of oppression produces an emancipatory politic. Applied to lesbianism as an identity, this would mean that every lesbian, because she has experienced oppression on the basis of her sexuality, holds political positions that oppose other forms of oppression against other disempowered identities she may or may not possess based upon identity categories such as race, ethnicity, religion, class, age, and disability. In a universe of perfected identity politics, there are no racist lesbians, no ageist women, no anti-Semitic African Americans, no disabled homophobes.

Identity politics has preoccupied much of recent progressive theory, but it occupies a privileged position in the development of contemporary lesbian theory. For example, as articulated in the early 1970s by the Furies, an influential lesbian-feminist collective, "Lesbians, as outcasts from every culture but their own have the most to gain by ending class, race, and national supremacy within their own ranks."[1] Lesbian poet and theorist Adrienne Rich similarly notes that as a "lesbian/feminist" any passive subservience to the order of men that has profited from slavery and imperialism, as well as enforced heterosexuality and misogyny, is against her own self-interest.[2] As expressed by lesbian historian Lillian Faderman, the 1970s desire for "Lesbian Nation" produced communities with "various dogmas" regarding "class, race, food, and ecology consciousness" and "political activity," which "were not unlike those of the hippie counterculture and New Left, but filtered always through a radical feminist awareness."[3] Lesbian attention to political issues other than lesbianism persists: the "struggle to take each other's cultures and systems of oppression seriously" continues.[4]

Yet even among its most fervent lesbian adherents identity politics prevails as a normative theory rather than a descriptive one. The statements by the Furies collective that lesbians have much to gain by resisting oppression and by Adrienne Rich that lesbians act against their own self-interest by accepting oppression are admonitions, not summaries of inherent or universal lesbian traits. Faderman's use of *dogma* to describe such political positions is used in the context of a discussion of *political correctness*, a term that has received subsequent widespread usage outside of the lesbian communities of the 1970s. The possibility of being politically incorrect for some violation of the code recognizes that a correspondence between sexuality and politics is neither imperative nor absolute. Any conflation of sexual and political identities conflicts with a premise at least as powerful as identity politics—the premise that lesbian existence is a quasi-universal phenomenon. Slogans such as "A Lesbian Republican Is an Oxymoron" compete with "We Are Everywhere" on T-shirts and buttons as well as in discourse. One can exist as a lesbian without possessing lesbian politics.

Thus, identity politics posits a series of expectations and aspirations rather than a claim to experiential reality; otherwise a criticism of any lesbian as politically incorrect for failing to satisfy standards of lesbian politics would be meaningless. The aspiration that is identity politics recognizes an ability to analogize between various identities.

When analogizing is not required, however, identity politics reveals its most powerful expectation, perhaps approaching a claim to reality. It would be reasonable to assume that when one's own identity is implicated one's politics will lean toward the emancipatory rather than the oppressive. Such a position, however, neglects both the struggles to define what is emancipatory and the effects of internalized oppression.

This most powerful aspect of identity politics, among others, was raised in the context of Clarence Thomas's nomination as Supreme Court Justice. Those of us who believed that an African American should be nominated to the Supreme Court upon the retirement of the Court's first African American, the civil rights champion Thurgood Marshall, did so because of a belief based upon Marshall's example: a justice with knowledge of racism would work to eradicate it. Clarence Thomas, an African American, nominated and confirmed as justice, described his own racially shaped experiences but did not demonstrate any commitment to the eradication of racism. Instead, his racial identity insulated him from investigation into his lack of commitment to eradicate racism.[5] His deployment of racist stereotypes—notably in his portrayal of his sister as a "welfare queen,"— was obscured. Clarence Thomas demonstrates that race as identity and race as politic are distinct. As African American theorist Cornel West expresses it, "Blackness is an ethical construct."[6]

The disjuncture between identity and politic is also evident in the lesbian context. In fact, Anne-Imelda Radice, former chair of the National Endowment for the Arts (NEA), was characterized as "the lesbian Clarence Thomas."[7] President Bush appointed Radice to replace John Frohnmayer, under whom the NEA had been mired in controversies surrounding the funding of lesbian and gay artistic and literary projects. Conservative Senator Jesse Helms successfully orchestrated a law forbidding arts grants to be used to "promote, disseminate or produce" art that included depictions of "homoeroticism" or was "obscene."[8] Congress subsequently amended this provision to provide that artistic excellence and merit are to be judged "taking into consideration the general standards of decency" and that "obscenity is without artistic merit, is not protected speech, and shall not be funded."[9] Radice, aptly described as "a lesbian even Bush and Helms could love," explicitly stated that under her leadership the NEA would continue to examine the sexual content of arts projects and that she would veto funding for any projects with "difficult subject matter" or "sexually explicit matter," phrases that are generally understood to pertain to lesbian and gay art and literature.[10] In the realm of political appointments Radice's sexuality is atypical, although perhaps not arbitrary.[11] In the realm of identity politics Radice is anomalous; a lesbian who not only does not share the progressive politics but also is hostile to lesbian sexuality.

A "lesbian even Bush and Helms could love" effectively falsifies any claim to universal truth that identity politics might assert. *Lesbian* cannot unfailingly operate as shorthand for a certain set of political positions. Identity politics, recognized as normative rather than descriptive, allows for the possibility of a lesbian Supreme Court Justice being antilesbian. This is the specter that any proposal for a lesbian Supreme Court Justice must contemplate.

Postmodernism as Postlesbianism

Not only is identity politics subject to dispute on the grounds that there is no necessary connection between one's identity and one's politics, it is also subject to a more devastating critique of the notion of identity itself. The critique of identity is largely derived from postmodernist critiques of subjectivity, positing the "death of the subject." As articulated by Fredric Jameson, one of the most respected American proponents and scholars of postmodernism, this position entails the notion that "individualism and personal identity is a thing of the past; that the old individual or individualist subject is 'dead'; and that one might even describe the concept of the unique individual and the theoretical basis of individualism as ideological."[12] From a postmodernist perspective any appeal to individual authenticity or even freedom is suspect.

This allows a postmodernist heterosexual male law professor to criticize a postmodernist lesbian law professor for not being sufficiently postmodern because of her views based upon the authenticity of her own experience. As a self-described "white male, heterosexual, forty year old academic of working class background," he can critique Patricia Cain's article "Feminist Jurisprudence: Grounding the Theories," in which Cain argues that postmodernism holds the most promise for feminist theory, because Cain's use of the "authentic self" is a "subtheme that runs strongly through the essay that compromises her commitment to postmodernism" and her sketch of freedom "is not postmodern in character or ambition."[13] His critique tellingly illustrates the failing of Cain's "modernist mentality": "She goes so far as to say that 'male homosexuality is a practice that contradicts the assumption of universal heterosexuality, but affirms male-centered reality.' Yet this surely denies the lived experience of many gay men. In a world of almost compulsory heterosexuality, their reality is equally marginal and invisible."[14] In this view postmodernism perfected renders the experiences of gay men and lesbians "equally marginal and invisible." I would suggest that only the most arrogant gay men would affirm that their own reality of marginality and invisibility is equal to the reality of lesbians in our world of gendered power. Any claim to "authenticity" or even "self" is suspect—especially, it seems to me, if it would disrupt accustomed power relations.

Postmodernist critiques of identity also argue that even assuming there is an individual subject any identities that inhere in individual subjects are the result of historically specific and contingent discourses of power. The work of Michel Foucault is considered an extended argument of this position. In his influential *History of Sexuality* Foucault argued that the *homosexual* was an invention of nineteenth-century medico-juridical discourses,[15] an argument that has gained ascendancy and is presently the legitimate version of identity. Foucault, himself a gay man, rejected the notion of sexual identity,[16] despite his involvement with gay liberation in America as well as France during the last years of his life.[17]

Sexuality has been fertile ground for the postmodernist contestation of the coherence of identity categories, in part because lesbian and gay theorizing has been profoundly influenced by all aspects of postmodernism. Such contestations can be rather grandiose. For example, lesbian theorist Judith Butler argues that the incoherency of sexual categories like lesbian are precisely their appeal. She states that she is "skeptical about how the 'I' is determined as it operates under the lesbian sign" and argues that identity categories such as lesbianism are "sites of necessary trouble":

> In fact, if the category were to offer no trouble, it would cease to be interesting to me: it is precisely the pleasure produced by the instability of these categories that make me a candidate for the category to begin with. To install myself within the terms of an identity category would be to turn against the sexuality that the category purports to describe.[18]

This is a rejection not only of any (pre)determined connections between lesbian identity and politics but also of any determinable connections between lesbian identity and anything else, except instability. Any sexuality that might be named *lesbian* is precisely too unstable to be named anything at all.

Postmodernism relegates lesbianism to a precarious position: postmodernism entails postlesbianism. The postmodernist instability of lesbian identity (as well the instability of gendered identity) makes possible a lesbian who has sexual relationships with men, or even a "lesbian man." Such postmodernist possibilities "make lesbianism, at least as we have known it, impossible."[19] A definition of lesbian as a woman who gives her erotic and affectional attention to other women rests on a gendered axis, an axis that postmodernists also dispute.[20] Yet lesbians also dispute the gendered axis, albeit with a result different from the dissolution of lesbianism. Perhaps the most famous among these is Monique Wittig, one of the first theorists who devastatingly deconstructed and antiessentialized gender. For Wittig, *woman* exists only in terms of men, only in terms of "heterosexual systems of thought and heterosexual economic systems," which leads Wittig to her famous pronouncement that "Lesbians are not women."[21] However, Wittig has been accused of being a "lesbian modernist," because she posits homosexuality (specifically lesbianism) as outside the "heterosexual matrix" and as a "purification," and thus as a unification of lesbianism.[22] Lesbian separatist and ethicist Sarah Lucia Hoagland, who has probably never been labeled a postmodernist, also contends that "woman" is a normative category to regulate female behavior and the "category 'woman' is not a reflection of fact but tells us how to determine fact."[23]

In addition to interrogating gender, lesbians have also interrogated the meaning of the erotic, the affectional, and sex relational categories that apply to lesbian interaction, albeit again resisting the conclusion that such relations are unstable and impossible.[24] As I, among others, have argued elsewhere, the cessation of the category lesbian is a grave potential danger. Yet the impossibility of lesbianism is precisely the goal of postmodernist philosophers; a goal that reverberates in common conversations in this postmodern era in which people eschew labels that might be applicable to their sexuality. Lesbianism, of course, is not uniquely impossible. All sexual identities, as well as gender and racial ones, are ultimately impossible. Within postmodernism's ambit even the identity of postmodernist is objectionable.

Repudiation of identity categories within legal theory has generally been more circumspect. In a pertinent, if obverse, example postmodernist theorist Jennifer Wicke argues that [lesbian and] gay advocates should be supported in any quest to extend marital rights to intimate relationships:

Marriage can be subjected to a withering critique as a transparently ideological institution, but in this case too the importance of reserving a vocabulary of 'rights' as a legal subject transcends those objections since the political objectives of securing [lesbian and] gay marriage outweigh any hesitance about the identities presupposed by the marriage.[25]

While I will discuss the issue of same-sex marriage more fully later,[26] for the moment I want to focus on the reply of Mary Joe Frug, the late postmodernist feminist legal theorist, who argued that it is precisely the law's preoccupation with enforcing identity that produces the injustice:

> Law requires all legal claimants to assume a particular posture—a partial identity—in seeking judicial assistance; we must leave aside much of the multiplicity and complexity of our lives to engage in legal discourse. Injustice occurs, as in the . . . [lesbian and] gay marriage campaign, when legal rules structure these particular postures in such a way that subordinate groups cannot squeeze into them at all. In these situations, legal rules need to expand the narrow and rigid character of the subject position they impose as a condition of admission to the legal arena.[27]

Thus, although disagreeing, neither Wicke nor Frug promote the abandonment of identity categories, apparently judging such categories necessary for social change. Interestingly, however, both conclude that conditions of the subordinate identity category—lesbians and gay men—would be improved by participation in an arrangement definitive of the dominant category—the heterosexual right to marry—a debatable assumption.

Claiming and Disclaiming Lesbian Identity

Much of the postmodernist impulse to transcend identity categories is certainly an understandable one, even as it arguably reestablishes the unique individual (a person beyond all labels) that postmodernism also rejects. This impulse approaches irresistibility in the context of sexual identity categories because these categories must be claimed explicitly.[28] Lesbian identity is generally not transmitted through cues from one's parents, as are cultural, religious, and gender identities, but is instead claimed in the coming-out process, often in direct contradiction to normative expectations.

Coming out is often thought to be a cornerstone of lesbian experience and theory. Its structure is a collective and individual narrative of identity, and, as later discussed, lesbian narrativity is paradoxical.[29] Although arguably identities are accessible only as narrative, the coming-out narrative is endemic to lesbian narratives. Despite individual variations, coming out is generally considered as a process through the stages of self-labeling, a communication of feelings or identity to others, a location and participation in a community, an integration of sexuality into the self, and possibly the proclamation of identity to friends, parents, children, employers, and the world at large. This narrative is constructed as an emancipatory (and implicitly irreversible) trajectory involving the recognition and claiming of one's authentic identity. Within the confines of such a narrative, not coming out—remaining "in the closet"—is an inauthentic, negative, and generally disparaged state. Not surprisingly, this narrative has been rightly criticized as simplistic.

Yet the rhetoric of coming out and closets has remained vital in lesbian/gay theory, even as it has proliferated beyond references to lesbian and gay identity so that now conservatives are only one of a number of groups that come out. However, one reason for the authority of the notion of claiming lesbian identity is the often dramatic consequences attendant to such a claiming. The claim can sunder previous relationships between the claimant and her family, friends, employer, and others in her social and professional circles. For example, a claim that one is a lesbian can mean a loss of employment, a loss that the law rarely deems actionable employment discrimination. Another reason for the continued vitality of claiming is the imperceptibility of lesbianism, given a combination of heterosexism, which presumes universal heterosexuality, and sexism, which assumes (at least some) women are asexual.

Claiming lesbian identity (or coming out) implies a volitional act, an implication that is not universal. Lesbian literature is replete with positive journeys toward lesbian identity but also contains instances in which lesbianism is initially exposed rather than confessed. There are centuries of accusations of lesbianism, accusations that often merit legal sanctions including death, banishment, or prison, as well as contemporary cases in which lesbianism is an issue. The outing controversies, prompted by the revelation of one's lesbian or gay status often by members of lesbian/gay communities for political purposes, is but the latest complicated development in the history of involuntary disclosures of one's sexuality caused by the necessities of claiming lesbian/gay identities.

The complications surrounding claiming and disclaiming lesbian identity have gained national prominence, foreshadowing the specter of a lesbian Supreme Court Justice. Despite the fact that, when elected, President Bill Clinton promised to appoint a diverse cabinet, any possibility that lesbian identity might figure among the diversities remained ultimately unrealized, although Roberta Achtenburg, former director of the National Center for Lesbian Rights and well-known figure in San Francisco politics, was finally appointed to a less-than-cabinet-level position. For the most part, however, it became important that any woman who might potentially be claimed within a lesbian identity category disclaim any lesbian identity.

For example, intimations of lesbianism attached to both Donna Shalala, Clinton's successful nominee for secretary of the Department of Health and Human Services, and Janet Reno, Clinton's third (and successful) nominee for attorney general. Donna Shalala's disclaimer of lesbianism occurred in an article in a local newspaper and was thereafter widely reported.[30] The particular quote attributed to Shalala is, "Have I ever lived an alternative lifestyle? The answer is no." The article portrays the rumors of lesbianism as being generated by "gay groups" who have subjected others "to this sort of attack." The article also concludes that "feeding the rumor was the fact that Shalala, at fifty-one, is one of the few high-profile, single women her age in town."[31] Being unmarried as a condition that necessitates a disclaimer of lesbianism also occurs in Janet Reno's case, although Reno handled it a bit differently by explicitly stating that she is "attracted to strong, brave, rational and intelligent men."[32] Shalala's singlehood as rumor nourishing and Reno's use of heterosexual interest to disclaim lesbian identity occurs in a legal context that equates an absence of heterosexual activity with lesbian identity.

Importantly, however, neither candidate relied upon any postmodernist incoherency of the category of lesbianism; one cannot imagine Shalala or Reno stating that "to install myself within the terms of an identity category would be to turn against the sexuality that the category purports to describe."[33]

Even more important, neither candidate proffered a statement that her sexual orientation might be irrelevant to the task at hand. As one commentator expressed it, supporters of Reno wanted to be "reassured that there aren't any culturally unacceptable hair-raisers of the Dykes-on-Bikes variety in her background."[34] A more delicate issue implicates the disclaimer itself: "Sources close to the investigation [of Shalala] insist the FBI check isn't a 'lesbian witch hunt,' but instead the FBI is trying to determine whether or not the HHS secretary-designate has lied about her sexual orientation."[35] This is the classic catch-22 that contaminates claiming and disclaiming lesbian identity: a claim of lesbian identity causes one to be discriminated against as a lesbian; a disclaimer of lesbian identity causes one to be discredited as a liar.

Problems of Essentializing and Analogizing Identities

The fact that lesbian identity is an identity that must be claimed implicates the problems of essentializing and analogizing lesbian identities. Within identity theories essentialism and (social) constructionism compete for explanatory primacy. Essentialism generally theorizes from the place of "biological force" while the oppositional theory of constructionism, or social constructionism, generally theorizes from the place of culturally defined constructs and labels. Reductively expressed, the conflict is one between nature and nurture. Despite accurate observations that the essentialism/constructionism dichotomy has outlived its usefulness, the dichotomy refuses retirement. Within lesbian and gay theorizing, however, social constructionism continues to be preeminent. Previous theories, such as lesbian-feminist theories of the 1970s, are often disparaged as essentialist, essentialism having become more of an insult than a viable competing theory.

This competition between essentialism and social constructionism is not limited to lesbian theoretical texts. In scientific discourse the preoccupation with an etiology for lesbianism is expressed as a contest between biological explanations and psychological ones. While lesbianism was once generally believed to be less biological and more psychological, a widely reported empirical study posits the likelihood of a lesbian "gene."[36] This well-publicized scientific debate, which reached the covers of national magazines,[37] informs and is informed by the political/legal debate, in which the contest usually devolves into a distinction between status and conduct. This has been most pronounced in the military context.

As is apparent in any of the arguments concerning discrimination, including military employment, the importance of deeming lesbianism as a status, preferably with biological roots, is derived from the primacy of analogizing identities. Racial and ethnic identities are arguably protected identities, based in part upon constitutional theories of equal protection derived from the Fourteenth Amendment, which provides that no state shall deny any person "equal protection of the laws." The contemporary interpretation of "equal protection" owes a great deal to a rather prosaic 1938 case decided by the United States Supreme Court, *United States v. Carolene Products*, which involved the interstate shipment of milk.

Footnote 4 of the Court's opinion—called by some the most famous foot-note in constitutional law—intimated that a "more searching judicial inquiry" might apply to statutes directed at "discrete and insular minori-ties," such as "religious or national or racial minorities." To be within what many call the "promise" of *Carolene Products*'s footnote 4, a discrete and insular minority must be a social minority that has been historically dis-criminated against and continues to be relatively politically powerless, the members of which possess immutable and identifiable characteristics. Thus, efforts at theorizing equal protection for lesbian and other sexual identities often focus on analyzing these *Carolene*-derived criteria, often attempting to argue lesbian identity within the criteria and often prob-lematizing the immutability requirement. Essentializing lesbian identity as immutable, fixed, and biologically determined results in the most tradi-tional compliance with the *Carolene*-derived criteria, yet such an essential-ism is inconsistent with much of current lesbian theorizing.

Analogizing is also problematic for lesbian identity within the context of the *Carolene*-derived criteria. Within equal protection discourse, the history of equal protection as intentionally and paradigmatically directed at racial identity results in lesbian identity being most often analogized to racial (or ethnic) identities. Arguments that lesbian identity is socially con-structed (rather than essential), attributable to psychology (rather than biology), and an activity (rather than a status) supposedly taint the analogy. Such a distinction obscures the extent to which all identities combine ele-ments of essentialism, including primordial ascription (what a person really "is"), and social constructionism, including optional affiliation (what one "chooses").[38] As critical race theorists have noted, race itself is a soci-etal construct.

Yet analogizing is not merely faulty because racial identity is likewise constructed. The positing of African American racial identity as the para-digm with which lesbianism must comport is rather pitiful, given the per-sistent political, legal, and societal discrimination against African Americans and other racial minorities. Thus, even a perfectly fitting anal-ogy would be imperfect because race is not a perfect paradigm given an emancipatory goal. Further, the act of analogizing racial and sexual iden-tities obscures the extent to which the identities overlap. All persons hav-ing racial identities have sexual ones as well, and vice versa; or, more specifically, there are many African American lesbians.

Moreover, paradigms of protectable identities are not limited to racial and ethnic identities. Religious identities are dissimilar to any racial/ethnic paradigm in many of the same ways in which sexual identities are dissimilar, especially in cases in which the religious identity is adopted in an adult conversion process. Thus lesbian identity might be more impeccably analogized to a born-again Christian identity, a protected identity.

Ultimately, however, the vitality of lesbian identity cannot rest upon its assimiability to another protected identity, whether based upon essentialism or constructionism. As previously argued, the analogues are hardly aspirational and the analogies are always analogies rather than duplicates. Further, what is essentialized is susceptible to alteration; what is constructed can be deconstructed.

Weight/lessness and Futuristic Fantasies

There is a weight and weightlessness to lesbian identities.

One type of weight is based in history. As Jacquelyn Zita argues, there is a "lacuna in postmodernist ontology and a failure to recognize the individual's real powerlessness" against "the historical gravity of a culturally constructed" body that "stubbornly returns with a weight that defies the promises of postmodernist fantasy and its idealistic denial."[39] The "weight" of lesbianism is as a historically disparaged and prosecuted identity, an identity that can serve as a punitive legal referent even when the individual denies its applicability. Even among those who argue that lesbian identity must be negotiable, the history of persecution and violence against lesbians requires that we live our lives "under a cloud of prior interpretation."[40]

Another type of weight is based in perception and process, more phenomenological than a claim to foundational reality. Lesbian identity is something I have known, have felt, have recognized across a room and across years. It is the river lesbian theorist and poet Gloria Anzaldúa utilizes to describe identities: changing, yet perceptible, flowing.[41]

Yet another type of weight is based in community. Although I do not posit lesbian identity as primarily forged in community, I do think there has been an intellectual confluence of discovery and creation of lesbian identities. This weight of our contemporary identities is subject to continuing scrutinizing: "At this point in the history of lesbian studies, it may be useful to step back from our 'cumulative discoveries' and examine them as our 'collective constructions.' "[42] There is also the weight of lesbian bodies, bodies in relation, in desire and sex. As French lesbian theorist Michelle Causse describes it, lesbianism, "a *face a face* between two lesbians . . .

between two subjects who are constantly inventing themselves outside of any referent," is a relation, a praxis.[43]

Paradoxically, perhaps, there is also a type of weightlessness to lesbian identities. Lesbianism is most present as an absence. The term *lesbian* itself is what lesbian theorist Marilyn Frye describes as a "quadrifold evasion" because of its fourfold referential framework: Lesbian as an inhabitant of the island of Lesbos, which in turn is a reference to the poet Sappho who is said to have lived there, which in turn is a reference to the fragments of her poetry that have survived, which in turn is a reference to the kind of person who might write such words.[44] And, further, there may be a kind of weightlessness to lesbianism as a claiming of space. As lesbian theorist Sue-Ellen Case writes, in our fast-approaching cyberworld, lesbianism is akin to a space and a "call to commitment to collectivization and dialogue from within a claimed space."[45]

It is against this weight/lessness that a lesbian Supreme Court Justice becomes a worthwhile suggestion. A lesbian Supreme Court Justice remains rather unimaginable. A Justice weighted with the history of lesbianism, with lesbian perception and process, with lesbian community, with lesbian desire; it is barely imaginable. A Justice existing in contradiction to the weightlessness of lesbianism, its imperceptibility; its unimaginability is precisely its attraction.

Yet the desire for a lesbian Supreme Court Justice also exhibits a startling lack of imagination. This lack inheres in the problem of identity and identity politics, embodied by a Supreme Court Justice who might not only be conservative but also be strategically used. But this lack of imagination also inheres in the identities—socially constructed—of those of us who are imagining. It is this construction that makes it difficult for us to imagine the most radical changes, changes that are not merely inserting lesbian interests into the existing structure.

Imaginings that do not take for granted a Supreme Court, or even a constitutional system, or even the "rule of law"—these are the imaginings that are the real challenge of lesbian legal theory.

2

Incendiary Categories: Lesbian/Violence/Law

Sl/ashes

Violence mediates all relationships between lesbians and law.

Yet when I am invited to talk or write about violence and lesbians and law, I am expected to produce ampersands and not slashes—I should provide sparks and not charred remains. I am invited as lesbian evidence toward the credentialing of a conference or collection as inclusive. I am invited to provide the "new" perspective, to speak about violence *among* women and how the law can (better) address this problem.

This inclusion disturbs. The paradigm of violence against women is a feminist conception of men's dominance over women, a dominance often enforced with overt violence and always enforced with subtle promises of violence. For some, violence among lesbians is merely an instance of lesbians appropriating male values. For others violence among lesbians produces a certain equal-opportunity violence. For most it seems that after the lesbian interlude the agenda can return to the "real" problem of violence against (heterosexual) women.

I do not mean to imply that the concern about the violence many men display toward many women is a small concern. It is not. Further, lesbians are not immune to the violence some men routinely exhibit in intimate situations toward women simply because we often inhabit a private realm without men. First, for many of us—especially those of us who are younger or impoverished—inhabiting a realm without violent men is impossible. Second, even if we can afford such a privatized realm, we experience male violence in public places like streets or workplaces.

Nevertheless, I think a focus on individualized and privatized violence is insufficient. The deficiency is especially apparent when our attention turns toward legal solutions for addressing violence between individuals. While we can propose legislation and fine-tune judicial responses and then react to the effects we may not have intended (such as mandatory arrest provisions in domestic violence statutes having a disproportionate effect in communities of color), I here want to engage with a different problem: the legal regime's own expressions of violence toward lesbianism. That the law is violent toward lesbianism cannot be seriously disputed: the law criminalizes our sexual activities, excludes us from what it considers to be important, and denies us protections.

But the law's violence toward lesbianism is only part of the picture. I do not wish to posit lesbians as victims of the violence of laws or men. Instead, I want to claim violence as an attribute of lesbianism. This claim is not based on incidences of violence between lesbians but on the existence of lesbianism as a violent denial to the law's system of heterosexual and male hegemony. To posit an identification between lesbianism and violence implies that lesbianism is bad (since violence is negative), as well as threatening the coherence of the term *violence*. But perhaps we can (re)interpret violence as fire.

Fire

Like violence, fire can be both good and bad, helpful or harmful. One's body remembers fire that has warmed and flushed the skin as well as fire that has burnt and curled the flesh. Fire is an image that recurs in lesbian theory and poetics, a metaphor to describe a lesbian as a "woman ablaze who is reborn from the essential of what she knows she is."[1] Fire is also an essential element that occurs in lesbian mythology, a connection between current colloquialisms and ancient rites. For example, lesbian writer and mythicist Judy Grahn connects the slang term *frig* (to rub a woman's genitals with the fingers) with the Latin term *fricatrice*, meaning "she who rubs" in the sense of friction and firemaking: "The ancient belief was that fire resided in the wood, coming out when the wood was rubbed in a particular manner and that creative/sexual fire resided in the female pudenda, also coming out when it was rubbed a certain way."[2] Grahn also connects the British slang term for a lesbian, *wick*, with the candles used in witchcraft ceremonies and voodoo rituals: "The wick, that part of a candle or lamp from which fire can be brought forth is . . . the very essence of the female sexual-creative force."[3] Fire is prominent in lesbian-feminist philosophizing, an image that permeates lesbian-feminist desire. For example, Mary Daly posits the "pyrospheres" as the second realm on women's journey to enter "metamorphosperes."[4] According to Daly, women need to develop themselves as "Volcanic Furies" who practice "pyromachy," a word taken from the archaic term meaning to "fight fire with fire" that Daly redefines as "Fighting with Fire/Desire."[5]

Fire is identified with women—women to the exclusion of men—in almost every cultural tradition:

> World myths, folk traditions, and anthropological studies agree that women first discovered how to use and produce fire. . . . Fire was the tool of tools; through its use foods could be dried and conserved for future use, and some poisonous plants and fruits made edible. It was women who developed all the early associated industries of cooking and ceramics in which fire was the critical tool.[6]

For example, in the Aboriginal language of Dyirbal, the schematization of reality results in the category of *balan*, a category that encompasses women, fire, and objects of violence.[7] This category exists in opposition to three other categories of experience/language, including the category of *bayi* that encompasses men, snakes, and the moon. Cognitive theorists explain the Aboriginal categorization present in the grammatical structures of the Dyirbal language, under a "domain of experience" theory.[8] For example, Aboriginal speakers of Dyirbal link women with fire with danger, and are capable of explaining these links in a narrative fashion: "Women is a destroyer. 'e destroys anything. A woman is fire."[9]

Fire is not limited to destruction, however, and fire's creative use is especially pronounced in Aboriginal culture. As Stephen Pyne, a cultural historian and scholar of fire notes, European colonizers reported a continent ringed with fire as Aborigines continued their tradition of using fire to communicate, travel, hunt, and, in general, to control their environment.[10] In Australia fire was both singular and universal: "It was almost everywhere and it was everywhere intensely felt," and the omnipresent firestick carried by the Aborigines symbolized Aboriginal life.[11]

The firestick was a symbol not only of the practical effects of fire but of the spiritual ones as well. Fire "differentiated the human world from the nonhuman, yet it bridged the mental world with the material." It was an archetype, of both power and danger, at the core of human existence. It was a cognitive center: "As a context, fire invited contemplation, and as an object, it demanded explanation."[12] While the Aboriginal emphasis on fire may be extraordinary, it is certainly not unique:

> The human revolution that fire helped make possible was ambivalent. Humans were not genetically programmed to start, preserve, use, explain, or otherwise live with fire, whose prevalence and power made it a profoundly variegated and even contradictory phenomenon, ideally positioned to explain and exemplify the specialness and ambivalence of human existence. So clearly, among the animals, was fire a uniquely human possession that its origins could be related to the origins of humans, and its exercise to the special duties and responsibilities incumbent upon humans. The possession of fire—at once both an extraordinary power and an exceptional danger—was an archetype for human behavior.[13]

Fire and violence. Extraordinary power and exceptional danger; the archetype of human behavior; the possibility of lesbianism.

Li(v)es Between the Slashes

Thinking of fire, as both negative and positive, as a metaphor for violence, the argument that all categories are a kind of violence seems reasonable. Categories operate to exclude and include, to totalize by repressing differences, and to insist on their own authority. Classical category theory is based on a perception that items within the category have shared properties:

> From the time of Aristotle to the later work of Wittgenstein, categories were thought to be well understood and unproblematic. They were assumed to be abstract containers, with things either inside or outside the category. Things were assumed to be in the same category if and only if they had certain properties in common. And the properties they had in common were taken as defining the category.[14]

On the other hand, cognitive category theory is based on a perception that prototypes within the category order categorization:

> Human categorization is essentially a matter of both human experience and imagination—of perception, motor activity, and culture on the one hand, and of metaphor, metonymy, and mental imagery on the other. As a consequence,

human reason crucially depends on the same factors, and therefore cannot be characterized merely in terms of the manipulation of abstract symbols.[15]

Despite differences in emphasis on properties or prototypes, both classical and cognitive theories of categorization share an implicit understanding that categorization enforces reality—"to change the concept of category itself is to change our understanding of the world."[16] The violence inherent in categorization is often conjoined with political violence: the power to determine what marks insanity, intelligence, or integrity becomes the power to punish or reward persons with institutionalization, education, or publication. But what of the category of law itself?

The Category of Law

The law's arbitration of violent interactions between individuals exhibits the law's own violence. The late legal scholar Robert Cover phrased the law's inherent violence most graphically, reminding us that we do not read court opinions because they are aesthetically pleasing or intellectually stimulating, but because they are written "in blood," given the fact that they are backed by military power.[17] For Cover, our "legal world is built only to the extent that there are commitments that place bodies on the line."[18] The political world of nation-states also places bodies on the line, although philosophers differ concerning the originary violence of political organization.[19] The law, however, is generally considered to be the instrument of the state that (violently) maintains state power. Scholars as different as Jacques Derrida, the paragon of deconstruction, and Richard Posner, the philosopher of law and economics, agree that the law is based on force and coercion: Jacques Derrida states that "there is no such thing as law that doesn't imply *in itself, a priori, in the analytic structure of its concept*, the possibility of being 'enforced,' applied by force,"[20] while Posner observes that "law is coercion rather than persuasion."[21]

The law manifests its violence in concrete terms: "A judge articulates her understanding of a text, and as a result somebody loses his freedom, his property, his children."[22] Lesbians experience these concrete manifestations of violence daily: we are more likely to be imprisoned than heterosexual women,[23] we lose property in courts that do not recognize our relationships, we have our children removed. Such expressions of concrete violence are supported by the law's symbolic violence in discourse. As feminist legal theorist Rosemary Coombe notes, "Legal interpretation is not something joined with the practice of violent domination, but an example of that practice; in other words, the process of legal interpretation can itself be seen as a practice of political violence, not simply a practice which has political violence as a likely consequence."[24]

Such violence is exemplified by the violent expressions contained in statutes such as the federal Hate Crime Statistics Act.[25] The federal act provides for the compilation of statistics of hate or bias crimes, specifically defined as "crimes that manifest evidence of prejudice based upon race, religion, sexual orientation, or ethnicity," and marks the first time sexual orientation as a category has been codified into federal law. While the federal act's inclusion of sexual orientation is a testament to the recognition of violence against lesbians, gay men, and bisexuals, as well as a linking of this violence with the violence perpetrated on the basis of other group identities such as race, ethnicity, and religion, it occurred amidst much controversy within Congress. The compromise necessary in Congress to preserve the sexual orientation category included a statement in the act that "the American family is the foundation of American society; federal policy should encourage the well-being, financial security, and health of the American family; and schools should not de-emphasize the critical value of American family life."[26] Any doubts about the function of this paean to the family operating as an antidote to the mention of sexual orientation is resolved by the statute's next section: "Nothing in this Act shall be construed, nor shall any funds be appropriated to carry out the purpose of the Act be used, to promote or encourage homosexuality." The federal Act also includes an antidote to any possible judicial interpretation that a law requiring the collection of statistics about the violence against us might mean that discrimination against us is disfavored: "Nothing in this section creates a right to bring an action, including an action based on discrimination due to sexual orientation."

The very Act that seeks to collect statistics about the violence against us is itself a manifestation of that violence. Many legal reformers believe that the repeal of statutes criminalizing lesbian sex and the passage of statutes protecting lesbians from discrimination are necessary steps in the quest to end violence against lesbians, but the Act specifically rejects these goals. The signing of the Hate Crime Statistics Act marked the first time openly gay men and lesbians were invited to the White House. Yet, under the very rule of law they had been invited to celebrate, lesbians cannot be promoted or encouraged or have any remedies against discrimination. Such ironies do not negate the federal Act as an advancement, but do indicate the violence against us that inheres even in rules of law that implicitly disapprove of the violence against us.

The federal Act also manifests violence against us through several strategies of categorizing our identities. First, the category "sexual orientation" is defined in the Act as "consensual homosexuality and heterosexuality." Perhaps consensual is meant to modify both homosexuality and heterosexuality, but even assuming such a charitable interpretation, the very inclusion of heterosexuality is problematic. The category operates to obscure power differentials between heterosexuals and "homosexuals." Second, the degendering of the category of sexual orientation is a violence against lesbians. The degendering that occurs usually results in the deemphasis, if not the imperceptibility, of lesbians. Although some documentation supports a conclusion that gay men are more likely to be victims of violence than lesbians, many reports reflect that lesbians are up to twice as likely to be victims of violence than gay men. More important than comparing incidences of violence between lesbians and gay men, however, is the effect that the imperceptibility of violence against lesbians has on lesbians. Lesbians are apparently much more accepting of the violence against us and thus less likely to report it or even believe it is anything other than daily life.[27]

The federal Hate Crimes Act is but a single example of the law's insistence that it control all categories, including the categories of relation among lesbians. For example, the law has uniformly denied lesbians (and gay men) the right to marry based upon its interpretation of the legal category of marriage. That the category of marriage may itself be an expression of legal violence does not cancel out the violence of its denial to lesbians. Further, the remaining categories of relation available to lesbians are also violent. Contract, for example, has been posited as an acceptable legal category and many lesbian advisers counsel lesbians to adopt relationship contracts, yet contracts are also rooted in patriarchal violence. As Jacques Derrida succinctly states, "There is no contract that does not have violence as both an origin and an outcome."[28] Even relatively benign legal categories without a history of violence, such as "attorney in fact" or "beneficiary," do violence to lesbians because they compress lesbian relationships into legal categories rather than lesbian ones.

The law's control of categories produces an insidious violence that is the domestication of lesbian existence. Domestication operates powerfully not only against the lesbians who are directly at risk of losing their freedom, property, or children because they have become actors on law's field of "pain and death."[29] We often believe, those of us who work within the law, that we are inured to the law's violences. Or we tell ourselves stories of struggle and progress. Stories we try to believe.

It is a Thursday afternoon. I am leaving my office at the law school to catch a plane to Texas for a conference devoted to the subject of violence and women and the law. Two of my research assistants, both lesbian law students, give me some legal research on lesbian issues from their weekly computerized search. One case in particular, one of them says to me, is worth reading. "What does it say?" I ask. She laughs, but her eyes glint somewhere between hard and hurt. "You'll have to read it yourself," she says and walks out of my office without saying goodbye. The other one follows.

The case is *Chicoine v. Chicoine*.[30] The court is the Supreme Court of South Dakota. The year is 1992. The case is domestic, an appeal of an award of restricted visitation to a lesbian mother. There is an opinion, dissenting and concurring, written by Justice Henderson, that quotes Leviticus and the Egyptian Book of the Dead, forsaking the more common Deuteronomy; it is an opinion reeking with violence:

> Lesbian mother has harmed these children forever. To give her rights of reasonable visitation so that she can teach them to be homosexuals, would be the zenith of poor judgment for the judiciary of this state. Until such time as she can establish, after years of therapy and demonstrated conduct, that she is no longer living a life of abomination (see Leviticus 18:22), she should be totally estopped from contaminating these children. After years of treatment, she could then petition for rights of visitation. My point is: she is not fit for visitation at this time....
>
>   There appears to be a transitory phenomenon on the American scene that homosexuality is okay. Not so. The Bible decries it. Even the pagan "Egyptian Book of the Dead" bespoke against it [citation omitted]. Kings could not become heavenly beings if they had lain with men. In other words, even the pagans, centuries ago, before the birth of Jesus Christ, looked upon it as total defilement. This case is in a divorce setting. If it were under the juvenile code of this state, rights to a child could be *totally terminated*, through a petition, by reason of "environment . . . injurious to the child's welfare imposed by parents upon a child [citation omitted]."[31]

There is a majority opinion that stuns with its violent reversal of the trial court: the overnight unsupervised visitation of the children with the mother is so liberal that it is an abuse of discretion, despite the condition that "no unrelated female or homosexual male could be present during the children's visit."[32]

This state supreme court enumerates the basis of its opinion that unsupervised overnight restricted visitation every other weekend was too liberal for Lisa Chicoine and her two children, James, age six, and Tyler, age five, with the following revelations from the record:

(1) Lisa has experienced a myriad of psychological problems including an eating disorder, depression, suicidal threats, sexual abuse as a child and active homosexual relationships with several female partners.

(2) In the last two years of marriage, Lisa was absent from the home frequently.

(3) Lisa openly admits that she is an active homosexual and that she had many sexual encounters with female partners *during* the marriage to Michael.

(4) Lisa and the children moved out of the marital home and into Lisa's lover's home.

(5) Lisa and her lover were affectionate toward each other in front of the children, caressing, kissing and saying "I love you."

(6) The oldest son reacted by saying "Mommy don't touch," or "Don't!" when Lisa and her lover held hands.

(7) Lisa and her lover were in an intimate position in bed when the oldest son entered the room. Lisa told her son to go back to bed and when questioned by her son why she was lying on top of the other women, Lisa told him she was telling secrets. Lisa did not stop the sexual act to comfort her son.

(8) On at least two occasions, Lisa took the children to gay bars in Sioux City when she was out looking for her lover.

(9) On some occasions when the children were not present, Lisa publicly danced with females, Kissing and caressing them on the dance floor.

(10) On some occasions, James and Tyler were allowed to get into bed to sleep with Lisa and her lover. Sometimes Lisa would be unclothed.

(11) Lisa and her lover discussed getting married and raising the children in a homosexual marriage.

(12) Lisa admits that it is inappropriate to hold hands, kiss and show affection to her lesbian partners in front of her children.

(13) Lisa has openly exposed her homosexual feelings in front of her sons on more than one occasion.

(14) Dr. Arbis testified that "unless Lisa blatantly and consciously encourages them [the children] to engage in sexual behavior, or blatantly exhibits her sexual behavior in front of them, they will not receive any adverse developmental messages in terms of their own sexual preferences."[33]

These chosen revelations reveal more about the court's violence toward lesbianism than about Lisa Chicoine's mothering. For example, the first listed revelation finds fault with the mother for being a victim of child sexual abuse—a violence from which the law apparently did not protect her. The court describes the violence of her own sexual abuse as her "psychological problem." Another psychological problem is her "active homosexual relationships with several female partners." The violence of the clinical word "homosexual" is inflamed with other sexual transgressions such as "active" and "several." Thus, Lisa Chicoine is exiled even from the "good homosexual" category that some courts have employed to shield monogamous and discrete "homosexuals" from the law's violence. For example, a New York court modified a custody decree in favor of a "homosexual" father, repeatedly using judgments like "discreet" "not flamboyant," "decorous, not blatant," noting that the father does not "flaunt," as well as that the father's relationship with a [single] partner as "stable and of eight years duration."[34] In contrast, the court in *Chicoine* makes it clear that her exile from any possible "good homosexual" category is warranted: she has demonstrated affection to her lover in front of the children.[35]

The court also finds noteworthy the audacity of Lisa to compare homosexuality to heterosexuality: "(11) Lisa and her lover discussed getting married and raising the children in a homosexual marriage," as well as her "admission" of misconduct: "(12) Lisa admits that it is inappropriate to hold hands, kiss and show affection to her lesbian partners in front of her children." The court's coupled revelations from the record comprise a mirror of wrongdoing. A lesbian mother cannot avail herself of attempts at respectability without being ludicrous, and even her attempts to conform her conscience to the dictates of the law are rendered evidence against her.

The legal standard applicable to judge Lisa Chicoine's capacity to visit with her children is the "best interests of the child[ren]." This seemingly innocuous standard has within it a violence toward lesbianism, toward any sexuality other than heterosexuality. The danger of Lisa Chicoine is that she might communicate any "adverse developmental messages in terms of their [the children's] own sexuality."[36] Adverse developmental messages are any messages that interfere with heterosexuality. Almost all custody cases involving lesbian or gay parents rest on the foundation that it is not in the best interests of any child to mature into anything other than a heterosexual.[37]

Lisa Chicoine's case results in her being denied the love of her children.

It is a daily violence that many lesbian mothers endure. The violent message of Lisa Chicoine's case is that lesbians are not sanctioned as mothers. The violence of this message is shielded by the lesbian law students; after all, they tell themselves, they live in New York and not South Dakota. Yet they have also read the same message in the more liberal cases in the more liberal states: lesbians can only be mothers if we are very very good girls.

The violence of the legal discourse in *Chicoine* is not limited to lesbian motherhood. The violence of such cases is the implicit pronouncement that lesbians, whether we are mothers or not, must be eradicated. What we understand—what the lesbian law students understand—when we read cases like *Chicoine*, and even more liberal cases, is that it is not in the best interest of anyone to be a lesbian. What lesbians know is that we are the children who did not mature into what the law mandated for us.

The Category of Lesbian

To incessantly engage in a defense of the category lesbian against assaults is to become inured in combating violence. As lesbian theorist Sarah Hoagland argues, to "define 'lesbian' is to succumb to the context of heterosexualism."[38] Yet as "lesbian" theorist Gloria Anzaldúa argues, the term *lesbian* "*es un problema*" "representing an English-only dominant culture" that can "subsume" persons from the nondominant culture under the category, although only by erasing color and class.[39] Thus, as Anzaldúa points out, the category of lesbian may be a privileged violence against others. This applies not only to other lesbians but to nonlesbians as well.

I am teaching a feminist jurisprudence class and students have read Ruth Colker's essay on authenticity, in which she reveals her previous lesbian state and her present involvement with a man.[40] I had expected the piece to provoke a response from the self-identified lesbians in the class. Instead, it is the heterosexual women in the class who express a visceral response to Colker's piece, speaking about their own wish to be lesbian, if only they "could," because "everything would be easier." Because I am the professor/facilitator, I do not react. But I want to scream. I want to speak of the violence endured in those lesbian lives where everything is easier. I want to speak of adolescents chained to radiators or sent to aversion therapy by their families, of lesbians assaulted and raped and knifed by gangs of men. Interestingly, as the heterosexual feminists experience the violence of exclusion, I ground their exclusion on experiences of violence.

Yet I do not believe that the category of lesbian should be grounded in the experience of oppression/violence at the mercy of others. It is not a victim status. Instead, I want to claim its violence. I want to claim its fire. I want to make an argument for arson.

On Arson

Our legal history is a history of fire. We have been burned at the stake in countless countries, in uncounted incidents, with the sanction of the law.[41] But even given the law's violence toward lesbians, we must avoid the temptation to relegate lesbians to the status of victims. This victim status might entitle us to glorification,[42] but that is a woefully inadequate diet for daily life.

Violence mediates the relationship between lesbians and law not only because the law is inherently violent and expresses some of that violence toward lesbianism but also because lesbianism is inherently violent and expresses some of that violence toward the legal regime. Lesbianism exists as a violent rupture in the law's enforcement of heterosexual hegemony. Lesbianism expresses its violence whenever it exists, even when this existence is not in direct resistance to the law's violence.

Interrogating whether lesbian violence or legal violence is originary is akin to asking the chicken and egg question: neither is very productive. Rather than being interested in whether legal violence mandated the violent resistance of lesbianism or whether lesbian violence produced the violent repression of the law, I am more interested in the survival and perpetuation of lesbianism. It is the violence of lesbianism that is responsible for its survival.

Violence is often considered illogical and noncognitive; it is outside the realm of language, so necessary for the act of definition: "Violence is the supreme gesture of closure toward the other. It constitutes a world of unreason where discourse is no longer possible."[43] Likewise, lesbianism may also be illogical and noncognitive; it may be a gesture of closure. Lesbianism may be a world of unreason where discourse with the other is closed to the extent that the discourse is a dialogic process about lesbianism.[44] But whether lesbianism is cognitive, linguifiable, unreasonable, or closed, I suggest that lesbianism must be non-negotiable. This non-negotiability may be enforced with violence or not, but it is itself violent.

Confronted with our own violence, the learned (domesticated?) response may be to recoil. This response is specifically enforced by rules of law that make it criminal to advocate violence against the rule of law.[45]

Our negative response to violence may also be derived from our experiences as victims and witnesses to violence. Thus, any new perspective on violence that urges lesbians to adopt violence may be illegal and appear to mimic the worst of male values. However, there is a helpful distinction drawn by Drucilla Cornell between "acceptable and unacceptable violence,"[46] which, I believe, would mean a distinction between a violence directed at emancipatory change and a violence directed at conservative order.[47] This distinction inheres in the element of fire. The fire that warms us and burns us. Both.

Thus, when I am invited to provide a "new" perspective on violence and women, a perspective that includes lesbianism, I am likely to answer, "Fire." Fire as an extraordinary power and an exceptional danger. Or I may say, "Arson." Recalling the fires set under the feet of women burned for their lesbianism.

But also recalling the possibility that lesbianism itself is arson. Slashes become our firesticks. Ashes are our lesbian lives; the law's lies. Having survived the fires of violence set to extinguish us, we continue to survive as an incendiary category. Within and without the law.

3

Convictions: Lesbians and Criminal Justice

In legal advocacy and theorizing about lesbian issues we have generally failed to address the multitude of issues provoked when a lesbian becomes a criminal defendant. Our failure to consider lesbian criminal defendants is derived from a variety of problems. In the explicitly sexual context the dominant assumption has been that lesbians were rarely, if ever, prosecuted for sexual crimes; I have argued elsewhere that this assumption is mistaken. In the nonexplicitly sexual context two contradictory assumptions coexist: first, that the pairing of "lesbians" and "criminal" is metaphorical at best,[1] lesbians inhabiting a gendered realm of privatized tranquillity; second, that the pairing of "lesbians" and "criminal" is stereotypical at worst, lesbians being stock characters in films and fiction about vampires, prisons, and ax murders. Yet these assumptions are not the only deterrents to theorizing lesbians as criminal defendants. More important, conceptualizations of equality and identity often operate as obstacles to theorizing lesbians accused or convicted of nonsexual crimes. We need to articulate and confront these obstacles as well as to begin theorizing the relationships between lesbianism and criminal justice, especially in the context of the prosecutorial uses of lesbianism against criminal defendants.

The Politics of Equality

Politically, it has seemed most urgent for lesbian/gay/bisexual legal theorists to theorize equality, so that many other projects are relegated to a subordinate status. But the political importance of theorizing equality is not only an obstacle in terms of allocating energies and resources. The theorizing of lesbians as criminal defendants may be incompatible with a political agenda of achieving equality.

To theorize legal equality is to theorize the necessity of a departure from legal censure, especially the criminal penalties that have attached to lesbianism. The criminalization of lesbians through statutes that outlaw our sexual expressions is often considered the foundation upon which our discrimination rests. Repeal of the so-called sodomy statutes has thus been an explicit goal of the lesbian/gay legal reform movement: distance from criminality is a necessary condition of equality.

The pursuit of equality has a rhetorical inconsistency with criminality. Focusing on equality, the lesbian and gay civil rights movement has sought to present images of what I call "but for" lesbians, who, "but for" their lesbianism, are "perfect." These "but for" images of lesbians are intended to contradict the pathological depictions of lesbians advanced by conservatives. However, conservatives have evinced the ability to pathologize even these "but for" images, often relying upon lesbian- and gay-produced theorizing, cultural production, and research. For example, lesbian and gay work on the economic status and political power of our communities is routinely harnessed against antidiscrimination laws in a strategy with disturbing similarities to stereotypical anti-Semitism.[2] Such a climate understandably produces a reluctance to theorize on issues so easily manipulated by conservatives. While our own theorizing might attribute the disproportionate number of lesbians on death row in the United States[3] to social biases and discrimination, conservative explanations would certainly link lesbianism and murder as social—and moral—pathologies, both deserving state condemnation through legal mechanisms.

The "but for" lesbian is not merely a rhetorical strategy; she is doctrinally necessary, especially as discrimination theory has developed in the United States. In the relatively rare event that there exists a legal bar to discrimination on the basis of sexual orientation, a discrimination plaintiff must demonstrate that "but for" her lesbianism she would have been granted the benefit, such as housing or employment. The lesbian with a criminal conviction is not a preferred plaintiff under these circumstances. As employers and others become more sophisticated, the articulation of an acceptable reason to "discriminate" becomes more important. A criminal conviction is not only socially unacceptable, it is enshrined in the positive law of many jurisdictions: conviction of a felony can foreclose the right to vote, own a firearm, and is admissible as evidence of veracity. Thus, the lesbian "criminal" is inconsistent with particular litigation to achieve equality, just as a more general focus on lesbian criminality is inconsistent with the overall rhetorical strategy of normalization to achieve equality.

The overarching nature of equality discourse is also implicated in a propensity to conceptualize lesbians as victims (persons being subjected to homophobic violence) rather than possible perpetrators of violence: rights for "innocent victims" are much more palatable than "special rights" for morally culpable actors. Even violence between lesbians is often articulated in terms of equality: the battered lesbian is entitled to the same social services, legal remedies, and criminal defenses as her heterosexual counterpart. The lesbian perpetrator remains relatively untheorized, except to the extent that she is implicitly subjected to an equality claim that she should be treated as *her* heterosexual counterpart—the male batterer—and prosecuted to the full extent of the law. She must thus be delesbianized: she is a "common criminal," a "stranger," a "man." In the context of criminal justice our theoretical and political energy is directed almost exclusively to the lesbian we can valorize as the victim.

Even when a lesbian perpetrator is theorized, she tends to be recast as a victim. The case of Annette Green is illustrative. Green is reportedly the first American lesbian allowed to raise a battering defense in the prosecution for the murder of her lover. The judge accepted the defense argument that battered "woman" meant battered "person," thus allowing evidence of battering. The prosecutor argued that the battering defense was inappropriate, despite his admission that Green had been "battered": "She was shot at before by the victim. She had a broken nose, broken ribs."[4] The jury rejected the battering defense summarily, taking only two and a half hours to deliberate, which included the time necessary to agree upon a jury foreperson. One interpretation of the failure of the battering defense in the case of a lesbian is due to simple bias on the part of jurors. As Green's defense attorney reports, prospective jurors were heard expressing the desire to be selected as jurors in order to "hang that lesbian bitch."[5]. Despite our own conceptualizations of lesbians as "victims" of inequality, lesbianism seems to operate to extinguish any defense based upon a being a "victim" of battering.

The lack of success of victimization as a trial strategy for individual lesbians is certainly worth exploring. However, I am here interested in the import of the strategy's insistence on a formal and neutral version of equality—as well as further reifying the already rigid American model of equality—that rejects (or hopelessly distorts) previous theoretical formulations of domestic violence, which rely upon a gendered dynamic of power. In the convoluted scenario exemplified by Annette Green, the perpetrator—this time the lesbian who has been murdered—is again relegated to the realm of the untheorizable.

The situation of Annette Green as well as many other lesbian criminal defendants demonstrates the disjuncture at the metatheoretical level between equality paradigms and criminal justice concerns. Theorizing lesbians accused of crimes does not fit neatly into equality structures because there is no congenial category of similarly situated persons who are consistently being afforded more favorable treatment. Feminists have confronted a similar problem in attempting to theorize female criminals; the male criminal is not an appealing normative category and may even be afforded less favorable treatment in some circumstances.[6] Further, many feminists have correctly identified equality itself as a problem rather than a solution for women. For example, women accused of murdering their male partners could rarely meet the classic male-defined criteria for self-defense. In response, feminists developed the battered woman syndrome defense, the same defense Green sought unsuccessfully to translate into the lesbian context.

Despite its problems, equality retains a fundamental appeal. Some feminist legal theorists have, for example, criticized the battered woman syndrome defense on the basis that it is predicated upon (and therefore perpetuates) female inequality.[7] Some feminist criminologists have posited an "equality" or "liberation" theory of female criminality linking women's claims for equality with hypothesized increases in women's criminal activity. Empirical findings that women are prone to be convicted more frequently, receive harsher sentences, and remain incarcerated for longer periods validate the theoretical subject of "women criminal defendants," just as similar empirical findings regarding lesbians in comparison to non-lesbian women validate the theoretical subject of "lesbian criminal defendants." Yet such invocations of equality suggest their own problems: the battered woman syndrome defense has assisted some women; the liberation theory is consistent with an antiequality backlash; contrary or inconclusive empirical data trivialize any theoretical inquiry.

The problems and appeals of theorizing equality have been articulated by feminists as the sameness/difference conundrum: does "equality" mean that the law should treat women exactly the same as men or does it mean that the law should recognize women's differences from men? Under a "sameness" interpretation of equality, an insurance company's denial of coverage for pregnancy benefits might be acceptable because women and men are being treated the same—all "pregnant persons" are being discriminated against. On the other hand, under a "difference" interpretation, an employer's exclusion of women from more lucrative positions might be acceptable because women's different biology or even interests must be taken into account. The conundrum results because neither treating women as the same as men nor treating women as different from men necessarily results in equality.

This conundrum also structures lesbian/gay legal theorizing and strategizing.[8] As many have argued, this conundrum, with its concomitant requirement of rights, often rigidifies our theorizing and stalls our activism. Such arguments have a magnified resonance in the criminal justice context. In criminal law the other side of the equality equation is always the state—not other criminal defendants. While there is an argument that the other side of the equality equation is always the state, even in civil litigation, however, such a recognition undergirds rather than diminishes the recognition of the state's explicit position in criminal law. We need to be especially skeptical of the capacity of "civil" rights equality discourse to dominate our theorizing and our ultimate goals in the criminal context.

In one circumstance, however, the politics of equality should be given more attention rather than less. The theorizer and theorized subject occupy a vexing relation of inequality. By theorizing, we risk exploiting and sensationalizing real lesbians involved in ugly and tragic events who often face prolonged incarceration. Such theorizing inures to the benefit of the relatively insulated and privileged academic or other writer and ultimately entertains (often through educative pleasure) the audience.

The most flagrant example is Aileen Wuornos, known (incorrectly) as the first female serial killer.[9] To even attempt to theorize about her is to risk further exploiting and sensationalizing a person who has been so repetitiously exploited and sensationalized that her very exploitation is sufficiently notorious to warrant a documentary film, *Aileen Wuornos: The Selling of a Serial Killer*. Most media accounts are not so self-conscious, of course. The media frenzy over Wuornos produced a superficially fictionalized American made-for-TV movie, *Overkill: The Aileen Wuornos Story*, as well as segments on U.S. TV tabloid shows such as *Hard Copy, Dateline,* and *Inside Edition,* a segment on *Court TV*, talk show interviews, and pieces in popular magazines such as *People, Glamour,* and *Vanity Fair*.

Such media exploitation and sensationalization are not independent of the legal process. In Wournos's case, for example, how is the legal process affected when sheriffs and an (ex)lover/codefendant are marketing the story, a public defender is negotiating a deal with a producer, a producer is paying childhood acquaintances for exclusive rights to their memories, and an "adopted mother" and new attorney are negotiating interviews from death row? Given such events, the court proceedings not only become secondary but may also become more subject to the forces of the market than the interests of justice.[10] Unfortunately, Wuornos's situation is not unique. In a case involving a death sentence of a woman for the kidnapping murder of a young girl with whom she had sex, the defendant argued at trial that she suffered from battered woman syndrome and had procured the girl and killed her at the insistence of her husband. In a recent appeal she contended that her attorney's negotiation of publicity contracts directly influenced his trial strategy. At trial the attorney conducted a four-day direct examination of the defendant, eliciting "lurid facts" previously ruled inadmissible. Such facts were central to his "copyrighted, 400-plus page 'appellate brief' which he has attempted to market as the basis of a book or movie."[11]

I am not suggesting that lesbian theorists occupy exactly the same position as those betraying confidences for movie deals. Neither am I suggesting that defendants or prisoners possess no agency, personality, or power; nor am I suggesting that lesbian theorists should refrain from theorizing about lesbian criminal defendants. What does worry me, however, is that our treatments of lesbians accused or convicted of murder will be distinct but not sufficiently different from more obvious types of exploitation. The power differentials between theorist and inmate are vast.

Our possible exploitation of theorized subjects is related to the political dangers of promoting an aestheticization of violence through sensationalism. This aestheticization has attached to our cultural notions of serial killers in particular, and murderers in general.[12] The social problems derived from being a woman, from being a lesbian, and from being economically disadvantaged are sublimated into a romanticized version of the outlaw. The outlaw is supremely individual, effectively erasing the "social" aspects of her condition. She can then be romanticized through true crime books, media reports, and even theories. She becomes an excitingly individual problem solved through resort to the rationalized procedures of criminal investigation and prosecution. Even as we criticize and theorize these criminal justice processes, her peril may still become our profit.

Conceptualizing Identities

In addition to the political and ethical problems with theorizing lesbians and criminal justice, there are methodological ones. These methodological problems are concretized versions of the postmodernist problematics of identity that have so preoccupied lesbian and queer theorizing. The first layer is the problem of identifying a lesbian presence in newspaper reports, trial transcripts, and appellate opinions: what criteria do we use? For example, the identification of lesbians on death row in the United States depends upon an (implicit) articulation and application of operative criteria. Of the forty-one women on death row in the United States, seventeen (approximately 41 percent) have been "implicated as lesbians," according to Victoria Brownworth.[13] Yet only a few have consistently maintained a lesbian self-identity before the circumstances leading to their conviction, during the trial and related proceedings, and continue to do so as prisoners on death row. While sexual identity is arguably always socially constructed, it is difficult to fathom more "constructing" circumstances than the threat of being executed. In other words, if one's very life is at stake, it seems one might reconceptualize one's identity to comport with identities that maximize the chance of survival—in other words, being heterosexual (and, if possible, being white and rich). At the very least, living on death row isolated from previous communities and intimacies might cause one to change one's sexual identity or to have sexual identity become largely irrelevant.

Any self-identity must always be evaluated in the context of the relevance of lesbian identity at trial. Lesbian identity can be important as part of the prosecution's theory of the case. Thus, I have come to believe that the prosecutorial uses of lesbianism against criminal defendants is the relevant inquiry, bracketing the defendant's own conception of her identity or my conception of her identity. If lesbianism is used as a prosecutorial strategy against a nonlesbian woman, it is still a concern for lesbians.

The prosecutorial uses of lesbianism to improve the chances of conviction are varied. In the example of murder the importance of the defendant's lesbian identity can vary with the gender identity of the victim. If the victim is a woman, then the (lesbian) defendant committed the crime out of sexual passion: the victim was the defendant's lover, former lover, or sexual threat to the defendant's relationship. If the victim is male, then the (lesbian) defendant committed the crime out of her antipathy for men.

A few recent murder prosecutions in the United States demonstrate this. In Annette Green's case the prosecutor secured her conviction for murder of her lover by stressing the intimate relationship of the defendant to the victim, alluding to sexual jealousy rather than self-defense as the motive for Green's violence. In the cases of Aileen Wuornos and Ana Cardona, both presently on Florida's death row for murdering males, the lesbian-as-man-hater is never explicitly articulated but virtually floats from the transcript pages, even in Cardona's case, in which the male victim is her child. Thus, sexualized banalities about lesbians—and women in general—as jealously possessive ("hell hath no fury") or man-haters may fluctuate with the gender identity of the victim but can be marshaled toward a finding of guilt.

Another problematic aspect of lesbian identity as deployed in prosecutions is its proof. In the cases of Green, Wuornos, and Cardona the defendant's lesbianism was not contested by the defense. In cases in which the defendant does contest her lesbian identity, the prosecutor must prove it in order to sustain that portion of the theory of its case. In the absence of a living lesbian lover who can testify to the existence of her relationship with the defendant—an issue discussed below—the evidence used to prove lesbianism is extremely troublesome and clichéd. One type of evidence is that of gender (non)conformity. The defendant "dressed like a man, kept her hair cut like a man, wore men's clothing, including men's shoes."[14] While this strategy may become less effective in contemporary urban courtrooms, many women remain imprisoned for crimes "proved" in part by such references. Another type of evidence is that of nonheterosexuality. The defendant has no apparent heterosexual activity—no "boyfriend"— so must therefore be a lesbian. This strategy may be gaining ascendancy, if its popularity outside of the criminal context is any indication.

Defining and applying criteria for lesbian identity does not entirely resolve the methodological issues posed by identity problems. An additional methodological difficulty arises from determining the relevance of lesbian identity. This question is usually posed to me as, "Are you saying that these women are convicted *because* they are lesbians?" While I cannot sustain any claim of legal causation, it would also belie credulity to maintain that lesbianism plays no role in convictions. One of the few empirical studies that has been done concludes that lesbians are more likely to be convicted and serve longer sentences than heterosexual women.[15] The statistical abnormality of the number of women "implicated as lesbians" on death row in the United States is also probative.[16] As one death row expert has cautiously opined: "All other things being equal, a female offender's lesbianism would be a disadvantage rather than an advantage in the capital punishment process."[17]

Nevertheless, numerical correlations are ultimately unsatisfactory for the purposes of theorizing lesbians as criminal defendants. Problems of methodology include not only defining lesbian identity but isolating lesbianism as a factor. Similar to other lesbians, a lesbian criminal defendant is not exclusively a lesbian. Statistically, a lesbian who is a criminal defendant is probably also a woman of color and disadvantaged economically.[18] Positing ethnic, racial, or class status as the *cause* of prosecution and conviction is facile; however, empirical data that point to the statistical overrepresentation of disempowered groups within the criminal justice system confirm a social observation. There is little reason to suspect that lesbianism operates radically differently from other minority identities as a derationalizing, dehumanizing wedge between the criminal defendant and the criminal justice system as embodied by prosecutor, judge, and jury.

In addition to its connection with other identities, it is difficult to isolate lesbianism as a consistent factor within the criminal justice system because crimes and their trials are exceedingly particularized. Variables include the circumstances of the crime, the situations of the defendant and victim, and the location of the trial. The manner in which lesbianism is deployed in one trial may be inconsistent with its deployment in a different trial, or even within the same trial. The criminal defendant may not be the only incarnation of lesbian identity and the prosecution may also have to grapple with lesbianism. In some instances the victim may be implicated as a lesbian; the prosecutor must thus maintain that a crime against such a person is worth punishing. In other instances the prosecution's star witness may be a lesbian, in which case the prosecution must maintain that she is credible. Neither the prosecution nor defense strategy in such situations can consist of a simple condemnation (or valorization) of lesbian existence. Thus, it becomes necessary to differentiate between good lesbians (worthy of protection and believable) and bad lesbians (worthy of punishment and disbelief).

As used by the prosecution, the tropes manipulated to differentiate between good lesbians and bad lesbians demonstrate an amazing versatility.[19] One of the most interesting manipulations occurs in the prosecution of Ana Cardona for the murder of her male child. Cardona is portrayed as a feminized, attractive, and popular lesbian as contrasted with her (former) lover, Olivia Gonzalez-Mendoza, who is portrayed as mesmerized by Cardona. Such a construction reverses the stereotypical one of identifying the "bad" lesbian as the more "male"-identified partner: lack of gender conformity being a sign of deviance and maleness being an indicator of a propensity toward violence.[20] Interestingly, however, the construction of Ana Cardona is consistent with the "femme fatale" trope so prominent in murder prosecutions of heterosexual women. Further, the femme fatale construction is conjoined in the Cardona case with another trope prominent in murder prosecutions of heterosexual women: the bad mother.[21] For although the defense argued that the actual murderer of the child was Olivia Gonzalez-Mendoza and there was testimony to support such an argument (especially at the separate penalty phase of the trial in which the jury considered the imposition of the death penalty), as the biological mother of the victim, Ana Cardona was the person prosecuted for a capital crime, convicted and sentenced to death. The state attorney offered Olivia Gonzalez-Mendoza a relatively generous plea bargain in exchange for her agreement to testify against Ana Cardona. As an editorial from the *Miami Herald* entitled "Deserved the Death Penalty" opined: "Cardona may have been the weaker partner in this union, but she was something that Gonzalez was not. She was Baby Lazaro's mother. She had the moral, legal, and every other responsibility for his welfare. She was not too weak to call the police, or HRS [the state agency responsible for child welfare], or somebody to come and get the baby."[22] In a similar case in California the court held that the biological mother's "legal duty" to protect the child from the behavior of her lesbian lover satisfied the requirements for first-degree murder, although there was no evidence the biological mother ever physically harmed the child.[23]

Yet lesbianism itself may be understood as a trope in the murder prosecution of Ana Cardona. From a different perspective, centering on the trope of "bad mother," lesbianism becomes an enhancement of that category. Especially in the press accounts of Ana Cardona's trial, *lesbian* functions as a suppressed intensifier, not unlike *cocaine user* or *selfish*. Similarly, in the prosecution and press coverage of Aileen Wuornos, *lesbian* functions as an adjective for *prostitute*, negating the possibility that Wuornos is any storybook heart-of-gold streetwalker. In both the Cardona and Wuornos cases the lesbian identity amplifies another identity—(bad) mother or prostitute—and becomes submerged into it.

This submersion of lesbian identity into another disparaged identity renders methodological purity impossible. Perhaps this submersion is a testament to the progress—or at least superficial shift—in contemporary life that renders it publicly treacherous to link lesbianism and murder as correlated pathologies. From a prosecutor's perspective, such an explicit linkage could risk losing the conviction (depending on the attitudes of the jurors, judge, or appellate judges) or some political prestige (depending on the attitudes of one's superiors, the local press, and voter population). Thus, as in discrimination discourse, legal actions that are detrimental to lesbians can appear to be only coincidentally related to their lesbian identities. The assertion of the irrelevance of lesbianism can serve the state's interest. For example, the state objected to the National Center for Lesbian Rights' motion for leave to file an amicus brief on behalf of Aileen Wuornos relating to the homophobia that may have denied her a fair trial. The state argued that lesbianism was irrelevant.

The danger for lesbian legal theorists, reformers, and activists is that we will be daunted by methodological complications. Theorizing lesbians within the criminal justice system is a rather messy project, given the blurring of lesbian identities and the relevance of such identities. Despite these methodological obstacles, and despite the political and ethical problems previously discussed, I believe we must move toward theorizing the connections between lesbianism and criminal justice systems.

Toward a Lesbian Legal Theory of Criminal Justice

Identifying the obstacles to theorizing lesbians and criminal justice marks a preliminary path. Some of the equality-related problems of theorizing lesbians as criminals can be surmounted by a more expansive and radical interpretation of equality. The adages about a society being appropriately judged by its treatment of its criminals and freedom being realized only when the least fortunate are free are applicable to lesbian legal theorizing. Theorizing for the exclusive benefit of "but for" lesbians is partial at best. Thus, I maintain that we must attempt to theorize—and incorporate in our legal reform agendas—lesbians accused or convicted of crimes, including violent crimes. While the project of theorizing lesbians and criminal justice with *lesbian* as its centrifugal force arguably reinstates the previously discussed obstacles to theorizing, lesbian legal theory must take up the case of criminal justice in general and criminal defendants in particular. If it does not, then it risks being a "but for" theoretical position, which, "but for" its lesbian emphasis, could be a normalized theory. Lesbian legal theory in this regard should take heed of feminist legal theory's history, a history considered by many to be marred by its accentuation of legal issues important to professionalized women. Nevertheless, in making criminal justice an important subject of inquiry and advocacy, we should not make equality a shibboleth that obscures the differences between civil rights and criminal justice.

Our ambitions of equality should also appropriately extend to our own work. Our theorizing must not only address but must reflect an attention to the possibilities of exploitation of criminal subjects. Further, we must be wary of the sensationalization and aestheticization of violence. Lesbians convicted of murder should not be glamorized as outlaws just as they should not be dismissed as irrelevant. Both options tempt the theorist, who can make particular crimes into a "sexy" presentation at a prestigious conference, or who can decide that the issue of crime is not one that deserves attention in the present scholarly climate.

The issue of advocacy in cases in which lesbianism is implicated also merits examination. While I believe our practical intercession in the area is important, I remain uncertain about the terms and conditions of that intercession. As always, it seems to me that subjecting our own involvements to rigorous reflection is extremely vital. I am not suggesting a spectacle of mutual trashing, or even self-flagellation. Instead, I believe we can aspire to (if not always achieve) an ethical consciousness about the impact and consequences of our own stake as theorizers in the realm of criminal justice.

Methodological obstacles resulting from the imposition of identity criteria can be surmounted by adopting expansive definitions. I suggest that we should be less interested in consistent or even articulated self-identified lesbian identities of various actors than in the specter of lesbianism whenever it is introduced into criminal justice proceedings, however obliquely. Ultimately, I am less concerned with whether or not an individual defendant is "really" a lesbian than with the manner in which her "lesbianism" becomes pertinent. The question I am thus interested in interrogating is to what effect is lesbianism—as trope, stereotype, theory of the case, prejudice—articulated during the criminal process?

This expansive definition of identity also means that combinations of identities, be they ethnic, racial, economic, or constructed as similar to *prostitute* or *bad mother,* also merit attention. Nevertheless, we must be wary of the way in which other identities are utilized to "trump" lesbian identity. Lesbianism becomes irrelevant for those who argue that a particular case is "really" about prostitution or mothering or economic status. My wariness extends to the manner in which theories of the female offender can suppress considerations of lesbianism. It is certainly not that prostitution or mothering or economic status or gender are irrelevant. It is simply that we must consistently entertain the relevance of lesbianism.

Further, we must expand our methodologies. We must address complicated and particularized situations as such. While statistics can be useful, we must be wary of reasoning from statistics. We should also be wary of adopting criminal justice definitions as our own. The very definition of crime needs to be vigorously questioned. Given the erratic and bizarre ways in which our sexual acts have been and continue to be "crimes," we have more than sufficient cause to be similarly distrustful of other constructions of crime. In terms of our inquiries, we must also expand our concerns from the more easily researched and potentially glamorous crimes such as murder to the more mundane crimes of shoplifting, fraud, and drug offenses. We must also expand the subject positions to be theorized. While the purpose of this chapter has been to focus upon lesbians as criminal defendants, the positions of all lesbians within the criminal justice system merit interrogation. The position of the lesbian as victim of a crime has received the most previous attention, and we should not abandon that project. But I believe further expansion is necessary. For example, what does it mean for a lesbian to prosecute other lesbians within the criminal justice system?

Theorizing lesbians and criminal justice requires an examination of the entire system in light of its impact upon lesbians and its use of "lesbianism" in the achievement of its own goals. Such a project can benefit from the extensive work done by criminal justice critics, including feminist criminologists who continue to examine the complicated impact of the criminal justice system on women and its use of gendered stereotypes. If we consider the criminal justice system from the perspective of lesbianism, what theoretical conceptualizations of criminal justice do we develop? If we apply our politics of equality and our interrogations of identity to the categories of criminal and justice as rigorously as we have applied them to the category lesbian, how do our theories of crime and punishment alter? Once we begin the serious task of taking criminal justice as a subject for lesbian legal theory, perhaps we will be be able to answer such questions. Perhaps we will be able to intervene in actual criminal trials in ways that will benefit those accused of lesbianism, although the crime charged in the actual indictment might be murder.

4

Embodiment(s)

The embodiment of anything like a lesbian legal theory occurs among other bodies: the bodies of feminist theory and the bodies of postmodernist theories, especially as those have become blended with the bodies of queer theories.

The confluence of feminism and postmodernism has been especially pronounced, and taken together feminism/postmodernism problematizes each component of the lesbian/legal/theory trinity. Can there be such a category as lesbian? Can law be relevant? Can theory be a coherent project?

While *postmodernism* has become a term so ubiquitous as to seem meaningless, postmodernist ideologies are rooted in the aesthetic (specifically literary and architectural) critiques of modernity's "ruthless denial of the past" and "standardization and rationalization."[1] The postmodern critique has extended beyond the aesthetic to encompass "political, social and cultural constellations,"[2] a predictable extension if a "postmodern artist or writer is in the position of a philosopher."[3] Postmodernism may be waning, but it remains the dominant intellectual discourse.

It is postmodernism that relentlessly objects to the term *lesbian*. Thus it is necessary to continually clarify any project that might be thought of as lesbian legal theory. For as soon as the word *lesbian* is uttered, the speaker is to relegated to essentialism and assumed to be theorizing from the place of "biological force." On the other hand, the oppositional theory of constructionism (or social constructionism) puts *lesbian* in scare quotes and generally theorizes from the place of culturally defined constructs and labels. Concurrently, postmodernism generally theorizes from the place of fragmentation, while modernism generally theorizes toward the place of culminated unity.

Yet it must be remembered that social constructionism and essentialism are both potentially dangerous to the existence of any lesbian legal theory. Social constructionism may reinforce attempts to eradicate lesbianism: if sexual identity is constructed, it may also be deconstructed or reconstructed. Essentialism may also reinforce attempts to eradicate lesbianism: if sexual identity is inherent, it is separate and other, and aberrant—a defect to be cured. Likewise, postmodernism and modernism are both potentially dangerous to the existence of any lesbian legal theory. Postmodernism may effectively silence by its insistence on relentless fragmentation, while modernism may effectively silence by the exclusion of lesbians or by the imposition of a monotonal definition of lesbianism.

Yet social constructionism and essentialism, as well as postmodernism and modernism, all possess emancipatory potential. To discover and value the emancipatory potential—above even trendiness or aestheticism—is the task I believe we must set for ourselves. In thinking about how to make this task concrete, I settled upon two examples, one grounded in the practice of law and another grounded in the practice of lesbianism. These two examples offer the glimpse of a site that can nurture lesbian legal theory: a site that insists on the viability of lesbian as a category but refuses its incarceration, a site that allows for the relevance of law but resists its imperialism, a site that tolerates both theory and practice. This site is shaded by both feminism and postmodernism, with the duplicity that shade implies, both necessary shelter from harsh sunlight and obscurant shadow in approaching twilight. To reach that site is to replicate a journey, using bodies as trope, problem, and hope, as they appear in the background, as text, as category, in the academy, in law, and as possibilities.

The Bodies in the Background

The questionings that are this text are products of concrete bodies. The bodies in the background of this text include mine, a body with a history of specific acts in the material world. But there are also other bodies in the background of this text, bodies that need to be foregrounded in more than a footnote of acknowledgment. For this text, perhaps more than most or perhaps not, began as the product of the intersection of three bodies. Three bodies endowed with the privilege to pursue theory, although each of us reside differently within that privilege. I have skin color that substantiates that privilege, a class background foreign to that privilege, a gender tenuous in that privilege, and a sexuality suspicious of that privilege. Each body has not only her own privileges, but her own interest, her own agenda, her own histories and theories to be tested and formulated.

Like bodies all over the country, all over the world, our three bodies have constituted ourselves into a group: a reading group, a study group, a group somewhere between a seriously sanctioned seminar and a klatch of gossiping friends, a group process somewhere between a postmodernist "conversation" and a feminist study group.

Our three bodies schedule themselves for thirteen three-hour sessions; we keep to our schedule, for the most part. We are aware, however, that our schedule, no matter how rigorous, is an interlude: a time of scholarship we have borrowed money to obtain.

We meet to discuss the texts we have chosen, to choose the texts we will discuss. The backgrounds for the bodies are the playgrounds of theory: academic lounges, trendy cafés, and cement benches slatted with sunlight. We drink caffe latte or herbal teas, staining our texts. We decide to meet inside or outside, dragging our texts.

Dragging our bodies. Bodies we learn to describe as "inscribed." We describe our inscriptions: we are gendered as female. We are politicized as feminist, arguing about whether politics is a "real" inscription. Two bodies describe their inscriptions as lesbian, the third body prefers the label *straight* to that of *heterosexual.* Two bodies describe their inscriptions as Anglo, one as Chicana; two bodies describe their inscriptions as American, one as Canadian; two bodies describe their inscriptions as being lower classed, one as professionally classed. We divulge our inscriptions, our sexual practices, our histories, gradually, as we contradict or confirm our texts.

Despite our attentions to our bodies, what we privilege is our texts. The texts are embodied goddesses that our bodies have come together to worship and criticize. Or the texts are not-goddesses that our bodies have come together to decipher and criticize.

The Bodies of the Text

Each text is a body. One my body has not known before, or one my body remembers, or one my body reminisces as some other body. My body approaches each text as if she were approaching another body: I bring libations (coffee or potato chips), I make a comfortable space (an outside chair or inside bed), I aim for an attitudinal mix of respect, attention, enthusiasm, and suspicion.

Some texts, like some bodies, are more seductive than others. I am seduced by the texts of Quebecois lesbian-feminist writer Nicole Brossard, again and again. Brossard, whose *La lettre arrienne* has been translated into English, is capable of such poetic pronouncements as "a lesbian who does not reinvent the word is a lesbian in the process of disappearing" and its corollary, "a lesbian who does not reinvent the world is a lesbian in the process of disappearing,"[4] both reminiscent of French lesbian Monique Wittig's poetic prescription for the seventies: "But remember. Make an effort to remember. Or, failing that, invent."[5] In Brossard's texts the theme of invention predominates: a lesbian "with her body, invents everything by the force of the attraction she has for other women."[6] Brossard not only refers to invention, she practices it. Her texts inhabit a new genre, a postmodernist feminist genre, that of fiction theory.[7] Fiction theory is echoed in legal theory. As feminist/postmodernist law professor Drucilla Cornell writes, the "reality of Woman cannot be separated from the *fiction* in life and in theory" and "feminist theory cannot be separately maintained from fiction."[8]

Yet the intertwining of fiction and theory cause the three bodies in the café some consternation. Despite the fact that we agree that fiction theory is a useful category to describe many of the texts we have been reading and admiring, other meanings funnel through our mouths and ears. One body is particularly insistent: "It isn't rigorous enough. There's no way to critically engage. I just get impatient." The body in the café who criticizes a genre I find inspirational is not solitary in her impatience. For example, feminist critic Susan Bordo compellingly notes that postmodern figures like the trickster are maddening "to one who wants to enter into a critical dialogue with them" and, further, such figures "refuse to assume a shape for which they must take responsibility."[9] Accused of being less than critical and less than responsible, my sensation is from adolescence: the discovery that not everyone thinks my new lover is as intransigently perfect as I do—in fact, they find her rather silly. As if entranced in equally adolescent images of democracy or dialectics, I look toward the third body, the one who has not spoken, the straight-defined one, as if she could break the tie or produce a synthesis. She does neither.

I revel in the irony—or perhaps it is only a self-perceived inconsistency—that I am the one in our trinity who has positioned herself as the least critical and least responsible. I consider myself the most practical, in part because I am the only one of us who has practiced law—inventing theories to countervail the theories that disempowered my clients. Yet despite such irony, I recognize that my body is particularly susceptible to fiction theory, as it privileges invention in the form of writing. While I struggle to situate my body—and the other two bodies—among our texts, I resist the notion that there is not a whit of difference between the world and the word. But although Brossard may equate the world and the word in the context of what lesbians must reinvent lest they disappear, Brossard is also explicit about the power of writing and its limits:

> Writing is memory, power of presence, and proposition. I also know that the act of writing permits me to exist within and beyond my biographical restraints. For in writing I become *everything*: subject, characters and narrative, hypothesis, discourse and certitude, metaphor and movement of thought. . . . In writing, I can foil all laws of nature and I can transgress all rules, including those of grammar. I know that to write is to bring oneself into being: it is *like* determining what exists and what does not, it is *like* determining reality.[10]

To write is *like* determining reality; to write is not to determine reality. Interestingly, Brossard's version of writing in the above passage also seems to be a writing *beyond* the body, beyond "biographical restraints."

The relationship between the body and writing predominates among feminist postmodernist writers and is especially typical among the French feminist proponents of *écriture féminine*. This grounding of writing within the female body is not unique, yet other postmodernist feminists are troubled by the Cartesian dualism that infects much of postmodernist French feminism despite its best efforts: by conceptualizing the body as the essential site of female language, French feminists attempt to transcend the mind/body dualism even as they reject it. While I agree with such critiques, I think it is important to remember that postmodernism did not introduce the critique of mind/body dualism to feminism; an analysis of the privileging of the (male) mind over the (female) body is integral to many feminist examinations of patriarchy. Thus, a postmodernist critique takes the form of questioning what a prelinguistic body could say; another feminist might articulate a critique in the form of questioning how else one could write, other than with the body. When I write I do not experience my body as either pre- or postlinguistic/conceptual. Instead, I feel the pen and see the words form themselves in my favorite black ink that smells like Chinese calligraphy block ink from a childhood neighborhood. Or, if

I type, I hear the computer keyboard and the hum of the machine supposedly in my power. I am hungry or my head hurts or I have to hurry because my body has to move itself through time and space to be somewhere else for some other body. It is difficult—impossible—for me to think of writing without the body.

Or is a disembodied writing what theory has always aspired to, if not accomplished? Always, that is, until feminism? And if feminism is preempted by postmodernism, how shall I write with my postmodernist antibody?

The Bodies of the Body

To ground writing in the body is to necessarily privilege the body in one's theory, including legal theory. The problem from the perspective of the development of a lesbian legal theory is the confusion between gender (a female body) and sexuality (a lesbian body). The body marks the site of the debate between essentialism and social constructionism.

Feminist texts influenced by the postmodernist tenet of social constructionism have criticized earlier feminist texts as essentialist. As expressed by one feminist who attempts to undermine it, gender essentialism is "a tendency in dominant Western feminist thought to posit an essential 'womanness' that all women have and share in common despite the racial, class, religious, ethnic, and cultural differences among us."[11] This judgment reverberates among our three bodies and settles on our caffe lattes. Feminism shaped our three bodies and its critiques are subject not only to textual analysis but to the memories our bodies carry. My memories are complex, and they include memories of essentialist expressions that hinged women's oppression on the bodily ability to "be raped" or "bear children" in ways that are not only essentialist, but racist and reductionist. Yet my memories do not confirm monolithic essentialism; I remember social constructionism as an ideology in the 1970s. My memories provoke investigation.

Apart from the other bodies, awake late into the night, I reread feminist texts that are now nearly twenty years old. Equipped with my 1990s theoretical vocabulary, I can label certain phrases essentialist. However, adjacent to those essentialist phrases are phrases that evince social constructionist tendencies: a woman assaulted by a rapist is not only targeted as a member of the class of women, but she is "restricted by her fragile sense of her own reality and worth" and the escape from rape for women is the freeing of "the imagination";[12] a woman is not only limited by her reproductive capacities, but "*society* has ultimately defined woman as a childbearer."[13] Surprisingly often, I find entire sentences that could have been lifted from books Foucault had not yet published, authored by feminists whose names have become synonymous with gender essentialism. "The discovery is, of course, that 'man' and 'woman' are fictions, caricatures, cultural constructs." So wrote Andrea Dworkin in 1974.[14] I cannot accurately accuse the early second-wave feminists of unabashed essentialism any more than I can accuse postmodern feminists of essentialism. And even as I agree that modernist feminism—as well as postmodernist feminism—has been marred by a middle-class white heterosexist solipsism, I am unconvinced that modernist feminism is ultimately any more classist, racist, ableist, and heterosexist than is postmodernist feminism. Comparing the "texts" of the two feminisms, I find the second-wave modernist texts to be much more diverse than I would have believed had I read only the postmodernist critiques—and often more diverse than the postmodernist texts themselves.

More confusing than my inability to be convinced of clear boundaries between essentialism and social constructionism is the mapping of shifting boundaries of essentialism when applied to gender as compared to sexuality (and other characteristics). Thus, a gender social constructionist may be judged an essentialist in other areas, as is Monique Wittig, a writer whose lesbian texts our three bodies return to repeatedly.

Wittig was one of the first women who devastatingly deconstructed and antiessentialized gender. Yet Wittig is criticized as leaving "intact" the "category lesbian" and thus committing the new transgression of lesbian essentialism: "What Wittig ought to be talking about is not lesbian culture, but lesbian *cultures*, not 'the lesbian body' (the title of one of her best-known novels) but *lesbian bodies*, not lesbian sexuality but *lesbian sexualities*."[15] Yet simple pluralization as a remedy for essentialism (or modernism) elevates form over substance. Wittig's novel *The Lesbian Body* is about nothing if it is not related to particularized differences: It contains several litanies of bodily elements, (THE BONES THE CARTILAGE THE OSTEOID THE CARIES THE MATTER THE MARROW), and provides descriptions of love that evoke cyborgs more than essentialized lesbians.[16] Wittig's work is often translated from the French with an italicized "I," for the French first-person singular pronoun *j/e*, but she expressed her commitment to the *bar* in the j/e of *The Lesbian Body* as a "sign of excess" so "powerful it can attack the order of heterosexuality in texts and assault the so-called love, the heroes of love, and lesbianize them" and consistent with antiessentialist suggestions to focus on *my* body rather than *the* body.[17]

While our three bodies find Wittig inspirational, the critiques of her work provide a necessary perspective. A lesbian legal theory is subject not only to the pitfalls of gender essentialism and modernism that have marred feminism and feminist legal theory; it must also avoid *lesbian* essentialism and modernism.

The Bodies of the Category

The problems and solutions posed by the dichotomies of essentialism/ social constructionism and modernism/postmodernism are those of unity, duality, and multiplicity.

Unity is the ultimate good in the modernist strategy, but, as many feminists have argued, the modernist unity is not only false, it is a male unity presenting itself as ungendered. Further, the modernist strategy is also necessarily dualistic, and this dualism is hierarchal. The logic of modernism "generates dichotomy instead of unity" because the "totalizing movement always leaves a remainder," which remainder is then devalued.[18] As applied to the category lesbian in any lesbian legal theory, the insight is that the category produces a hierarchal structure that reveres— perhaps ironically—the "remainder" of lesbianism rather than privileging that which is "totalized" by heterosexuality.

Dualism infects the postmodernist strategy no less than the modernist one, however, and the postmodernist strategy is no less hierarchal. The very valuing of the postmodernist perspective rather than the modernist one creates a dualistic hierarchy. For example, within feminist legal theory, this dualistic hierarchy is evidenced by the shared understanding that to be denominated an essentialist is an insult, that to have one's theory deemed essentialist is a censure. Dualism, however, can also be a solution and need not be hierarchal. As it relates to lesbian cultural experience and theory, dualism may be inherent in lesbianism as the "butch-femme" flirtatious couple. As Sue-Ellen Case argues, "The butch-femme couple inhabit the subject-position together" and is comparable to Wittig's "j/e or coupled self" with a constant seduction of the sign system, and emphasizing "the lesbian bar."[19] This generous view of duality as a flirtatious couple is rare in postmodernist-influenced discourse and contradicts the notion that any duality is necessarily hierarchal.

Multiplicity, as the postmodern feminist solution, relates to lesbian theory on three levels. The first level is by categorizing lesbianism as a category much like race that is often excluded from feminist theory; the solution is therefore that feminist theory incorporate lesbianism. This has been advanced within feminist legal theory. For example, Leigh Megan Leonard notes that lesbian existence is either omitted, subject to token allusion, or sexualized in feminist legal theory and advocates the "inclusion of lesbian existence in feminist legal theory."[20] Similarly, Pat Cain observes that feminist legal scholarship has violated its own method of "listening to women and believing their stories" in relation to lesbian experience.[21] In dividing feminist legal theory into three stages, Pat Cain is optimistic that the third stage—postmodern feminist legal theory—can "reflect the real differences in women's realities," including "differences of race, class, age, physical ability and sexual preference."[22]

The second way in which the multiplicity solution affects lesbianism is by the investigation of any false unity using the "heterogeneity" methodology. This attention to heterogeneity is hardly new to lesbian theory. Lesbian theorists have often claimed that lesbians exist in all times, cultures, and classes, a claim captured in the slogan "we are everywhere." Ironically, however, it has been lesbianism's very claim to heterogeneity— to cross-cultural and transhistorical existence—that has prompted accusations of essentialism.

The third manner in which the multiplicity solution implicates lesbianism is at the very core of lesbian identity: sexual practices. While there are a plethora of definitions advanced for lesbianism, all rest significantly upon some sort of sexuality, although this sexuality can be variously expressed as eroticism, attention, or emotional commitment. The duality of butch/femme eroticism provoked debates within lesbian-feminist communities, yet the question was whether butch/femme roles were sufficiently feminist; it was never questioned that the roles were lesbian. The current debates are more invested in the very definition of lesbianism. For example, a multiplicitous and heterogeneous approach to lesbianism would embrace lesbians who have sexual and intimate relations with men. Yet this extension of multiplicity threatens the definitional boundaries of lesbianism: a woman who is sexually engaged with women (through eroticism, attention, or emotional commitment) is a lesbian, a woman who is sexually engaged with men is heterosexual (and not a lesbian), and a woman who is sexually engaged with women and men is bisexual (and not a lesbian).

Such definitional certainties reassuringly bound multiplicity. Yet definitions are disembodied. When they become embodied—when one of the lesbian bodies in the background misses a scheduled meeting because she has to go for a pregnancy test when we know she is not attempting to become pregnant—then problems of unity, duality, and multiplicity pause for test results. Negative. She is happy. She is not pregnant. But is she still a lesbian?

Will she be if she decides she is in love, with *him*?

Moves in with *him*?

What stake do the other two bodies have in her lesbian identity? When will she cease being a lesbian?

Lesbian identity is problematized by unities/dualities/multiplicities of the self, yet it is also preoccupied with the identity of someone other than the person sought to be described. In its grossest form, the decision whether or not one is a lesbian can be based on the gender of the person(s) one desires as sexual partner(s). That one's identity may not rest within one's self but rest outside one's self may mark lesbian identity (as well as all sexual identities) as ultimately postmodernist.

The Bodies of the Politic

To the extent that postmodernism proscribes lesbianism as a category it is an antiemancipatory politic that forecloses the possibility of an embodiment of any lesbian legal theory. The fragmentation of the operative category disenables categorical analysis. The insistence on radical heteroglossia effectively silences.

The postmodernist and feminist demand for historicism and contextualization is revealing when applied to postmodernism itself. Feminists in many disciplines note that postmodernism is a movement concurrent with the loss of white male hegemony. For example, feminist philosopher Susan Bordo wonders whether postmodernist feminist "gender-scepticism" actually operates in the service of nonfeminist goals, believing that it is "no accident" that such scepticism about the ability to make categorical claims for female reality appears at the point at which feminists are beginning "to get a foothold in those professions which could be most radically transformed by our (historically developed) Otherness and which have been historically most shielded from it."[23] Feminist psychoanalyst Jane Flax is "deeply suspicious of the motives" of postmodernists advocating fractured subjectivities "at the same time as women have just begun to re-member their selves and to claim an agenetic subjectivity available always before only to a few privileged white men."[24] African American feminist literary critic Barbara Christian discusses how the obscurant language created by the postmodernist literary theory "surfaced, interestingly enough, just when the literature of peoples of color, of black women, of Latin Americans, of Africans began to move to 'the center.' "[25] And three feminist anthropologists comment that postmodernist ethnographies replay "a time in which Western white males were of supreme importance in the lives of the 'other' just at this moment when the anthropologist fears his irrelevance."[26] In various disciplines feminists agree that in "the postmodern period, theorists 'stave off' their anxiety by questioning the basis of the truths they are losing the power to define."[27]

The anxiety that is postmodernism is also evident in its insidious and relentless elitism. To quote Susan Bordo:

> Indeed, it is possible, as we all know, to advance the most vociferously anti-totalizing theories, and yet do so in the context of an intellectual discourse and professional practice (governing hiring, tenure, promotion, publications, etc.) whose very language requires membership to understand, and that remains fundamentally closed to difference.[28]

Bordo's worry that "concrete others" are being excluded from the conversation is well-founded,[29] especially since in postmodernisms—and increasingly within certain feminisms—the body of the politic is confused with the body of the academy.

The Bodies of the Academy

The university becomes the universe.

The elitism of the universe of the university excludes "concrete others" from the conversation. It is difficult to argue that the "merit" standard for student admissions and faculty hiring, promotion, and tenure are not—by definition—elitist. The exclusion of concrete others also occurs in the academic "conversations" that include references only to other academics, preferably to other academics with prestige in accordance with institutional affiliation, race, and gender. The university's elitism also dictates the contents of the conversation of those not excluded. For example, in the literary academy postmodernism may deflect feminist women of color from writing about contemporary writing by women of color so that they can critique the "nature of reading itself" through an examination of white Western masterpieces.[30]

While the academy may be inherently and historically exclusionary, postmodernism's academic agenda is not only exclusionary and diversionary, it may also be appropriating. The ideas of women of color may be appropriated even as the identity women of color becomes a symbol of another identity. For example, postmodernist feminist Donna Haraway credits Chicana theorist Chela Sandoval, who becomes gradually displaced,[31] in a work in which the women of color" are gradually displaced by the more trendy "cyborg" identity.[32] For Haraway, cyborgs are "a kind of disassembled and reassembled, postmodern collective and personal self" of "ether and quintessence" who must refuse the "feminist dream of a common language" as a "totalizing and imperialistic one."[33] Haraway uses the writings of Chicana Cherríe Moraga; that Moraga is a lesbian remains unmentioned by Haraway, perhaps because Moraga might be interpreted as privileging her own lesbianism: "My lesbianism is the avenue through which I have learned the most about silence and oppression, and it continues to be the most tactile reminder to me that we are not free human beings."[34] Instead, Haraway focuses on Moraga's language, which " is not 'whole'; it is self-consciously spliced, a chimera of English and Spanish, both conquerors' languages."[35] But, again, Moraga's own words remain unquoted: "What is my responsibility to my roots—both white and brown, Spanish speaking and English?" to which Moraga answers, "I am a woman with a foot in both worlds; and I refuse the split."[36] Can it be Moraga voiced an impermissibly modernist refusal of a split and quest for unity? Likewise, Native American lesbian writer Paula Gunn Allen argues in her writing for recognition of a spiritually based Native American conception of "reality where thought and feeling are one, where objective and subjective are one, where speaker and listener are one, where sound and sense are one."[37] If the words of these women of color are given credence, their cyborg identity is not necessarily consistent with Haraway's conviction that "cyborg feminists have to argue that "we" do not want any more natural matrix of unity and no construction is whole."[38]

Judith Butler has also been tellingly criticized for the (mis)appropriation of the ideas of women of color, specifically those of Cherríe Moraga. In her excellent critique Paula M. L. Moyo argues that "Butler extracts one sentence from Moraga, buries it in a footnote, and then misreads it in order to justify her own inability to account for the complex interrelations that structure various forms of human identity." Moyo thus charges that the

EMBODIMENT(S) 55

voices of women of color have been used merely instrumentally.[39] As critic Vivien Ng notes, the trouble with texts like Judith Butler's *Gender Trouble* is not gender but "the absence of the voice(s) of lesbian feminists of color" or, when there is not a complete absence, a marginal or misrepresented presence.[40]

Ng asks whether it is possible that some theorists have been "dismissed" as "too essentialist" because of their "persistent (and consistent) self-identification as Black lesbian feminists" and specifically mentions both Barbara Smith and Audre Lorde.[41] Haraway laudes Audre Lorde as a "Sister Outsider"[42] even as she accuses Lorde of having "restricted too much what we allow as a friendly body and political language" by "insist[ing] on the organic."[43] While I am not suggesting that criticism is disrespectful or that one must adopt all of someone's ideas or none, I am nonetheless concerned about the manner in which we exercise selectivity. The elitism that is appropriation provoked this response from Lorde in 1979: "Did you ever read my words, or did you merely finger through them for quotations which you thought might valuably support an already-conceived idea concerning some old and distorted connection between us? This is not a rhetorical question."[44]

Another question that is necessarily not rhetorical is the extent to which any appropriation not only contradicts but effectively disempowers. In terms of language, appropriation can effectively co-opt the disempowered into "speaking a language and defining the discussion in terms alien to and opposed to our needs and orientation."[45] In terms of identity, appropriation can deny the disempowered any expression of a unitary self because all selves must be expressed as fragmented. For those who have been prohibited from expressing (or possessing) a unitary self, this "loss" may be contrary to the desires of the disempowered selves.[46]

Lesbians have been subjected to appropriation when they are women of color but have also been appropriated qua lesbians. Postmodernist academic discourse about lesbians—often authored by lesbians themselves— posits lesbianism as metaphoric, fragmented, and even mythically invisible. For example, as Catharine Stimpson writes, "Is lesbianism a metaphor? . . . 'Lesbianism' might represent a space in which we shape and reshape our psychosexual identities, in which we are metaphoric creatures. . . . The lesbian, like some supernatural creature of myth and tale, shows that no identity is stable enough to claim the reassurances of permanent visibility."[47] In the definitions Stimpson discusses I become a "metaphor," a "space," an "invisible" and "supernatural" creature. To what extent do such definitions appropriate me—*whose* metaphor am I? existing in *whose* space? for *whom* am I invisible? in *whose* myths? To what extent am I sanitized, denied, disempowered, disembodied? A metaphor does not need a job; a space does not need protection on the streets; a supernatural creature does not need health care.

To mention such mundanities as employment, safety on the streets, or adequate health care is to commit postmodernist heresy; such issues are not on postmodernism's agenda and not apparent in the texts we put under our steaming caffe lattes. When they make their way into our communication (Did they call you about that job? Is it too late to stay here? Did the insurance cover the costs of that test?), they are less within the postmodernist paradigm of conversation than within the "trivialities" that marked feminist consciousness-raising. But if we believe our bodies to be inscribed, we must believe such issues give content to some of those inscriptions. And inscribed into those other bodies we once inhabited as comfortably as our own: our mothers.

Each of our three bodies carries a mother's body with us wherever we go, just as we were once carried in a mother's body wherever she went. For the two of us from relentlessly nonacademic backgrounds, carrying our mother's bodies embodies us as trespassers in the halls of academia. Our mothers' bodies would not only be concerned with our (lack of) jobs, safety, and health, they would also be critical of our elitist and exclusionary conversations even as they admired our comfortable residency within the buildings and languages of academia. Our mothers' discomfort and our comfort—our status as the daughters of mothers from the "lower" classes or the "darker" ethnicities—mark the site of the postmodernist anxiety as historicized.

But just as postmodernism expresses anxiety, it assuages it. My body finds it seductive, soothing. The complexity of postmodernist discourse is compensatory. The third-grade teacher who mocked the grammar I spoke naturally at home and called my background "unfortunate" is vanquished whenever I articulate "textual strategies that can deconstruct essentialist epistemologies." The college professor who advised me of the rumors of my lesbianism and called my activities "destructive" is subjugated whenever I articulate "discursive inscriptions on historically situated bodies as disruptive of the socially constructed heterosexual matrix."

While disempowered classes have not rushed to embrace postmodernist discourse, disempowered sexualities have. We look for protection in strange places. Feminism once provided political justification for my body's desires, but, now that politics is passé, theoretical rigor is required to ensure credibility. I believe it is no accident that lesbian/gay/bisexual studies has enthusiastically adopted postmodernism. No matter how queer we are, if we (re)present our queerness on our bodies in a trendy enough style, if we wear the right footnotes like accessories, if we express the body's desires in a manner complicated and oblique enough, then maybe our bodies will be tolerated within the body of the academy. Tolerated as metaphoric, unstable, and invisible.

The Bodies of the Law

Like the nonlegal academy, the legal academy has been exclusionary. Again, it is difficult to argue that the merit standard for student admissions and faculty hiring, promotion, and tenure are not—by definition— elitist, an elitism that is reinforced for admitted students. Again, the exclusion of concrete others occurs in the academic conversations that include references only to other academics, preferably to other academics with prestige in accordance with institutional affiliation, race, and gender. Again, the legal academy's elitism also dictates the contents of the conversation of those not excluded.

Unlike the nonlegal academy, the legal academy has evidenced exclusionary and diversionary customs so entrenched that appropriation has been relatively rare as a matter of legal scholarship. The legal academy has adopted postmodernist strategies, however, that attempt to ensure that viable alternative legal theories will never exist. Two examples from my own experience with lesbian legal theory are illustrative.

The first example illustrates the anxiety of those who are dominant and seek to disable challenges to their position. The site is an interview for a law school faculty position. The topic was my recent scholarship in lesbian legal theory.

"Surely," the interviewer said, "you aren't advancing that there be a separate animal such as lesbian legal theory. If you are, then where will it all end? Shall we have a legal theory for left-handed Albanians? Shall we have a legal theory for green-eyed golf aficionados? And why don't we have a theory for white male law professors like myself?"

"Surely," the interviewer said after I had voiced a reply to which he did not listen, "you aren't suggesting that all lesbians are the same. You can't presume yourself to speak for Russian lesbians, can you? You can't speak for poor or Black lesbians, can you?"

Apart from his assumptions that I was not Black or poor or Russian, apart from the conflation of golfers and lesbians as if it were illegal to play golf and not illegal still to engage in lesbian sex in many states and many countries, and even apart from the nonrecognition that there is a legal theory for white male law professors to which he subscribes even as he engages it with his postmodernist critiques, there is anxiety.

The second example illustrates the anxiety of those who may be temporarily subordinate and seek to disable any obstacles to resumption of their traditional dominance. The site was an after-class discussion with a law student in a required family law and relations course that I was teaching at City University of New York School of Law.

"Of course," the student said, "you aren't saying that lesbian couples need a different theory from heterosexual unmarried couples. What next? I mean, should interracial couples have their own theory? Should Marxists? And why don't we have a theory for law students?"

"Of course," the student said after I had voiced a reply to which he did not listen, "you aren't saying that all lesbian couples are the same. I mean, I *know* some lesbians, and they are all different. Some lesbians might disagree with your conclusions."

Apart from his assumptions that I would find it offensive that Marxists might need a different theory of coupledom, true that the existing theory is not for law students, or revelatory that some lesbians might disagree with me, there is anxiety.

This anxiety is expressed with postmodernist strategies that are different in type but not in kind to earlier strategies designed to dissuade the development of an alternative legal discourse; once it was "dangerous" to devote attention to such scholarship, now it is not sufficiently avant-garde. That both the professor/interviewer and the student are men is predictable; that both are white men is even more predictable; that both consider themselves progressive, sympathetic, and maybe even radical is less common in legal academia but also ultimately predictable in terms of postmodernism. Even in progressive legal academic circles the legal academy reproduces its own elitist version of itself. The theory produced by progressive legal academics has been no less self-referentially elitist: feminist legal theory has been rightly criticized as being white and heterosexual; progressive critical legal studies scholarship has been rightly chastised as classist and racist for its failure to consider how the "deconstruction" of rights might effect real people.

Real people.

The bodies of real people. Of the three bodies sifting through postmodernist texts, only mine has practiced law. While we have each been trained in the law, only my body has shifted in courtrooms, sweating in clothes that feel like costumes, consoling or celebrating with the real people who are my clients. In these present conversations in cafés a continent away from the women in poverty I represented and re-represented, but less than a block from other women (and men) in poverty, the practice of law seems nothing less than unseemly. Our three bodies talk more about sexuality than about the practice of law. Law practice seems more physical than sex, more grimy, more taboo.

For if we privilege our texts, then practice is necessarily unprivileged. As Gayatri Chakravorty Spivak says, "A notion of generalized textuality would say that practice is, as it were, the 'blank part' of the text, but it is surrounded by interpretable text."[48] That legal practice is the "blank" part, or at the very best, unprivileged, is evidenced by the hierarchal arrangements of the legal academy.

The practice of law, however, insulates me from the potency of the threat of dire consequences should my surrounding interpretable texts succumb to essentialism. I take theorizing extremely seriously and believe that if I choose to participate in an academic totalizing epistemic regime I must accept the consequences of my participation—consequences that I believe are real and potentially destructive. Yet, no matter how seriously I take theory, to believe that all my privilege to engage in lesbian legal theory can paralyze lesbian existence the way a single cop can is to be misguided.

The law enforces its quest for modernist unity and its essentialist reasoning with the power of the state. The law employs the category lesbian or lesbianism in a punitive manner, often relying upon essentialist and modernist strategies. The following three examples demonstrate this proclivity.

The first example is that of the criminalization of lesbian sexuality: to admit to being a lesbian is to admit to criminal conduct in many states. The law may thus falsely unify or essentialize a person as a lesbian, despite other social realities. Audre Lorde suggests that if she and Mary Daly were to "walk into a classroom of women in Dismal Gulch, Alabama, where the only thing they knew about each of us was that we were both Lesbian/Radical/Feminist," race would determine many reactions.[49] Yet to validate Lorde's perception of racism—of varying reactions provoked by lesbians—is not to invalidate the reaction provoked by lesbians. Further,

Lorde and Daly are not only essentialized according to race and sexuality by the women in the classroom, but their sexuality is essentialized by what might be referred to as the "prevailing legal discourse" of the Alabama statute that declares all homosexual activity to constitute the crime of sexual misconduct.[50] The discourse of the legal regime is that both women as lesbians admit to criminal conduct; to acknowledge that the discourse will be implemented along race, class, and other lines is to acknowledge that the discourse is part of the dominant culture. That the law in Alabama, and in many other states and countries, currently enshrines the criminalization of lesbianism essentializes and unifies lesbians, at least with respect to any sexual practices, even if such practices are merely presumed.

The second example is related to the criminalization of sodomy but addresses the problem that sexual activity is by definition an act rather than an essence or unity. Interpreting the army's former regulation (before Clinton's "Don't ask, don't tell policy") that disqualified homosexuality as it "includes an individual who is an admitted homosexual but as to whom there is no evidence that they [*sic*] have engaged in homosexual acts either before or during military service," a United States court of appeals has no trouble upholding the regulation. In *Ben Shalom v. Marsh* the court's opinion reflects the vitality of essentialism within legal reasoning:

> It is true that actual lesbian conduct has not been admitted by the plaintiff on any particular occasion, and the Army has offered no evidence of any such conduct. [United States District] Judge Gordon found no reason to believe that the lesbian admission meant that plaintiff was likely to commit homosexual acts. We see it differently. Plaintiff's lesbian acknowledgment, if not an admission of its practice, at least can rationally and reasonably be viewed as reliable evidence of a desire and propensity to engage in homosexual conduct. Such an assumption cannot be said to be without individual exceptions but . . . the Army need not try to fine tune a regulation to fit a particular lesbian's subjective thoughts and propensities.[51]

For this court any disparity between an essentialist or falsely unifying label such as *lesbian* and a prohibitable activity is a distinction without a difference. The law, after all, cannot be expected to "fine tune" itself in accordance with subjectivities.

The third example participates in lesbian essentialism and modernism but also partakes of the gender essentialism and modernism that marks legal discourse. In this instance a court is comfortable elevating its own essentialist and modernist definition of lesbianism over the self-definition of the person to whom the label is being applied. In *Perez v. State* a Texas appellate court considering an appeal from a murder conviction accepts as evidence of lesbianism photographs and testimony that the defendant "dressed like a man; kept her hair cut like a man; wore men's clothing, including men's shoes."[52] The defendant's presentation of her own identity, her denial of her lesbianism, is insufficient to overcome the legal presentation of her lesbianism, evidence based on stereotypes of lesbianism and gender transgressions. The theory of the prosecution in a murder trial is thus supported by modernist and essentialist strategies; the conviction is affirmed on appeal.

The three preceding examples demonstrate how the essentialism and modernism of the prevailing legal regime can penalize lesbianism. The uses of essentialism and modernism reify lesbianism into the wearing of inappropriate attire "including men's shoes." Yet while I worry about the theoretical strategies employed in the legal discourse, I am more troubled by the results.

The substitution of constructionist underpinnings for essentialist ones does not ensure different results. Reasoning from the place of biological force is not necessarily more repressive or more powerful than reasoning from the place of cultural labels. For example, the United State Supreme Court in *Bowers v. Hardwick* did not use an essentialist rhetoric of biological force to support its finding that "homosexual sodomy" was not constitutionally protected; the Court relied almost entirely on acknowledged culturally constructed meanings.[53] The Court rejected any claim that "homosexual sodomy" was "deeply rooted in this Nation's history and tradition" or "implicit in the concept of ordered liberty" and buoyed its opinion with a reading of history that supported the "ancient roots" and common-law antecedents of proscriptions against sodomy. The closest approximation to an essentialist argument made by the Court was in the context of distinguishing precedents protecting certain privacy rights: "No connection between family, marriage, or procreation on the one hand and homosexual activity on the other has been demonstrated."[54] Of these categories, family and marriage are obviously socially constructed. The potential for procreation provides the only possible essentialist argument with some biological force that distinguishes heterosexual from homosexual activity. While some of the "majority sentiment about the morality of homosexuality" vindicated by the Court's opinion may be based on biological differences between procreative and nonprocreative sexual activity, the Court does not rest its reasoning on any rock of essentialist meanings.

Further, a constructionist approach fosters repressive laws intended to prevent the "promotion of homosexuality," such as Great Britain's Clause 28. Section 28 of the Local Government Act 1987–1988, which passed into British law in 1988, provides in part that a local authority shall not "intentionally promote homosexuality or publish material with the intention of promoting homosexuality" or "promote the teaching in any maintained school of the acceptability of homosexuality as a pretended family relationship." As Anna Marie Smith argues, the supporters of Clause 28 unanimously agreed "that sexuality is not fixed biologically at birth and that virtually every child and teenager is vulnerable to sexual corruption through 'improper' teaching" and that because sexual orientation is not fixed, but only stabilizes in a person's twenties, school-age persons remain "open to seduction" and "must be protected."[55] Thus, the social constructionist argument can be employed to support discrimination against lesbians in education.

Similarly, the substitution of postmodernist strategies for modernist ones does not ensure different results. Reasoning from mandated unity is not necessarily more repressive or more powerful than reasoning from mandated multiplicity. For example, in *White v. Thompson* the Mississippi Supreme Court rejected a lesbian's claim that the chancery court had erred in finding her "unfit, morally and otherwise" to have custody of her children because of her lesbianism.[56] The appellate court employed a multiplicitous strategy to enlarge upon the factors relied on by the chancery court, rendering lesbianism as one factor among many despite the fact that the chancery court may have "relied almost entirely" on it. The court's successful employment of the postmodernist strategy of multiplicity results in the lesbian losing custody of her children to her ex-husband's mother and stepfather and the lesbian's inability to legally visit with her children in the presence of her lover. Further, postmodernist proclamations such as "There is nothing outside the text" can result in an analysis of the text of *White v. Thompson* to the exclusion of concrete actions to empower the person whose loss is documented in the pages of the *Southern Reporter*.

While the privileging of practice over theory can be as dangerous as the vanguardism of theory, I believe some pragmatic perspectives are necessary. The case of *White v. Thompson* involves An White, a lesbian, who lost something that is important to her. A theory that can discredit White's not atypical loss based on a belief that motherhood is inimical to lesbian existence must still consider Miriam Ben Shalom. And if a theory can discredit Miriam Ben Shalom's loss because lesbians should refuse to serve in the armed forces, then there remain lesbian lovers who have been separated through the legal regime. And if a theory posits coupledom as destructive for lesbians, then it must at least attend to the lesbians who have been legally executed for their lesbianism.

In all these cases, however, I want to use the theories of essentialism and constructionism, modernism and postmodernism, in ways that further rather than hinder lesbian existence under the rule of law.

The Bodies of Possibilities

Essentialism as a tenet of modernism poses a serious danger to lesbian existence, to the embodiment of any lesbian legal theory. Essentialism entraps me as lesbian or not, either/or. It makes me static. Bounded. Imprisoned. Modernism defines my lesbianism for me, or, perhaps even worse, it defines a unified existence intolerant of the deviance of lesbianism.

Constructionism as a tenet of postmodernism also poses a serious danger to lesbian existence, to the embodiment of any lesbian legal theory. Constructionism promises that I can be "deconstructed," no longer tolerated when the fashion for tolerance fades. Postmodernism defines my lesbianism for me, or, perhaps even worse, it defines a relentlessly heterogeneous existence rendering lesbianism insignificant or invisible.

But in addition to their dangers, both essentialism (modernism) and constructionism (postmodernism) present possibilities for an emancipatory enterprise such as a lesbian legal theory.

Essentialism and modernism can be used as strategic choices. If "it is not possible, within discourse, to escape essentializing somewhere,"[57] then this may validate my choice to essentialize in the somewhere (everywhere?) that lesbian bodies exist. Gayatri Chakravorty Spivak analyzes the work of a group to retrieve a specific minority consciousness as "a strategic use of positivist essentialism in a scrupulously visible political interest"[58] and posits the requirements for this strategy to be successful. As appraised by Diana Fuss, Spivak's wisdom is that "the permissibility, if you will, of engaging in essentialism is therefore framed and determined by the subject position from which one speaks."[59] The relevancy of the subject position from which one speaks results in a "politics of location"—to use Adrienne Rich's phrase of the early 1980s—and can resist the forces of the dominant culture that would "fragment" everyone outside of that culture's ideal.[60]

Constructionism (postmodernism) can also be used as a strategic choice.

All politics demand contextualization: the category lesbian is such a contextualization. Once contextualization begins, however, one realizes that "contextualization is never completed; rather one reaches a point where further contextualization becomes unproductive."[61] Determining the point at which contextualization becomes unproductive is a delicate judgment call that invites disagreement.

Somewhere between the fragmentation of the unrelentingly particular and the imperialism of the totalizing universal is a place where I can speak a language that might be lesbian legal theory. It is a place that allows the insistence upon the viability of lesbian as a category and it is a place that realizes that lesbian does not mean a person who conforms to one specific ideology or specific bodily configurations and inscriptions. It is a place of unity and specificity, without privileging one or the other. To exercise the prerogative of such judgment is scary: almost everything in my life counsels against such an assumption of power and such an assumption of risk and responsibility.

But not everything. As I survey my life, I find two interstices, two practices, two bodies, that provide an insight into the ways in which such power, risk, and responsibility might be assumed in a collaborative and respectful manner.

A PRACTICE WITHIN THE LEGAL CORPUS

One possibility is located in the practice of law. More specifically, in law as I practiced it with the goal of making changes for the real people who were my clients. This possibility is the litigation procedure known as the class action. Conservatives have increasingly realized the class action mechanism for the tool of social change it can be and have thus attempted to curtail its usage, especially on behalf of poor people.[62] Nevertheless, the possibility of class actions remains encoded in the Federal Rules of Civil Procedure, Rule 23, and similar state rules generally modeled on the federal rule.

Rule 23 provides for the bringing of a lawsuit as a class action having multiple parties. Thus, the class action was a harbinger of postmodernist multiplicity in the modernist "unitary concept of the civil action [in which] litigation was strictly a two party affair—one plaintiff and one defendant."[63] The class action is a theoretical anomaly in the inherently individualistic Anglo-American legal system, although it has roots in medieval group litigation. As a modern procedural rule, class actions have been revised and restudied by legal scholars on several occasions, and in 1966

Rule 23 was amended into its current form and adopted by the United States Supreme Court for use in the federal courts.[64] The class action device is most often justified in terms of judicial economy and most frequently considered a civil rights tactic, although its use by consumers and corporate shareholders is also frequent.

Under the present federal rule a class action needs to meet all of the prerequisites of Rule 23(a) and to conform to one of the categories of Rule 23(b).[65] While there are current prominent recommendations to continue the evolutionary trend toward abolition of categories such as those in Rule 23(b), the prerequisites for maintaining a class action have remained fairly consistent. These prerequisites are outlined in Rule 23(a):

> One or more members of a class may sue or be sued as representative parties on behalf of all only if (1) the class is so numerous that joinder of all members is impracticable, (2) there are questions of law and fact common to the class, (3) the claims or defenses of the representative parties are typical of the claims or defenses of the class, and (4) the representative parties will fairly and adequately protect the interest of the class.

Additionally, these prerequisites imply that a "class" must be definable and that class representatives must themselves be members of the class. The prerequisites for a class action provide useful images of sites of unity and multiplicity, of essential qualities and constructed ones.

While the four explicit and two implicit prerequisites for a class action can be divided into two groups—those that concern the membership of the class and those that concern the representatives of the class—in another sense all the prerequisites "tend to merge."[66] Considering the prerequisites distinctly, however, might more concretely demonstrate the capacity of each prerequisite to reveal particulars about contextualizations and categorization.

The implicit requirement that there be a definable class is derived from the theory of class action itself and also implicates due process considerations. One common manner in which this implicit prerequisite is expressed is that a (plaintiff) class must be definable in terms of having been injured by the defendant. However, this articulation emphasizes the victimization of the class members; a more empowering definition might be that of shared purpose or common goal. As one commentator stresses, a class in a class action suit is a "temporary litigative entity" that grants class members a "form of power."[67] Despite concerns for empowerment, however, some courts have interpreted definability in a rather limited way, i.e., in an "objective" manner that excludes "state of mind" from the realm of definability. Thus, a class consisting of "all black persons who were discouraged" from applying for sales positions with a certain company has been deemed too "abstract or nebulous" and "too imprecise and speculative" because it requires "an inquiry into that individual's state of mind."[68] However, a class consisting of women who "desire or may desire" an abortion has been deemed sufficiently definite.[69]

Further, the so-called numerosity prerequisite contained in Rule 23(a)(1) operates expansively on the implicit requirement of definablity because it allows for speculative class members who are not presently definable. In its most straightforward sense this explicit prerequisite seeks to ensure that a class action may only be maintained when there are so many class members that other rules of civil procedure such as joinder[70] are not better suited procedurally. Numbers of class members alone are insufficient evidence of this prerequisite's satisfaction. Courts routinely consider factors such as geographic dispersion, the nature of the action, and the size of the claims. The fact that the nature of the action and size of the claims are considered factors is attributable to judicial considerations of whether the members of a class are realistic litigants, that is, whether deprivation of class certification would be tantamount to deprivation of judicial remedy. Interestingly, this same judicial consideration prompted one court to regard "stigma" as a factor contributing to numerosity in a class designated as patrons of a gay bar.[71] Thus, the numerosity requirement means that contextualization stops when one reaches the de minimis point at which the category only contains a few persons and yet allows for the contingency that a category need not be disregarded if it only contains a few persons by allowing for the consideration of other factors.

The second prerequisite of Rule 23(a) requires common questions of law or fact. This commonality requirement is not one of identity or exclusivity: a single question of law or fact in common among all class members is sufficient. As one commentator expresses it, the standard is "qualitative rather than quantitative."[72] The qualitative nature of this commonality is often based upon the defendant's actions, but, as in the existence of a definable class, the emphasis can be changed from victimization to empowerment. For example, even if a government defendant can point to differences with regard to its own actions in awarding entitlements to individual class members or to disparities in individual medical situations, the class may develop a legal theory and demand a form of relief that focuses on their commonality. Thus, the class is empowered to construct its own theory in order to reach the goal it articulates. In its applicability to any lesbian legal theory, I find this method of categorization to be valuable.

The remaining three prerequisites, both implicit and explicit, of Rule 23(a) concern the characteristics of the class representative. Analogized to problems of categorization in lesbian legal theory, the class representative corresponds to the advocate; the lesbian as speaker, writer, artist, and activist who speaks publicly and privately as a lesbian qua lesbian. The requirements of Rule 23(a) thus not only provide some guidelines to evaluate contextualizations but also some guidelines to evaluate those who advance such contextualizations.

Rule 23(a)(3) requires that the class representatives' claims be typical of the class. This typicality requirement "tends to overlap" with the commonality requirement of (a)(2), except that the emphasis is on the relationship between the class representative and other class members instead of among all class members. Again, however, it is the goal for which the class is being maintained that is determinative rather than coextensive identity. In the previously mentioned gay bar case, for example, the court rejected the claim by the police department defendant that the claims of the named representatives were "not typical of those class members who may not be homosexuals" and found that the typicality requirement was satisfied by the class's theory based upon a violation of constitutional rights of all those present in the bar when the police raid occurred.[73] Thus, the class representative is judged by the goal articulated by the class; again, a valuable insight for categorization problems in any lesbian legal theory.

Rule 23(a)(4) requires that the class representative fairly and adequately represent the class. Generally, this consists of a two-pronged test: whether the class representative has a conflict of interest with other class members and whether the class representative's attorney will adequately protect the class. The second prong, regarding attorneys, is irrelevant for analogizing purposes, but the first prong is pertinent because although it again "tends to merge" with previous requirements, it ensures that the class representative not have goals that are at odds with the rest of the class members. I think of this as the "different agenda" or perhaps "personal aggrandizement" disqualification, and I think its applicability to categorization within any lesbian legal theory would be worthwhile.

The implicit requirement of Rule 23 concerning the class representative is that any representative be a member of the class. While this appears obvious if the prerequisites of typicality and adequacy are to be satisfied, in fact, the requirement is less rigid than one might suppose. For example,

although "Richard Ragsdale" is not within a class described as "all women
in Illinois of child-bearing age who desire or who may desire an abortion,"
the court found Dr. Ragsdale to meet the requirements of Rule 23 because
as a physician he had standing to assert the claims of his women patients as
a constitutional matter,[74] and likewise corporate clinics have been deemed
adequate class representatives for classes of similar women.[75] As applied to
categories of persons who advocate for lesbians, this implicit requirement
allows flexibility in terms of identity.

Considering all the above discussed prerequisites to maintaining a class
action under Rule 23, the procedural device displays some promising tendencies. The class need not be "some existential class with a determinate
membership" but only a group of people sharing a common controversy.[76]
A class is capable of being described, must have definite but not absolute
boundaries and can contain speculative members. It is understood within
the circumstances of a specific project and the power to define the project
rests with the class. Representatives must be typical of the class and adequately and fairly represent it. A class description makes a claim to reality
but not to ontology; it makes a claim to accuracy but not to exclusivity.

Of further benefit to the usefulness of the class action analogy is the
fluid relation between classes. If class definitions do not meet the com-
monality-related prerequisites of Rule 23(a), subclasses may be certified[77]
or a class action may be maintained by two different classes. For example,
in the case of the class of women who might desire abortions in Illinois, the
court simultaneously certified a class of physicians "performing or desiring to perform" abortions in Illinois.[78] These two classes joined together to
pursue a common goal in a litigative analogy to the coalition activity currently pursued by many lesbians. Yet these classes intersect not only
through a common goal but also shared membership: there may be
women physicians who are "performing or desiring to perform" abortions
even as they are women "of child-bearing age who desire or who may
desire an abortion." Exclusivity must not be implied if the class action
analogy is to have vitality.

Class action doctrine as discussed above would support a class composed of "all persons who might be prosecuted under a state sodomy law"
or "all unwed mothers who were asked for the father's name in order to
have a birth certificate issued" or "all black females who applied for an
employment position at a national company" or "all lesbians who have
been terminated from academic support positions at a state university" or
"all consumers who purchased a Sonnet electric toaster during 1995–7" or

"all persons who might drive intoxicated on Route 80." A hypothetical black lesbian toaster-buying mother who may have too much wine at the next potluck could count within all these classes.

The example of class actions is not a panacea but a concrete practice that might assist in the determination of relevant contextualizations. The difficulty of categorization, naming, and definition must not be underestimated. Even with a directed and narrow goal (having a statute declared unconstitutional, getting a job, obtaining a refund of money paid for a defective toaster), articulation of a class raises numerous practical and theoretical issues, as I think anyone who has ever drafted a class action complaint can attest. Thus, even within the law, Rule 23 can be said to "ask more questions than it answers. It is neither a set of prescriptions nor a blueprint. It is, rather, a broad outline of general policies and directions."[79] Further, the instrumental reason involved in consideration of the purpose for which the class is being described raises the specter that theorists will become tacticians rather than thinkers. Nevertheless, I think more focus on the contextualizations for our contextualizations might allow room for practical and respectful theoretical categories. As a site of possible theorizing, Rule 23 speaks by way of analogy (not prescription) to problems posed by essentialism and constructionism as well as by the unitary insistence of modernism and the multiplicitous fragmentation of postmodernism.

A PRACTICE WITHIN THE LESBIAN CORPUS

Another possibility is located within the practice of lesbian bodies. More specifically, in lesbianism as I have been able to practice it with other lesbians in America in the latter decades of the twentieth century. Even more specifically, in lesbian sexuality.

There is no citation that I can neatly footnote here. There are no centralized or provincial rules. There have been no impressively credentialed commissions appointed to recommend and review procedures, no supreme court to adopt standards. Although there have recently been texts that aspire to authoritative stature on the subject of lesbian sexuality, these texts—unlike Federal Rule of Civil Procedure 23—do not ultimately invoke the authority of the government; quite the opposite. Further, again unlike Rule 23, I am not interested in origins, history, or precedent, or even specific case studies that might be illustrative.

Lesbian sexuality is a possible site of unity and specificity that does not privilege either; a site in which the recognition of lesbianism is possible without its idealized enforcement.

This is not an argument that sexuality defines lesbianism, or even that sexuality is a proper "signifier" for lesbian "sex."

This is not an argument that lesbian sexuality is unique or oppositional.

This is not an argument.

This is an attempt to articulate a site in which I have been located, in which I am located. A site in the center, on the margins, outside. A site that Nicole Brossard describes as a hologram[80] but that for me is a site in which shape is shapeless. It is a site of presence, not absence.

A site I know as well as the back of my hand. I need no maps to navigate here. This place *is* a map.

A site in which I am continually lost. Maps would be useless here. There is no navigation.

A site as an awkward evocation of desire. A glance not dependent on vision; a touch not dependent on mobility.

There are narratives about how I got to this site, ones that I clutch tightly and ones that I change on whims. There are explanations. But within the site trajectories and random patterns are equally interesting. I do not care how I got here: perhaps some biological core of sexual identity forced my propulsion; perhaps some social conspiracy orchestrated my arrival.

I cannot use language to take you here.
Language: Maybe one of the ways I got here. For I have been a literate lesbian who has been a devourer of the products of the women-in-print movements. This site is surrounded by the language of the lesbians I have read and loved: Barbara Deming, Cheryl Clarke, Adrienne Rich, Nicole Brossard, Audre Lorde, Barbara Wilson, Gloria Anzaldúa, Dorothy Allison, Michele Cliff, Beth Brant, Pat Parker, Barbara Smith, Minnie Bruce Pratt, Mab Segrest, and the anonymous women who wrote those wonderful Dutch lesbian erotic novels I read when I was sixteen.

But in this site I have met and loved many lesbians who do not travel with words. Lesbians who have never read a lesbian novel. Lesbians who have never read. Lesbians who cannot read or write. Lesbians who are the "nothing" outside the postmodernist's totalizing "text."

And in this site language is only one of the multiplicity of ways in which communication is possible. Sometimes there are no words when we make love. Sometimes there are only words.

here: Not a place, and, even if a place, not one place. Even with the same person, repeatedly, under control circumstances, there is multiplicity. Even among moments. Even as there is unity, duality.

In this transitory site: shifting. We shift as we are shifted.

In this site that endures within me even when I am not there. An ever-present memory. An ever-expanding memory that I bring like a gift to each site, from each site. Inhering in the body, if not inherent.

Other bodies, with whom I have not visited this site, also inhere. I can hear her critical voice, steaming around the latte: "There's no way to critically engage." She is right. But why should we privilege critical engagement? I am still waiting in vain for the third one to produce synthesis.

In the cafés we spent days and days arguing and rearguing a passage from an interview with lesbian theorist Michele Causse:

> A lesbian body, one might think it's a knowing body *a priori* a body of knowledge, a body of innate science, well I've discovered there is no knowledge, there is an instinct, an intuition, but it's not always followed by erotic knowledge. . . . But it is true that the quantitative plays a role in the knowledge that we have of our *semblables-différentes*. Knowledge is acquired on the body of others and from one's own body, for me it's capital, I would not be who I am today if I had not known bodies who were themselves bearers of knowledge and sometimes of non-knowledge. . . . I have followed words which were incarnated, a body had to speak to me and speak to me lesbianly, not evade me, not distance me from what is pregnant for me, that is from my perceptions. Next, difference sets in, that this is so is the happiness of lesbianism. And one will never say enough about it. The enormous difference there is . . . even if its an unhappy difference, the richness of this difference remains, it's what dazzles me in every lesbian relationship. Difference frightens, seduces, astonishes, stupefies and in the end it is absolutely instructive. I believe that fundamentally a lesbian body is a body which wants to learn indefinitely and to its dying day. Lesbianism, is, it seems to me, the only way which allows a woman to know more about this difference, and to bet on it, whatever the avatars and the difficulties encountered.[81]

Two of our three bodies are critical of the "capitalization" metaphor. So mercantile. I am wary of the manner in which economics colonizes lesbianism, just as I am wary of the manner in which economics colonizes law. A different pair of us worry over the valorization of the lesbian body; will the one without one be offended?

But the more our three bodies ponder Michele Causse, the more we are seduced. Knowledge, as capital, acquired from the bodies of others. The mercantile analogy becomes less prominent. A similar analogy is Joan Nestle's reference to the "accumulated wealth" of sexual knowledge: "I do have my own person, my own body, that has led me to a lifetime of new places, new resistances, new compassions. This accumulated wealth of sexual self-knowledge that many of us have is not often discussed in our communities and, thus, we are still learning about the political and personal implications of our sexual wisdom."[82]

Nestle's articulation serves to flatten as cliché the commercial aspects of Causse's statement. What becomes highlighted is a relation we speak of as sexual: "I would not be who I am today if I had not known bodies who were themselves bearers of knowledge and sometimes of non-knowledge." A relation of difference: "difference sets in, that this is so is the happiness of lesbianism."

What this means for the embodiment of a lesbian legal theory is not that any one of us can speak for lesbians other than herself; it means that "self" is in fact composed of others (just as these others are composed of others). Causse reminds me that the richness of difference between lesbians is what "dazzles," what "frightens, seduces, astonishes, stupefies and in the end it is absolutely instructive." I agree with Causse that this difference between lesbians can be "bet on, whatever the avatars and the difficulties encountered."[83] In the site where difference is at its most intimate, there is every possibility.

The Bodies Disembodied

The bodies in the background came to the foreground, then dispersed. We left each other, left our group; before our conversation was completed, before our consciousnesses were raised. We left the cafés, the cups of coffee and tea still served are no longer for us.

We have to work.

The body has to be maintained. Not only its desires, but its needs. Food. Shelter.

We have to work.

We each work differently; we each maintain differently. We sell clothes, we buy them. We are teachers or students. We borrow money or we lend it. We are separated by thousands of miles, a triangle that letters traverse but do not transcend.

Our bodies now discuss texts with other bodies. Bodies with different skin colors. Different class backgrounds. Different sexualities. Different ideas.

But we miss the particularized differences we shared. We miss our temporary privileges, our schedule, our discussions, our texts. In the guise of missing each other, we miss our own bodies, as they were inscribed, problematized, and desiring in those particularized and generalized times and spaces we shared.

5

Reflections and Taxonomies: The Feminist

Jurisprudence Question

Asked to participate in a feminist jurisprudence bibliography project as the person responsible for collecting and writing an introductory essay on "gay and lesbian" legal scholarship, my first reaction is a rush of pleasure. I am personally pleased in the sense of being flattered, but I am also more generally pleased that "gay and lesbian" issues are being included. Perhaps as a by-product of having attempted research on lesbian legal issues only to be confronted by locked cabinets caging the paucity of "HQ" books (HQ being the bibliophilic classification for sexual matter), I still welcome any efforts at cataloging and disseminating lesbian and gay materials. And I am specifically heartened that the editor of a feminist jurisprudence collection considers it necessary to include sexual orientation issues. Although such inclusion is no longer rare, I know I would be among the first to criticize any feminist jurisprudence text that omitted lesbian issues.

Sometime after these initial delights—when I have agreed to the task and the deadline is approaching—a second sentiment surfaces. A mirror image of the initial reaction, this second sentiment is as unpleasant as the first was pleasurable. It is what might be called a rush of resentment. In its personal aspect, the perception of compliment is now a perception of stultification; I am a rube who has been duped into the boring and thankless task of acting as an encyclopedist and commentator. As for the feminist jurisprudence text itself, I cynically conclude that lesbian and gay issues are only being inserted in a tokenist move to forestall any criticism that would occur in an instance of omission.

The sentiments of resentment start to fade as soon as I begin to actively engage in the work itself. After reading the guidelines for the overall project and gathering materials, the real intellectual process begins with the attempt to formulate with some precision the question the essay will address. In this case the question seems relatively simple: What is the state of lesbian and gay legal scholarship?

Likewise, the answer to the question seems relatively uncomplicated. In the past two decades a scholar doing research is no longer confronted with those few pieces in locked HQ cabinets but can locate hundreds of articles and several books concerning legal issues relating to lesbianism, gay male sexuality, bisexuality, and transsexuality/transgenderism—what might be called les-bi-gay-trans legal scholarship. With some notable exceptions, such as the work of Professor Rhonda Rivera, most of this proliferation occurred after the United States Supreme Court's regrettable 1986 decision in *Bowers v. Hardwick*,[1] in which the Court upheld Georgia's sodomy law against a constitutional attack. In response, law reviews virtually exploded with analyses of the majority, concurring, and dissenting opinions, the vast majority of articles criticizing the decision. While many of these articles now seem unoriginal and redundant, one must credit, if one believes in the relevance of legal scholarship to legal change, even the most derivative and superficial case note criticizing the Court's decision in *Bowers v. Hardwick* as part of a progressive political process.

For ten years later, as I prepare to write the essay, the United States Supreme Court has again rendered a momentous opinion in the area of les-bi-gay-trans rights.[2] In *Romer v. Evans*,[3] the Court held an amendment passed by voter referendum to the Colorado state constitution—Amendment 2—unconstitutional as violative of equal protection under the Fourteenth Amendment to the United States Constitution. Amendment 2 prohibited all legislative, executive, or judicial action at any level of state or local government designed to protect "homosexual, bisexual, or lesbian" persons or activities. Affirming the Colorado Supreme Court, a majority of the Court, in an opinion authored by Justice Kennedy, held that Amendment 2's classification did not further a proper legislative end but sought to make a class of persons unequal to everyone else and a "stranger" to the state's laws. We can expect to witness an outpouring in the law journals similar in quantity to that provoked by *Bowers v. Hardwick*, only this time most will probably commend the opinion and reserve their criticisms for the scathing dissent authored by Justice Scalia and joined by Thomas and Rehnquist. Thus, in terms of les-bi-gay-trans rights, ten years have brought a burgeoning of legal scholarship and some success.

From this perspective, then, the answer to the inquiry about the state of les-bi-gay-trans legal scholarship can be conveyed as a narrative of progress. Yet neither the answer nor the question seem particularly satisfying. The attitudes of the anticipatory phases of the project, both the pleasure and the resentment, resurface with nagging authority. But now the focus is not on authorial ego or editorial motive, but on the intellectual domain itself. The essay must not only contextualize itself, but it must justify itself. Simply put, the question is this: What is the relationship between les-bi-gay-trans legal scholarship and feminist jurisprudence?

This question becomes more interesting when I realize that there is little else written that is direct and expansive on this issue, although the legal scholarship does reveal some explicit statements, a plethora of assumptions, and some tantalizing omissions.

As I consider the legal scholarship, both les-bi-gay-trans and feminist, my mode of analysis is distinctly Aristotelian: I begin categorizing the multiplicity of answers to the question of the relationship between les-bi-gay-trans scholarship and feminist jurisprudence. That these answers are often revealed as a matter of implicit practice rather than as a declaration or pronounced theoretical stance makes the categorizing exercise more interesting. Finally I settle on four distinct albeit at times overlapping strands, which I decide to label as follows: the no apparent relation mode, the lesbian-feminist link, the sexual orientation (is) (is not) gender debate, and the alternative theories approach.

The No Apparent Relation Mode

The most obvious strand to detect is the one that assumes there is absolutely no relation between les-bi-gay-trans legal scholarship and feminist legal theory, or at least any relationship worthy of mention. This approach would be favored by any feminist legal theorists who might argue that les-bi-gay-trans issues are beyond the scope of feminism; thankfully this is absent from the scholarship in feminist legal theory. What has been present, however, in disturbingly large quantities, is feminist legal scholarship that proceeds as if its audience were exclusively heterosexual. This "heterosexual presumption" has been tellingly criticized by legal scholars such as Mary Dunlap, Patricia Cain, and others.

The no apparent relation mode is also favored by those scholars writing les-bi-gay-trans legal scholarship who do not connect their own scholarship with feminist legal theory, including feminist jurisprudence's most rudimentary insight: women exist as legal subjects. This oversight has not been as rare as feminist scholars might expect. For example, in the numerous articles on *Bowers v. Hardwick*, only a few even mention lesbianism and sometimes this mention is to specifically exclude it. The legal analysis and theoretical perspectives proceed as if the criminalization of nonmarital sexuality or nonheterosexuality affected only male homosexuals. This phenomenon marks a gendered divide within lesbian/gay legal scholarship itself. Sodomy laws and their reform can be considered "male" issues, given the stereotype that only men engage in and are prosecuted for sex. On the other hand, custody of children can be considered "female" issues, given the stereotype that only women desire relationships with children. Further, many of the articles fail to consider the relevance of the critiques by feminist legal theorists concerning constitutional privacy, the theory that was primarily advanced on behalf of Hardwick. Thus, on a most concrete level (the existence of lesbians) and on a wider theoretical level (the relations between the theories being advanced) feminist legal theory and les-bi-gay-trans legal scholarship can inhabit parallel universes.

Linguistically, the gender failings so evident in the *Bowers v. Hardwick* scholarship have not prevailed. Current les-bi-gay-trans legal scholarship purports to be much more gender inclusive. However, this does not mean that it is necessarily more gendered in any feminist sense. Much of the legal scholarship proceeds with inclusive language but an absence of any application of the concept of gender that might reveal complexities. Yet gender is not the only social construct ignored and les-bi-gay-trans legal scholarship certainly faces the same challenge that has faced feminist jurisprudence: the solipsism of its creators who may be privileged by racial, ethnic, economic, physical, or other group status.

Equally—if more perplexingly—egregious is the absence of gendered analysis that can occur in feminist inclusions of gay/lesbian issues. For example, lesbians can be relegated to a section on "lesbian and gay" issues in which "lesbian and gay" becomes an ungendered category. Thus, paired with "their men" in a move mimetic of heterosexuality, the unique legal issues and perspectives of lesbians become eclipsed and erased. Yet the inclusion of lesbian/gay legal issues in feminist legal theory texts, law journals, conferences, symposia, and surveys marks an understanding that there is some coincidence between the interests of les-bi-gay-trans legal scholarship and feminist jurisprudence.

The Lesbian-Feminist Link

A second strand of the relationship between feminist jurisprudence and les-bi-gay-trans legal scholarship focuses on the overlapping role of lesbianism as a marker of both a specific sexual orientation and gender. In terms of feminist legal theory, this might be understood as part of the diversity pattern. Sexual minority identification—lesbianism, bisexuality, and perhaps transgenderism—is another difference between women, much like racialized and ethnicized identities/constructs are differences between women. These sexual differences, like other differences, are part of the feminist project per se given that the feminist project is concerned with all women, which by definition includes lesbians. Thus, as previously mentioned, feminist jurisprudence would be underinclusive as a theoretical project to the extent it excluded lesbian perspectives.

However, another consequence of this diversity model is that any legal scholarship on issues specific to lesbians might fit within the feminist jurisprudence rubric. The legal scholarship on lesbian custody of children, for example, has been prolific, including excellent articles examining how lesbians (and gay men) fare in custody disputes with their heterosexual coparents as well as groundbreaking articles advocating legal reforms to accommodate lesbian coparenting.

Within this diversity model all articles focused on lesbians would be included. Thus, articles on lesbian battering, for example, would be just as appropriate as articles on battered women whose batterers are presumably men. Yet given the gendered explanation for domestic violence developed by many feminist scholars, the problem that immediately surfaces is whether an article on lesbian perpetrators of violence would also fit within feminist jurisprudence. The answer must undoubtedly be affirmative, in the same way that articles about female perpetrators of other crimes, such as infanticide, are matters of feminist jurisprudence. Thus, legal scholarship about lesbian relationships—with other lesbians, with children, and with the State—must be a matter of concern to feminist jurisprudence. Although many of the law review articles on lesbian issues—like law review articles on other issues—devote themselves to doctrinal exegesis and do not employ critical theoretical frameworks, feminist or otherwise, these articles are important to the feminist theoretical project because they elucidate the legal landscape. Further, when primarily doctrinal articles do evoke a theoretical perspective, feminist jurisprudence is certainly one of the favored frameworks in the panoply.

The very evocation of feminist perspectives, however, also marks divisions within lesbian legal scholarship as well as les-bi-gay-trans legal scholarship. For example, such a division has occurred in the scholarship relating to the issue of same-sex marriage. Some lesbian legal theorists arguing that the availability of marriage between same-sex couples should not be a priority for lesbian/gay liberation rely on feminist critiques of the legal institution of marriage. For example, Professor Nancy Polikoff, who situates herself as a "lesbian feminist," argues that an "effort to legalize lesbian and gay marriage would make a public critique of the institution of marriage impossible."[4] On the contrary, legal advocate Evan Wolfson surveys the debate within the gay/lesbian community, and notes that lesbians and gay men are "a remarkably diverse group," but does not adequately explore any differences caused by gender constructs.[5] Yet this is not to suggest that only authors who ignore feminist jurisprudence ultimately conclude that entitlements to same-sex marriage would be a positive legal reform for gay men and lesbians. Here, as in other areas, feminist jurisprudence has multiple inflections.

Thus, scholarship that involves lesbians and lesbian issues is integral to feminist jurisprudence, whether or not a particular feminist jurisprudential perspective is invoked. However, even scholarship that is not exclusively or even partially devoted to "women," for instance, legal scholarship that explores the situation of transgendered persons, gay men, and bisexual men, can be important for feminist legal theory. While as persons some persons may not fit into that elusive category women with which feminism is concerned, the theoretical issues raised by their legal treatment certainly stimulate exploration of a core issue of feminist legal theory: the legal meaning of the construct of gender.

The Sexual Orientation (Is)(Is Not) Gender Debate

A third strand of analysis relevant to the relation between feminist jurisprudence and minority sexualities seeks to clarify, at a theoretical level, the relationship between the constructs of sexual orientation and gender as those constructs are applied in the law. For some this occurs in an attempt to explain sexual orientation in terms of gender, especially in the context of discrimination. Others argue that the law has perpetuated a confusion between sexual orientation and gender. Both of these arguments implicate broader inquiries into identity.

The argument that sexual orientation is a subset of sex/gender occurs in some of the earliest legal scholarship on sexual orientation. Under this argument, an end to discrimination based upon sex would engender an end to bias based upon sexual orientation. Not surprisingly, such an argument would be attractive to a feminist jurisprude, for it maintains feminism as a grand theory and a fundamental claim. Yet gay male legal scholars also adhere to this theory, notably Professor Marc Fajer. Further, this view may be expressed in a complex manner that avoids rigid subordination of "sexual orientation" to "gender." For example, in her thoughtful article, "Refashioning the Unfashionable: Claiming Lesbian Identities in the Legal Context,"[6] Professor Diana Majury provides a telling example that a possible consequence of arguing lesbian discrimination as sex discrimination rather than sexual orientation discrimination might be the possibility for legal reform that is more profound.[7]

The argument also has a possible doctrinal efficacy given the prohibition of "sex" discrimination in Title VII and other laws. Arguments concerning the relation between sexual orientation and gender often require specific facts such as gender nonconformity or the adoption of a gendered understanding of sexual orientation. However, arguments concerning the relation between transgenderism/transsexuality and gender can have a more immediate logical and intuitive appeal; the argument that it is gender discrimination to fire a person who was hired as a man because the person is now a woman rests only upon a change in gender. Nevertheless, courts interpreting Title VII have relied upon congressional intent and have rejected any inclusory claims by plaintiffs who assert that discrimination on the basis of their sexual orientation or on the basis of their transsexuality would be encompassed by sex discrimination.

Despite a long and uniform history of disappointment for those who argued for the judicial acceptance of sexual orientation discrimination as included in sex discrimination, the Hawaii Supreme Court recently accepted just such an argument. In *Baehr v. Lewin*, the "Hawaii same-sex marriage case," the court relied upon its state constitutional provision prohibiting sex discrimination to invalidate the Hawaii statute that imposed an "opposite sex" requirement for couples to obtain a marriage license.[8] Interestingly, however, the court did not exactly equate sexual orientation discrimination with gender discrimination, but rather disin-

genuously relied upon a dissonance between sexual orientation as sex/
gender, stating:

> "Homosexual" and "same-sex" marriages are not synonymous; by the same
> token, a "heterosexual" same-sex marriage is, in theory, not oxymoronic. A
> "homosexual" person is defined as "[o]ne sexually attracted to another of the
> same sex." Taber's Cyclopedic Medical Dictionary 839 (16th ed. 1989).
> "Homosexuality" is "sexual desire or behavior directed toward a person or
> persons of one's own sex." Webster's Encyclopedic Unabridged Dictionary
> of the English Language 680 (1989). Conversely, "heterosexuality" is
> "[s]exual attraction for one of the opposite sex," Taber's Cyclopedic Medical
> Dictionary at 827, or "sexual feeling or behavior directed toward a person
> or persons of the opposite sex." Webster's Encyclopedic Unabridged
> Dictionary of the English Language at 667. Parties to "a union between a
> man and a woman" may or may not be homosexuals. Parties to a same-sex
> marriage could theoretically be either homosexuals or heterosexuals.[9]

Nevertheless, the Hawaii marriage case may have the effect of resuscitat-
ing the doctrinal purchase of arguments that sexual orientation discrimination is within the ambit of prohibitions of sex discrimination.

A contrary approach argues that many problems flow from our confusion of sex as gender and sex as sexual orientation. For example, Professor
Francisco Valdes concludes that although the law did not "invent" the
conflation of sex, gender, and sexual orientation, legal culture's acceptance
of the conflation facilitates a systematic denial of protection to those seeking it and subverts the "grand, formal promise of equality."[10] A related
approach is taken by Professor Mary Anne Case, who explores the legal
position of the "effeminate man, i.e., a man usually perceived to be gay."[11]

At a metatheoretical level, the gender (is) (is not) sexual orientation discussion is concerned with the more fundamental issue of "identity"—an
issue that has preoccupied both feminist jurisprudence and les-bi-gay-
trans scholarship. For lesbian and gay legal scholarship, the issue has been
most often explored in the context of specific legal consequences, such as
the availability of equal protection under current constitutional doctrine
and the status/conduct distinction employed by the United States government, especially the military, in its expulsion of lesbian and gay employees.
However, like feminist jurisprudence, les-bi-gay legal scholarship has not
been immune to the theoretical currents of postmodernism affecting those
working in nonlegal disciplines. Within legal scholarship there are those
who argue that lesbian and gay identity is similar to an "ethnic" identity as

well as those who dismiss such ethnic parallels as essentialist and argue for a more performative construction of identity, including identities of bisexuality and transgenderism. Perhaps ironically, both the essentialist paradigm and the performative/constructionist paradigm lend themselves to the creation of larger theoretical paradigms.

The Alternative Theories Approach

In my Aristotelian taxonomy the final category that facilitates the consideration of the relationship between feminist jurisprudence and les-bi-gay-trans legal scholarship requires contemplation of whether les-bi-gay-trans legal theories are compatible and equal theoretical perspectives to feminist jurisprudence. In my own work I have clearly posited an answer to this query, at least with regard to lesbian legal theory, nevertheless the categorical impulse leads to an examination of whether or not there may be a "queer" legal theory, a specifically "lesbian legal theory," a "bisexual jurisprudence," or a transgender legal theory, any of which might be a perspective illuminating a specific legal problem that might also be—or not be—within the circle of light cast by feminist jurisprudence.

Most easily identified are the instances in which the alternative legal theory conflicts with some tenets of feminist jurisprudence. For example, in the area of pornography Carl Stychin has elucidated a gay male theoretical position from which to consider the legal regulation of pornography.[12] Similarly, in their coauthored article Tamara Packard and Melissa Schraibman have argued for the necessity of lesbian pornography to the production of lesbian community and theorizing.[13] Finally, Ann Scales has considered the Canadian experience accepting many of the feminist arguments against pornography and thereby adopting an antipornography law that has been disproportionately applied to regulate lesbian and gay materials at independent lesbian/gay bookstores.[14] Although feminist legal theory is certainly not monolithic in its perspectives on the legal ramifications of pornography, it is not necessarily true that these articles are simply a gloss on a rift within feminist jurisprudence itself. Instead, these articles, as well as articles concerning hate speech and privacy considerations related to "outing," attempt distinct conceptualizations of particular problems that may be relevant to feminist jurisprudence, while drawing on wider theoretical currents in lesbian and/or gay scholarship.

More problematic are the instances in which there is substantial overlap between a feminist jurisprudence and les-bi-gay-trans legal theories.

For example, despite much scholarship and many panels denominated lesbian legal theory, it is unclear to what extent any lesbian legal theory would overlap with queer legal theory or with bisexual jurisprudence. As Ruth Colker argues, a bisexual jurisprudence should be a "dynamic, inclusive jurisprudence which serves to understand society's control of our sexuality in all of its dimensions,"[15] thus including aspects of lesbian legal theory as well as queer legal theory. Further, the very denomination queer is generally interpreted to include lesbian, gay, bisexual, and transgendered issues, persons, and practices as well as some of the less normative aspects of heterosexuality. And the very notion of a transgendered jurisprudence could encompass feminist legal theory's interrogation of gender as well as aspects of queer theory.[16]

Certainly, it is quite possible that doing scholarship requires one to be conversant with a wide variety of theoretical perspectives. For example, in her work on contract ideology, Kellye Teste demonstrates tremendous aptitude at moving between theoretical perspectives she denominates as feminist jurisprudence and lesbian legal theory as applied to the area of contract doctrine, also incorporating critical race theory and postmodernism.[17] While one could rightfully pose the question whether all these overlapping theoretical perspectives are necessary, one might then be led to the unenviable task of choosing a single theory as guarantor of liberation of a wide range of minority sexualities. And if les-bi-gay-trans legal theorists can learn anything from the history of feminist jurisprudence, it is that a grandiose theory will not be effective—or tolerable—for very long.

But isn't every theory grandiose? And what do we mean by theory anyway? I realize that my conclusion perpetuates an obfuscation contained in the question posed and its responsive hierarchal taxonomy—the slippage between doctrinal analysis and theory. For at the very core of the enterprise are assumptions not only about feminist jurisprudence, les-bi-gay-trans legal scholarship, and the possibility of lesbian legal theory but also about the nature of theorizing itself. These assumptions bubble throughout the explication of the taxonomy and result in the implicit (or not so implicit) devaluation of work denominated as mere "doctrinal exegesis." This occurs in spite of my belief that one cannot accomplish doctrinal exegesis, mere or not, without resort to some theoretical perspective, and most likely more than one.

Yet these inquiries are beyond the assignment, although vital to the questions I have posed for myself. After the article is submitted and the peculiar joys of taxonomic exercise have subsided, these questions coalesce into a much more specific problem: what are the real differences between feminist jurisprudence and lesbian legal theory?

Didi Herman, critiquing the possibilities of lesbian legal theory, argues that the separation of lesbian legal theory from feminism may reinforce the very problems the separation attempted to solve, because, "ironically," such a separation would mean the inability to consider lesbians as *women*.[18] However, I am less convinced that such an inability is inherent in the project, just as I am unconvinced by Herman's other assertions that lesbian legal theory must homogenize lesbians or that lesbian legal theory rejects an ethic of solidarity with heterosexual feminists or gay men. Further, Herman's concerns are applicable to any theory, including feminist jurisprudence. For one could argue (as many did) that feminist jurisprudence results in an inability to consider women as human, that feminist jurisprudence homogenizes women, and that feminist jurisprudence rejects an ethic of solidarity with other oppressed peoples, such as working-class men or men of color. Yet these dangers seem to me to be dangers attributable to a narrowly imposed version of reality, rather than inherent in the theoretical perspective itself. Further, it seems to me that much of the anxiety surrounding the positing of a lesbian legal theory (including my own anxiety) is the specter of the label *separatist*. To bear the badge of lesbian separatism is to be marked as reactionary, racist, and definitely retrograde. Yet I find it interesting that such anxieties are provoked whenever the term *lesbian* appears without partners or modifiers.

Nevertheless, I am ultimately less concerned with the tagging of a theory than with its perspective, content, and ultimate goals. One reason that I became interested in a lesbian legal theory is that I found feminist legal theory cramped, and this constriction was not limited to its weak inclusion of lesbian issues. Thus, although I certainly agree with Diana Majury's suggestion that arguing lesbian inequality as sex discrimination rather than as sexual orientation/lesbian discrimination would yield a different analysis and result, I am struck by her example. Majury argues that applying a sex equality analysis in the so-called spousal benefits cases (cases in which a benefit such as health insurance or pensions are available only to married partners), a sex equality perspective would more clearly expose the gendered assumptions of need and dependence upon which such benefits are premised and would thus "open up the larger question" of whether such benefits should in fact be distributed on a gender-neutral assessment of need and dependence and probably provide the grounding for arguments about universalized benefits.[19] This is certainly a version of feminist jurisprudence that would earn my loyalties, and it is also a version of lesbian legal theory that I have advocated, reaching a similar conclusion through the route of considering lesbians who are not in partnered or coupled relationships to question whether such relationships should determine the availability of benefits. In such cases there is little relevant distinction between certain conceptions of feminist jurisprudence and certain conceptions of lesbian legal theory—at their very best, they both "open up the larger question." But then again, shouldn't all theories do that?

Which brings me back to the question of theory itself. Long before I pondered the existence of lesbian legal theory, of feminist jurisprudence, or even a career in law, I recall participating in extended and complicated discussions among my fellow students about differences between what we called "reform" and "revolution." A few of us may have called these conversations "theory" (or, more likely, "political philosophy," given that many of us were philosophy or political science majors), but mostly we were concerned with change and something we amorphously called "liberation." Some of us were feminists and some of us were Marxists, some of us were queer and some straight, and at least one a self-proclaimed celibate, some of us were anti-imperialist and some of us Afrocentric, a few of us were anarchists and a few were "democratic pluralists." And these things divided us, not only from each other but also within each of us as individuals. But the larger division—and the one that caused the most heated of our arguments—was the degree and rate of change we believed was necessary to achieve what we called "liberation."

And perhaps that is still the case.

6

Beginning From (My) Experience: The Paradoxes

of Narrative

The shaping of experience into narrative is a staple of progressive legal theorizing, including lesbian/queer legal theorizing. The importance of narrative rests upon two intertwined beliefs. First, it rests upon the belief that the extant legal theories and doctrines are impoverished because they are based upon the experiences of only dominant groups, those who have had the power to construct the theories and doctrines. Second, the importance of narrative rests upon the belief that the present legal landscape can be improved if those persons outside the dominant group make public our experiences. In short, the argument provides that lesbians and other queers, faced with a dominant legal regime to which we are essentially "foreigners," can effect change in the law by telling our stories.

The Beginning

Let me begin again, this time with a quotation:

> What would happen if one woman told the truth about her life?
> The world would split open[1]

To include such a reference is to lay the foundation for a personal revelation: what feminists would name experience, what Foucault might call an engagement in the confessional mode, what postmodernists would label narrativity, and what legal theorists might entitle storytelling or outsider jurisprudence.

And, like most quotations, this one probably has more resonance for its user than for its audience. The first time I heard these words, they were being read aloud not by their author, the poet Muriel Rukeyser, but by a fellow student of mine in a women's literature course. We were using the then-newly published anthology, *No More Masks! An Anthology of Poems by Women*,[2] and the very idea that there were enough poems written by women to fill an entire book seemed rather exciting. Part of each class consisted of a student presentation: a student would select a poem and read it aloud, talk about what the poem meant to her personally, and then facilitate a class discussion about the poem. In these discussions we never mentioned line breaks or meter, and students almost always talked about our lives. Although it could not be graded in a traditional manner, we knew that telling and listening to our experiences was a fundamental portion of the course.

"Käthe Kollwitz" is the title of the poem by Muriel Rukeyser that my fellow student read aloud. Käthe Kollwitz was a visual artist working in Germany between the world wars, most famous for her pacifism and her woodcuts. Her life was the subject of a biography, published a few years later.[3] In the Rukeyser poem Kollwitz becomes an embodiment of the dilemma of the woman artist—caught between her female gender and her "masculine art." The poem provoked stories from the women in the class, a large proportion of whom were then called "returning women." These returning women spoke about their struggles to do the reading for classes and attend to their demanding husbands and children; their tales were full of topless toothpaste tubes and televisions.

"If one woman told the truth about her life, the world would split open," the woman who had read the poem aloud paraphrased. Her voice was sharp as she spoke very eloquently about being prescribed Valium when she told her physician husband that she felt her life was empty and wanted to go to college. I remember she spoke a long time, longer than had become customary. I remember looking across the circle at one of the other younger students in the room, trying to catch her eye and looking away when I did. I remember the sympathetic expression on the professor's face. I remember it was spring, but I was still wearing boots. I remember tamping down my own reactions to what I saw as her economic privilege; I remember thinking that she could have sold the Valium on a street corner or on campus and I could tell her some good locations; I remember thinking that she was lucky to have toothpaste, topless or not. But this is what I remember most of all: no matter how much truth she told about her life, the world did not split open. At least not for me.

Because what I understood Muriel Rukeyser to mean, even allowing for poetic excess, was that the world was as susceptible of being ruptured by the story of an ordinary woman in the same way a chicken could be cleaved in half by the sharp knife of a skillful chef. And every evening, in the restaurant where I waitressed, I could hear bones cracking as the chicken breasts were being sundered and sliced. Sometimes I would proffer this experience as the basis for my vegetarianism. I might even crack my knuckles as a soundtrack.

Beginning Again

Let me begin again, because I have digressed, as telling a story often leads one to do. What I want to discuss is the current state of narrativity in lesbian/queer legal theorizing. But any attempt at this discussion leads me to the role of experience in theorizing, especially in feminist theorizing. For although lesbian/queer narratives often accompany feminist narratives as well as racialized and ethnicized narratives—under the rubric of "outsider" scholarship—the explicit links between the feminist emphasis on experience and the present popularity of narrativity often remain unexplored.

From Epistemology to Experience

This is not to say that experience as epistemological method and the critiques of such are originary with feminists. To theorize at all, even if such theorizing is labeled ontological, is to engage the questions of epistemology—how we know what we (think we) know. In the ancient Chinese philosophic tradition the most famous example is Chuang Tzu's story of the man who dreams he is a butterfly: "How can I tell whether I am a man who dreamt he was a butterfly or a butterfly dreaming she is man?" Similarly, Plato's allegory of the cave points to the partiality of perception—experience—for apprehending reality.[4] Building on both Chinese and Greek traditions, Hegel sought to explain experience as "the dialectical process which consciousness executes on itself,"[5] meaning that experience was both the mind's apprehension of a thing and the thing itself. Both before and after Hegel, countless other philosophers, including Kant, Husserl, Heidegger, Hume, all struggled with the role and reliability of experience in theorizing, yet most of these thinkers concentrated on ontological matters. Karl Marx, however, eschewed ontology for an imposition of the dialectical "history of consciousness" onto the experience of economics and state power.

Yet we do not necessarily think of Chuang-tzu or Plato as authorities on experience, at least in the sense that we have come to think of experience. In its contemporary usage, experience is not the perception of objects qua objects but is a more complicated—and personally unique—process involving a host of interpersonal relationships, social conditions, environmental interactions, and events. The critiques of subjectivity, however, apply equally forcefully to experience as perception of objects and experience as personal history. In both cases experience presupposes a fully constituted individual: perception and experience are something a person has.[6]

Nevertheless, it is also widely recognized that experience constructs subjectivity. Even in a traditional philosophic dialectical process consciousness itself is transformed by the apprehension of the object. In Marxist terms "life is not determined by consciousness but consciousness by life."[7] Similarly, we routinely relate specific experiences in our personal histories as a way of explaining our current personalities, and we speak of transformative experiences.

For feminists of the 1970s consciousness-raising—the sharing of personal experiences—was itself postulated as a transformative experience. Hearing one's own story spoken by oneself and recognizing one's own story in the stories of other women was itself an experience that would lead to a reconceptualization of the way one thought of one's own life and one's identity as a woman. The relevance of experience, shared in the context of consciousness-raising sessions (whether formally named as such or not), has been called a core concept of feminism.[8] The reliance of women on individual experience allowed them to question previously held "objective" notions such as that women were not oppressed as women. Perhaps ironically, it was individual experience that formed the basis for shared identity–by speaking about individual problems women were to realize that these experiences were not in fact individual in the sense of being unique "personal" problems but were part of larger patterns. According to an early 1970s "working sheet" for a beginning consciousness-raising group: "The consciousness raising process is one in which personal experiences, when shared, are recognized as the result not of an individual's idiosyncratic history and behavior, but of the system of sex-role stereotyping."[9] Or, as stated two decades later by feminist theorist Catharine MacKinnon:

> The analysis that the personal is political came out of consciousness raising. It has four interconnected facets. First, women as a group are dominated by

men as a group, and therefore as individuals. Second, women are subordinated in society, not by personal nature or by biology. Third, the gender division, which includes the sex division of labor which keeps women in high-heeled low-status jobs, pervades and determines even women's personal feelings in relationships. Fourth, since a woman's problems are not hers individually but those of women as a whole, they cannot be addressed except as a whole. In this analysis of gender as a nonnatural characteristic of a division of power in society, the personal becomes the political.[10]

There are many pitfalls and problems with consciousness-raising. First, the process as a means to its proclaimed end is debatable. Although many feminists posited the slogan "the personal is political" as a retort to New Left nonfeminists who interpreted consciousness-raising as simply personal therapy, some feminists themselves expressed doubts as to the relationship between relating personal incidents and the achievement of political solutions. For example, as early as 1971 Carol Williams Payne published her piece about leaving her consciousness-raising group because she "felt nothing could be accomplished by becoming more and more intimate with a small group of women."[11] Furthermore, once a group abandoned the group therapy model, the ability to take concrete action was often hampered by the group's devotion to the leaderless, "structureless" mode of organization.[12]

Moreover, like any methodology that posits experience as a path to truth, consciousness-raising possesses a fundamental flaw—the inability to account for women who experienced their own experiences as different from the political "truth" being proffered by others. This flaw lead to an adoption of the concept of false consciousness,[13] the state inhabited by those who did not (yet) understand their condition in feminist terms. Yet because feminism itself attacked the existence of objective and singular truth (heretofore male), the positing of a singular truth necessary to render false consciousness "false" was problematic. Further, the version of truth was deemed partial, having been based only upon a relatively privileged and predominantly white group of women.

Despite the problems with consciousness-raising and the role of experience in feminist theorizing, it is important to remember the roots of the practice of relating individual experiences. Sharing experiences was intended to foster recognition of shared conditions and reject the notion of individual pathologies. The goal was to forge an understanding that women's lives were constrained by political forces. It was not necessary that this goal be achieved by the particular method of sharing experience through consciousness-raising; what was necessary was that this understanding lead to political action to improve women's lives. Thus, the sharing of experience was never in and of itself a goal.

Coming Out

The closest parallel to feminist consciousness-raising in the lesbian/queer context is coming out. The stereotypical coming-out narrative constructs an individual's experience as a linear progression, culminating in the revelation of one's lesbian or queer sexual identity. As lesbian theorist Judith Roof notes, the "quintessential lesbian narrative is the coming out story, not because there is something inherently lesbian about it, but because it is both ubiquitous and proclaimed as such by lesbians."[14] In lesbian literature the coming-out story is the common bildungsroman.[15] A professor in a lesbian studies course may have the students "share" their "coming-out stories." Lesbian legal scholar Mary Dunlap has suggested that in order to evaluate scholarship it is necessary that an author adhere to an ethical duty to elucidate his or her own experiences that are pertinent to the subject.[16]

Yet, although there is a sharing of stories in literary and other modes of cultural production, I do not believe that coming out is necessarily a narrative process in and of itself. As Kenneth Plummer suggests, narrative is important in the production of individual as well as communitarian sexual identities, but it is not the same as "life."[17] Thus, although coming out can be constructed as a story, and often results in the reconstruction of a narrative of one's experiences, it is distinguishable from consciousness-raising because one does not necessarily come out through the revelation of one's own story and a recognition of its commonality with the other stories one is hearing. Further, coming out does not necessarily have the required "beginning, middle, and end" of narrative structure because we often refer to "coming out" to denote a declarative statement about one's sexual identity rather than a retelling of a story of which the claiming of an identity is the end.[18] Additionally, coming out is not always the self-construction of a narrative, as the possibility of being "outed" demonstrates. My argument is that coming out is not necessarily or fundamentally a narrative process; one may just as easily come out in the context of non-narrative experiences such as going to bars or flirting or engaging in sex, although certainly those incidents can later be narrativized.

This is the point at which I am permitted to engage in my own coming out story.

I have a confession: I often find such stories tedious. Including my own coming out narrative; especially my own narrative.

I have another confession: I am always tempted to pretend that my own narrative is so extraordinary—extraordinarily intense, or painful, or embarrassing, or funny, or wonderful, or even pathetic—that its specialness must be guarded.

This is my final confession: I am sometimes even tempted to construct and tell as true an extraordinary narrative—one that is intense and wonderful, or perhaps painful and pathetic—as long as it is interesting.

For that is narrative's ultimate imperative: to be fascinating. The formal structures of narrative, codified since Aristotle, are merely techniques to accomplish narrative's task of engaging our attention. This attention may ultimately be erotic. In the phrasing of literary theorist Peter Brooks, narrative is equated with desire: "Narratives both tell of desire—typically present some story of desire—and arouse and make use of desire as dynamic of signification."[19] Similarly, Teresa de Lauretis exclaims that "narrative is desire"[20] and Roland Barthes famously explicates upon the pleasures of the text.[21] The correlation of narrative with desire relies upon Freudian concepts of psychoanalysis, yet one need not subscribe to psychoanalytic theories to accept the rather prosaic notion that narrative's imperative is to be interesting.

Legal Narrativities

In the legal context, however, narrative has an additional function. In advocacy narrative is harnessed to the goal of success. Integral to strategy, narrativity is a technique employed by the advocate who evaluates testimony and evidence and constructs a story that will achieve the client's desired outcome. This is nothing new: "It would hardly shock lawyers who lived before the era of high critical theory in American academia to discover that the winner in some trials is the more sophisticated or compelling storyteller."[22] While there might be many competing narratives that one can choose for a particular case, part of advocacy training is learning to select and hone the narrative that will best achieve the desired outcome. The advocate conveys the narrative theme in pleadings, during the trial through questioning, and, felicitously, most coherently during closing arguments. If one is successful, the narrative that one has chosen is the narrative that the jury accepts as "truth." On appeal, an advocate crafts a persuasive "statement of facts" in the brief and hopes that these will be reproduced as the "facts" in the judicial opinion. Such narratives may be explicit and specific or may implicate larger issues of justice. For example, in the death penalty context an advocate may advance a narrative that a specific client should not be executed as well as a narrative that executions are unjust.[23]

Outside the litigation context legal theorists are also enamored of narrative. While such has always been true, in the last decade or so storytelling, narrativity, and autobiography have been more explicitly proffered as scholarly methodology. Such scholarship is related to the so-called law and literature movement, but, as Robert Chang perceptively notes, the distinction is that law and literature scholarship "talks about narrative" as opposed to "doing" narrative.[24] Nevertheless, before "doing" narrative, legal scholars have often engaged in an explanatory exegesis of the value of narrative. While there are no previous specifically lesbian pieces, queer scholarly contributions have been made by Marc Fajer,[25] William Eskridge,[26] and most recently Larry Cata Backer.[27] These contributions are contextualized among the work by many legal scholars of color and feminist legal scholars—having become loosely grouped into a genre known as "outsider narratives."[28]

Like other outsider narratives, lesbian/queer narrative legal scholarship rests upon the two intertwined beliefs previously mentioned at the beginning of this article. First, it rests upon the belief that the extant legal theories and doctrines are impoverished because they are based upon the experiences of only dominant groups, those who have had the power to construct the theories and doctrines. So, for example, Marc Fajer argues that the law is based upon certain "pre-understandings," or stereotypes of queers, and that for queers themselves to tell our stories is an effective way to combat these stereotypes. In his groundbreaking article, Fajer identifies three important preunderstandings "about gay people: the sex-as-lifestyle assumption, the idea that gay issues are inappropriate for public discussion, and the cross-gender assumption."[29] That such preunderstandings are in fact themselves the result of narrative processes is made clear by the work of Larry Cata Backer, who demonstrates that gay men have been relegated by sodomy jurisprudence narratives into categories he names predator, pied piper, whore, and defiler.[30] Implicit in both Fajer's and Backer's arguments is that such cultural and judicial categories have been forged apart from the influence of persons known to be sexual minorities.

Second, queer narrative legal scholarship rests upon the belief that the present legal landscape can be improved if those persons outside the dominant group make public our experiences. In short, this belief is that lesbians and other queers, faced with a dominant legal regime to which we are essentially "foreigners," may be able to effect change in the law by telling our stories. Thus, Fajer assembles narratives from a wide variety of sources—personal experiences, judicial opinions, lesbian/queer texts, and newspaper accounts—to combat the harmful preunderstandings he has identified. Additionally, there is strong sentiment that succumbing to the pressure to suppress our narratives will not ensure legal—or personal—success.

Reviewing the Critiques of Narrative Legal Scholarship

The genre of narrative legal scholarship has provoked rather virulent debate. The work of some scholars of color, as well as some feminists, became the subject of the initial critiques,[31] although the critiques quickly became focused exclusively on outsider narratives.[32] These critiques in turn provoked compelling responses[33] and subsequent practitioners of narrative scholarship seemed compelled to engage with the critique.[34] While the initial critiques avoided any substantive engagement with lesbian/queer legal issues,[35] as the debate developed, it began to include work of sexual minority scholars, specifically Fajer and Eskridge. Before discussing what I consider to be certain paradoxes implicated in the possibilities of lesbian/queer narrative legal scholarship and lesbian/queer narrativity more generally, it is necessary to indulge in a brief rehearsal of the current controversy. The present terms of the debate encompass five basic arguments: the accuracy argument, the representative argument, the special voice argument, the nonobjective argument, and the evaluative argument.

First, the accuracy argument against narrative entails the objection that narrative, especially any purportedly autobiographical narrative, does not allow a reader to confirm the truth of the narrative because there are no external or objective sources readily available. The accuracy of narrative is posited as important in legal scholarship because a misrepresentation of events is "perilously close to what is known in other fields as research fraud: doctoring data to fit your thesis."[36] Critics "have been concerned about the risk that stories can distort the legal debate, particularly if those stories are atypical, inaccurate, or incomplete."[37] Legal academic scholarship is paralleled to litigation in which a lawyer is not being able to offer her own testimony at trial or vouch for the credibility of a witness,[38] and

the "facts" have been subjected to an adversary process.[39] While this epistemological anxiety does not trouble all critics, it is a significant objection
by the critics of narrative in legal scholarship.

There are several responses to the accuracy critique. One overall theme
of such responses is that the accuracy of a narrative is not comparable in
importance to the accuracy of empirical data. For some the function of the
narrative in the general account determines the stress to be placed upon
issues of accuracy; for others it is not necessarily the factual accuracy but the
integrity or coherence of the narrative that counts. Further, as Fajer points
out, in law we "regularly use fictional hypotheticals to further [our] analyses and engage in discussions assuming facts to be true arguendo."[40] Fajer
also makes several concrete and constructive suggestions to enable scholars
constructing a narrative to minimize the credibility issue. There seems to
be an agreement that "under the assumptions of form" of narrative a reader
may not be able to compare the author's story with an external account of
the event, but defenders of narrative argue that stories can provide the
reader with a "flash of recognition." Thus, while there is some agreement
that narratives should be accurate unless denominated differently, the
importance of accuracy and the methods of verification are contested.

Second, the representative argument, often discussed as a question of
typicality, disputes any claim that a narrative can reveal itself as either customary or aberrant. This argument is composed of two intertwined but
distinct problems: the narrative may not be representative of the writer's
other experiences and, even if the narrative is representative of this writer's
experiences, this may not be representative of the experiences of other
(similarly situated) people. The critique again interprets narrative as
empirical data and questions whether it is "statistically significant."[41] A
powerful narrative may become particularly suspect because "individuals
assume that dramatic or easily remembered events are typical," which
means that they have a tendency to "overestimate the likelihood" of such
an event and likewise overestimate the prevalence in other members of the
population of such an event.[42] In short, people stereotype.

However, if Fajer and others are correct that one function of narrative
is to combat stereotypes, then the criticism that a narrative may not be representative is largely irrelevant. In other words, even if the narrative is
considered to be a singular event in an unusual person, it can operate to
undermine the stereotype. Additionally, the tendency toward typicality,
likelihood, and prevalence is counterbalanced by a certain status quo solipsism. As Robert Chang expresses it, because people have convinced them-

selves that the ugliness of racism does not exist, at least in blatant forms, they can dismiss Chang's narratives of discrimination against him as a Korean American as "isolated incidents."[43] Thus, critics and supporters of narrative in legal scholarship have divergent opinions about whether representativeness is an appropriate criterion of assessment.

Third, critics dispute any claim that any group of narrators possesses a special "voice." Critics reject any claim that an outsider narrative is based upon group experiences, because there is neither a distinct nor unitary voice possessed by any group. Critics use theories of social constructionism and antiessentialism, developed by many outsider theorists themselves, to dispute the existence of any coherent perspective possessed by any particular group. Defenders, in fact, may agree: some defenders of narrative aver that "voice" is an "unfortunate metaphor"[44] or a false issue.[45] Alex Johnson, however, in supporting a "Voice of Color," argues that "voice" is not some essentialist possession but a result of the social construction of the categories of race itself: the "Voice of Color" is thus "socially constructed as different or minority—as 'other' or 'them,' never as 'same' or 'us.' "[46] Or, as Jane Baron contends, one need not assert the existence of any "essentially" different voice to explain why those who lack power or represent people who do might be particularly focused on one of power's "most important forms, the story."[47] Thus, both supporters and critics of narrative may seek to distance themselves from the sin of essentialism. In this distancing there does seem to be at least a superficial agreement that outsider narratives are not simply special because they are written by persons who are members of what might be described as outsider groups. Nevertheless, supporters of outsider narrative would maintain that group membership can be important and that a narrative can demonstrate the significance of group membership.

The special voice argument has two additional aspects. First, the special voice argument tends to collapse outsiders and narratives: not all "outsider" scholars practice narrative and not all practitioners of narrative are outsiders. Second, combined with the previous representative argument, it places any narrator with a group identity (which I suggest would be every narrator) between Scylla and Charybdis. The narrator is either not representative of her group, in which case her narrative should be dismissed as aberrant, or else she is claiming to possess a special group "voice," which does not exist.

Fourth, critics raise arguments concerning the nonobjective nature of narrative. In some sense the nonobjectivity argument underlies the criticisms of narratives with regard to accuracy, representation, and voice. This criticism implicitly contrasts narrative with logical argument, implying that narrative is flawed because it is not capable of an authoritative interpretation. Yet, within the debate, this argument has a rather unique twist, devolving into a claim by critics that although practitioners of outsider narratives claim their texts are susceptible of multiple meanings the practitioners themselves insist upon a singularly correct interpretation.

This argument is related to another nonobjectivity argument: that narratives, especially personal ones, foreclose rather than enhance scholarly (objective) debate. On this view, the inclusion of a personal narrative makes it difficult to challenge the author's point without questioning the author's "emotional stability or veracity"[48] or being construed as an ad hominem attack.[49] In response, defenders of narrative point to the very existence of the critical scholarship making the argument to defeat the claim that such criticism is foreclosed as well as noting that considerable scholarly discussion exists regarding the work of scholars who employ narratives extensively. More specifically, Marc Fajer outlines a number of civil and scholarly responses that could be made by those who are skeptical about a particular narrative.[50]

In sum, while questions of objectivity are implicated in the other criticisms of narrative, the struggles regarding objectivity are not simply between those professing an objective stance and those asserting that all stances are contingent. Rather, arguments regarding interpretative authority and the conditions of scholarly debate reflect very different postulations of the academic enterprise and legal scholarly "community."

The last argument also involves issues rather exclusive to the academy. The evaluative argument, or what I would prefer to name the tenure difficulty, expresses doubts about whether narrative scholarship can meet the criteria of "excellence" employed by academic arbiters with the power to award tenure, as well as promotion and initial faculty appointments, and, if so, under what criteria. Critics of narrative argue that the claim of some theorists that traditional criteria should not apply to narrative contains several unsustainable contentions. First, aesthetic considerations cannot be determinative because the focus of the legal academy is law and not literature. Second, a claim that outsider narratives should be judged according to their "ability to advance the interests of the outsider community" is akin to a political litmus test: the confusion of scholarship with politics is not necessarily transformative, but "can be merely tragic."[51] And third, any claim that traditional evaluative standards are biased or inapplicable to certain persons is beyond discussion. The lowest common denominator of agreement regarding standards applicable to the evaluation of narrative within the legal academy might be that narratives in the context of legal scholarship should be somehow related to legal concerns.

Obviously, disputes involving tenure, promotion, and even initial appointment can lead to ugly conflicts within a law school as well as within any larger university in which a law school might be established. In an attempt to forestall such difficulties, Arthur Austin has sought to situate narrative scholarship within the three stages of legal scholarship—vocational, doctrinal, and interdisciplinary—and to remind us that legal scholarship is a relatively new field.[52] Given such a background, the implicit suggestion is that legal academics need to be less defensive and less critical and begin the work of formulating concrete standards. Austin proffers his own criteria: that the scholarship must deliver the message with clarity, that the scholarship must add something to the existing body of knowledge, that the scholarship opens or is part of an ongoing dialogue, and that specifically narrative scholarship must satisfy the aesthetic requirements of narrative qua narrative.[53] Austin elaborates these criteria and applies them to specific examples, making his project practically useful to his goal of contributing to making an effective response to the "deepening fragmentation of scholars into special interest groups."[54] Yet however "concrete" the standards, they cannot pave over the fundamental disagreement between critics and practitioners of narrative, particularly outsider narrative. For critics, the academic project is a greater "understanding" of law;[55] for supporters of outsider narrative, the project is one of changing the law.[56]

The foregoing outline of the debate surrounding narrative in legal scholarship and, specifically, outsider narratives is necessary background for any discussion of lesbian/queer legal narratives. While the critiques of narrative make some interesting points and have opened up a discussion, I do not find the critiques of narrative compelling and often find them reactionary and rude. Nevertheless, I do have some concerns about relying upon narrativity as a strategy to accomplish progressive legal change relating to lesbian as well as queer issues. My misgivings encompass narrative as used in legal scholarship but also in the theorizing that occurs in places other than academic law reviews, as well as narrative more generally. As I hope is clear, I write as one who is enmeshed in narrative, both in legal scholarship and in traditionally narrative forms such as the novel, in which I write as well. Further, I depart from the contours of the current critiques, with their binary attentiveness to a presumed opposition between narrative and logical argument, which probably have more in common with each other than lyricism and, certainly, nonlinguistic communications have with either.

My trepidation is derived from the possibility that a reliance upon narrative may undermine what we seek to accomplish because of certain paradoxes of narrativity. These paradoxes relate to the male/heterosexuality of narrative structure itself, the ubiquity of narrative, the contrast of narrativity with feminist consciousness-raising, the interplay between individual and collective narratives, the tendency of narratives to provoke counternarratives, the lure of self-censorship, and, finally, the fact that we may be at the end of the period in which narrativity is a relevant undertaking.

Seven Paradoxes

1.

First, it may be paradoxical—and unworkable—to use narrative to advance lesbian liberation because narrative itself may be inescapably male and heterosexual. For those theorists who rely upon psychoanalytic models of narrative as equatable to desire, this desire is constructed as male. As Teresa de Lauretis notes, it is male desire that structures narrativity and results in its singular plot: the male hero's quest, which has a woman as the reward/object.[57] The heterosexuality of this model is made more explicit by lesbian theorist Judith Roof, who argues that "our very understanding of narrative as a primary means to sense and satisfaction depends upon a metaphorically heterosexual dynamic within a reproductive aegis."[58] Roof is not arguing that there cannot be narratives with lesbian content, or even narratives with "positive" lesbian content, but rather that the structure of narrative is ineluctably male and heterosexual. This may explain some of the dissatisfaction with the revolutionary potential of current lesbian narratives, even when such narratives seek to disrupt sex or gender categories. As Roof states: "Something in the way we understand what a story is in the first place or something in the way narrative itself operates produces narrative's 'heterosexually friendly' shape."[59] While not invoking objections of masculinity or heterosexuality, Fredric Jameson's analysis of the "commodification" of narrative is pertinent.[60] In Jameson's analysis narrative's Aristotelian arrangement into beginning-middle-end is a reifying and consumptive structure whereby the end determines every portion of the narrative, which portions are themselves consumed under the narrative beginning-middle-end model.[61] If Roof is correct in her assertion that narrativity only tolerates lesbianism in its perverse middle,[62] then Jameson's insight about the relative irrelevance of every aspect other than the end means that lesbians can exist as consumable objects within narrative but that our existence cannot be narrativity's end/purpose. Thus, although we may believe that narrative is preferable to doctrinal rules for accomplishing favorable legal change for lesbians, it may be that narrative is as male and heterosexual a structure as rationalist legalism.

2.

A second and related paradox is that the oppositional stance of narrative may not be oppositional at all. Barthes has famously stated that "narrative is international, transhistorical, transcultural: it is simply there, like life itself."[63]

Similarly, Hayden White has stated that to even "raise the question of narrative itself is to invite reflection on the very nature of culture and, possibly, even on the nature of humanity itself."[64] By using narratives we often believe we are presenting a specific account as distinct from an abstract theory, but the very structure of narrative may be undermining its content, no matter how distinctive. As Judith Roof argues, narrative "is a structural defense against a chaotic world"[65] and in its attempt to impose order it may be more like a logical system than not. The beginning-middle-end structure of narrative is the same structure employed in Enlightenment and modernist pursuits of history, economics, science, and law. For example, one of Hegel's central notions was that "history is the story of the development of human freedom."[66] This development is inextricably bound to law and the formation of the nation-state, which, in fact, enables the conditions for narrativity. As Robert Weisberg explicates, according to Hegel,

> Only where there is law can there be a subject or kind that lends itself to narrative, or a legal subject to serve as that agent, agency, and subject of historical narrative. The urge to tell stories derives either from an urge for national law and order or a desire to challenge that law and order. . . . Hence narrative deals with law, legality, legitimacy, or more generally authority. The desire to narrate is the desire to represent authority, whose legitimacy depends upon establishing certain grounding facts.[67]

Such philosophizing, indeed all of Hegel's philosophizing, typifies the grand narrative or metanarrative that postmodernism rejects. Postmodernism's rejection, however, does not encompass "smaller" narratives, which are often celebrated as a method to oppose scientific, abstract, or even legal systems.

Yet these smaller narratives—by being narratives—replicate the structure of the grand narratives being rejected, albeit on a smaller scale: my afternoon at a lesbian bar is substituted for the global human struggle toward freedom. Yet even my small story of my afternoon at a lesbian bar requires me to "emplot the events according to the principles informing the structures of distinctive story types or genres."[68] This so-called emplotment—structuring the events with a beginning, middle, and end—will occur whether I later write the afternoon as a fictional scene, whether I later "truthfully" narrate "what I did today" to my lover, or perhaps even as I remain silent but simply understand/remember that specific afternoon at that specific bar. What I am suggesting is that it may be the very act of emplotment, the narrativizing itself, that is problematic rather than simply the scale or subject of the narrative.

Just as narrative seems transhistorical, transcultural, and even "natural," so too does domination and subjection. What if there is a link between the structures of narrative and the structures of domination?

In other words, what if a condition of lesbian emancipation is a state without a *necessary* end? Or, as Roof expresses it, a rejection of narrative may allow us to understand that which has always been there but that we have never counted because it did not lead to "closure or production."[69] Or, perhaps even more radical, what if the condition of lesbian emancipation is a state without *any* end? If "every story is over before it begins" because narratives "report a completed past which they cannot alter,"[70] then lesbian liberation in the here and now may demand a rejection of narrative.

3.

A third, and less abstract, paradox of narrative in legal scholarship is elucidated by its comparison with feminist consciousness-raising. Although narrativity makes a claim to experience, it is not generally utilized in law similar to the feminist process of consciousness-raising in which one should recognize one's own life. Instead, narrativity is often proffered as a process in which one is requesting that the listener achieve empathy.[71] It is thus based upon difference rather than likeness. It asks that the listener reject his or her own experience and replace it with the experience of another person, the teller of the tale. Yet perhaps we listen to the stories of others only to fortify the narratives we have constructed for ourselves. According to the writer and critic Charles Baxter,

We are like Ivan Illych's friends who, upon hearing of his death, think: Well, at least it wasn't me. We seem to know ourselves, socially at least, only by comparing ourselves to someone else, to others. We knit together what comparative context we can.

In day-to-day life we play these little games of comparison-contrast in which we are usually the contrast. I wouldn't have done it that way. I wouldn't have done that at all. Look at him, the one who did it, sinking. *At least it wasn't me!* By telling stories in this manner, we become narratable. We find a story for ourselves. We spin around ourselves, in what seems to be a natural form, the cobweb of a plot. We move our own lives into the condition of narrative progression.[72]

Even if Baxter is only partially correct, what his insight demonstrates is that a lesbian narrative intended to promote understanding may have the effect of making a listener more smug about her or his heterosexuality. As Lucie White notes, practices of empathy (such as acquiring knowledge about another person) are often also practices of domination.[73] Thus, we may believe that telling our lesbian stories has achieved empathy, but what we have gotten is pity. From my perspective, pity is not only insufficient, it is unwelcome.

Even more bleak is the possibility that empathy is unachievable. In his work on narrativity and intelligence Roger Schank posits that a listener's "understanding" is a process of "mapping the speaker's stories onto the listener's stories": "Since we can only understand things that relate to our own experiences, it is actually very difficult to hear things that people say to us that are not interpretable through those experiences."[74] Thus, to the extent our lesbian narratives are not capable of being mapped onto preexisting narratives, they are unintelligible. To the extent our lesbian narratives are mapped, they may become something other than lesbian.

4.

A fourth paradoxical effect of our reliance upon narrative is the effect that it can have on our communities and movements. A reliance upon the narratives of individual experience as a touchstone can lead to a solipsism that separates us from each other and inhibits understanding of operations of power. For example, our discussions theorizing important issues such as same-sex marriage begin–and often end—with statements about the specific effect it would have (or not have) given one's present situation. Compare these two statements:

"I support gay marriage because my lover has a good insurance plan and I am self-employed and I need the insurance because when I was ill last year and had to go to the hospital the bill was outrageous and if we were heterosexual and married I would have been covered by my lover's insurance."

"I don't support gay marriage because I just broke up with my lover and if we had to go through a divorce it would have been terrible, just like it was when I was heterosexual and my husband and I divorced and he took me to the cleaners, getting the house that I had worked hard to fix up and even my mother's silver bracelet."

Such statements are collapsed narratives, often approved because of their specificity and grounding in personal experience. Further, neither speaker is presuming to speak for any community, the existence of which is contestable at best. The "end" of each statement—the political position in support or not of same-sex marriage—is narrativized by the preceding incidents related by the speaker. These narratives, both structurally and in their appeal to personal experience, cannot only preclude logical argument; they may, more importantly, preclude each other and a collective politics.

Personal narratives may seem more specific, contingent, and contested than Hegelian grand narratives or Aristotelian logics, but they can be equally essentializing. This essentializing movement is bound with psychoanalytic structures, processes, and language. As Kenneth Plummer argues in his study of sexual stories,

> Therapy provides a major instance of the power of essentializing stories in personal lives, where sexual stories weave together past, present, and future into an identity. They help to clarify personal problems, the story lending a (maybe only momentary) coherence to a life. . . . Narrative plays a key role in the healing process. It can provide answers to the questions "Why me?" . . . and also "What can be done?"[75]

This invocation of the therapeutic is not arbitrary, especially for lesbians. As one national survey has reported, three out of every four lesbians in the United States has been in therapy at some point in her life.[76] Even if this statistic is inflated, over the last two decades therapy has gained prominence in "Western middle classes and leftist liberal communities in general" and certainly among lesbians.[77] While once lesbians, queers, and feminists opposed the discipline of psychology on political grounds, now psychology seems to have subordinated politics. As Celia Kitzinger and Rachel Perkins argue in their book, *Changing Our Minds*, the political goal

of changing the world has been replaced by the therapeutic goal of changing ourselves.[78] Thus, the exploration of the questions "Why me?" and
"What can be done?" do not lead to an exploration of common conditions
or of political, economic, or legal structures, as in the process of consciousness-raising. Instead, there is the development of healing personal narratives. Violence against women is the addressed through anger-manage-
ment counseling for rapists, racism becomes "something to get off your
chest in a counseling workshop," and oil spills are remediated by hiring a
counselor for the affected persons.[79] Legal, economic, and political patterns that enforce subordination of women and people of color or support
ecological pollution remain untheorized and virtually unnoticed.
Revolution may still be desirable, but it will occur at the end of specific personal narratives, with the individual attainment of "self-esteem" as cure.[80]

Thus, although we may proffer our individual narratives as a specific
rebuke to present constructions of power, this very offering occurs in a
therapeutic climate that valorizes individual pathologies. While my story
of being discriminated against by a specific university ("We don't know if
we're ready for a lesbian on our faculty") might be meant to provoke political outrage, perhaps it is only intelligible within a psychological framework that will attend to my feelings of hurt or, at most, pathologize the
"homophobia."[81] Likewise, political positions on the desirability of same-
sex marriage become intelligible only as the product of individual narratives. Our discussions among ourselves about political change are thereby
inhibited. Paradoxically and, I think, mistakenly, the narratives of our personal experiences no longer simply inform or "ground" our politics; such
narratives can become our teleologies.

5.

Another paradoxical effect is that our counternarratives provoke other
counternarratives, often directly incorporating and responding to les-
bian/queer produced narratives. The conservative right's notorious video
The Gay Agenda is largely a reproduction (and editing) of lesbian/queer
narratives.[82] As lesbian theorist Didi Herman notes in her excellent book,
The Anti-Gay Agenda, conservative material "makes frequent use" of "the
texts of gay writers themselves," to support its themes of disease and seduction.[83] Gay "success stories" of achievement, especially economic achievement, are harnessed by conservatives to demonstrate their claim that sexual minorities do not suffer discrimination.

The use of counternarrative also occurs in a recent law review article entitled "Wigstock and Kulturkampf: Supreme Court Storytelling, the Culture War, and *Romer v. Evans,*"[84] arguing that the landmark case of *Romer v. Evans* is both incorrect and irrelevant. The author includes an awkwardly crafted section entitled "A Personal Narrative" that contains personal declarations, although not structured in any recognizable narrative form, as well as a more narratively structured explication of the facts involving a landlord who sought to evade nondiscrimination laws through a religious exemption.[85] Further, the author sprinkles the piece with footnotes from the Bible, which is itself composed of narratives.

I am not arguing that the narrative form is especially susceptible to being countered, either through the production of oppositional stories or through appropriation. For example, the author of "Wigstock and Kulturkampf" also seeks to reverse categories, positing religious persons" as the "true outsiders" and the "gay elite" as insiders.[86] Further, the author uses a quotation from Gertrude Stein to critique the majority opinion in *Romer v. Evans,*[87] although whether the use of a quotation from a famous lesbian writer to critique the Court's first favorable lesbian and gay decision is ironic or simply unintentional is not obvious. Conservatives routinely utilize statistics and scientific studies to bolster their theologically derived arguments. What I am arguing, however, is that the use of narrative is not sufficiently special to insulate it from contradictory uses, and that the uses of narrative cannot be confined to emancipatory purposes.

6.

The use of *Wigstock: The Movie*—a visual narrative—in a very antiqueer piece of legal scholarship points to yet another paradox of using narrative. The author uses the movie, which he describes as "a documentary about the drag queen festival held on Labor Day in—did you need to ask–New York City" and as "screamingly funny and wrenchingly sad" to illustrate what he calls a "homosexual fundamentalism" and to illustrate what he presumably finds (most?) objectionable about queer culture.[88] This usage demonstrates that if we wish to challenge his stereotypes with counternarratives, then we can be forced to select the most antistereotypical, conforming, and palatable narratives.

So, for example, in Marc Fajer's attempt to counter what he has identified as the "sex as lifestyle" "pre-understanding," he quite reasonably chooses to emphasize stories about long-term relationships. Yet, as he notes, he risks "accusation" that he is "in some sense 'selling-out,'" that he is "saying we have to model ourselves after non-gay ideals to be accepted." Fajer defends himself against this possible accusation by arguing that he is being descriptive: "In many important respects, many of us *are very much like heterosexuals* in our aspirations, our relationships, and many other aspects of our lives."[89] But even assuming this is true, it seems to me that it requires suppression (or at least deemphasis) of the stories that might confirm the preunderstanding. Thus, an attempt to combat the sex-as-lifestyle stereotype requires a rejection of the lesbian/queer stories involving experimentation or explorations of our sexuality.

The preference for respectable narratives also occurs in reform litigation. It does, of course, appear to be the best strategy to select what I call the "whitest and brightest" lesbian clients or "but for" dykes as plaintiffs to challenge an oppressive legal rule. Yet such a tactic is ultimately divisive and does not afford legal protection for the diversities of lesbian lives.

Focusing on litigation narratives that might combat stereotypes also can have the effect of desexualizing lesbians. For example, in much of the litigation challenging military regulations barring homosexual conduct, advocates have advanced arguments that a declaration of homosexuality does not necessarily mean sexual conduct, thus betraying "the celebration of sexuality for which the gay rights movement once stood."[90] Further, the possibility that an individual narrative can remain sexual and yet adequately confront the narratives of sexual depravity and criminality entrenched in our current jurisprudence is bleak.[91] Even further, as Julie Shapiro has demonstrated in the child custody context, the stories that are acceptable may not only exclude sexuality but affection.[92] Thus, paradoxically, our reliance on narrative to combat stereotypes threatens to divide us from each other and also encourages self-censorship.

7.

Finally, and perhaps most paradoxically, narrativity itself is an extremely troubled practice. What I have been calling the "narrative" of the movie *Wigstock* is in fact barely a narrative at all. Despite the ubiquity of narrative, not everything is narratively structured. *Wigstock: The Movie* is a documentary of an event, and its structure is more of a pastiche—a collection of relatively random images, though making use of repetition—than of a narrative that leads ineluctably from beginning to end. While legal argument could be said to have a narrative structure, we generally distinguish between logic and story, between analysis and facts. In our celebration of narrativity the category can expand to include almost everything, thereby losing its explanatory power.[93]

More fundamentally, it is paradoxical that we might proffer narrative as a successful strategy at the end of narrativity itself. As lesbian theorist Sue-Ellen Case argues in *The Domain Matrix: Performing Lesbian at the End of Print Culture,* the current age is engaged in a "contest between two orders, previously perceived as alphabetic and visual but technologically represented by print and screen."[94] Case makes it clear that print/alphabetic culture is associated with traditional narrative structures and that screen/visual culture is associated with the non-narrative: "The printed page, by the nature of its technology, enforces the sequential development of ideas, whereas the computer screen offers multiple arrangements of data."[95] Although a printed book, Case attempted to emulate screenic qualities in the design and production of *The Domain Matrix*, encouraging the reader to "surf" through the text rather than be constrained by its linearity and including boldface text meant to mimic hypertext links available on a computer. Hypertext, which can be defined as "text composed of blocks of words (or images) linked electronically by multiple paths, chains, or trails,"[96] itself "challenges narrative and all literary forms based upon linearity" and calls into question ideas of plot and story current since Aristotle."[97] Hypertext makes problematic the notion of beginning, which becomes increasingly arbitrary, as well as the notion of ending, which may rest more upon fatigue than satisfying closure. Perhaps most at risk, however, is the Aristotelian idea that beginning, middle, and end form a coherent whole with a definite "magnitude."[98] A hypertext experience is constructed by the "reader" rather than the text; its length and unity are optional at best.[99]

Those who venerate technological culture are not the only ones who argue that computerization is troubling to narrative coherence. If Hayden White is correct in equating narrativity with culture,[100] then the arguments against "technolopoly" as destructive of "traditional narratives and symbols" and offering only "technical expertise and the ecstasy of consumption" are certainly pertinent.[101] White's linking of narrativity with culture, and even humanity, is similarly implicated by the work of the critic Sven Birkerts in *The Gutenberg Elegies*, eloquently arguing that the rise of the computer and the decline of the reading of books threatens our culture and our humanity.[102] Discussing his displeasure with hypertext, Birkerts argues that its promise to deliver the reader from the "univocal linearity" of the book is not enticing because the very reason Birkerts reads "fixed acres of print" is to be subjected to an author's masterful narrative.[103]

Both paeans and reproaches to the end of print culture, however, may be overstated. One is reminded of discussions of the struggle between oral culture and so-called alphabet culture. In the Platonic dialogue *Phaedrus* Socrates relates a story of the Egyptian god Theuth whose offer of the art of writing to the wise king Thamus was rebuked because the king believed that writing's usurpation of orality would be the demise of memory and wisdom.[104] According to a contemporary philosopher, the transition from pictographs, hieroglyphics, and other visual representations to a phonetic alphabet ruptured the human and nonhuman worlds, divorcing human semiotic meaning from the narratives of nature.[105] This divorce is finalized with the invention of the printing press, both because of the replacement of calligraphy by standardized type and the widespread availability of written texts. As compelling as these arguments may be, they have not meant the death of memory, nature,[106] or narrative but only change, however dramatic.

Similarly, both the paeans and reproaches do not unequivocally reject narrative. Claims that narrative will be "reconfigured"[107] by hypertext are not necessarily the same as claims that narrative will cease. A narrative supplied by reader rather than author is nevertheless a narrative. While the classical definitions formulated by Aristotle are certainly implicated, there is no certainty that the structure of beginning-middle-end or the coherence of unity are absolutely necessary for narrativity in the new millennium.

Yet it is undoubtable that narrative is troubled. It is paradoxical that we might proffer narrative as a path to emancipation at a time when the continuation of narrative as we have known it is becoming increasingly suspect. We may be telling our stories at the end of the story of storytelling.

Beginning at Last

It is too late to begin again, but I want to return to the returning woman who read aloud the Muriel Rukeyser poem about Käthe Kollwitz. Because there is something else I remember. Something else besides her toothpaste tube and her television set and her physician husband. Something else besides the Valium and the sharp voice. Some other detail necessary to this story.

This something else happened later. It was warm; I remember that. We were outside, tucked into a stand of trees on the knoll of a hill behind the library. Perhaps we were working on a project together, maybe for the same class, maybe even on Muriel Rukeyser's poetry. I really don't remember, and I could offer the excuse that it was more than twenty years ago, but I probably didn't remember these details the next semester. But what I did remember, the next semester and even now, is that she was wearing a yellow shirtdress and her sandals had ankle straps. I remember that her slip was full and white and soft and underneath it her bra felt like cardboard. I remember her underpants were not cotton, but something synthetic and unpleasant.

I remember the sex.

And what I learned from that experience was what her narrative sought to convey. I learned what it meant to be a returning woman. I learned what it meant to have a husband and children and a life one didn't enjoy. I didn't learn everything, of course, and I didn't learn articulable details about toothpaste tubes. But in a certain slope of the shoulder, a shudder of sweat, I experienced an empathy that had previously eluded me.

I also experienced her beyond empathy. And I assume she experienced me that way. Inhabiting a space that does not have a male/heterosexual structure, a place that is originary and original. In that uncontestable site where narrative is absolutely absent. Bordering being neither individual nor collective, and not subject to being countered or censored.

In that compelling moment when it seems as if the world just might split open.

This did not make for a lasting relationship, or any relationship.

After that semester, the only other time I saw her, she was in the restaurant where I waitressed. She was part of a party of five, drank three daiquiris, and ordered chicken cordon bleu.

I do not know how she fit the sexual episode into the narrative of her own sexual history and identity. I fit it into mine as another escapade that I would not mention to my then-girlfriend, despite our commitment to being honestly nonmonogamous.

And now, of course, I try to reconstruct that bodily engagement here—as a narrative about the paradoxes of narrative.

The paradoxes in which I am interested do not speak of narrative's inferiority to logical argument. Logical argument cannot capture sandals with ankle straps, women's sweat, and sex. And sometimes, yes, sometimes, narrative can. But only paradoxically.

Thus, I am not suggesting we eschew narrative any more than I am suggesting we abandon rationality.

I confess I love them both.

But I am arguing that we must never reject or neglect our sexual energy in all its various expressions. And we must unfailingly preserve and honor the illogical, nonverbal, nonarticulate, non-narrative beauty of our lives.

7

The Codification of Lesbian Relationships:

Examples from Law and Literature

In this postmodern era celebrating diversity, admitting fragmentation, and arguing for polymorphous perversities, there is nevertheless a trend in the United States as well as in other common-law nations toward the codification of lesbian relationships. By codification I mean the process of developing and prescribing normative rules as well as the set of prescriptions that result from such a process.[1] These normative understandings shape our judgments about lesbianism and lesbian relationships. We decide which incidents fit within the category of "lesbian relationship." We then make further judgments about those incidents that do fit within the category, dividing them into subcategories such as "acceptable" or "not acceptable."

It could be argued, however, that there have always been such rules regulating lesbian relationships, including two longstanding and contradictory edicts: lesbian relationships do not exist and lesbian relationships are sick. Happily, although these rules still operate, they no longer possess the regulatory force they did a mere twenty, perhaps even ten, years ago.[2] Yet the movement away from these very restrictive rules does not necessarily mean a movement into greater liberty. Ironically, the very repressiveness of these twin rules of invisibility and perversity at times created a space for freedom and experimentation. In some instances, this space allowed for rather undesirable conditions, such as a normative rejection of all norms or a rigidly enforced set of alternative norms; the critiques of lesbian cultures on these bases are well known.[3] Nevertheless, there could be the possibility and subjective sense of "making up the rules" rather than conforming behavior.

The current process of codification is much more diffuse, as befits its postmodernist stage. Certainly, there is no totalizing body of regulation that is indexed and titled like the civil and criminal codes of many nations. There is also no conspiracy of codification that meets on a board, panel, or committee to review and promulgate regulations. Nevertheless, it does seem as if there are particular "laws," understood as such, that benefit those who comply with them and cost those who defy them.

While this process of codification may occur in many sites, this chapter concentrates on the fields of law and literature, not because these two pursuits are either the most blameworthy or most important but because of my idiosyncratic situation. I work within both these fields, and during this work I have been struck by some similarities that I did not expect.

I have also been marked by my own participation in these processes of codification as well as the participation of colleagues who I like, respect, and admire. Thus, I am not arguing that either law or literature is some repressive force "out there"; I am more interested in our complicities. For example, in the legal field, we make decisions about what cases to take, what arguments to advance, what scholarship to write. Likewise, in the literary field, we make decisions about what to write, how to write it, where (if anywhere) to publish it, what to review, and what to read. The normative channeling that occurs is often expressed in terms of our "success" within these fields. In the law, we choose the cases we think we can win, the arguments that will prevail, the scholarly topic that will be published, or make a contribution, or be acceptable for tenure. In literature, we revise and market our work, we read the work of others that has received acclaim, and we engage in public criticism.

Given such shared pursuits and concerns, it seems natural that a set of shared values would develop among the participants who might constitute an "interpretative community."[4] Yet I think it is vital to remember that not all members who participate in a community are situated equally. In fact, a disturbing propensity in the United States context is toward smaller and smaller concentrations of power, despite the postmodernist perception of diffusion. In the lesbian legal context in the United States, there are a handful of gay/lesbian advocacy organizations that effectively decide which cases are worthy of a devotion of resources, which arguments are advanced, and which issues should be the subject of legislative lobbying.[5] Similarly, in the literary context, the publishing industry in the United States is more and more an "industry," with the vast majority of books published by eight huge media conglomerates more devoted to entertainment profits than to literature.[6]

Independent publishing houses and independent bookstores, once cultural institutions within lesbian, gay, feminist, and progressive communities, now struggle for existence.[7] While mainstream publishers are supposedly looking for the "big gay book," this book is not literature or serious nonfiction but a "celebrity" book.[8] And while megachain bookstores often have a "gay" shelf, the bookshelf may feature only the titles from mainstream publishers who have provided substantial discounts to have their books included in stock.[9]

Keeping in mind the above explanations, qualifications, and disclaimers, I now turn to what seem to me to be some of the developing rules of lesbian relationships and their problems.

Rule 1: Lesbian Relationships Are Mimetic of the Myths of Heterosexual Marriage and Romance

Under this normative prescription, lesbian relationships are deemed subject to the same aspirations and expectations as the heterosexual romantic tradition that posits "true love" and defines it as "forever" and "only." Thus, lesbian relationships—as normatively prescribed, if not normatively experienced—must exhibit longevity and exclusivity.

In the legal realm, longevity and exclusivity have been the twin pillars that support the recognition of lesbian (and gay) relationships. In a groundbreaking case in the United States involving the tenancy of a rent-controlled apartment in Manhattan, the court was willing to consider the named tenant's lover as fitting into the category of "spouse or other family member" based upon evidence of the duration of the relationship and the fact that it seemed exclusive.[10] Thus, Michael Braschi was able to forestall an eviction from the apartment he shared with his lover because the testimony showed that the pair were monogamous and had been together a suitable length of time (eleven years). Presumably, a relationship that was not mimetic of the aspirations of heterosexual romance—a relationship that occurred between three people, for example, no matter how mutually committed the parties were, or a relationship that had been for some lesser period of time, would not have qualified Michael Braschi for the rights of tenancy.

There is a similar emphasis on exclusivity and longevity in domestic partnership registrations. Beginning in the mid-1980s, municipalities, some other government employers such as universities, and progressive corporations began to offer so called domestic partnership benefits to their employees.[11] Such benefits generally include bereavement and family leave, which would embrace the domestic partner, and medical, dental, and vision insurance supplied by the employer, which would generally only be extended to an employee's legal spouse and dependent children. By the late 1990s, the availability of these benefits has spread, perhaps to as many as 10 percent of private employers,[12] and to many municipalities[13] and a few states.[14] All such employers define domestic partner with requirements that the relationship meets a minimum time frame (usually six months), that the relationship is intended to be enduring, and that the relationship is one's "only" domestic partnership.[15]

Should legal marriage become possible in the United States as a result of the ongoing situation in the state of Hawai'i, as discussed more fully in chapter 8, "States of Marriage," this would further enforce the codification of lesbian relationships as mimetic of traditional heterosexual ones. In legal marriage the expectation of longevity is conveyed by the difficulty of the process of dissolving the marriage; even in the most simple of cases (no property, no children) divorce is a legal process governed by strict rules.[16] Additionally, one of the traditional grounds for such a dissolution is adultery—nonmonogamy,[17] which remains a crime in many states.[18] Adopting marriage as the model for lesbian relationships results in the primacy of the dyadic couple. "Lesser" relationships, such as "mere" roommates or "mere" friends, are not really relationships, and are not deserving of legal respect. Thus, the legal trend toward marriage and domestic partnerships codifies lesbian relationships as mimetic of traditional heterosexual romance, which ends in marriage.

This trend is also part of contemporary lesbian literature. The romance novel has become the normal genre for serious lesbian literary fiction in ways that we can barely recognize. At one time the norm was the coming out novel in which a woman fell in love with another woman as a way of recognizing her true identity as a lesbian. As lesbian critic Bonnie Zimmerman noted in her classic *The Safe Sea of Women: Lesbian Fiction, 1969–1989*, early lesbian coming-out novels conformed to the classic bildungsroman, while post-Stonewall and lesbian-feminist novels expanded to include the picaresque, the quest tale, and even the religious motif of exile and revelation.[19] In all coming-out novels, however, the major dramatic tension is the protagonist's realization of her lesbianism.

For readers well past the coming-out stage themselves, such narrative structures can become tiresome relatively quickly. But it is difficult not to succumb to a certain nostalgia for coming-out novels when compared to the crop of contemporary novels that read as romances. For it does seem as if the coming-out novels did contain a wider affirmation—even if it was an innocent and essentialist affirmation—of lesbian identity and existence.[20] This is true despite the fact that many coming-out novels appear to be romances themselves; as Zimmerman notes, "Most heroes of lesbian coming out novels end their quests by falling in love and setting up housekeeping with another woman."[21] If the first myth of lesbian literature is the creation of the "lesbian self," the second "recounts the formation and definition of the lesbian couple."[22]

Yet this coupling is distinct from heterosexual coupling, especially as it is portrayed in heterosexual romances. As Ann Barr Snitow theorizes, mass-market romances have as their subject the sexual difference between men and women:

> The novels have no plot in the usual sense. All tension and problems arise from the fact that the Harlequin [the Canadian company that is the major publisher of mass-market romance books] world is inhabited by two species incapable of communicating with each other, male and female. In this sense these Pollyanna books have their own dream-like truth: our culture produces a pathological experience of sex difference.[23]

On the contrary, the lesbian novels about which Zimmerman writes are not based upon the "institutionalized inequality" of gender.[24] Further, and perhaps even more important, these novels also participate in what Zimmerman calls the third myth of lesbian literature—community. Even in a classic novel titled with reference to a couple, June Arnold's *The Cook and the Carpenter*, the notion of community is integral. While in heterosexual coupling novels the woman's "achievement" of marriage marks her acceptance within mainstream society (a fact so assumed it bears little exposition), in lesbian novels the relationship sets the couple apart from mainstream society, making the existence of an alternative community vital.

Community in these lesbian novels, however, is not subservient to the couple. As Zimmerman notes, the plots of such classic American lesbian novels as Maureen Brady's *Folly* (1982) and Ann Allen Shockley's *Say Jesus and Come to Me* (1982) "revolve around the creation of feminist political networks."[25] The bar serves as a focus for lesbian community and the setting for multitudes of characters in much of Lee Lynch's work, including *Toothpick House* (1983), as well as in Nissa Donnelly's novel, *The Bar Stories* (1989). In these novels and many others published in the 1980s lesbian romance is situated in a larger political context; a context that distinguishes itself from the myths of heterosexual romance. Additionally, there were many novels that portrayed struggles against the acceptance of these myths. For example, in *The Medusa Head* (1983), by the Canadian writer Mary Meigs, three women characters struggle with preserving their three-way love affair. This struggle against heterosexually defined romance also resulted in a spate of novels of speculative fiction, including *Les Guérillères,* the classic by the French writer Monique Wittig,[26] as well as in novels such as *The Wanderground*, *Retreat*, and *Paz*.[27]

More recently, however, the trend seems to me to be an absolute acceptance of the myths of heterosexual romance, including the myth of isolation. As Snitow noted in her analysis of mass-market heterosexual romances, even the ideal of female virginity is

> without a history, without parental figures to support it or religious convictions to give it a context. Nor can anyone say money is a value; rather it is a given, rarely mentioned. Travel and work, though glamorous, are not really goals for the heroine either. . . . Of course, the highest good is the couple . . . . Everyone is young . . . . There is no context, no society, only surroundings. . . . The realities of class—workers in dull jobs, poverty, real productive relations, social divisions of labor—are all, of course, entirely foreign to the world of the Harlequin [novel].[28]

Comparable to Harlequin, the largest publisher of lesbian fiction in the United States, the Naiad Press, continues to emphasize novels that proudly proclaim their status as romances and routinely become best-selling lesbian novels. For example, in *Seasons of the Heart* (1996) by Jackie Calhoun and *Courted* (1996) by Cecila Cohen the "highest good" is undoubtedly the couple, and romantic fulfillment occurs in a social vacuum.

Comparing lesbian romance novels to heterosexual romance novels may yield predictable results, and it is probably unfair and elitist to expect more of lesbian romances than their heterosexual counterparts. Disturbingly, however, the myths of heterosexual romance are also evident in so-called literary novels. The myths of heterosexual romance may be at their most poignant, in fact, in recent literary novels that might be termed antiromance, such as Sarah Van Arsdale's *Toward Amnesia* (1996) and Carol Anshaw's *Seven Moves* (1996). In both these novels the protagonist deals with the loss of a lover. Readers are meant to understand the loss as devastating because it violates the norms of heterosexual romance. The codification of lifelong monogamy means that anything other than life-long monogamy is a loss; it is lesser and amounts to a failure. Thus, the lesbian protagonist is meant to be sympathetic because the normative aspiration that the relationship should not have ended has been violated. Unfortunately, little else in these novels arouses interest. There is no community. There is no work; both protagonists abandon their jobs without financial qualms in reaction to the loss of the lover. There is no context; only surroundings.

In some ways the mimetic quality of lesbian relationships in both the legal and literary realms appears harmless, and perhaps even beneficial. Part of our oppression has always been that lesbian relationships were deemed to be not as valuable or meaningful as heterosexual ones. Yet it will only be a partial liberation if our relationships are valued to the extent that they mimic heterosexual traditions and myths.

Rule 2: Lesbian Relationships Are Apolitical

Lesbian relationships are increasingly being codified as apolitical. To even consider a lesbian relationship as political has become rather ludicrous, conjuring up stereotypes that in the United States would invariably include a pair of indistinguishable women with certain food habits (vegetarianism), footwear (Birkenstocks), hair styles (short), and tones of voice (shrill). As I have elsewhere argued, this mandate of an apolitical appearance is related to capitalism, consumerism, and commodification. As lesbian theorist Robyn Wiegman expresses it, "products" have become equated with "political progress,"[29] and the notion of "political" itself becomes not simply impoverished but erased. For example, as Sue O'Sullivan brilliantly argues, the present media images of how "cool it is to be a dyke" depend upon the retreat of the "boring old lesbians" who represent not only "unattractiveness" but "politics."[30] Similarly, American lesbian journalist Alisa Solomon explains that the rejection of lesbian politics is because "political analysis has become equated with political correctness—as if hairy legs and flannel shirts had been reduced to an official lesbian-issue uniform and everyone had lost sight of the underlying intentions to free ourselves from objectification and restricted movement."[31] As Sue O'Sullivan notes, however, to collude with the denunciation of the stereotyped image of the outdated political lesbian is to reject the "radical political agenda of feminism, including its analyses of the social, cultural and economic."[32] It is this trend toward the apoliticalization of lesbianism that I here want to discuss in terms of its regulatory force in law and literature.

In the legal realm, the normativity of apoliticism was strikingly evidenced in the famous litigation surrounding Sharon Kowalski.[33] After a car accident that rendered Sharon Kowalski severely disabled, the legal issue became whether her lesbian lover Karen Thompson could be her legal guardian. Originally denied this status in favor of Sharon Kowalski's parents, Thompson continued to litigate, and the lesbian and gay community supported her in her struggle. This support became an issue for the court, however, which denied Thompson guardian status even after Sharon Kowalski's parents withdrew their claim. The court's reasoning was based in part on the fact that Thompson participated in political activities and took Sharon Kowalski to some of these events, all of which were a method of gaining the support of the lesbian and gay community. The trial judge found that such political activities constituted harm to Sharon Kowalski by revealing her sexual orientation, although this was fortunately disregarded on appeal.[34]

The mandate of apoliticism is also pronounced in cases involving child custody or adoption, including so-called second parent adoptions. The good lesbian parent has a level of politics that stops at parent-teacher conferences. Any sort of political activity, meaning any activity on behalf of lesbian or feminist issues, is considered as potentially embarrassing to the child and thus detrimental and not in the child's "best interests."[35] As Professor Julie Shapiro notes:

> Typically, courts are especially critical of openly lesbian . . . parents, contrasting them with those who are secretive, "discreet," or closeted. Thus, a lesbian mother who shields her children from all knowledge of her sexual identity is seen as less problematic than a lesbian mother who is involved in a relationship of which her children are aware. Most problematic of all is a lesbian mother who is open about her lesbianism, so that others in the community as well as her children are aware of her identification. The reasons why courts find an open lesbian mother more problematic than one who is "discreet" are directly related to the underlying concerns that motivate the court. If, for example, neither the child nor the surrounding community is aware of the mother's sexual identity, then the mother's identity poses no problem in terms of the child's sexual identity, gender role, or potential exposure to stigma. If the child is aware of the mother's sexual identity, but

the surrounding community is not, then at least the problem of stigma may be nonexistent. If the child and the community are aware of the mother's identity, then all of the potential problems may be implicated. Thus, the concerns may be seen to arise not from the mother's [sexual] conduct (which at least theoretically could be kept sufficiently private) but from her identification as a lesbian.[36]

Even more disastrous than participating in political activities so that one's sexual minority status is public is including the children in that participation. As one appellate court declared, in upholding a denial of custody and restricting visitation:

> We are not presuming that Wife is an uncaring mother. The environment, however, that she would choose to rear her children in is unhealthy for their growth. She has chosen not to make her sexual preference private but invites acknowledgment and imposes her preference upon her children and her community. The purpose of restricting visitation is to prevent extreme exposure of the situation to the minor children. We are not forbidding Wife from being a homosexual, from having a lesbian relationship, or from attending gay activist or overt homosexual outings. We are restricting her from exposing these elements of her "alternative life style" to her minor children. We fail to see how these restrictions impose or restrict her equal protection or privacy rights where these restrictions serve the best interest of the child.[37]

Community activities, especially if the children have knowledge of them or attend them, can result in a lesbian mother being denied custody or visitation.[38] Thus, being apolitical is the normative good, rewarded with the label of good parent and the legal status of custody.

The proscription against political activity is also inherent in the United States military regulations that allow the discharge of lesbians on the basis of their revelation of sexual identity.[39] The United States military's present "Don't ask, don't tell" policy is a liberalization of previous policies in which the identity need not have been *self*-revealed, resulting in accurately named witch-hunts. Nevertheless, a revelation of lesbianism sufficient to satisfy the "tell" portion of the policy can consist of a political activity, such as attending a lesbian/gay pride parade. Thus, the Senate Report specifically notes that activities such as "frequenting gay bars, reading gay literature, or marching in a gay rights parade are non-verbal statements which show a propensity to engage in homosexual acts."[40] Further, there is, of course, the argument that the affirmation of lesbian identity is itself a political act. As Kenneth Karst has observed, "Especially in the context of the central expressive function of the Army's exclusion regulation, coming out is not just an act of self-definition but an act of political expression."[41]

In literature, disapproval of many lesbian novels is certain if the novel is deemed "politically correct."[42] For characters in a relationship to have a political discussion, it would have to survive the pencil of editors who readily proclaim that political discussions are unrealistic and bore the reader. Certainly, there have been many lesbian novels in which the political discussions were boring. For example, in Heather Conrad's *NEWS* (1987), a character takes the stage to give a speech and the fictional speech is then reproduced for seven pages.[43] The problem, however, is not political writing, but a lapse in good writing—a speech on any topic, no matter how engaging, is usually tedious in a fictional narrative context.[44]

In the current climate, if political dialogue or action survives beyond the editorial impulse and appears in serious lesbian fiction, critics often deride or ignore the work. A case in point is Sarah Schulman's novel *Rat Bohemia* (1995) a novel many people expected to win a Lambda Literary Award, the "Academy Awards" of the U.S. gay/les/bi/trans book industry, yet, although it was nominated, it did not win. In talking with gay/les/bi/trans booksellers, editors, publishers, and writers—the people who serve as judges of the award—the overwhelming objection to the book was that it was "too political." Comments from persons I had always considered serious readers included judgments that the lesbians and their relationships in the book were "too serious," "not funny enough," "really downbeat," and "not personal enough," always followed by some reference to politics as not really interesting.

As Schulman herself noted in a recent interview, she "got incredible pressure to change the political content" of her work: agents were telling her "write formula, throw in a murder, write an erotic thriller; political books are dead; your career is over; let's bring in a book doctor."[45]

I am not arguing that lesbian relationships, either in law or literature, are best perceived through a relentlessly political lens. I am also not arguing that all or even most lesbian relationships should be characterized as political. What I am contending, however, is that a normative valuing of lesbian relationships, in either the legal or literary contexts, that is based upon the extent to which such lesbian relationships are apolitical is a disturbing trend. It is at least as disturbing as any previous trend toward valuing lesbian relationships to the extent to which such relationships could be characterized as political; although I do think it is worth noting that such a trend was never evident in legal realms and only sporadically evident in literary ones. Thus, the codification of lesbian relationships as apolitical is not simply explicable as a pendular compensation. In any case, however, this codification of lesbian relationships imposes a particular norm upon our relationships in which those that are apolitical reap the rewards available in the legal and literary realms.

Rule 3: Lesbian Relationships Are Sexually Privatized

It might seem that public acknowledgment of the sexual content of lesbian relationships is at a pinnacle. There are various media representations, including advertising campaigns for products, mainstream movies, television serials, and the ubiquitous talk shows featuring descriptions of all variety of sexual encounters. Nevertheless, a demarcation between good lesbian relationships in which sexuality is privatized and less than good lesbian relationships in which sexuality is allowed to be public is evident in both the legal and literary contexts.

In the law, much of the codification comes from cases involving children. Courts often make much of the issue of whether or not the lesbian couple ever "demonstrated affection" in front of the child—a public and therefore wrong expression of sexuality. As Professor Julie Shapiro has demonstrated, while it is "an undeniable fact of life that most parents have sex lives," when those parents are lesbians "conduct which would be deemed irrelevant to parenting abilities if engaged in by two adults of opposite sexes (holding hands, for example) may become determinative" in custody and visitation decisions.[46]

Perhaps the most well-known example in the United States occurs in the notorious *Bottoms v. Bottoms* litigation in which Sharon Bottoms lost custody of her child Tyler to her mother, Pamela Kay Bottoms. In *Bottoms,* the trial judge's brief judgment noted that Sharon Bottoms "readily admits her behavior in open affection shown to April Wade in front of the child. Examples given were kissing, patting, all of this in presence of the child."[47] That kissing and patting in front of a toddler are inappropriately public displays of lesbian sexuality is apparently accepted by the highest court in the state of Virginia, which affirmed the trial judge's ruling (reversing an intermediate appellate court that had reversed the trial judge) and included in its recitation of relevant facts Bottoms's testimony that there were signs of affection displayed in front of the child.[48] Importantly, the legal standard applicable in Bottoms was "unfitness": this was not a custody dispute between two parents with an equal presumption of custody but between a grandmother, a legal third party, who had to overcome a presumption of custody in the legal parent, Sharon Bottoms, by showing her unfit.[49] Thus, the public display of affection within a lesbian relationship can support a finding of unfitness to be a parent.

Bottoms and similar cases exemplify a codification of an extreme privatization and expansive definition of sexuality within a lesbian relationship. In *Bottoms*, the public characterization is accorded to acts that occur within the privacy of a home, but are public because they are witnessed by a toddler. The sexualization of displays of affection such as kissing and patting, activities that can span a range from perfunctory to erotic, is assumed, perhaps because of the lesbian context. In *Bottoms*, the enforcement of this norm is the enormously harsh sanction of loss of child custody. In other cases, the enforcement of this norm can have criminal consequences.

Although there are varying nomenclatures, in every jurisdiction in the United States, as well as in many other nations, public sex is a crime. Such public sexual activity is often criminalized under statutes that criminalize "lewd" behavior,[50] although there is also criminalization of the exposure of certain bodily parts, including breasts.[51] The definition of public is expansive. It can include a private house, if such acts are observable from the outside of the home[52] or by persons within the home.[53] For the lesbian and gay community, the prosecution of sex in public lavatories has been especially widespread. For example, the Supreme Court of Nevada upheld convictions for open or gross lewdness and/or indecent or obscene exposure based upon the homosexual activities of several men in a park lavatory, although these activities were observable to the "public" only through surreptitious technological surveillance.[54] Interestingly, *public* is interpreted to mean "the place" in the case of a "public" lavatory, while *public* is interpreted to require the observation of persons in the home cases.

The enforcement of the norm of sexual privatization does not occur exclusively through prohibition. Much of the rhetoric and a few of the successes in the U.S. and global controversies concerning sex statutes rest upon the legal rock (or pebble) of privacy. Such arguments tend to conflate privacy and autonomy, so that the private realm is a quasi-sacred enclave protestable against governmental intervention.[55] While there are various positions concerning the doctrinal efficacy of such arguments, I am here interested in the manner in which privacy-based arguments solidify the norm that acceptable sexuality is privatized. Furthermore, sexual matters then become relegated to the private sphere—a sphere beyond the reach of any positive interventions from the state—as feminists have compellingly demonstrated.[56] Such a relegation can result in a privatization of lesbian relationships per se, resulting in a restriction of the public sphere to a display of heteronormativity.[57]

This display of heteronormativity can lead not only to a privatization of our sexual activities but to a denial of them. As Teresa Bruce argues in her piece "Doing the Nasty: An Argument for Bringing Same-Sex Erotic Conduct Back Into the Courtroom,"[58] the doctrinal development in the United States distinguishing homosexual conduct (permissibly regulated under *Bowers v. Hardwick*)[59] and homosexual status (perhaps not permissibly regulated, despite the military's continued ban on homosexuals), has lead to a desexualization of lesbians, gay men, and bisexuals. While a common argument in the military context has therefore been that simply because a woman has declared she is a lesbian this is "not compelling evidence that she will engage in same-sex erotic activity while under the jurisdiction of the army, unless you believe that, as a lesbian she is simply incapable of self-control," Bruce finds this argument "intellectually and emotionally dishonest."[60] Further, Bruce concludes that such an argument

> endangers the health and well-being of individual members of the gay community by dismissing as insignificant the erotic relationships they share with one another, by abdicating the celebration of sexuality for which the gay-rights movement originally stood, by feeding the tradition of secrecy that surrounds homosexuality, and by providing a foundation upon which anti-gay activists can attack same-sex erotic conduct.[61]

Thus, the privitization of our sexuality can be equivalent to its erasure.

In the nonlegal public sphere, the situation seems rather different at first glance, and it could be argued that lesbian sex is no longer privatized in the arts as it is in the law. Yet although there is certainly a proliferation of lesbian literary erotica, there has been a simultaneous desexualization of so-called literary lesbian fiction as well as other genre fiction. It is generally understood that in order for a book to have mainstream appeal the lesbian sex must be minimized. For example, in the antiromance novels previously discussed, the cessation of the relationship means that any sex is recalled, usually diffusely. Even in the romance novels, the sexuality is scant. Thus, in nonerotic lesbian literature, the lesbian sex increasingly occurs "off the page," and in the genre of mystery novels, the very relationship often occurs off the pages. This is not a problem for readers who can fill in relationships or their sexual aspects that do occur off the pages, but if one is not able or does not desire to fill in the details, then the message is that one should not be reading serious lesbian fiction, or even detective novels. Instead, one should be reading erotica.

The process of codification here results in a demarcation between fiction and erotica. In practice, a lesbian author who has written a piece of short fiction will be faced with a choice concerning its publication and a dilemma. Submitted to a collection of erotica, the piece may be rejected or edited if there is too much nonerotic content. Also at issue is the definition of erotic—an erotic narrative is supposed to provoke sexual feelings—and not just literary meanings—from the reader. In other words, as the submission criteria will request and the jacket copy later attest, the story must be "hot." On the other hand, submitted to a collection of nonerotica, the piece may be rejected or edited if there is too much sexual content, especially because sexual narrative is easily criticized as irrelevant, off-putting, or possibly offensive to potential nonlesbian readers. Obviously, the judgments about the acceptable quantity of sexual content are subjective—how much is "too much" lesbian sex in a serious lesbian novel? The answer in many mainstream novels seems to be about one-half of a page. If one wants more, the message seems to be that what one wants is erotica.

Thus, the codification of lesbian sex as privatized results in a demarcation between literature and erotica, with erotica becoming the category in which sexuality is allowed and literature becoming the category in which lesbian sex is privatized beyond the page. In this construction, the norm and its transgression are symbiotic. The norm, however, still occupies the privileged position, for although erotica is often popular, its popularity is transgressive. In other words, the publication of erotica depends upon the privatization of sexuality in other types of fiction, the types of fiction that are normalized and valorized as serious and meritorious. The types of fiction suitable for a bookshelf in a house in which lesbian parents wanted to retain custody of their child.

Rule 4: Lesbian Relationships Are Definitional of Lesbianism

Perhaps this is not a rule at all, but the assumption that underlies the other rules. In discussions about lesbianism, in both law and literature, a slippage often occurs so that the discussion turns into one about relationships. My argument is not that lesbian relationships are irrelevant to lesbianism; my argument is simply that the conflation of lesbianism as a category is disserved by an exclusive focus on lesbian relationships, a subcategory. In other words, it is a mistake to assume that a part adequately represents a whole.

Lesbianism as a category can be legally relevant. For example, in the few jurisdictions that allow a claim based upon sexual orientation discrimination, proving that one is a lesbian or perceived as such would be a necessary element of one's claim.[62] In a less attractive circumstance, a prosecutor might attempt to prove that the complaining witness in a rape is a lesbian, in order to rebut the male defendant's defense that the victim consented to sex.[63] As an offensive matter, a person in a custody dispute might want to prove that the other person with a claim to the child is a lesbian, a definite disadvantage.[64]

The manner in which lesbianism is most often proved is through a relationship. The woman herself testifies not only that she is a lesbian, but that she has a lesbian sexual relationship. Or, better yet, another woman testifies that she has had a lesbian relationship—meaning, again, a sexual one—with the woman in question. In some cases, the absence of a heterosexual relationship can render a woman a lesbian by default because the existence of *some* sexual relationship is assumed.

The view that relationships are definitional of lesbianism is also evident in legal reform movements. With marriage taking the front seat of the legal reform movement in the United States, it is almost as if the "right to marry" becomes definitional of civil rights. According to much current rhetoric, the right to marry will guarantee other rights, including equality in employment and child custody.[65] This is considered logical given the conclusion that it is our relationships that are the basis of the discrimination against us. Yet such an articulation obscures the fact that it is not simply our relationships but often our sexual practices, either within or without relationships, that are relevant. Much of the antigay propaganda in the United States centers upon "homosexual" sexual practices.[66] Additionally, it is often—although not always, of course—true that if women's relationships are considered asexual a level of tolerance might accrue.[67]

Furthermore, the fight for the right to marry seeks to codify certain lesbian relationships as definitional of good lesbianism, relegating other relationships to a lesser status. While it is true that marriage would not be compulsory, and one is always "free" not to marry, codification does not always operate through compulsory measures. The method of enforcing the norm of a certain relationship will be an award of benefits to those who comply and a concomitant disadvantage to those who do not comply. Interestingly, it is the availability of these benefits and costs at the present time that make the argument for marriage compelling; I do not expect that they will evaporate as normative channelers once the "right" is available. In other words, the availability of marriage will channel lesbian relationships into those deserving of legal protection and those not deserving. While the arguments on this issue have been well-developed and cannot be fully rehearsed in this limited space,[68] I would note that the fact that marital status can result in discrimination is well recognized; some jurisdictions in the United States prohibit marital status discrimination.[69] Interestingly, an ordinance has been proposed in San Francisco to update the city's nondiscrimination policy to not only include marital status but also to prohibit domestic partnership discrimination.[70] A landlord who refused to rent to a lesbian couple because they were unmarried or not in a registered domestic partnership (either because the landlord believes in the sanctity of marriage or simply prefers to rent to a "stable couple") does not seem to me an improvement over a landlord who refused to rent to two women because they were lesbians.[71]

In literature, also, lesbian relationships become constitutive of lesbian fiction. While there are many recent novels that can serve as examples, I would like to indulge in an anecdote from my own experience. It concerns my own work, a novel, entitled *Another Mother*, published by a mainstream publisher in 1995. The main character is Angie Evans, a high-profile lesbian attorney who represents lesbian mothers, first in custody cases and eventually in a few murder prosecutions. Part of what I wanted to write about in the novel was work, the costs, rewards, and consuming nature of political work. Part of what I wanted to write about was also class, for Angie comes from an impoverished background but is now a successful attorney. Part of what I wanted to write about was mothering; Angie's clients reverberate with ties to their children and their mothers, which is refracted through Angie's own relationship with her adopted daughter and difficult mother.

Angie is not a sympathetic character because she has an underdeveloped capacity for coming to terms with her own history. Given her unsympathetic role, it was necessary for her to have a foil—both in terms of conventions of the novel as a genre and to avoid certain conventions of lesbian stereotypes. That foil is her lover, a character named Rachel.

The anecdote I wish to relate is about Rachel. The following conversation occurs while the novel is still a manuscript with a lesbian who has some power to ensure that the manuscript becomes a published novel.

"Rachel needs development," she says.

"How so?"

"We need to know more about her. How she became a lesbian. Her background. She needs her own chapters."

"But she's a minor character."

"She can't be a minor character."

"Can't?" (I resist the urge to say it's my book I can make her anything I want).

"Of course not. She's the protagonist's lover."

"Well, yes. But the novel isn't about them."

"Of course it is. What you don't understand is that this is a serious lesbian novel, and serious lesbian novels are about relationships."

"They don't have to be."

"Of course they do. What else would they be about?"

As it turns out, I didn't add much about Rachel or give her chapters or explain why she became a lesbian. But when the book was finally published the reviews most often focused on . . . the relationship between Rachel and Angie. The reviews gave only a passing mention to Angie's work, and few even mentioned her impoverished background. Instead, the book was interpreted as the saga of the relationship between Angie and Rachel. Given this interpretation, a few reviews opined that the book was weak—which seems to me the correct assessment if one has mistaken subplot for plot. More disturbingly, however, many reviews thought the book was a compelling story about a relationship in trouble. And so it seems to me now that the lesbian who advised me that "serious lesbian novels are about relationships," was prophetic. As I writer, I overestimated my ability to subvert strictures and control the manner in which my work would be interpreted.

There are some who might argue that not only lesbian novels are about relationships, but that all women's novels are about relationships. There are even some who might argue that not only are all women's novels about relationships, but that all novels are about relationships. Certainly this is true if we abandon our romantic dyadic definition of relationships and include all intrahuman interactions as well as extrahuman ways of relating. We must read lesbian novels and other fiction allowing for these broader interpretations. Recalling lesbian literary critic Bonnie Zimmerman, we must remember that the couple is only one of the several myths of lesbian literature[72]—it should not be reduced to the singular one. Further, we must not be limited to the previous myths of lesbian novels. Although, as British lesbian writer Jeanette Winterson notes, "these are

hard times" for experimental writing of any kind,[73] as writers and readers—and as lesbians—allowing our literature and ourselves to be defined
by romantic relationships is to restrict the possibilities of what we could be.

Concluding Thoughts

I have argued that there is a legal/literary trend toward codification of lesbianism as meaning lesbian relationships and toward lesbian relationships
as being most properly mimetic of heterosexual romantic traditions, apolitical, and sexually privatized. While normative rules are not an inherent
evil, it seems to me that this particular process of codification narrows our
lesbian choices. This narrowing also seems to me to occur at a point in history at which we have an opportunity to expand our experimentation and
multiplicitous attempts to construct lesbianism and our relationships. At
its most timid, my claim is that we can afford to be more creative than we
are presently being in law and in literature. At its most bold, my claim is
that we cannot afford to be otherwise.

8

States of Marriage

The struggles for lesbian equality (as well as for gay, bisexual, and transgendered equality) often focus on the state as capable of providing the remedy. Increasingly, this struggle has highlighted marriage as a practical and symbolic guarantee of equality. Yet our notions of the state as well as marriage are often blurry, derived more from sentimentalized cultural notions fostered by recitations of the pledge of allegiance and jump rope rhymes than by our attempts at rigorous theorizing. Further, because we live surrounded by the state and by marriage like proverbial fish in water, it is often difficult to be self-conscious about our conceptions of them. In thinking about the state and its role in lesbian liberation, including the possibility of same-sex marriage, my own attempts at conceptualizations have been advanced by conversations with lesbians from other common law countries, notably Canada, Australia, and New Zealand/Aotearoa; I therefore try to bring those perspectives to bear on this discussion of the state, the developments regarding legalized same-sex marriage, the implications for governmental structures raised by the controversies surrounding same-sex marriage, and, finally, the relation of legalized same-sex marriage to our quest for equality, including a proposal for the abolition of marriage.

The State

Our struggles for sexual equality embody undeveloped and contradictory notions of the state. Like other advocates pursuing justice for minorities, we argue both that the state should refrain from regulating us and that the state should act to ensure our rights.

The argument that the state should refrain from regulating us (by criminalizing our sexual practices) is a rather entrenched and comfortable position and is based upon a conception of the so-called negative state. Under this quasi-libertarian view, the less state intervention that occurs, the better. Such a view is predicated upon the specific history of state regulation of sexual minorities, including raids upon our gathering places and resultant arrests, prosecutions of persons for wearing less than three items of clothing of the "appropriate" gender, and prosecutions for sexual relations. According to the argument, if the state were to remove its proscriptions against our sexuality, we would attain some measure of equality. While many nations have decriminalized our sexuality, many more—including the United States—have not.[1] At present, almost half the states in the United States continue to criminalize certain homosexual practices.[2] In Australia the controversy in the state of Tasmania over its sodomy statute also concerns a government's attempt to regulate sexual practices with the countervailing argument that the state should not be allowed to interfere in such private realms.[3]

The antisex statutes have symbolic status, but we should not assume that such draconian restrictions are anachronisms. Criminal prosecutions for sexuality still occur in many parts of the United States.[4] Further, even when prosecutions do not occur, the criminalization of sexual practices is often the linchpin upon which other sorts of discrimination may rest. So, for example, in a child custody trial, an attorney can cross-examine a lesbian mother on the basis of her "homosexual" practices and procure an admission that she is an "admitted criminal."[5] Portrayed as less than law-abiding, the parent is thus not the best person to serve as a role model for any future-citizen child, even apart from any moral or sexual concerns.[6] Under a theory of the negative state, the solution is for the state to absent itself from sexual regulation: without criminal sex statutes, there would be no prosecutions and no cross-examinations as to criminal status.

Coexisting with the negative state is the contradictory notion of the positive state—a government that could and should take positive steps to ensure equality for sexual minorities. Under this quasi-socialist view, state intervention for the public good is preferable to maintaining undesirable social conditions. In the context of sexual minorities, such a view may be predicated upon the specific history of state intervention on behalf of other minorities. So, for example, many laws prohibiting discrimination on the basis of sexual orientation are often amendments to preexisting laws that prohibit discrimination on the basis of race, color, nationality, or "sex"[7] or, even if protections for gay men and lesbians against discrimination are freestanding, such laws are modeled after laws pertaining to other minorities.[8] Similarly, the advent of state recognition of crimes against lesbians, gay men, and transgendered persons as "bias crimes"—crimes based upon an animus toward sexual minorities—has been linked to the recognition of crimes committed because of racial, ethnic, and religious hatred.[9]

Importantly, however, the notion of the positive state employed to ensure equality for sexual minorities is also related to a recognition that the state regulates all sorts of "social" relations. In the United States this recognition is often fleeting due to an antisocialist tradition. As discussed below, arguments that our equality will be furthered by state recognition of same-sex marriages implicitly rest upon a comparison of lesbian relationships with heterosexual relationships in terms of state recognitions and benefits. But whatever one thinks about same-sex marriage, or enhanced penalties for crimes committed with a showing of bias, or antidiscrimination laws that might also prevent lesbian organizations from "discriminating" against heterosexuals, the notion of the positive state is certainly important in the struggle for equality. Also vital, however, if we want our sexual practices not to be subject to criminal penalties and resultant stigmas, is the notion of a negative state. In other words, we want to prohibit the state from enforcing its morality when that morality prohibits our sexual practices, yet we also want the state to enforce its morality against others when that morality is the ethic of equality. While there are arguments that would seek to distinguish sexual morality from civil rights, such arguments often collapse of their own weight and fall into conflicting liberal conceptions. Instead, I think that we must directly confront the reality that these conceptualizations—the state as both positive and negative—are both necessary and inconsistent.

Such an inconsistency is troubling because it makes our positions on disparate issues such as antisex statutes and antidiscrimination statutes difficult to ground with foundational arguments about state and state power. We want theoretical clarity, but we also want specific results. While I do not suggest that we abandon the quest for theoretical clarity and consistency, we need to recognize that the state itself employs inconsistent conceptions of its own power. Some of this inconsistency is due to the fact that although we talk about *the* state, the state is not unitary. This is especially true in governmental systems that seek to allocate power between different governmental entities (such as federal and state in the United States and Australia and federal and provincial in Canada) as well as between different branches (usually the legislative, executive, and judicial branches).

An elucidating example of inconsistent conceptions of the state and contrary positions between different facets of the government is *Romer v. Evans*, also known as the Colorado Amendment 2 case, decided by the United States Supreme Court on May 20, 1996.[10] Romer v. Evans is a landmark because it is the very first time that les-bi-gay-trans equality issues have been successful in the United States Supreme Court. This success arrives after some stunning defeats. In *Bowers v. Hardwick*, ten years earlier, the Court gave a constitutional imprimatur to state statutes that criminalized homosexual practices. Perhaps less well known but equally offensive was the Court's decision in *San Francisco Arts and Athletics v. United States Olympic Committee,* in which the Court held that the United States Olympic Committee "owned" the word *Olympics* and could seek an injunction against the Gay Olympics for infringement, despite granting the use of the term *Olympic* to other groups (such as the Explorer Olympics) and its failure to enforce its right against other groups (such as the Crab-racing Olympics).[11] Similarly, in *Hurley v. Irish-American Gay, Lesbian and Bisexual Group of Boston*, the Court overruled the Massachusetts Supreme Court, which had held that the group organizing Boston's St. Patrick's Day Parade violated state laws by excluding gay, lesbian, and bisexual Irish-Americans from the St. Patrick's Day Parade, because the parade organizers had a first amendment right to determine the content of the parade.[12]

In terms of conceptualizations of state power, *Bowers v. Hardwick* and *San Francisco Arts and Athletics v. United States Olympic Committee* are inconsistent with *Hurley v. Irish-American Gay, Lesbian and Bisexual Group of Boston* in terms of the arguments relied upon by the advocates for sexual minorities as well as in terms of the rationales adopted by a majority of the Justices of the Court. In *Bowers v. Hardwick* and the Gay Olympics case, sexual minority advocates argued that "the state" should not be interfering with the lives of gays, lesbians, and bisexuals. In contrast, in *Hurley,* sexual minority advocates argued that "the state" should be interfering to protect the rights of gays, lesbians, and bisexuals.[13]

Yet we can easily accept that different cases warrant different arguments. Thus, it may be more useful to consider the disparate arguments in the context of the situation involving Colorado Amendment 2. The Amendment 2 controversy reveals the ruptures and fragmentations of an entity that could be labeled the state. In order to understand these complexities, further discussion of the background of the case is necessary.

Amendment 2 was an amendment to the state constitution of the state of Colorado, passed by voter referendum.[14] The Court's majority opinion by Justice Kennedy most properly begins a discussion of the history of Amendment 2 with references to antidiscrimination ordinances passed by some progressive municipalities within the state, such as Aspen, a popular ski resort, and Boulder, site of the University of Colorado. Such ordinances prohibited public and private discrimination based upon "sexual orientation." There was also an executive order, promulgated by the governor, that prohibited discrimination on the basis of sexual orientation in state employment.

Such positive steps by the state provoked a response—or what might be termed a "backlash"—from conservative opponents such as the Coalition for Family Values. Such well-funded organizations, known as part of the religious right, obtained sufficient signatures to have a referendum placed on a statewide ballot. The referendum provided that the state constitution would be amended to prohibit any "statute, policy, ordinance" that allowed sexual minorities a claim to minority status. The referendum was supported by an intense media campaign that sought to persuade the populace that the amendment would prevent "special rights" for gay men and lesbians. The campaign implicitly alleged that special rights were always problematic in a democracy but explicitly focused on the two reasons gay men, lesbians, and bisexuals were especially undeserving of any special consideration. First, "gay people" (presumably including bisexuals and lesbians) did not deserve protection because they did not need protection: they were already more privileged economically than the rest of the population and had higher disposable incomes because of their childless status and better education. Second, "gay people" did not deserve protection because they were not worthy of protection: they were moral degenerates who flaunted the conventional, spread disease, and posed a danger to children.

At the time Amendment 2 was being considered in Colorado, similar rhetoric—and referenda—were being attempted in other states, including Maine, Oregon, and Washington. The difference was that in Colorado the referendum was approved and Amendment 2 became part of the Colorado state constitution.

Amendment 2 was immediately challenged by advocates for lesbian and gay organizations, joined by the cities of Aspen and Boulder. Ironically, the named defendant in the case was Roy Romer, governor of

Colorado, who had publicly opposed Amendment 2 when it was a referendum. The case was brought in the state courts on many grounds, including federal constitutional ones. The Colorado Supreme Court—the highest court in the state of Colorado—ultimately found Amendment 2 unconstitutional under the United States Constitution.

Because the Colorado Supreme Court rested its decision on federal constitutional grounds, its decision could be reviewed by the United States Supreme Court as ultimate arbiter of the United States Constitution. The governor of Colorado—the same governor who had publicly opposed the amendment—authorized the state to pursue the only type of appeal allowed, a petition for a writ of certiorari directed to the Court's discretion. The United States Supreme Court granted review but affirmed the decision (if not the reasoning) of the Colorado Supreme Court and held Amendment 2 unconstitutional as violative of the equal protection clause of the Fourteenth Amendment to the United States Constitution.[15]

This brief procedural recap of Amendment 2's history demonstrates the fragmented nature of the state. What precisely do we mean when we say "the state" in the context of Amendment 2? We might mean municipalities such as Aspen and Boulder, although despite their status as "creatures of the state," these municipalities seem to position themselves as "other," although surely the conservatives who objected to the antidiscrimination ordinances realized that the municipalities were exercising state power. We might also mean the executive, which had an order prohibiting discrimination, and whose head officer publicly opposed the amendment, but which appealed a ruling from its own judicial branch to a federal court. And we might also mean the judiciary, which we sometimes seem to include in our notions of the state and sometimes expect to be positioned "above and beyond" the rest of government. In a more typical situation, surely we would mean the legislature, which is peculiarly absent in the Amendment 2 controversies. In the case of a referendum, then, we must certainly mean the citizens of the state—those voters who passed Amendment 2.

In federalist systems the state is further complicated by two coexisting systems of government—the federal and state. In the United States context a vacillating notion of dual sovereignty is freighted with the unfortunate history of states rights. Despite a recent contrary trend, an assertion of states rights is understood in the context of race relations, including the Civil War, Reconstruction, and the 1960s civil rights movement during which racial desegregation was enforced (imposed) by the federal government against the (Southern) states. Indeed, some of the rhetoric in the Amendment 2 controversy was marked with this history, although with a Western "frontier" state inflection rather than a Southern one.

Thus, at the very least, it is necessary to be precise when referring to the state. For as we have long realized, and the Amendment 2 controversy demonstrates, the state is a multifaceted creation. Yet, interestingly, the recognition of this multiplicity is often paired with a conception of a pure and unsullied state that must be preserved through reclamation of that portion of the state that had been "captured" or "commandeered" by special interests alien to it. In the Amendment 2 case, gay and lesbian advocates implicitly argued that voters were captured by religious special interests, while conservatives, including Justice Scalia, argued that the antidiscrimi-natory ordinances as well as the appeal to the judiciary's powers to interpret the United States Constitution were products of the powers of a concentrated "gay elite." Scalia, dissenting in an opinion joined by Justices Rehnquist and Thomas, argued that the Court's characterization of "homosexuals" as a politically unpopular group was " nothing short of preposterous" given their "enormous influence in American media and politics" and the fact that although "composing no more than 4% of the population had the support of 46% of the voters on Amendment 2." Scalia also specifically berated the members of the Court who joined the majority opinion:

> When the Court takes sides in the culture wars, it tends to be with the knights rather than the villains—and more specifically with the Templars, reflecting the views and values of the lawyer class from which the Court's Members are drawn. How that class feels about homosexuality will be evident to anyone who wishes to interview job applicants at virtually any of the Nation's law schools. The interviewer may refuse to offer a job because the applicant is a Republican; because he is an adulterer; because he went to the wrong prep school or belongs to the wrong country club; because he eats snails; because he is a womanizer; because she wears real-animal fur; or even because he hates the Chicago Cubs. But if the interviewer should wish not to be an associate or partner of an applicant because he disapproves of the applicant's homosexuality, then he will have violated the pledge which the Association of American Law Schools requires all its member-schools to exact from job interviewers: "assurance of the employer's willingness" to hire homosexuals. Bylaws of the Association of American Law Schools, Inc. s 6–4(b).[16]

Thus, Scalia is relying upon a negative conception of the state, but, to whatever particular aspect of the state we refer, any argument must include an exhortation to embody either a positive or negative conception of the state. For example, the arguments of lesbian and gay advocates predominantly rested on a positive conception of the state, specifically the judiciary, which should ensure equality. Yet the arguments of gay and lesbian advocates also embodied a negative conception of the state, at least regarding an electorate that should not be allowed to enforce its majoritarian prejudices in this realm. Similarly, the arguments of those seeking to uphold Amendment 2 predominantly rested upon a negative conception of the state, specifically the judiciary, and any other organ of government that might seek to recognize the "special interests" of gay men, lesbians, and bisexuals. Such arguments, however, also embodied a positive conception of the state, at least regarding an electorate that can act to interfere with other organs of the state.

Thus it is evident that the state is fragmentary and duplicitous and that to theorize about the state is to theorize reductively and unhelpfully. Yet further specificity is not necessarily curative. The conflict between the positive state and the negative state is real, but I believe we must be wary of how these conceptions are employed. The positive/negative oppositional framework cannot be a foundational principle that would be employed consistently. It is not employed consistently by opponents of les-bi-gay-trans equality and it is not employed consistently by the state itself—to restrict ourselves to a consistent position would be ludicrous.

Nevertheless, in terms of lesbian theory and advocacy, I do believe we must continue to search for foundational principles beyond liberalism that might ground our theories and legal arguments. In this search, I suggest that we consider two things. First, we should take into account our own complicities with the state, as activists, as voters, as educators, as lawyers, and as agents of state power. Too often, we view the state as something external to our own agency. Second, and somewhat contradictorily, we should honor our historic opposition and outsider position vis-à-vis the state, so that we might have a modicum of freedom to develop alternatives and because someone has to perform that role—lest we have a state without opposition, which is usually called a tyranny.

Developments in the Quest for Legalized Same-Sex Marriage

Our complicities and oppositional stances are both apparent in the drama of legalized same-sex marriage, a drama that occurs on the stage of the state. Although it may seem as if the quest for legalized same-sex marriage is incredibly recent, it is not quite so new. First, it is important to recognize that many legalized same-sex marriages have occurred, although only because the state assumed that a male-female dyad was involved. Second, the arguments during the 1970s against the ERA—the federal constitutional amendment that would have prohibited discrimination based upon sex—were rife with references to the specter of "homosexual marriage." In fact, such litigation was occurring on the state level, although even in states that had a "little ERA"—a state constitutional amendment prohibiting sex discrimination—the courts had little difficulty rejecting the claim for same-sex marriage.[17]

The issue of same-sex legalized marriage seemed dormant for many years, although there were rumblings in the form of domestic partnership legislation in the United States and Scandanavian nations, as well as from universities and corporations that began to haphazardly extend some of the benefits given to married couples to "domestic partners." In the mid-1990s, however, the issue of legalized same-sex marriage regained vigor.

Much of this energy in the United States context is attributable to a ruling by the Hawai'i Supreme Court in *Baehr v. Lewin*,[18] holding that the denial of a marriage license to a same-sex couple must be evaluated under the Hawai'i state constitution's equal protection clause, which includes discrimination on the basis of sex.[19] The Hawai'i Supreme Court found that unless the state could prove a compelling state interest the denial of a marriage license to same-sex couples constituted a denial of equal protection and remanded the case for trial. At the 1996 trial the Honorable Kevin Chang found that the sex-based classification in the Hawai'i statute was unconstitutional on its face and as applied under the state constitution's equal protection clause.[20]

The possibility of one state recognizing same-sex marriage raised the probability that such marriages would be valid throughout the United States. The *United* States has generally meant that legal judgments valid in one state, such as marriage and divorce, are valid throughout the nation. This general understanding is expressed in Article IV of the United States Constitution, in the full faith and credit clause, discussed below. In light of this potential, individual states, and then Congress, began adopting statutes intended to prevent recognition of legal same-sex marriages. Congress enacted the Defense of Marriage Act, DOMA,[21] which provides that states need not recognize same-sex marriages of other states[22] and further provides that the federal government will only recognize marriages between members of "the opposite sex."

At this same time the legal regimes in many other nations are confronting the issue of legalized same-sex marriage. In May of 1996 the High Court of New Zealand/Aotearoa rendered *Quilter v. Attorney General* and declined to find that the female plaintiffs were entitled to obtain a marriage license and marry.[23] Although the applicable act, the Marriage Act of 1955, does not explicitly prohibit same-sex marriages or explicitly require male-female marriages, the court concluded that "it must be Parliament which chooses to enact the necessary law."[24] In Canada an Ontario judge declared the Family Law Act unconstitutional to the extent that it excludes same-sex couples from alimony provisions.[25] This newest Canadian decision follows Canadian Supreme Court cases such as *Mossop*, denying family status to same-sex couples for purposes of bereavement leave,[26] and *Egan*, denying old age benefits to a same-sex partner of forty-five years,[27] as well as flurries of activity in the provincial legislatures,[28] all amidst a sophisticated legal theory of gay and lesbian equality.[29] The Attorney General of New South Wales, Australia, stating that he would advocate a same-sex domestic relations act, and with the approval of the Australian federal cabinet, in the 1996 census counted same-sex couples as "family," while the Supreme Court of New South Wales rendered an important decision regarding termination of a lesbian relationship.[30] In Europe, the Republic of Iceland joined Sweden, Norway, and Denmark in including same-sex couples in their respective Registered Partnership Acts. The Kingdom of the Netherlands passed a Marriage Bill that includes same-sex marriage.

Such developments regarding legalized same-sex marriage are important. They are important because they raise a host of jurisprudential issues that embrace the structure of government itself and the government's relation with its citizens/inhabitants, including lesbians. They are also important because they allow us to focus on the question of legalized same-sex marriage and its relation to our quest for equality.

Jurisprudential Issues Raised by Same-Sex Marriage

THE STRUCTURES OF GOVERNMENT

Claims to legalize same-sex marriage often challenge the structures of legitimate government. For example, the New Zealand High Court in

Quilter abdicated responsibility for individual rights to Parliament, as if New Zealand were not a common law nation with an independent judiciary but a civil law state with an especially stunted notion of judicial review. Despite the High Court's conclusion that the Marriage Act did discriminate on the basis of sexual orientation in contravention of the Bill of Rights, the Court nevertheless refused to interpret the Marriage Act consistent with the Bill of Rights, because that would require the Court "to interpret the law in a way I do not perceive Parliament to intend."[31] Under such a view, the Court could never declare an Act of Parliament invalid in contravention of the Bill of Rights if the Court found that Parliament intended to contravene the Bill of Rights. While this may be an unnecessarily harsh view, especially given section 4 of the Bill of Rights, which provides that the courts cannot "decline to apply any provision" of a parliamentary enactment "by reason only that the provision is inconsistent with any provision" of the Bill of Rights,[32] it nevertheless seems to me that a judicial perception that "social policy" is a matter for Parliament even when the Bill of Rights requires redress renders the judiciary expendable and certainly subservient to the legislature.

In contrast, Judge Epstein of the Ontario Court of Justice considered the uneven Ontario legislation with regard to recognizing same-sex couples and concluded that the legislature's failure to act in this specific instance made the judiciary's obligation to remedy the discrimination even more pronounced.[33] While Judge Epstein's reasoning has special force under the Canadian constitutional scheme incorporating the Charter of Rights,[34] the role advanced for the judiciary is the role inherent in a democratic society. As stated by Canadian Supreme Court Chief Justice Lamer and quoted by Judge Epstein:

> As for the suggestion that judges intrude into the legislative sphere, the truth is that many of the toughest issues we have had to deal with have been left to us by the democratic process. The legislature can duck them. We can't. Think of abortion, euthanasia, same sex benefits, to name a few. Our job is to decide the cases properly before us to the best of our abilities. We can't say we are too busy with other things or that the issue is too politically sensitive to set up a royal commission. We do our duty and decide.[35]

Under Justice Lamer's view, a judiciary that does "duck" an issue is not doing its duty in a democratic society.

In the United States context, struggles around the issue of same-sex marriage have also involved the very structure of government. By passing

DOMA, Congress implicated the constitutionally mandated federalist structure of the nation. The federalist relation between the states themselves as well as federalist relations between the federal government and the states are altered by DOMA.

Like other federalist governments, the United States employs concepts that order the operations of laws between its various states.[36] The proper scope of relations between the states of the United States is expressed throughout the text and structure of the Constitution, but occurs notably in the "full faith and credit clause," which provides that full faith and credit shall be given in each state to the public acts, records, and proceedings of every other state.[37] Marriage certificates obviously fall into this category and the long-standing law has been that a marriage valid in one state is valid in every other. This has been true despite the fact that laws differ between states. So, for example, if the minimum age for marriage in one state is fourteen years of age, a fourteen year old validly married in that state still has a valid marriage even if she or he were to move to a state in which the minimum age for marriage is sixteen. Such problems can also be analyzed under conflicts of law doctrine, which recognizes "public policy" exceptions to recognizing the effects of laws from other jurisdictions. The interface of the full faith and credit clause and choice of law doctrines has prompted much scholarship, given the prospect of same-sex marriage in Hawai'i.[38] What DOMA attempts to do, however, is to usurp these interstate conflicts to the federal legislature.

Unlike most other federalist nations, in the United States domestic relations and family law are considered matters to be governed by the general powers of the state rather than the specific constitutionally enumerated powers of the federal government. Most federal statutes that utilize marital relations, including social security and tax codes, rely upon state definitions of marriage. Thus, the determination of whether a person is married or not for purposes of the federal tax code, for example, would depend upon the state laws where the marriage was validated. Again, the difference between state laws in this area was not considered to be a vital federal interest.

The experiences in New Zealand/Aotearoa, the United States, and Canada demonstrate the manner in which a challenge to the marriage statutes implicates the very structures of government. The respective roles of the judiciaries and legislatures can become entangled, an entanglement especially pronounced in the instance of controversial issues such as same-sex marriage. In a federalist system such as the United States the respective roles of the states and the federal governments can also become involved.

Nevertheless, while the state's structures contend with each other, the root of this conflict is the state's relation to the persons claiming that the state is acting unjustly.

INDIVIDUAL RIGHTS

Perhaps the most important jurisprudential issue raised by same-sex marriage is the legal regime's relation with its citizens, especially its citizens who do not belong to dominant groups. The legalization of same-sex marriage can be a litmus test of the state's willingness to recognize its sexual minority citizens as full members of the polity. From the perspective of the state, marriage is a civil relation of the highest order; withholding marriage is thus an indication of the status of any persons for whom marriage is not legally available.[39]

In New Zealand/Aotearoa the Human Rights Act prohibits discrimination on the basis of sexual orientation, which is defined as "a heterosexual, homosexual, lesbian, or bisexual orientation."[40] Such a provision indicates that the nation of New Zealand/Aotearoa holds its sexual minority members in a regard equal to its other citizens. Honoring such a ban on discrimination would require the reinterpretation of any statutes, practices, or policies that discriminate on the basis of sexual orientation. In the instance of the Marriage Act, the act did not limit marriage to members of the opposite sex and was thus not facially discriminatory. For the plaintiffs to prevail in *Quilter*, the High Court needed only to require the registrar general to apply the Act in a nondiscriminatory manner.

Instead, the High Court became entangled in tangentials.[41] The High Court looked to the "traditional common law view" of marriage concluding that "judicial dicta" since 1795 limited marriage to "one man and one woman."[42] The Court then referred to other statutes, most of which referred to husbands and wives, and reasoned that such statutes should not be "interpreted in a way where language and ordinary interpretation rules have to be strained to produce the result sought."[43] Based upon the traditional common law view and statutes other than the one directly applicable, the Court concluded that the Marriage Act should not be interpreted in a manner consistent with the Bill of Rights. The result of *Quilter* is that the Bill of Rights ban on discrimination on the basis of sexual orientation is meaningless if it is contrary to "judicial dicta" or ancillary statutes. Such an impoverished interpretation of the right to be free from discrimination on the basis of sexual orientation exhibits a fundamental dismissal of gay and lesbian persons as equal to heterosexual persons in the polity.

In the United States context, DOMA exhibits a similar fundamental dismissal of the equality of gay and lesbian persons. Even the name of the act, Defense of Marriage Act, expresses a particularly parochial paranoia constructing gay men and lesbians as a threat that must be defended against. The legislative history of DOMA elaborates on this theme, stating that the "appropriately entitled" act is a "modest effort" to "combat" the "orchestrated legal campaign by homosexual groups to redefine the institution of marriage," which is a "radical proposal that would fundamentally alter the institution of marriage."[44] Such a fundamental alteration would occur, according to the House of Representatives Committee on the Judiciary, because marriage exists for the procreation of children.[45]

Even the Hawai'i Supreme Court in *Baehr v. Lewin* fails to accord full respect to gay and lesbian persons. The Hawai'i Supreme Court acknowledged that although there is a fundamental right to marry, this right does not extend to same-sex couples.[46] Furthermore, in a rather disingenuous footnote, the court distanced its opinion from sexual orientation[47] and in another footnote accused the state attorney general of injecting the issue of homosexuality into a case in which it would be otherwise absent.[48] The Hawai'i Supreme Court's reliance on gender as a category can thus be interpreted as a failure to adequately consider the issue of sexual orientation by masking the issue as one of gender unrelated to sexuality.

Gender

As the Hawai'i Supreme Court opinion in *Baehr v. Lewin* indicates, legal responses to same-sex marriage can elucidate the government's position on the relevance and respect of gender categories. The jurisprudence of sex discrimination is elucidated in same-sex marriage situations in which the nonexistence of a sexual orientation discrimination provision requires the argument to proceed on the theory of sex discrimination. Under the sex discrimination argument, prohibiting same-sex marriage is sex discrimination because it is a prohibition that is based upon the sex of one's chosen partner. This is precisely the argument accepted by the Hawai'i Supreme Court in *Baehr v. Lewin*. However, most previous courts held that the prohibition of same-sex marriage was not sex discrimination because it applied equally to both sexes, even in instances in which there was an explicit state constitutional provision prohibiting sex discrimination.[49]

The meaning of gender is explored not only through doctrines of sex discrimination but also through precedent regarding transsexual marriages. For example, in *Quilter* the High Court had no difficulty distinguishing the transsexual cases, commenting that "in New Zealand for a marriage to take place there must be parties who visually at least are male and female."[50] The Court's emphasis on the visual could be interpreted as an interest in mere appearances, except that the preceding sentence focuses on situations in which "one of the parties has undergone reconstructive surgery, by the removal of a male penis and the construction of a vagina in its place or the construction of a penis from a female vagina."[51] Such an approach is similar to the United States cases, the most notorious one being *M.T. v. J.T.,* a divorce case, in which a New Jersey appellate court held a marriage valid where one party was a postoperative male-female transsexual and the other party was male.[52] In one sense, the court applied a liberal nonessentialist definition of gender and reached the conclusion that a previously male person could become female. In another sense, the court's conservatism mandated that marriage include persons of the "opposite sexes" and made gender determinations based upon stereotypical sexual functioning. As the court stated, "It is the sexual capacity of the individual which must be scrutinized," requiring the "coalescence of both the physical ability and the psychological and emotional orientation to engage in sexual orientation as either a male or female."[53] Such scrutiny not only reifies gender roles, of course, but dictates heterosexuality.

Thus, legalization of same-sex marriage raises jurisprudential issues concerning the structure of the government, the state's treatment of its minorities, and the state's understanding of sex/gender. It is also important, however, to explore the legalization of same-sex marriage from another direction—the direction of the lesbian, gay, bisexual, or transgendered citizen and her or his relation with the legal regime, as well as his or her intimate and community relations.

The Question of Legalized Same-Sex Marriage

The jurisprudential issues of same-sex marriage must also be addressed from the perspectives of those to whom it would apply. Of course, I am not advocating a single nonperspectival perspective or even a majority perspective among those to whom it might apply.[54] The debates within lesbian (and lesbian, gay, and bi communities) regarding marriage demonstrate the existence of a multitude of opinions on this subject.[55] Nevertheless, any jurisprudential analysis of the legalization of same-sex marriage is incomplete without at least an attempt to theorize the issue from the subject positions of those to whom it would apply.

Invoking such theoretical perspectives involves an interrogation of the purposes of same-sex marriage for lesbians. Based upon the arguments, discussions, and discourse surrounding same-sex marriage, it seems that for lesbians the availability of legal marriage is an avenue toward solving three sets of problems often expressed as desires. First, we want our relationships not to suffer in comparison to heterosexual relationships. Second, we want the legal system to be responsive to solving disputes among ourselves. And third, we want the reality and perception of equality. These problems are discussed in turn.

THE DESIRE THAT OUR RELATIONSHIPS NOT SUFFER BY COMPARISON

Comparative suffering can occur when our relationships are rendered irrelevant because other relationships are legally recognized. The situation of Sharon Kowalski exemplifies this problem.[56] In November of 1983 Sharon Kowalski was in a car accident and suffered extensive physical and neurologic injuries limiting, among other things, her ability to communicate. Until her accident she had been living with her lover Karen Thompson in a house they were buying together. After her accident the persons legally responsible for her were her parents, parents who did not believe that their daughter was a lesbian or could be involved in a lesbian relationship with anyone, including Karen Thompson.[57]

The prospect of not being allowed even to visit with her lover prompted Karen Thompson to bring an action in court. In one of the many court papers filed in the litigation, a doctor testifying on behalf of Sharon's parents stated that "visits by Karen Thompson would expose Sharon Kowalski to a high risk of sexual abuse." Eventually, Sharon's parents withdrew their claim to be her guardian, but the trial judge still refused to name Karen Thompson as guardian. The trial judge expressed concerns that Sharon's parents still objected to Karen as guardian (in part on the basis of her lesbianism), that Karen has been involved with at least one other woman in the years since Sharon's 1983 accident, and that Karen invaded Sharon's privacy by revealing her sexual orientation to her parents and by taking her to lesbian and gay gatherings. Rather than naming Karen as guardian, the judge named a supposedly neutral third party.

Reversing, a Minnesota appellate court relied on the uncontroverted medical testimony that Sharon Kowalski had sufficient capacity to choose her guardian and had consistently chosen Karen Thompson.[58] The court also noted that Karen Thompson was "the only person willing to take care of Sharon Kowalski outside of an institution." In a phrase that the lesbian and gay press reiterated in tones of victory, the appellate court also confirmed the trial court's finding that Sharon and Karen were a "family of affinity which should be accorded respect."[59]

Although there was a successful outcome in the case, eight years of litigation and perhaps permanent damage to Sharon's possibility of rehabilitation exemplifies the suffering that nonlegal recognition of our relationships can perpetrate. Advocates of same-sex marriage correctly point out that if Sharon and Karen had been legally married rather than simply "exchanging rings" in an extralegal ceremony Karen Thompson would have been Sharon Kowalski's legal guardian absent unusual circumstances.

A milder form of comparative suffering occurs when we cannot avail ourselves of the benefits available to married heterosexual persons. Such benefits may include those imposed by laws, such as tax differentials for married couples, inheritance laws, the ability to sue for wrongful death, entitlement benefits such as social security, and citizenship/immigration regulations, as well as those afforded by private interests recognizing the legal category of spouse, such as insurance benefits. Advocates of same-sex marriage argue that same-sex couples should be entitled to the same benefits as couples who can marry. Again, the availability of marriage would solve this problem.

THE DESIRE THAT THE LEGAL SYSTEM BE RESPONSIVE TO OUR DISPUTES

Second, we want to have legal rights as against each other. Such a desire stems from the problem that not all our relationships are eternal and of those that end, many do not end on amicable terms. Gay men and lesbians, like other members of society, may look to the legal system to solve disputes regarding the distribution of property accumulated during the relationship or to make decisions about custody or visitation of children. Because the legal system does have rules for dissolution of marriages, the exclusion of gay men and lesbians from the divorce process could be theorized as "suffering by comparison." Nevertheless, I think it is more accurate to acknowledge that what we want is for the legal system to protect us from ourselves.

The "selves" from whom we desire protection are not the selves willing to use alternative dispute resolution forms such as mediation.[60] The gay men and lesbians at issue are those more likely to use problematic arguments against their former partners. For example, the Australian case of *W v. G* decided in 1996 by the Supreme Court of New South Wales involved the termination of a lesbian relationship in which the plaintiff sought portions of real and personal property and "equitable compensation" for two children born through alternative insemination.[61] The defendant argued that the relationship was one of "room-mates or flat-mates" and that any child support should be claimed from the legal father—the sperm donor—and not from her. The defendant through counsel further argued that

> the formation of stable families is a socially desirable necessary aim; and to visit legal obligations upon non-parents to support a child in a homosexual or lesbian relationship is contrary to public policy in that: it will encourage the conception of children by artificial insemination in the absence of a father; will present as "normal" a relationship which is not recognized by the child maintenance legislation; it will encourage the evasion of provisions of the Human Tissue Act; and will encourage the bringing into the world of children without a father.[62]

The present state of the law, in Australia and elsewhere, encourages a gay man or lesbian to use objectionable—and even homophobic—arguments to escape responsibilities.[63] For proponents of same-sex marriage, the solution to such destructive arguments and situations is marriage. Legalized marriage would mean legalized dissolution of marriage and child custody/support determinations. Thus, we would be in the same position as our heterosexual counterparts, an end that is seen as desirable in and of itself in terms of equality.

THE DESIRE FOR THE REALITIES AND PERCEPTION OF EQUALITY

Third and last, we want equality.[64] The desire for equality permeates the first two desires, but is also an independent desire. It can also override some of our own misgivings about the institution of marriage, especially as it has been persuasively criticized by feminist scholars. In common law countries legal marriage historically meant the union of a man and a woman into a single entity—the man. Until the Married Women's Property Acts in the 1900s, married women were not thus not considered persons with enough legal status to own property or enter into binding contracts. The children of the marriage were likewise owned by the father. In contemporary times divorce—the termination of the marriage relation—continues to be controlled by the state. While marriage is considered contractual rather than a consequence of status, there are three parties to this contract—the man, the woman, and the state. Although the man and woman have limited power to alter the terms of the marriage agreement, through prenuptial agreements, for example, the state retains enormous power. A change in the state's understanding of the contractual terms can have devastating effects on women; witness the phenomenon of the "displaced homemaker," women who were married in the 1950s, when the marriage contract terms included being a full-time housekeeper, raising children, and supporting the husband's career in exchange for a promise of longevity enforced by alimony, and who were divorced thirty years later when the revised marriage contract included a year of rehabilitative alimony to allow the former wife to attend secretarial school.

Yet critiques of marriage, feminist or otherwise, are fundamentally irrelevant to the equality argument. Analogizing marriage to an American automobile, such as the Ford Pinto, illustrates the irrelevance. One might criticize the Ford Pinto for its design flaws, which caused injuries and accidents resulting in protracted litigation.[65] On such evidence one might refuse to purchase a Ford Pinto. However, it is easy to imagine one's reaction to a legal system that limited the availability of Ford Pintos to a certain select group. For those outside the group the Ford Pinto would become a symbol of their exclusion, just as for some of those included in the group the Ford Pinto would become a symbol of their preferential status. The relative merits of the Ford Pinto become secondary when the issue is equality. Thus, arguments about the problems inherent in marriage as an institution are not convincing to those who perceive marriage as a symbolic issue of equality for gay men and lesbians.

Abolishing Marriage

It seems to me that all three of the goals lesbians seek to accomplish through legalized same-sex marriage would be more completely realized by the abolition of any state-sanctioned marriage. For lesbians, the abolition of marriage would mean that our relationships would not be in a different legal category from other relationships. This would solve the problems of suffering by comparison and the larger issue of equality in this segment of the law. In terms of a desire to have rights as against each other, and which rights those would be, this would be subject to a revisiting of the scheme of ordering intimate relationships through legal processes.

While the abolition of marriage may seem radical,[66] it must be remembered that the reference is to legal marriage. As such, the abolition of marriage could easily be accomplished through a swift legislative act. Perhaps it could happen in Congress, although perhaps it would require individual states to act. Or the judiciary in numerous nations could logically declare legal marriage as a contravention of many individual rights, not limited to discrimination on the basis of sexual orientation, but including gender and marital status discrimination. Such abolition of marriage would not mean that marriage as a social, as a spiritual or religious, or as a psychological matter would be outlawed.

Instead, the abolition of legalized marriage would mean that the state would not relate to its citizens on the basis of their intimate relations. Most of us would agree with the state's articulated practice of nondiscrimination on the basis of gender in pay scales in public employment as well as with the state's imposition of nondiscrimination on private employment. The practice of discrimination, however, was a product of thinking not only of gender roles but also of the "family wage" system that provided more pay for men who were supporting families. It seems to me that contemporary practices based upon familial relations are similarly problematic.

Abolishing marriage would also mean that a nation could not resort to formalistic legal relations to determine the rights of its citizens. This is especially pertinent in the national engagement with minority populations, including ethnic minorities and indigenous populations. The state sanctioning of intimate relations is an imperialist and colonizing act. Even when the state seeks to recognize "common law" marriages, it forces persons into categories that may not accurately reflect social realities. The example of Hawai'i is instructive in that the categories of family and marriage are plastic and performative, kinship is attributed to those who act as kin, including friends and lovers.[67] It is not simply a matter of concluding that some cultures have a more expansive definition of family but a recognition that for some cultures family is not a meaningfully inherent category.[68] The imposition of marriage as the paramount legal relationship, even if such marriages could include same-sex couples, does violence to the configurations of intimate relations as experienced.

Further, the abolition of marriage would assist the governed in resisting the privatization of government responsibilities toward individuals. Much of the contemporary privatization discourse seeks to encourage family responsibility while allowing the government to escape from its obligations. As Jane Kelsey notes in the New Zealand/Aotearoa context, attacks on the welfare state are rhetorically coupled with blaming break-downs in traditional patriarchal family structures for all social ills.[69] Moreover, specific reforms aimed at dismantling the welfare state often take direct aim at those who dare to be unmarried. For example, the government of New Zealand/Aotearoa altered the universal allowance for students over twenty to target unmarried students under twenty-five, whose eligibility would be based upon parental income, whether or not the students lived at home or came from a nonuniversity town.[70] A typical pattern in privatization is to limit support for "single adults" because such people possess no dependents and then to limit family support because the disadvantage such people suffer is attributable to the lack of a married couple to head the requisite two-parent family. Thus, while no one is forced to marry under present legal regimes in the common law nations, the choice to marry is loaded with various incentives and disincentives that are enforced by state power.

The abolition of marriage would prevent the state from using marriage as a conduit to accomplishing its own ends, be they fiscal reorganization or the maintenance of dominant gender, ethnic, racial, or sexual configurations. This is not to argue, however, that the individual as unit is not without severe political and philosophical problems.[71] However, the problems inherent in individualism are not solved by permitting the state to vary its relations to individuals based upon their marital status.

Thus, the same-sex marriage issue is an opportunity to challenge not only the status of lesbians but the status of the state's recognition and imposition of intimate relations for its subjects through its legal regime. While legal regimes are presently confronting the issue of same-sex marriage and reaching disparate results, the larger question of the wisdom of legal marriage has yet to be seriously addressed by such regimes. The present state of marriage includes the state as a necessary actor: it is time to question whether all of us are being served by such an inclusion.

9

Resisting the Family: Repositioning Lesbians

in Legal Theory

The demand to redefine the family has become a pervasive panacea in liberal legal scholarship. Lesbians as well as gay men are a usual and symbolic focus of this redefinition effort. Lesbian and gay legal theorists and advocates have also been proposing that our relationships be understood within the rubric of the (redefined) family. While such a redefinition has practical benefits, I nevertheless want to challenge the inclusion of lesbians in any family, redefined or otherwise. Further, I want to challenge conceptualizations of lesbian relations as correlated—either by inclusion or exclusion—to the family.

I am suggesting that the position of lesbians with regard to the family's location within legal theory be one of resistance. While it might be argued that the existence of lesbianism is—in and of itself—a form of resistance to the paradigmatically heterosexual family, I want to propose that lesbian resistance to the family should not content itself with the descriptive or definitional. Instead, lesbian resistance should become more elemental: resistance to being either included or excluded, resistance to the power of the category of family within legal theory and legal practice to define, redefine, sanction, and appropriate lesbian existence. This proposition is a normative one, a political one, and perhaps even an ethical and aspirational one, grounded in a desire to promote lesbian survival as encompassing both the material survival of individual lesbians and the more discursive survival of lesbian communities, cultures, and theories.

Given the ultimate objective of fostering fundamental resistance to the family, we need to remind ourselves to problematize the family and discuss some of the obstacles to problematization, as well as to consider the interface between lesbian relationships and family in current political and legal discourse. In doing so, I will discuss three cases implicating redefinitions of the family inclusive of lesbians. Elaborating on these cases, I argue that the legal notion of family domesticates lesbians through its strategies of demarcation, assimilation, coercion, indoctrination, and arrogation. Finally, I want to return to the possibilities of lesbian resistance.

The Problem Family

Problematizing the family is not novel—feminist, lesbian, and socialist theorizing have long problematized the family, regarding it as an oppressive institution and linking it to the patriarchal state. The link between the family and state is not unique to such theorizing but is a prominent feature of much American political thought. For example, the "founding fathers" grounded national morality in private families, viewing the family as an important link in the chain of authority, and later nineteenth-century thinkers proclaimed the family as the bedrock of American civilization.[1] Contemporary political discourse continues to focus on the family, especially as it relates to the state of the nation. Recent legal scholarship continues to theorize the family as constitutive of the American system of government.

Much of current lesbian legal theorizing seems to have abandoned previous critiques of the oppressive and political nature of the family in favor of advocating recognition for "our" families, often leaving the concept of family unproblematized. Within lesbian cultures the celebration of the family accompanies a general depoliticization and privatization of lesbianism, mirroring the general depoliticization and privatization that have been so prevalent in the last decade. Where once we theorized community, tribe, and perhaps even "nation," we now theorize family. Certainly our communities were not idyllic—they were often stifling— but it seems as if we have forgotten the lesbian-generated critiques of family as equally stifling, as oppressive and often violent to the point of being deadly.

Such a decontextualization (by depoliticization) is accompanied by an overcontextualization (by personalization). This personalization is exemplified by a therapeutic movement concerned only with individual lesbians in terms of our individual families of origin as recapitulated in their present relationships. With the tools of therapy, any lesbian—any therapeutic client—can assess her present situations in light of her "dysfunctional" family of origin. The dysfunctionalisms remain private, personal, and insulated, despite their standardization and the proliferation of self-help groups and books. Thus, family ideology becomes indistinguishable from members of our particular (and dsyfunctional) families.[2]

Such personalization is not limited to lesbians who accept the therapeutic paradigm. Many others of us confuse a critique of the family with a rejection of the persons whom we would confine within that category. This confusion is further accentuated by the role of family members for many lesbians and feminists marginalized by racial, ethnic, religious, and economic status. This is a necessary consideration: the history of denial of the ability to preserve important relationships is linked to the denial of the status of family under oppressive social conditions, the extreme paradigmatic case being slavery. Thus, histories of oppression imbue *family* with additional layers of struggle and meaning. Further, critiques of the family have often assumed a white middle-class norm, thus positing a false universality. However, responses to those critiques often consist only of references to the love one has for particular persons. Interestingly, these particular persons—such as a favorite "aunt" who is not related by blood or marriage—may be excluded by even liberal definitions of family.

More important, however, the very oppressive social conditions that denied family status to certain relationships was itself often justified with reference to family, as in the case of slavery's "happy plantation family." As Margaret Burnham argues, "the 'one big happy family' image celebrated by slavery's adherents" portrayed plantation relations as "as organically interconnecting ones" that echoed "the idealized nineteenth-century view of the family as refuge and safe haven." Burnham quotes a South Carolina court, which stated, "Unless there be something very perverse in the disposition of the master or the slave, in every instance where a slave has been reared in a family there exists a mutual attachment. . . . The tie of master and slave is one of the most intimate relations of society."[3]

Both the depolitization and personalization phenomena occur because we have difficulty remembering that family is a cognitive category. Appeals to reality so dominant in redefinitions of the family mask the cognitive process of categorization that occurs. Thus, empirical "facts" such as "only one in four families is traditional" necessarily presupposes a generic category of family in which traditional is only a subset. One could easily argue for a generic category of family as either more or less expansive and without changing the meaning of *traditional* produce empirical facts such as "only one in one thousand families is traditional" or "every family is traditional."

Because family is a cognitive category subject to cultural as well as political constructions, it does not appear as a term in some languages; nevertheless a person who does have family as a cognitive category will explain all perceived relations with reference to the organizing category of family. As feminist anthropologists have noted, outside observers may easily delimit family boundaries in any and all societies, but the natives themselves may not employ such boundaries, or may employ other categories altogether.[4] For lesbians who have been enculturated in societies that subscribe to the cognitive category of family, the description of lesbian relations can reflexively occur in the language of family. According to one lesbian theorist of family, family is a "Rome term" to which "all roads lead," although there are "as many variants of the motive as there are roads."[5] Yet even if family is a "Rome term," it was never true that all roads led to Rome; the roads on the island of Lesbos led only to each other. To make the Rome proposition true, we must conceptualize Rome and roads in a way that redefines them toward that objective. Similarly, to make family a category to which all our lesbian motivations lead, we must conceptualize family and lesbian relations in a way that redefines them toward that objective. This teleological redefinition has a tendency toward the symbiotic: both family and lesbian relations are subject to modification toward the ultimate goal of having lesbianism be one of many paths to family.

Thus, I am arguing that family must be problematized as a nonessential, cognitive, and contested category rather than an unproblematized "reality" of "lived experience." This postmodernist stance can be quite difficult to sustain given the omnipresence of "family," an omnipresence that is startling when observed in its particularities in daily experience. For one day I monitored the incidents of family within my own social relations. I did not expect to find many references, perhaps because I was trying to take a vacation—in a two-family house. In casual conversations the term *family* recurred throughout the day: with a group of adults trading "family stories," with a child asking if pets could really be part of a family. Reading was no refuge from the family, even if one reads "progressive" magazines instead of the conservative *Family Circle,* especially if there are advertisements: there were advertisements for a "family car," with plenty of room for the family to grow, and advertisements for homeopathic "family medicines" made from all-natural ingredients; in the newspapers there were advertisements for "family department stores," grocery stores that can "handle any family," and parks that guaranteed "family fun." The commodification of the family is almost as pervasive as the commodification of sexuality: the family is appropriated to sell almost everything except liquor and cigarettes. The nonadvertising text of the magazines and newspapers also relied upon the family, even if in a supposedly subversive or critical manner: in a lesbian magazine there is a cartoon called *The Chosen Family* and a critique of family values rhetoric; in the newspaper there are cartoons like *The Family Circus,* a selection of "summer family recipes," and several articles discussing the modern family. Tired of reading, I took a solitary walk on a nature trail, where I am soon presented with an official parks department placard that labels a particular tree as a "Sibirica—a member of the dogwood family"—thus assuring me that family is a formation of the natural world. That evening I had to decide whether to eat at a recommended "family restaurant" and later whether to view a presentation that proclaimed itself as "family entertainment."

The presence of family in the legal world is equally ubiquitous. For example, in the United States Code, the term *family* appears no less than 2,086 times. In addition to obvious examples derived from a social welfare system that is almost entirely predicated upon the category of family, the category of family is used in a myriad of other situations: compensation for Congress, furniture for the White House, agricultural products and trade, fire protection, immigration, the military, bankruptcy, banks, housing, the census, consumer credit, national parks, conservation, copyright, crimes, witness protection, sentencing, tariffs, museums, libraries, education, student loans, drug abuse, foreign service, highway safety, Indians, labor, mineral rights, currency, patents and trademarks, "patriotic societies and observances," veterans, the postal service, territories, transportation, and national security. The "family farm," the "family corporation," "Aid to Families with Dependent Children," and other federal statutory creations exist despite the principle that "family matters" are reserved to state—and not federal—legislation. A consideration of only two states, California and New York, reveals even more regulation of the family. Although the term *family* appears in the New York statutes 2,149 times—only slightly more than the federal statutes—the term appears in the California Statutes 4,139 times. Judicial interventions and interpretations of family are even more extensive. There are also a plethora of casebooks, textbooks, articles, reporters, and newsletters devoted to family law as well as many professional organizations.[6]

Thus, any inclusion of lesbian in the (re)definition of the family subjects our relationships to an immense regulatory scheme. Yet the *exclusion* of lesbians from the (re)definition of family also subjects our relationships to regulatory schemes. Often the same ones. Given the immense power of law to bestow or deny concrete benefits as well as the law's symbolic stature, it is perhaps predictable that the ideological contestations concerning the relationship of lesbians to the family are often located within the legal system.

Family Quarrels

The contest over the terrain of family occurs within a legal and political regime hostile to lesbianism. This seemingly self-evident point is worth stressing because it is so obvious as to be ignored. In conservative political rhetoric the phrase "family values" is generally understood to connote an opposition to lesbianism and other "deviations." This conservative oppositional strategy is codified in the federal statutes: the first time the category "sexual orientation" appears in the United States Code it is explicitly contrasted with "the American family," despite the irrelevancy of such a contrast given the statute's purpose to collect statistics on bias crimes.[7]

The conservative definition of the family as oppositional to lesbianism and other deviations provokes the liberal (re)definition. The liberal (re)definition strategy stresses inclusion and diversity, specifically attempting to expand the conservative family to include previously excluded formations. This (re)definition strategy is essentially an argument that no opposition exists because family does—and must—include lesbian and other alternative families. This argument often rests upon a liberal politic that stresses diversity, plurality, and self-determination and upon an empirically derived "fact" that only a minority of contemporary families are within the traditional family definition. Thus, the liberal (re)definition argument appeals to the belief that the law should be both normatively grounded (plurality as aspiration) and descriptively grounded (diversity as reality). Stated in more generic theoretical terms, the conservative position employs the formalist approach: family is defined with reference to formal relationships, usually dictated by law or some other equally formal structure. Correspondingly, the liberal position employs the functionalist approach: family is defined with reference to the functions or attributes or "realities" operative in the relationships.

The confrontation between the conservative and liberal definitions of the family being waged in the law includes conflicts in the courts. Three landmark cases are illustrative of the judicial battle over the terrain of the family. *Braschi,*[8] *Kowalski,*[9] and *Alison D.*[10] are each important examples of litigation, supported by the lesbian and gay legal reform movement, in which there was an attempt to gain specific benefits reserved to family members. Because these three cases and the scenarios they represent are the focus of much feminist and lesbian legal theorizing about (re)defining the family, they merit specific interrogation.

In *Braschi,* the only case of these three to involve a gay man rather than a lesbian, Miguel Braschi occupied a Manhattan rent-controlled apartment with his lover, Leslie Blanchard, for approximately a decade. Shortly after Blanchard's death, the owner of the building threatened to evict Braschi, because only Blanchard was the tenant of record. The litigation, which reached New York's highest court, centered on a New York City rent-control regulation disallowing eviction of "either the surviving spouse of the deceased tenant or some other member of the deceased tenant's family." The issue for the courts was whether Braschi was within the protected category, "surviving spouse or some other member of the deceased tenant's family," and thus entitled to remain as a tenant in the rent-controlled apartment.

In considering the familial status of the gay men's relationship, the court approvingly referred to factors such as the exclusivity and longevity of the relationship, the level of emotional and financial commitment, the manner in which they conducted their everyday lives and presented themselves, and the reliance they placed upon each other for "family services." The court relied upon underlying facts such as their cohabitation for ten years, their regular visits to each other's relatives, and their joint status as signatories on three safe deposit boxes, bank accounts, and credit cards. Because the rent control regulation did not define *family,* the court could fashion its own definition upon a "foundation" of "the reality of family life." In stressing that it was "realistic" to consider family as including two lifetime partners "whose relationship is long-term and characterized by an emotional and financial commitment," the court concluded that its (re)definition of family comported with "society's traditional concept of 'family' and with the expectations of individuals who live in such nuclear units."

Although *Braschi* involves the interpretation of the term *family,* the model is clearly one of an adult coupled sexual relationship similar to a traditional heterosexual marriage. The court specifically stated that the men "regarded one another, and were regarded by friends and family, as spouses" and that they were viewed as "a couple." One could almost substitute "spouse" for "family" in most of the court's other pronouncements, although the court did not interpret *spouse* in the rent control regulation, only *family*.

More complex is the final judicial pronouncement in the controversy surrounding the well-publicized case of Sharon Kowalski, a lesbian severely disabled by a car accident, discussed in chapters 7 and 8.[11] The litigation involved a guardianship contest between Kowalski's lover and Kowalski's parents. Eight years after the initial accident a Minnesota appellate court awarded guardianship of Sharon Kowalski to her lover, Karen Thompson. The pertinent Minnesota statute provided that in selecting a guardian "kinship" was not a conclusive factor but should be considered to the extent "relevant" to explicitly mandated factors such as the ward's preference, the interaction between the ward and the guardian, and the guardian's ability to provide for the ward's needs, medical care, social requirements, training, and rehabilitation. Sharon Kowalski expressed her preference to live with Karen Thompson, although Kowalski's ability to express a preference was contested. By the time the almost decade-long litigation reached its conclusion, Karen Thompson was the only person willing and able to assist Sharon Kowalski in living outside an institution. On the preference and ability basis alone, the Minnesota appellate court could clearly have named Karen Thompson the guardian. Nevertheless, the court found it important to include its judgment of "fact that Thompson and Sharon are a family of affinity, which ought to be accorded respect."

The court's reliance on the reality of "fact" for its conclusion of familial relationship parallels that of the court in *Braschi*. The court's rendering of the relationship of Kowalski and Thompson, however, is less clearly based on the model of the adult sexual couple. The court's pairing of "Thompson" and "Sharon" as the members of this "family of affinity" connotes a relationship more akin to caretaker and dependent, with unequal status and formality attached to their names. Interestingly, however, the caretaking/dependent model may have made Karen Thompson's non-monogamy more palatable to the appellate court than it was to the trial court. The trial court had heard evidence that Karen Thompson had an affair—or perhaps more than one—sometime after the 1983 accident and the 1990 hearing and held that this created a conflict of interest. Reversing, the appellate court noted Karen Thompson's testimony that "anyone who is involved in her life understands that she and Sharon are 'a package deal.'" Yet the appellate court also relied upon expert testimony that "it is not uncommon for *spouses* to make changes in their personal lives while maintaining their commitment to the injured person."[12]

When the family model invoked is clearly that of parent-child, litigation efforts on behalf of lesbians have been less successful. For example, in *Alison D.* one member of a lesbian couple gave birth to a child through alternative insemination. After the adult couple's relationship dissolved, the biological mother eventually refused to allow her former lover to visit with the child. Decided by the same court that rendered *Braschi*, the court found that a lesbian nonbiological mother was not within the definition of parent and so had no standing to bring a petition for visitation against the child's biological mother. In *Alison D.* the court rejected the claim to reality in the form of "de facto parenthood" as insufficient to overcome the legal definition of parent. Only the dissenting judge, the highly regarded feminist jurist Judith Kaye, gave credence to an empirical approach; in the first paragraph of her opinion she refers to estimates that "more than 15.5 million children do not live with two biological parents, and that as many as 8 to 10 million children are born into families with a gay or lesbian parent." Judge Kaye explicitly appealed to *Braschi*'s formulation of criteria, noting that the court had the competence and authority to formulate criteria in this instance.[13]

Braschi, Kowalski, and *Alison D.* demonstrate attempts to (re)define the family to include "nontraditional" relationships. Within liberal theorizing *Braschi* and *Kowalski* are judged "good" cases because the courts expanded the concept of family to include the lesbian or gay relationship and the right result was reached. On the other hand, *Alison D.* is judged a "bad" case, because the court was unnecessarily restrictive and the wrong result was reached. Most theorizing is not so simplistic, of course, but it can be more simplistic—and perhaps more detrimental—than I believe lesbian existence deserves.

Redefining Families, Redefining Lesbians

Explicating the consequences of *Braschi, Kowalski,* and *Alison D.* within the context of feminist and lesbian legal theorizing elucidates some of the methods by which family redefinition becomes lesbian redefinition. *Braschi*'s restrictive criteria are the most obvious demarcation of those of us whose relationships will qualify as family from those of us who will be excluded. The court's use of criteria marks the liberal functional approach, departing from the more conservative formalist approach limited to legal relationships. While the conservative formalist approach excludes Miguel Braschi as well as any lesbian lover (unless otherwise related) from family membership and its concrete benefits, the liberal functionalist approach is also exclusionary. As expressed in *Braschi*, the requisite familial functions mimic the most traditional of marriages, including its economic practices within capitalist culture. The primacy of the economic function is not limited to judicial pronouncements but also surfaces in liberal legislative or quasi-legislative attempts to (re)define the family. For example, even the most progressive domestic partnership policies typically require affirmations related to financial interdependency, often with specific requirements. For example, the University of Iowa's Affidavit of Domestic Partnership requires an affirmation that at least three of the following conditions apply:

A. This relationship has been in existence for a period of at least twelve (12) consecutive months.
B. We have common or joint ownership of a residence (home, condominium or mobile home).
C. We have at least two of the following:
   1.) Joint ownership of a motor vehicle
   2.) Joint checking account
   3.) Joint credit account
   4.) Lease for a residence identifying both partners as tenants.
D. The domestic partner has been designated as a beneficiary for:
   1.) University of Iowa Group Life Insurance
   2.) Retirement Contract
   3.) Employee's will
E. A "relationship contract" has been executed which obligates each of the parties to provide support for the other party and provides, in the event of the termination of the relationship, for a substantially equal division for any property acquired during the relationship.

Thus, at least two-thirds of the criteria necessary to be satisfied to establish a domestic partnership are linked to property or property rights, and a domestic partnership may be established entirely on a property basis.

While there are only a few policies relating to nonbiological children, such policies also recapitulate the formal relations of parent-child, again stressing the economic. For example, Stanford University employees may "enroll an unmarried same sex Domestic Partner" and the "Domestic Partner's child(ren)" in the university medical, dental, accident insurance, and tuition grant program if the child meets all of the following eligibility requirements:

A. The child is primarily dependent upon you, the employee, for support, and

B. A parent-child relationship exists between you and the child based upon the following:

    1. The child must be unmarried and reside in the same household as you . . .

    2. You must assume full parental responsibility and control, including any and all debts incurred by the child (i.e., charges for health care and supplies.)

    3. A parent-child relationship will only be considered to exist between you and your Partner's child when both your Partner and the child are dependent upon you for support.

    4. You or your Partner must have a court-appointed legal relationship with the child (i.e., guardianship, adoption, foster child), or your Partner must be the biological parent, or the step-parent of the child.

These criteria not only emphasize the economic but also require that the economic relationship mimic the most conservative family construction consisting of one "breadwinner" adult and all other family members as dependent.

Economic relations as a hallmark of family weaken functionalism's appeal to reality, if such a reality is to be inclusive of lesbians. Most lesbians do not live in material comfort in Manhattan's Upper East Side sharing the keys to their safe deposit boxes, and many do not have the level of economic privilege necessary to obtain joint bank accounts and credit cards. A critique of *Braschi* (as well as domestic partnership policies) is that certain economic benefits (such as housing or insurance) depend on family or spouselike status, which is in turn proven through other economic accomplishments (such as joint bank accounts). This critique prioritizes the problem of collective inequities in the distribution of wealth over the individual's problem of an inequitable position within the wealth-distribution system. In other words, to use the example of health insurance, this critique is that obtaining a benefit such as health insurance should not be dependent upon being "related" to an individual sufficiently privileged to have insured employment; the problem is not simply that some people (who would be insured but for their lack of legal relation to an insured worker) are denied insurance but that *anyone* is denied insurance. Such an argument is more easily discernible in the spouselike context than in other contexts, but is no less applicable. Class-based criticisms are vital in this context, especially given the gender, racial, cultural, and ability disparities in the wealth distribution system, although such critiques often provoke accusations of being deflective or Marxist, or both.

Further, economic critiques are importantly considered in nonmaterial requirements such as exclusivity. The patriarchal link between marriage and women as property so devastatingly criticized by generations of feminist theorists is resuscitated and reified in familial functionalism. *Braschi*'s factors including the "exclusivity and longevity of the relationship," *Kowalski*'s attention to and ultimate excusing of nonmonogamy, and the domestic partnership affidavits mandating affirmation that the other is one's "sole domestic partner" all demonstrate the property model of relationship by valorizing exclusivity in sexual relations. In *Braschi* the narrowness of the court's conception of family as limited to coupledom is further evidenced by the court's comparison of its other decisions of functional familialism, those involving zoning restrictions limiting land use to "families." These zoning cases, which bring within the rubric of family any group of individuals that is the "factual and functional equivalent" of the family, like a group home for adults—and perhaps several lesbians sharing an apartment—are specifically rejected by the *Braschi* court.[14] The not-so-implicit message is that lesbian/gay relationships will be accorded the status of family only to the extent that they replicate the traditional husband-wife couple, a tradition based in property relations.

Nevertheless, critiques of capitalism can seem less pertinent in situations like the ones at issue in *Kowalski* and *Alison D.*, which place at issue "benefits" like caring for or visiting with a loved one. Certainly, not all of us have lovers who have been disabled by a car accident like Sharon Kowalski and not all of us have coparented a child with a biological mother, but the vagaries of our realities and functions in such cases may seem undetermined by economic and other privileges. The argument that Karen Thompson should be accorded any operative "kinship" preference and Alison D. should be accorded a parental claim for visitation rests on claims to reality as functionalism. Didn't Karen Thompson prove she was—in reality—the best guardian and functioning as true family by supporting her lover even after the biological family members had abandoned Sharon Kowalski to institutional care? And didn't Alison D. argue she was—in reality—the other parent and functioning like any parent in the constellation of the lesbian family? Yet both realities are situated within economic and other specificities, such as sufficient resources to care for a disabled person or to arrange visitation of a child. Further, both realities are situated within a legal regime that propertizes persons by allowing the legal exclusion of others through the mechanisms of guardianship and custody/visitation.

Enshrining realities through the functionalist approach to family reifies the family and conceptualizes relationships in instrumental terms, terms that are culturally constructed and enforced. While the functionalist approach may seem more fluid than the formalist approach, upon closer examination the functionalist approach reveals only a more complex rigidity. The functions that serve as criteria to determine family recapitulate the formal relations of either spouse-spouse or parent-child. These formal relations emphasize the economic, perhaps not surprising given our capitalist culture.

The criteria developed from spouse-spouse and parent-child relations are not only culturally determined but also aspire to universality and centrality. Such claims cannot be sustained. Feminist anthropologists and psychologists have convincingly disputed the universality and centrality of familial functions.[15] Within feminist legal theorizing arguments that adult sexual intimacy is foundational[16] compete with arguments that the mother-child dyad is similarly constitutive.[17] Similarly, arguments that (hetero)sexual relations are the grounding of women's subordination compete with arguments that reproduction/mothering are the roots of women's oppression. These contradictions may reveal schisms within feminist legal theory, but they also reveal the problem of claims to universality and centrality of any functions ascribed irrevocably to family formations and functions.

The functionalist approach also directly contradicts another tenet of the family redefinition agenda. This tenet is crystallized in the faith that lesbians can enter the family and transform it by our very existence, or at least our aspirations to transform it. But the functional criteria used to determine whether or not relationships are within the rubric of family guarantee exclusion of the very relationships that might transform the functions. Further, the transformation of family functions is disapproved even by feminist theorists who argue for the transformation of family participants. For example, feminist legal theoretician Martha Minow, discussing her work on Alison D.'s behalf to have her considered a de facto parent, concludes that "people should be able to choose to enter family relationships, but not free to rewrite the terms of those relationships."[18]

Even when functionally (re)defined, the family redefines lesbians by demarcating, assimilating, coercing, indoctrinating, and arrogating us. Demarcation occurs when familialism becomes a division between us, as well as when it serves as a convenient division between "good" lesbians and "bad" ones for the dominant culture. The danger of demarcation has been eloquently expressed by lesbian theorist, writer, and activist Joan Nestle, who writes of the temptation to see ourselves as the "clean sexual deviant" and dissociate ourselves from public sexual activity, multiple partners, and intergenerational sex and cloak ourselves in the image of "monogamous long-term relationships, discrete at-home social gatherings, and a basic urge to recreate the family." As Nestle notes, the safe image is not the reality for all of us, "not now and not in the past" and allows some of us to be scapegoated for the protection of others.[19]

Demarcation can occur only in a climate in which assimilation is coercive. The offer of concrete benefits like retaining a rent-controlled apartment is an example of such coercion, but the coercion also has a strong undercurrent of physical violence. For example, gay conservative Andrew Sullivan's conclusion that the formation of families through "gay marriage" is not a "denial of family values" but "an extension of them" is buttressed with a chilling argument: "Since persecution is not an option in a civilized society, why not coax gays into traditional values rather than rail incoherently against them?"[20] Such "coaxing" must be situated with reference to the historical persecution and execution of lesbians as well as the continuing violence against lesbians. Thus, the conservative argument contains an implicit promise of protection to lesbians if we conform our relations to traditional family values and a threat of persecution if we do not.

To avoid the disadvantages of not conforming, we are also required to display our indoctrination. Thus, it is not only sufficient to structure our relations *like* familial ones; we must indicate our belief that our relations *are* familial ones. One of *Braschi*'s criteria and the criteria of almost all functional family definitions is that the putative family members present themselves as family; they must indicate that they conceptualize themselves as a family. While this may be interpreted as extending family membership only to those who willingly choose it, the choice involved is coercive not only against the background of concrete benefits and fears of persecution but also with respect to mandating demonstration of our own indoctrination. We must not only conform our actions, we must be true believers.

One aspect of the true belief in the assimilability of lesbian relations in the redefined family is the arrogating of lesbian relations to heterosexual ones. The heterosexually defined family thus remains the norm, even in the redefinition. This results in the theoretical position adopted by some lesbian theorists that lesbian relations are "commensurable" to their "heterosexual counterparts." For example, Kath Weston argues that it is our family formations that introduce the basis for rendering heterosexuality and lesbian or gay identity "commensurable," and, interestingly, she echoes gay conservative Andrew Sullivan's argument by justifying some of the need for such commensurability as leading to a reduction of the "othering" of lesbians and gay men that makes the violence against us palatable.[21]

Heterosexuality as the norm must be as subject to critique in lesbian legal theory as masculinity as the norm has been subject in feminist legal theory. Any argument that equal comparisons between heterosexuality and lesbianism are possible ignores the power differentials between the regime of heterosexuality and the subordination of lesbianism. Outside of a lesbian-centered perspective, comparisons between lesbians and heterosexuals necessarily arrogate lesbianism to heterosexuality.

The arrogation of lesbianism is not limited to heterosexuality. Lesbianism is also arrogated to feminism, or even to familialism. Many feminist legal theorists routinely theorize that feminist legal theories based on the category of gender must merely be extended to incorporate the category of sexual orientation. Further, in a prominent and often excellent book devoted to feminist legal theorizing, the only section specifically devoted to lesbians, "Lesbian-Gay Rights and Social Wrongs," is encapsulated in a chapter entitled "Competing Perspectives on Family Policy." This positioning and resultant text arrogates lesbian issues to family ones.[22]

Demarcation, assimilation, coercion, indoctrination, and arrogation of lesbianism redefine lesbianism as the family is being (re)defined. This domestication of lesbianism must be resisted.

Possibilities of Lesbian Resistance

The family is certainly not the only categorical agent of lesbian domestication. Nevertheless, the family does lend special significance to the gendered connotation of the term. Domestication connotes the relegation of women to the domestic sphere, a private place that can facilitate being dominated and inhibit collective action. For lesbians, this domestication is doubly gendered, for we are relegated to a domestic sphere devoid of a correlative male sphere and our relations are valued only to the extent that they are derivative. Domestication also connotes other systems of hierarchy, the circumscribing of one's potential to the service of another, as when animals are domesticated for human use.

As I am using the term, *domestication* describes the plethora of methodologies by which an ideology like family appears to be a factual reality. We attempt to argue ourselves into legal categories such as family for strategic survival reasons including the receipt of concrete benefits, the protection from persecution, and the desire to belong. Yet we also (re)define our own relations as family because family is a category made prominent in our thinking by the process of domestication that we endure as we live in the world.

The domestication of lesbians as we are subjected to the hegemony of the family and its strategies of demarcation, assimilation, coercion, indoctrination, and arrogation can make resistance seem impossible. Yet domestication has within it the idea of its opposite. To have been domesticated, one must have once existed wild, and there is the possibility of a feral future. To be feral is to have survived domestication and be transformed into an untamed state.

I believe postdomesticated lesbian existence is one purpose of a lesbian legal theory: by examining the family's power to domesticate our legal theories and lives, we can begin to resist our domestication.

Resistance is not a monolithic activity with a predetermined result. Although some postmodernist-influenced feminist theorizing might resist the very notion of the possibility of resistance, Foucault's formulation of resistance stresses its integrity as well as its multiplicity.[23] Foucault's formulation also posits that such "mobile and transitory points of resistance" are capable of "marking off irreducible regions" in individuals, in "their bodies and minds."[24] Resistance is the struggle to make lesbianism such an "irreducible region" in our "bodies and minds."

Resistance to our domestication requires the abandonment of our reflexive adoption of the category family to explain and organize our relationships. Attending to the automatic quality of reference to family and contemplating the absence of such a ready referent are important forms of resistance to the power of family to domesticate lesbianism. While a critically strategic adoption of the category family within legal discourse can be an important form of resistance, one wonders what a resistance to the category of family might mean. Rather than lesbians requesting inclusion into the privileged legal category of family, what if lesbians advocated the abolition of benefits based upon family status, or even the abolition of the category family itself?

Any contemplation of the abandonment of such a culturally central category can cause consternation: *If not the family, then what?* An attempt to answer this question could also be an important form of resistance, assuming that the effort would be to reconceptualize rather than merely replicate. As Michele Barrett and Mary McIntosh argue, any synonymous institution would suffer all the defects of the present institution. In answering the question "what would you put in family's place?" Barrett and McIntosh insist "nothing" and offer their solution:

> What is needed is not to build up an alternative to family—new forms of household that would fulfil all the needs that families are supposed to fulfil today—but to make family less necessary, by building up all sorts of other ways of meeting people's needs. . . . [We must] transform not the family, but the society that needs it.[25]

If we are no longer "riveted" to the extant categories, there is the possibility that we can create new categories that reflect lesbian diversity.[26]

We have learned the power of naming and renaming by naming, renaming, and reclaiming our situations, problems, strengths, and precursors. Lesbians have invented new forms and resituated old ones in our relationships, cultural formations, literature, art, and spirituality. Within feminist legal theorizing we have originated categories such as sexual harassment, comparable worth, and the category of feminist legal theory itself. The formulation of a new category could be an important form of resistance and could allow us to reconceptualize ourselves and our relationships in as yet unimaginable ways.

In addition to renaming categories, legal theorizing has also banished categories, accomplishing a virtual unnaming of the situations they once represented. For example, we no longer theorize about gendered harms from breaches of promise to marry or seduction.[27] It is not only that the law and cultural conditions have changed but that few of us would use such categories in a serious manner to conceptualize contemporary events, despite the fact that we might know women in the circumstances these categories were meant to describe.

Unnaming the family may be the most conceptually radical form of resistance to the family's power to domesticate lesbianism. The idea of unnaming is evocatively presented by feminist writer Ursula LeGuin in a story about Eve unnaming the animals.[28] Unnaming is an important, if underutilized form of resistance. Resistance to the domestication of lesbians within the legal realm requires that we theorize a lesbian jurisprudence that *unnames* the family. As long as family—in whatever form it takes—remains a named category, lesbians are positioned as either outlaws or inlaws.

IO

The Third Sex, Third Parties, and Child Custody

Lesbians have been called the third sex—persons relegated to a place outside the heterosexual dyad. Similarly, in terms of child custody, lesbians have often been relegated to an unpreferred place outside the heterosexual dyad by third party doctrine, which rests upon an assumption that legal scholar Karen Czapanskiy has called the Adam and Eve model—that a child has two parents—one of each gender—no more and no less. Because of the third party doctrine's fundamentally flawed origin in a male-female dyad, as well as its continued perpetuation of that heterosexual dyad, it must be discarded.

In considering the pragmatic application of third party custody doctrine, it is necessary to examine three categories of possible third parties: the lesbian nonlegal mother, the sperm donor, and the grandparents or other biological relatives. An examination of the cases shows that there is no instrumental or pragmatic reason to retain third party doctrine. Even when third party doctrine should operate to the benefit of lesbians, it often does not. So, for example, while a lesbian may be in a privileged position as a member of the Adam-Eve model at the time of a child's birth, third parties—such as grandparents—have been able to overcome the disability of being third parties and obtain custody. Like the notion of the "third sex," third party doctrine needs to be abandoned.

A Short History of the Notion of the Third Sex

The "body and soul of a woman, the spirit and strength of a man," "a third sex which has not yet got a name," is the fictional self-description of the narrator of the 1835 French novel *Mademoiselle de Maupin* by Theophile Gautier.[1] The sort of "men" who might guard Oriental harems, those members of "the third sex," is the uncomplimentary description of feminist reformers in the 1886 Congressional Record.[2] Despite its influence on literary and legal conceptions, however, the term *third sex* originates in neither discipline. Instead, the term *third sex*, along with the companion term *sexual inversion*, is a product of nineteenth-century science, specifically medicine and the developing discipline of psychiatry/psychology.[3] As encapsulated by lesbian historian Lillian Faderman:

> A lesbian, by the sexologists' definition, was one who rejected what had long been the woman's role. She found that role distasteful because she was not really a woman—she was a member of the third sex. . . . All her emotions were inverted, turned upside down: Instead of being passive, she was active, instead of loving domesticity, she sought success in the world outside, instead of making men prime in her life, she made first herself and then other women prime. She loved womankind more than mankind.[4]

The definition of the female members of the third sex began in 1869 when the German psychiatrist Carl von Westphal published the first study of female "sexual inversion."[5] His disciples include the British psychiatrist Havelock Ellis, author of the influential text *Studies in the Psychology of Sex*,[6] and Richard von Krafft-Ebing, author of *Psychopathia Sexualis*.[7] Such physicians and their American counterparts,[8] collectively known as sexologists, sought to apply scientific methodology and rigor to the study of sex. Concentrating on sexual variance and pathologies, among their investigations was the subject of homosexuality, which they conceptualized in medical-psychological terms. Under the medical model, homosexuality is reconceptualized as a medical condition rather than a crime or a sin, although the theorizing of the sexologists occurs within a religious and legal context. For example, in Havelock Ellis's chapter on sexual inversion in women in *Studies in the Psychology of Sex*, he justifies his conclusion that homosexuality is "not less common in women than in men," by referring to a "Catholic confessor, a friend tells me, informed him that for one man who acknowledges homosexual practices there are three women."[9] He also notes that "a remarkably large proportion of the cases in which homosexuality has led to crimes of violence, or otherwise come under medicolegal observation, has been among women," specifically detailing two American murder cases.[10] While the sexologists' attempt to remove homosexuality from the realms of law and religion could be interpreted as a liberalization[11]—an interpretation that led the Nazi regime to persecute them[12]—the medicalization of homosexuality operated less as an ultimate liberalization than as a shift in the modes of regulation. In his ground-breaking study and collection of documents related to gay and lesbian lives, historian Jonathan Katz devotes a substantial section to the treatment of lesbians and gay men by psychiatric-psychological professionals.[13] As he notes, among the treatments are "surgical measures: castration, hysterectomy, and vasectomy. In the 1880's, surgical removal of the ovaries and clitoris are discussed as a 'cure' for various forms of female 'erotomania,' including, it seems, Lesbianism. Lobotomy was performed as late as 1951."[14] Katz also notes that varieties of drug therapies have also been used, including hormones, lsd, sexual stimulants and sexual depressants, as well as shock treatments and aversion therapy.

The sexologists' deployment of the notion of third sex/sexual inversion rests upon a strict antipodal relation between gender identity and gender object choice as well as the assumption of a heterosexual hegemony. The sexologists posited that if one was sexually attracted to women, one must be a man; even if a man inhabiting what might appear to be a woman's body. This "appearance" of being a bodily woman merited further interrogation by the sexologists, who concluded that the female members of the third sex did not appear *entirely* feminine, but evinced masculine traits. The articulation of these masculine traits was extremely racialized or ethnicized as well as being class-coded. For example, Havelock Ellis uses body hair and musculature as indicators of female sexual inversion. Ellis concludes that "there seems little doubt that inverted women frequently tend to show minor anomalies of the pilferous system, and especially slight hypertrichosis and a masculine distribution of hair."[15] He then describes a "very typical case of inversion" in an "Italian girl of 19" with "down on the arms and legs" and "very abundant hair in the armpits and on the pubes." Ellis further notes that a "woman physician in the United States who knows many female inverts similarly tells me that she has observed the tendency to growth of hair on the legs."[16] Ellis connects his observations regarding body hair to sexual inversion by supposing that both are controlled by an "abnormal balance in the internal secretions," although he does admit that his observations may be complicated by ethnic varieties in the distribution of body hair, if not cultural variances in its removal. Concerning muscle tone, Ellis does not speculate that such a diversity might be attributable to physical exertion, including work.[17]

Further, as lesbian historian Lillian Faderman notes, the sexologists' case studies of female inversion were derived from "a captive population in prisons and insane asylums, daughters of the poor," and did not exhibit an understanding that poor servant women "might have more difficulty surviving" if they were more feminine acting.[18] Perhaps even more problematic is the fact that not only is the identification of masculine traits racialized, ethnicized, and class-coded as it related to notions of masculine/feminine polarized sex characteristics, but the very identification of sexual expression is similarly culturally determined. In a regime that regulated female sexuality in accordance with race, ethnic, and class status,[19] any expression of sexual interest is pathologized. In addition to a reliance upon culturally determined and perceived traits to assess masculinity, the sexologists emphasized the masculine invert while failing to adequately account for her only possible partner within their heterosexualized theory: a nonmasculine woman.[20] Of course, not all Ellis's masculine attributes are coded. For example, "Inverted women are very often good whistlers," although Ellis cautions that mere "whistling in a woman is no evidence of any general or physical or psychic inversion."[21]

While the sexologists' definition of female members of the third sex stressed the twinned scientific subjects of biology and psychology, it was not without its political implications. Thus, although the sexologists labeled a woman who had a sexual relation with another woman as a "congenital invert," a "victim of inborn 'contrary sexual feeling,' " possessing a condition attributable to "tainted heredity," passed on by parents who themselves "lacked the appropriate strong sex characteristics,"[22] such characteristics could be linked with the political movement of feminism. For some sexologists, who subscribed to a biological etiology of lesbianism, this connection was carefully negotiated. For example, Havelock Ellis noted that although the women's movement of emancipation is generally "wholesome and inevitable," it has "certain disadvantages" when applied to the sexual sphere. He further stated that while the influences of "modern movements cannot directly cause sexual inversion," they can "develop the germs of it, and probably cause a spurious imitation."[23] As Carol Smith-Rosenberg observes, the "connections Ellis drew between what he believed was a rising incidence of middle-class lesbianism and feminist political and educational advances reveal a man troubled by changes he could not in principle oppose."[24] For others, feminism as a political ideology itself became theorized as an almost organic defect.[25] For many, including Freud[26] and United States senators, lesbianism and feminism became linked as pathologies. Although this linkage might not be solely responsible for the failure of first-wave feminism, it was certainly one strategy of antifeminist rhetoric in the early 1900s.[27] This strategy was also exhibited during second-wave feminism of the late 1960s and 1970s, and is still practiced today.[28]

While we no longer conceptualize lesbians as members of the "third sex," the importance of the sexologists' conception of the "third sex" cannot be underestimated. It certainly influenced the entire field of psychology,[29] lesbian literary production,[30] and continues to influence our contemporary notions of lesbian and gay identities, including the legal implications of such identities.

Further, the sexologists' rather tortured theoretical stance is not a historical curiosity.[31] Instead, it was a fundamental preservation of a well-established heterosexual hegemony that continues to demand the integrity of two separate and distinct genders. This demand is necessary so that sex—and perhaps the entire natural world—can be conceptualized with reference to the norm of heterosexuality. As queer theorist Michael Warner writes, heterosexual culture conceptualizes itself as the elemental form of human association, the model of gender relations, and the means of reproduction. Warner illustrates his point with reference to a drawing placed on NASA's Pioneer 10 spacecraft designed to convey human society: a drawing of a man and a woman, immediately recognizable as "a heterosexual couple," testifying to the depth of cultural insistence that "humanity and heterosexuality are synonymous."[32] Thus, although we no longer employ the term *third sex* to describe lesbian (or gay male) relations, we continue to deploy its underlying premise of paradigmatic heterosexuality. This premise spills into legal doctrine, including the doctrine of third party custody.

Third Party Custody Doctrine

Third party doctrine in the realm of child custody is a tortured doctrine that seeks to preserve the heterosexual matrix and the notion of two separate and distinct genders. At its most fundamental, third party doctrine posits that each child has one mother and one father—no more and no less. Outside of these two parties necessary to complete the heterosexual matrix, others occupy the less privileged position of third parties. Like the sexologists' theoretical stance, this legal doctrine is predicated upon current notions of biology.[33]

Also like the sexologists' notions of the third sex, third party doctrine is often convoluted and disparate.

The general rule—that third parties are in a less privileged position with regard to claims to children as compared with parents—is derived from "natural" law that has found expression in constitutional principles. While natural law is often invoked, common law doctrines that are products of particular patriarchal cultures are also relevant. For example, the notion that a biological parent has a claim on a child is arguably based upon the notion of children as property, often legally expressed as the notion of family unity or autonomy. Family unity ideology proclaimed the husband/father as head of the household and all other members as subject to his economic and physical control. When constitutionalized, such common law and "natural law" principles deem parenting a "fundamental right" inasmuch as it is a liberty interest protected by the due process clauses of the fifth and fourteenth amendments to the United States Constitution. The origins of parental rights as fundamental rights are generally traced to *Meyer*[34] and *Pierce*,[35] two cases that reached the United States Supreme Court during the 1920s, both involving conflicts between parents and state regulations regarding the education of children: *Meyer* involved a Nebraska statute that prohibited the teaching of any modern language other than English at any public or private grammar school; *Pierce* involved an Oregon statute mandating attendance at public schools, which did not include any private schools not operated by the state. In *Meyer* the Court expounded upon the liberty guarantee of the fourteenth amendment's due process clause as including "the right of the individual to contract, to engage in any of the common occupations of life, to acquire useful knowledge, to marry, establish a home and bring up children, to worship God according to the dictates of his own conscience, and generally enjoy those privileges long recognized at common law as essential to the orderly pursuit of happiness by free men."[36] The Court in *Pierce* relied upon *Meyer* to posit "the liberty of parents and guardians to direct the upbringing and education of children under their control," stating with a rhetorical flourish that the "child is not the mere creature of the State; those who nurture him and direct his destiny have the right, coupled with the high duty, to recognize and prepare him for additional obligations."[37] Importantly, as in *Meyer*, the Court in *Pierce* did not rely solely upon parental rights; in *Pierce* the Court also credited the liberty interests of the private institutions that would be deprived of property should the state statute mandating education at public institutions be deemed valid.[38]

Despite the problematic precedential pedigree of *Meyer* and *Pierce* in freedoms of liberty and contract prevalent in the discredited *Lochner* era, during which time the United States Supreme Court invalidated approximately two hundred state statutes attempting to regulate economic relations,[39] after remaining relatively dormant for several decades, *Meyer* and *Pierce* have been resuscitated in contemporary privacy doctrine. In familial—and later individual—privacy doctrine the fundamental parental right becomes not only the right to make choices relating to the performance of one's parental role but also the right to make choices relating to whether or not one will assume a parental role.[40] This development results in the continuing line of contraception and abortion cases that give various effect to the freedom to decide whether or not one will become a parent. As most recently expressed by the Court, these "most intimate and personal choices a person may make" are "central to the liberty protected by the fourteenth amendment."[41]

Related to contemporary privacy doctrine as inclusive of contraceptive and abortion decisions affecting whether or not an individual will assume a parental role are cases in which the parental right involves the state's termination or nonrecognition of an individual's parental status. In the termination context, the recognition of a fundamental parental right serves as a constitutional regulation of state procedures in which the state is seeking to terminate an individual's parental status. For example, in *Lassiter*, although the Court recognized a fundamental parental right when the state was seeking to terminate parental rights, the right seemed to suffer in comparison to the more tangible liberty interest implicated by imprisonment. Thus the Court held that appointment of counsel was not constitutionally mandated in a termination of parental rights proceeding.[42] A year later, in *Santosky*, the Court recognized that a fundamental parental right is especially vital during termination proceedings and thus declared that due process required a showing of a relatively high standard of proof—clear and convincing evidence—before parental rights could be extinguished.[43] In the context of the recognition of parental status, the problem centers on identifying individuals who merit a fundamental parental right rather than on an interpretation of the contours of any fundamental right. Such cases—which can be collectively referred to as the "unwed father" cases[44]—result from contemporary challenges to traditional ideology that bestows parenting status according to a gendered disparity: women are deemed parents through the biological "fact" of giving birth, while men are deemed parents through the legal "fact" of a formal relationship such

as marriage with the woman who gave birth.[45] Despite erratic recognition
of fundamental parental rights to unwed biological fathers, the uneven
application of such rights in the context of parental termination proceedings, and the volatile predicament of contraceptive and abortion rights, the
notion of a fundamental parental right grounded in the liberty guarantee
of the due process clauses of the fifth and fourteenth amendments remains
firmly entrenched in constitutional doctrine.

The constitutional principle recognizing a fundamental parental right
is indisputably not a solitary principle but is situated within the complexities of constitutional contexts in which the child is also accorded a measure
of legal recognition. First, within a due process analysis the parents' fundamental right is subject to infringement by the state if such infringement
is narrowly tailored to serve a compelling state interest. The state's assertion of the best interest of the child is considered a compelling state interest; the state's interest and the child's interest become coextensive because
the state relies upon its role as *parens patriae* in the assertion of the child's
welfare.[46] Second, within any constitutional analysis there is the possibility
of conflicting individual constitutional rights. So it is possible that the parent's constitutional rights would conflict with the child's constitutional
rights, necessitating a balancing of rights. However, this approach has
been relatively rare, perhaps because the state is invested with parens
patriae status to assert the child's rights or possibly because minors' lesser
constitutional rights ensure that any parental fundamental right would
dominate. For example, in cases involving abortions requested by minors,
there is discussion both of the rights of the parents of the minor and of the
minor's less-than-adult constitutional rights.[47]

Against this backdrop of constitutional principles, individual states
have taken different approaches to recognizing any fundamental parental
rights in the custody and control of children by privileging parents over
nonparental third parties. One commentator divides the state approaches
into three distinct clusters: the parental rights standard, the parental presumption standards (including various types of presumptions), and the
best interest standard.[48]

The vast majority of states explicitly accord some privileged position to
parents in comparison to nonparents in custody determinations. Although
the expression of this privilege differs, typically the privileging requires
the establishment of some reason to depart from the general rule that parents are entitled to custody of their children. For example, in New York
this principle is articulated as a requirement that "exceptional circum-

stances" are necessary for a court to create an exception to the recognition of rights afforded to both parent and child in their relationship.[49] Nonrecognition of a parental privilege, perhaps best expressed as a "pure" best interest standard—in which courts "focus solely on the best interest of the child" without giving any preference to the child's legal parents—is a relatively rare minority position.[50] Nevertheless, the rhetoric of best interests of the child can also privilege natural or legal parents. The best interest of the child standard accomplishes this privileging through the general rule that it is within the best interests of any child to be in the custody of her or his natural or legal parents. The best interest standard's privileging of parents usually contains a caveat allowing for proof that the general rule might not be true in this particular instance.

Third party custody doctrine has thus developed into a rather arcane and convoluted set of preferences, presumptions, rhetoric, and caveats. Commentators have expressed dissatisfaction with the doctrine, employing examples such as unwed fathers, stepparents, foster parents, grandparents, and "surrogate mothers" to illustrate the incoherency of the doctrine in a society in which the doctrine's underlying premise of the nuclear family is no longer accurate.[51] For lesbians and our relationships with children, the underlying premise of third party custody has never been accurate, and its application is ill-equipped to serve our interests.

Third Party Doctrine and Lesbian Relations with Children

The doctrine of third party custody is deemed applicable to three categories of lesbian relationships with children. The first category is embodied by the lesbian nonlegal mother and occurs in the context of her efforts to obtain custody or visitation in the case of a rupture of her relationship with the legal mother as well as in the context of her efforts to adopt the child of the legal mother. In this category the notion of third party can operate to bar the lesbian nonlegal mother from being recognized as a legal parent to her child. The second category of third parties is putative fathers, especially sperm donors. These third parties are often extraneous to the lesbian legal mother, her partner who shares parenting as the lesbian nonlegal mother, as well as to the child. Nevertheless, largely due to their biological status, these third parties may be deemed not to be third parties and thus may be erroneously privileged as parents.

The third and final category consists of grandparents and other relatives of the child. Often motivated by disapproval of the legal mother's lesbianism, these third party relatives assert a right to custody and often prevail, despite their less privileged status. Thus, taken in its entirety, third party doctrine does not simply disadvantage or advantage lesbian mothers. This inconsistency might be explained by the various positions lesbian mothers occupy, yet it is also explainable on the basis of the underlying male-female dyad as a basis for third party doctrine. The inapplicability of the very notion of third parties is demonstrated by a further examination of cases within each of the three categories.

THE LESBIAN NONLEGAL MOTHER

The lesbian nonlegal mother, usually the lover or former lover of a child's legal mother, challenges the heterosexual matrix of third party custody by being the "other" mother in an ideology that admits of only one mother, the third party in an ideology that admits of only two parents, one of each gender. I prefer the term *nonlegal* rather than the more common *nonbiological* for two reasons. First, many lesbian mothers become legal mothers through adoption rather than biological birth. Second, and more important, the issue is exactly the legal identity of lesbians as determined and enforced through law. Although the term *nonlegal* as well as *legal* may seem to foreclose the very issue to be decided, both terms are contingent as well as based upon interpretation rather than fact. As feminist legal scholar Isabel Marcus notes in the context of marital identity, to the extent that legal categories are ascertainable with "relatively minimal effort, they are treated as self-evident or natural" and then this "apparent self-evidentness reinforces the sense of the cultural appropriateness of the category and the boundaries embodied in that category," which "reinforces existing power relations": "At best, a particular argument about a hard case involving the margin of a socially constructed category may be left for the judge or scholar."[52] Thus, to denominate a mother as biological naturalizes what is a legal decision and relegates nonbiological mothers to "hard cases."

While there have always been lesbians who have shared their lives with children,[53] within the last two decades lesbians have explicitly challenged the hegemony of the only-one-mother ideology in law[54] as well as in other forms of lesbian writings, including literature. Whether the challenge of the nonlegal mother is fundamental or superficial is, of course, debatable, as is the nature of the challenges posed by any lesbian "family" formation.

For example, litigation involving sundered lesbian relationships in which the nonlegal mother is seeking custody or visitation—and, importantly, the legal mother is denying such custody or visitation—enforce the notion of a heterosexual dyad to exclude the lesbian nonlegal mother. In these cases the other mother is a third party nonparent. Despite a plethora of theories that have been advanced in support of the nonlegal mother's parental status, scholarly critique of judicial denial of parental status to the nonlegal mother, and legal scholarship that persuasively argues for expanded conceptions of parental status,[55] the general rule is that the non-legal mother is a third party, whatever her current or past relationship with the child.

Perhaps the most famous of these cases is *Alison D.*,[56] decided by New York's highest court.[57] The factual background of *Alison D.* illustrates the typical scenario at issue in these cases: one member of a lesbian couple gave birth to a child through alternative insemination. After the adult couple's relationship dissolved, the legal mother eventually refused to allow her former lover to visit with the child. In the *Alison D.* litigation the New York courts uniformly held that the lesbian nonlegal mother was not within the definition of parent and so had no standing to bring a petition for visitation against the child's biological mother.[58] The high court rejected the claim to reality in the form of "de facto parenthood" as insufficient to overcome the legal definition of parent.[59] The sole dissenting judge, Judith Kaye, argued that the court imposed an unnecessarily restrictive definition of parent. She also criticized the court for rejecting the tradition of interpreting the law to promote the welfare of children and overlooking the significant distinction between visitation and custody proceedings.[60]

A few months later the Supreme Court of Wisconsin decided *In re ZJH, (Sporleder v. Hermes).*[61] In *ZJH* the two women lived together as lovers for approximately eight years. As described by the court, "after an unsuccessful attempt to have a child through the artificial insemination of Sporleder, they decided that Hermes would adopt a child."[62] When the couple separated, Hermes's formal adoption was completed and she prohibited her former lover Sporleder from visiting the child. The court upheld previous pronouncements that Sporleder had no standing to bring an action for either visitation or custody. The court first reasoned that Sporleder did not fit into any of the statutory categories allowing third parties to bring actions for visitation or custody, including circumstances in which "neither parent is fit and proper to have custody of the child" or in which "compelling circumstances" defined by precedent as similar unfitness on the part of the parent such as "abandonment, persistent neglect of parental duties, or extended disruption of parental custody" prevail.[63] The court then reasoned that Sporleder was not within the statutory category of parent, including any theory of "in loco parentis."[64] As a nonparent, Sporleder was without standing to bring an action for custody and was similarly without standing to bring an action for visitation.[65] Dissenting, Justice Shirley Abrahamson stressed the need for a hearing to examine the contract between the adults and the best interests of the child.[66] A court of appeals in Minnesota reached a similar result, although based upon a more liberal statute applied to more complicated facts. In *Kulla v. McNulty*[67] a referee had found that Kulla established a prima facie case under the Minnesota third party custody statute, but a court concluded otherwise and dismissed Kulla's petition for visitation with the child K.R.M. The child had been born to McNulty while she was in a lesbian relationship with Kulla, who became the child's caregiver, at least while McNulty was "away from home working as an airline attendant."[68] McNulty, however, subsequently resumed a relationship with the child's biological father and later married him. She specifically disavowed any implication that her relationship with Kulla was serious: "McNulty contends that she entered into the relationship [with Kulla] initially out of curiosity as to the gay lifestyle, and although she was fond of appellant [Kulla], McNulty asserts that the extent of her feelings were that she found appellant merely amusing and enjoyable for a time."[69] Applying the three prongs of the Minnesota third party visitation statute, requiring the court to find that visitation be in the best interests of the child, that the petitioner and the child had established emotional parent-child ties, and that the visitation would not interfere with the custodial relationship between the parent and the child,[70] the court upheld the trial court's finding that the third factor was not satisfied as within the trial court's discretion. Responding to Kulla's argument that satisfaction of the third factor was practicably impossible and could be effectively prevented by a biological parent's noncooperation, the court noted that absent the statute Kulla would have absolutely no right to petition for visitation.

Of the reported cases considering a nonlegal mother's right to petition for visitation, only a few do not per se exclude the nonbiological mother as a nonparental third party. For example, in *A.C. v. C.B.*,[71] a New Mexico appellate court stressed the fact of the parties coparenting and custody agreement, but also noted that the nonbiological mother had made a "colorable claim of standing to seek enforcement of such claimed rights" of visitation.[72] In *Holtzman v. Knott*, the Wisconsin Supreme Court set out critiria by which a nonlegal mother could claim parental status for visitation.[73]

Several theories of parenthood emerge from these cases as arguments to circumvent the harsh consequences of third party doctrine, especially in the absence of a statute. Almost all these theories are explicitly considered by the California appellate court in *Nancy S. v. Michelle G.*[74] Again, the factual details are excruciatingly typical. Nancy S. and Michelle G. lived together since 1969; Nancy S. gave birth to one child conceived through alternative insemination in 1980 and to a second child conceived through the same method in 1985. Both children have birth certificates that name Michelle G. as "father," were given Michelle G.'s "family name," and referred to both Michelle G. and Nancy S. as "Mom." When Michelle G. and Nancy S. separated in 1985, they agreed to a joint custody arrangement that was successful for three years. After disagreements, Nancy S. instituted an action to declare Michelle G. as "not a parent of either child."[75]

In arguing that she is a parent, Michelle G. relied upon the theories of de facto parenthood, in loco parentis, equitable estoppel, and the functional definition of parenthood. All of these theories are arguments that Michelle G. should be deemed a parent and thus forestall the operation of third party doctrine that would place her a position of considerably less entitlement than Nancy S.

The court considered and rejected the merit of each of these theories, although not necessarily disagreeing with their factual relevance. For example, the court found that Michelle G. might factually be entitled to the "the status of a 'de facto' parent," but that de facto parental status was not equal to legal parental status.[76] Specifically, the court considered the de facto parent as a third party, and applied its third party doctrine to conclude that "custody can be awarded to the de facto parent only if it is established by clear and convincing evidence that parental custody is detrimental to the child."[77] Similarly, the court decided that the concept of in loco parentis, even if it was factually relevant, was irrelevant in the context of custody decisions. Further, the court declined the invitation to declare Michelle G. a parent by equitable estoppel, a doctrine under which a court could preclude (estop) Nancy S. from asserting the claim in the interests of fairness (equity). Michelle G. argued that the legal mother, Nancy S., should be equitably estopped from denying Michelle G.'s parental status because of Nancy S.'s prolonged encouragement and support of the parental relationship. The court rejected this argument by noting that equitable estoppel had never been applied in California "against a natural parent" and that occasions of such applications in other states rested upon important considerations not present in this case. Regarding equitable estoppel in other states, the court considered the application of the doctrine to prevent a wife from denying paternity of her husband. The court noted that this use was rooted in one of the strongest presumptions in law: that a child born to a married woman is the legitimate child of the marriage.[78] The court then declared that "no similar presumption" applied to this case.[79] The court's failure to analogize the lesbian relationship illustrates my argument that the third party doctrine, even in its exceptions, results from the mandate of heterosexuality in the form of a male-female dyad. The logic of the court thus relegates the third sex relationship to third party status. Finally, the court considered the last theory proffered by Michelle G. and rejected any legal parental status derivative of functional parental definitions,[80] ostensibly because the acceptance of functional parenthood would be impracticable.[81]

In addition to family law doctrines of parenthood, the specter of constitutional privacy of the parental relationship haunts *Nancy S.* as well as the other cases involving lesbian nonlegal parents.[82] Such a haunting serves to constitutionalize third party doctrine by conceptualizing it as state protection of the parent-child relationship from third party interference. In this construction constitutional recognition of a parental fundamental right does not operate as a bulwark against state intrusion into parental rights but as a preservation of parental right against persons with noncognizable legal claims. As one court observed, to the extent it grants rights to the nonbiological parent, it would "diminish the rights of legal parents."[83]

Even in the rare case in which a nonlegal mother is allowed to make a claim for parent status in the form of visitation, the nonlegal mother must satisfy criteria sufficient to overcome her third party status. As articulated by the Wisconsin Supreme Court in *Holtzman v. Knott*, the nonlegal mother must demonstrate that the legal mother consented to and fostered the nonlegal mother's "parent-like relationship" with the child, that the nonlegal mother and the child lived in the same household, that the nonlegal mother and the child had a sufficient length of time together so that bonding has occurred, and that the nonlegal mother assumed responsibility for the child's care, including financial responsibility.[84]

The Wisconsin Supreme Court's formulation is an exception, and, interestingly, the same court rendering this exceptional decision had previously refused to legalize the avenue by which the nonlegal parent could have transformed herself into a legal parent—so-called second-parent adoption.[85] Given the prevalent application of third party doctrine to deny lesbian nonbiological or nonlegal parents visitation or custody, the adoption solution changes the status of the nonlegal mother to that of a legal parent so that she would no longer be a third party. Explicated, outlined, and advocated as a necessary reform in the legal literature before appearing in the courtroom,[86] "second-parent" adoptions are gaining some judicial acceptance. In allowing these adoptions, courts have struggled with the strict heterosexuality of parenting ideology, which does not contemplate lesbian parents. This heterosexual ideology is often implicitly articulated in the statutory requirements for adoption. For example, in the first reported second-parent adoption case, *In re Adoption of T. & M,*[87] the District of Columbia court had to construe the district's code section providing that a final decree of adoption terminated the relationship between the child and his or her natural parents except in the case in which one of the natural parents is the "spouse of the adopter."[88] Through the use of the term *spouse* as the only exception to terminating parental rights, the code section reinscribes (heterosexual) marriage as well as the notion of heterosexual parenting. In struggling with this issue the District of Columbia court declined to read the statute literally; instead it read the termination provision as directory rather than mandatory, analogizing the situation to a spousal, stepparent adoption and stressing the best interest of the child.[89] Similarly, New York trial courts, first in *Evan,*[90] and later in *Caitlin and Emily,*[91] a New Jersey trial court in *J.M.G.,*[92] as well as the supreme courts of Vermont and Massachusetts in *B.L.V.B. & E.L.V.B.*[93] and *Tammy,*[94] all construed the applicable statutes as not requiring the termination of the legal parental relationship, relying on the stepparent analogy and the best interests standard.[95] While the favorable results in these cases are far from uniform,[96] they do portend a practical solution in some cases[97] to the problems caused by third party doctrine, which relegates nonlegal parents to disfavored status in custody proceedings. The interwoven nature of the relation between third party doctrine and second-parent adoptions has not gone unnoticed by the courts.[98]

Nevertheless, although this intertwined relation has practical benefits, at a more theoretical level, the solution of second-parent adoptions to the problem of third party doctrine poses at least two problems. First, taken together third party doctrine and second-parent adoptions mutually reinforce not only each other but structurally sustain the dyadic nature of parenthood. Although the successful second-parent adoption cases certainly advance an emancipatory agenda for lesbians by not perpetuating sexual orientation discrimination,[99] lesbians must nevertheless carve themselves out as exceptions to the heterosexual mandate while remaining analogous to stepparents.[100] This performance requires lesbians to satisfy the most traditional and stereotypical terms of the heterosexual marriage mandate: the relationship between the two lesbians must be long-term, committed, and monogamous. The opinions invariably include in the recitation of relevant facts—often as the first sentence—a satisfaction of this implicit criteria: "The petitioners, Diane F. and Valerie C. have lived together in a committed, long term relationship, which they perceive as permanent, for the past fourteen years";[101] "[In both adoptions], the couples have lived together in committed, long term relationships for nine and twelve years respectively. Each couple viewed its relationship as permanent, akin to marriage";[102] "The plaintiff and E.O., the biological mother, have been in a committed relationship for approximately 10 years";[103] "Appellants are two women, Jane and Deborah, who have lived together in a committed, monogamous relationship since 1986";[104] "Helen and Susan have lived together in a committed relationship, which they consider to be permanent, for more than ten years."[105]

Further, there must be a maximum of two lesbians: there can be a second parent, but a third lesbian cannot be a third parent, she must be a third party. It is difficult to imagine a court bestowing even its limited generosity to a configuration of three or more lesbian parents. Thus, because of its insistence on a dyad, second-parent adoption suffers from many of the same ideological shortcomings as same-sex marriage.

Second, the second-parent adoption cases reinforce a dominate social structure based upon economic stratification. Just as the sexology theory—and its consequences—differed markedly for women of the higher and lower classes, so too does the requirement that the dyad be heterosexual seem to relax with economic privilege. Typically, immediately after noting the dyadic nature of the relationship evidenced by its longevity and mutual commitment, the court recounts the indicators of the lesbians' elevated class status including professional occupations and home ownership. For example, following the court's recitations concerning the dyadic nature of the relationship, the respective courts declare: "Diane, age 39, is an Assistant Professor of Pediatrics and an attending physician at a respected teaching hospital. Valerie, age 40, holds a Ph.D. in developmental psychology and teaches at a highly regarded private school";[106] "Plaintiff is employed part-time by a cable T.V. network and is the primary caretaker of the child. E.O. is an executive vice-president for a large communications company. They jointly own a home and other properties for investment purposes. They have a low six-figure combined income";[107] "In June, 1983, they jointly purchased a house in Cambridge. Both women are physicians specializing in surgery. . . . Both women also held positions on the faculty of Harvard Medical School."[108] In *Caitlin and Emily* the New York family court judge first describes the circumstances relating to the conception of the children and the appointment of law guardians before the judge provides the indicators of class status of the two lesbian couples. The first couple, one of whom is an environmental engineer, live with the children in "a large two-story 100 year old house in excellent repair, in a quiet neighborhood on a tree-lined street. The second couple are relatively less advantaged, although certainly not disadvantaged, one member of the couple being employed at a "large local corporation," and the couple living with the children "in a nearby suburb in a neat and well-furnished raised ranch."[109] A relative rarity is the Supreme Court of Vermont's opinion, which does not contain indicators of economic status.[110] While the absence of economic facts may be attributable to the trial court's rejection of the adoptions on legal grounds, causing the record to be devoid of factual findings, this opinion as well as *Caitlin and Emily* demonstrate that economic evidence can be irrelevant or minimized. However, in *Tammy* the Supreme Court of Massachusetts explicitly includes a resultant economic benefit, in the form of trust funds to which the child will become entitled, as part of its best interests of the child determination, finding it important enough to include in its opinion that "Susan indicated that the adoption is important for Tammy in terms of potential inheritance from Helen. Helen and her living issue are beneficiaries of three irrevocable family trusts. Unless Tammy is adopted, Helen's share of the trusts may pass to others. Although Susan and Helen have established a substantial trust for Tammy, it is comparatively small in relation to Tammy's potential inheritance under Helen's family trusts."[111] Thus, because of its emphasis on economic privilege, second-parent adoption again suffers from many of the same ideological shortcomings as same-sex marriage.

The lesbian nonlegal mother, usually the lover or former lover of a child's legal mother, whether adoptive or biological, has the potential to challenge the heterosexual dyadic model of parenting. However, when she is deemed a third party her challenge is unsuccessful because third party custody doctrine relegates her to an irrelevant or disadvantaged position. On the other hand, when she is accorded status as a second parent, her challenge is diluted, because second-parent adoption doctrine assimilates her to the dyadic model of parenting. While in practical terms the otherwise nonlegal mother may prefer second-parent status[112] to third party exclusion, especially in the event of a dissolution of the parenting dyad, lesbian legal theory must confront the ideological structures that produce this "practical" result. Politically and ethically, it is problematic that the practical protections are often necessary because one member of the former dyad is enforcing her desires through legal formalism. Theoretically, it is significant that the practical solution ultimately reinforces the dyadic structure of parenting, which is responsible for the problem requiring a solution.

THE SPERM DONOR

In all of the so-called second-parent adoption cases, the sperm donor or biological father as the potential second-party to the parent dyad is either implicitly or explicitly relegated to impossibility. When the sperm donor or biological father is not so relegated, but instead sues for visitation or custody, he threatens to assume the status of a member of the parental dyad rather than a third party, even if the child has a lesbian dyad in the parenting role.

Biology threatens to become determinative of social realities when *sperm donor* and *father* become synonomous terms. While biological paternity is not always legal paternity under constitutional doctrine, statutes regulating "artifical" insemination usually exclude the donor from paternity only when the recepient is a "married woman" and the insemination is performed by a licensed physician.[113] Thus, the biological paternity achieves its greatest social stature when it is necessary to establish the heterosexual parenting dyad: if there is another male to occupy the male half of the dyad, then the donor is irrelevant. For example, in a visitation proceeding brought by the sperm donor C.M. against the legal mother C.C.,[114] the court declared C.M. the natural father and awarded him visitation, reasoning that

> in this case there is a known man who is the donor. There is no husband. If the couple had been married and the husband's sperm used artificially, he would be considered the father. If the woman conceives a child by intercourse, the "donor" who is not married to the mother is no less a father. Likewise, if an unmarried woman conceives a child through artificial insemination from semen from a known man, that man cannot be considered to be less a father because he is not married to the woman. . . . There was no one else who was in a position to take upon himself the responsibil-

ities of fatherhood when the child was conceived. . . . It is in the best interests of the child to have two parents whenever possible.[115]

While such an outcome is not inevitable,[116] it can be the same even when
the consideration of the donor as one-half of the parental dyad potentially
excludes the lesbian nonlegal parent. For example, in one of the first
known lesbian parenting cases, *Jhordan H. v. Mary C.*,[117] the court awarded
the sperm donor visitation over the objections of Mary, the legal mother,
and Victoria, a "close friend who lived in a nearby town," who had participated in the selection of Jhordan as the sperm donor, agreed "to raise the
child jointly," with the legal mother, and assisted in the pregnancy and
birth.[118] The court applied both the marital status limitation and the physician requirement of the artificial insemination statutes to declare inapplicable any of the protections from donor interference.[119] Further, the court
specifically rejected the contention by Mary and Victoria that, with the
child, they "compose a family unit," which should be accorded family
autonomy, because the court deemed that they did not constitute a family
unit. Perhaps unusually, however, especially given the relatively early
occurrence of this case in terms of the sperm donor cases, the court did recognize Victoria's position as a psychological parent, although it declined to
declare her a "de facto parent," and it recognized her right to visitation.
Importantly, however, this situation would certainly have been different if
Mary C., as legal, biological, and custodial parent, had attempted to
exclude Victoria, as in the California case of *Nancy S. v. Michelle G.*, three
years later. In addition to statutory interpretation, the court based its conclusion that any family formation must include the sperm donor on a
"record which demonstrates no clear understanding that Jhordan's role
would be limited to the provision of semen and that he would have no
parental relationship."[120] Facts deemed relevant by the court included the
legal mother's failure to object to Jhordan's monthly visits after the birth
and his prebirth collection of baby equipment and establishment of a trust
fund.[121]

The question of the quality and quantity of "facts" necessary to transform the biological paternity of the sperm donor into the person of a legal
father as well as issues of legal interpretation are presented in *Thomas S. v.
Robin Y.*[122] Rendered by a New York trial court in 1993 and reversed on
appeal, this case has attracted much legal and community attention and
dissension.[123] In *Robin Y.* the child in question was born in 1981, into a
household of two lesbian parents and another child born to her nonlegal

mother the previous year. After several years both children met their sperm donors, considering them as family friends but knowledgeable as to the men's status as sperm donors or biological fathers.[124] After a disagreement, Thomas S., a gay male attorney,[125] brought an action arguing that as the child's "proven biological father," he was "absolutely entitled to an order of filiation and also entitled to an order of visitation."[126] In resisting the request for filiation and visitation, the lesbian mother(s)' arguments included one that the doctrine of equitable estoppel should preclude Thomas S. from asserting his parental rights at this late date. The court accepted this argument, applying it as a common law principle relevant to adjudicating paternity "for families whose reality is more complex than a one mother, one father biological model."[127] In so doing, the court stressed the factual details of the case. Thus, although the trial court's opinion in *Thomas S.*, supports lesbian parenting, it is problematic because it leaves unresolved the quality and quantity of facts necessary to establish legal fatherhood. The particularity of the factual details in the opinions demonstrate this problem. Further, the particular factual details preferred by those who disagreed with the opinions are also demonstrative. In reporting on the decision in the *Lesbian and Gay Law Notes*, editor Professor Arthur Leonard related the facts as including that "a relationship was established" with visits, calls, cards, and letters between the parties and also surmised that as the child "grew older and her relationship with Thomas S. became more extensive, her mothers apparently became concerned about the encroachment on their New York based family unit and sought to limit contact."[128] Letters in response included direct factual disputes: "It was the plaintiff's [Thomas S.] homophobic and insulting demand to introduce his biological daughter to his family in the absence of her mothers, whom he was 'not comfortable' including, that brought about this litigation,"[129] as well as criticism that Professor Leonard departed from the trial judge's findings. Other letter writers related their personal knowledge concerning Thomas S.'s "fatherly relationship,"[130] and among such writers was Thomas. S.'s trial attorney, who submitted quotes from letters and cards and conclusions relating to the mothers' intentions.[131]

Given such factual disputes—and disputes regarding the relative weight to be placed on particular facts—this cannot be a satisfactory solution to the problems inherent for lesbians' relations with children.[132]

Importantly, however, any decision awarding a sperm donor joint custody threatens to be a very tortured valorization of the interlocking and inconsistent analytics of biology and heterosexuality, as well as the preservation of male hegemony.[133] It is clear that a biological valorization would occur if the court accepted the sperm donor's argument that he is absolutely entitled to an order of filiation based upon his biological connection. Less clear are the intricacies of heterosexism and sexism should the sperm donor prevail, which are perhaps obscured by the identity of the sperm donor as a gay man.

In a situation in which a child is parented by a dyad, as in the situation in *Thomas S.*, *but for* the fact that the dyad is a lesbian one rather than a married heterosexual one, Thomas S. would have no viable claim. The declaration of the sperm donor as a father—even if the sperm donor is not himself heterosexual—reestablishes heterosexuality as normative, natural, and inevitable through the "real" heterosexually coupled parents. Further, the disparity between the treatment accorded the male member needed to complete the heterosexual dyad and the "third party" nonlegal lesbian mother irrelevant to the heterosexual dyad is instructive. Seemingly, the sperm donor can establish himself as a legal father with sufficient "facts," but no amount of good facts on the part of the nonlegal mother can establish her as a parent.

Even apart from sexual orientation constructions, the factual basis for declaring parenthood is gendered. It is difficult to imagine a judicial recognition of several visits—even many visits—over a period of ten years as an indication of *mother*hood. That custody determinations occur and reflect disparate power between the genders is well known;[134] less explored is how this gendered dynamic operates among lesbians and gay men.[135] Additionally, Thomas S. argued that a failure to accord him legal fatherhood status will "brand" the child "illegitimate."[136] This argument seeks to capitalize upon and enforce antiquated notions of morality that are sexist as well as heterosexist.[137]

In arguing that their status as sperm donors entitled them to the privilege of parenthood, Thomas S., Jhordan K., and C.M. relied upon dyadic notions of parenthood, which would exclude any nonlegal mother from the dyad as well as install themselves within the requisite heterosexually composed dyadic formation that is parenthood. If the sperm donor is not successful, he is relegated to a third party, a person outside of the parenting dyad, without recourse unless he can overcome the presumptions accorded to legal parents.

GRANDPARENTS

Grandparents are classic third parties, however, in custody cases involving lesbian parents these third party grandparents have been granted custody over the objections of the lesbian legal mother. The third party doctrine that should protect lesbian legal mothers is not applied to their advantage. Instead, the preference accorded to legal parents is overcome by reference to lesbianism, either explicitly or covertly.

The situation of Sharon Bottoms, which received extensive media coverage,[138] exemplifies this predicament. In the early 1990s a Virginia trial court granted a maternal grandmother's petition for custody of her grandchild based upon the fact that the child's mother—her daughter—was a lesbian. The attorney representing the grandmother, Pamela Kay Bottoms, called as his first witness Sharon Bottoms, and after establishing her identity as the child's legal mother and the identity of his client as the child's grandmother, immediately focused his questions on lesbianism:

> Q: Now, in the juvenile court you stated that you are in a lesbian relationship with whom?
> A: April Wade.
> Q: Now, for the record, would you tell me your definition of a lesbian relationship. What does it mean?
> A: It means two people of the same sex are together.
> Q: In what way are they together?
> A: In a relationship.
> Q: Now, you say a "relationship," does that entail sex?
> A: Yes.
> Q: Hugging and kissing?
> A: Yes.
> Q: Sleeping in the same bed?
> A: Yes.
> Q: Now then, you're not at all ashamed of that relationship, is that correct?
> A: No, sir.[139]

Delivering his oral judgment, the trial judge stated that

> this dispute presents the question of whether the child's best interest is served by a transfer of the custody of the child from her mother to her maternal grandmother, Kay Bottoms. That's the ultimate issue on the bottom line that we come to.
> The mother, Sharon Bottoms, has openly admitted in this court that she is living in an active homosexual relationship. She admitted she is sharing a

bedroom and her bed with another, her female lover, whom she identified by name as April Wade. Sharon Bottoms in this courtroom admitted a commitment to April Wade, which as she contemplates will be permanent, and as I understand her testimony, long lasting if not forever.

   She readily admits her behavior in open affection shown to April Wade in front of the child. Examples given were kissing, patting, all of this in the presence of the child. She further admits consenting that the child referred to April Wade, her lover, as to quote the words "Da Da."[140]

The trial judge then stated that the "mother's conduct is illegal" rendering her "an unfit parent."[141] While cognizant of the "presumption in the law being in favor of the natural parent," the court found that Sharon Bottoms's "circumstances of unfitness" were of "such an extraordinary nature" that they were sufficient to rebut the presumption of parental custody.[142] The court then denied overnight visitation to the legal mother as well as any visitation in the presence of April Wade.[143]

   On appeal Sharon Bottoms contended that the evidence was insufficient to overcome the parental presumption and award custody to the third party grandmother, arguing as well that the court did not apply the required best interests of the child standard after it had decided the legal parent and nonparent should receive equal consideration.[144] The trial judge relied upon a Virginia Supreme Court opinion that applied a per se rule disqualifying a lesbian mother in a custody contest with the child's father.[145] In so doing, the judge gave little effect to the state court's articulation of the third party custody standard. This standard, as applied in a case cited by the trial court, would deny a grandmother custody of her grandchild in a situation in which the child's custodial parent continued to live with a killer, in fact the killer of the child's other parent.[146] As expressed by the appellate court, such circumstances, although a matter of concern, do not constitute an "extraordinary reason" to deprive the legal parent of custody.[147]

   The Virginia Court of Appeals as well as the Virginia Supreme Court affirmed the trial judge's ruling and Sharon Bottoms continues to be deprived of her child.

   The amount of press coverage devoted to the Bottoms situation might lead one to believe it is an aberration. However, the courts of Mississippi confronted a similar situation. In *White v. Thompson* the paternal grandparents sought custody of their grandchildren on the grounds that the mother was an unfit parent.[148] The bulk of the testimony concerned the mother's lesbian relationship, which prompted the trial court to find the mother "unfit, morally and otherwise, to have custody of her children."[149] On appeal to the Mississippi Supreme Court the mother argued that the trial court's finding was impermissibly predicated solely on her lesbianism. The Mississippi Supreme Court finessed the issue of her sexuality, deciding not to reach the issue of whether lesbianism alone was sufficient to render a parent unfit and allow the court to award custody to third parties:

> Although the predominant issue in this case seems to have been Mrs. White's lesbianism, and the chancellor may have relied entirely upon this, we find that a review of the entire record and the circumstances present . . . shows that the chancellor's decision that Mrs. White was an unfit mother, morally and otherwise, was not against the substantial weight of the evidence.[150]

The circumstances included some testimony that the children had not been properly supervised, clothed, or fed.[151] The level of such impropriety remains vague, and thus vaguely troubling. Further, considerations of class are again relevant: the label of unfit applied by the judiciary is as class-coded as was the label of third sex applied by the sexologists. As the dissenting justice in *White* begins his opinion, any neglect of the children is "no more than one would expect to find in any case where a twenty four year old mother with but a high school diploma and no independent means" is attempting to support her children.[152] Yet such neglect was sufficient to satisfy the state standard for rebutting the presumption of custody accorded to a legal parent.[153]

The message of *White* is that a court can deflect the contentious issue of lesbianism with reference to more vague and class-coded standards. Such an approach could be applied in *Bottoms*,[154] in which the appellate court could credit the grandmother's testimony that the two-year-old child once "cursed" and stood in the corner.[155] Thus, even if the Virginia appellate court departed from a per se disqualification of lesbian mothers as parents, it could nevertheless affirm the trial judge's ruling.

Importantly, in both *Bottoms* and *White*, the heterosexual dyadic model of parenting did not operate to the legal mother's benefit. In *Bottoms* the child's legal father had never expressed an interest in the child[156] and the attempt at any reconstruction of a dyadic parent model with April Wade was deemed criminal.[157] Likewise, in *White* the children's legal father was not a contender for legal custody,[158] and again any attempt to reconstruct a dyadic parenting model with a woman was deemed unacceptable. In *Bottoms* the grandmother did not have a heterosexual mate at the time of the hearing;[159] in *White* the paternal grandparents presented themselves in the heterosexual model. Thus, while the dyadic model of parenting should have operated in favor of the lesbian legal mothers, relegating others to less favored third party status, because the legal parents could not satisfy the implicit heterosexual requirement of the dyad, these members of the third sex become equated with third parties.

Certainly, preferences for legal parents over grandparents or other third parties can operate in favor of a lesbian legal mother.[160] Nevertheless, such preferences are certainly no guarentee—or even adequate insulation—against lesbian legal parents being deprived of relations with their children. Further, third parties can gain an advantage by invoking the most powerful third party of all—the state—to regulate the relationships of lesbian mothers.[161]

No Third Sex, No Third Parties

Thus, an examination of the application of third party doctrine in the context of lesbian relations with children reveals that the doctrine can operate both to the benefit and detriment of lesbians. Rather than attempt to refine the doctrine so that it might better accommodate lesbians, I suggest that the doctrine's theoretical underpinnings in a notion of parenting as a heterosexual dyad render it problematic for lesbians, and objectionable. Just as we no longer speak of lesbians as members of a "third sex," we should abandon the language of "third parties" in the lesbian context. Perhaps a rejection of the underlying heterosexism and sexism of the dyadic model of parenting will not be far behind.

I I

Neither Sexy Nor Reasonable

These days it seems as if everyone thinks he knows something about lesbians. Including Richard Posner, a judge on the Seventh Circuit Court of Appeals and one of the foremost proponents of a legal philosophy known as law and economics. Law and economics theorizes human beings as rational actors incessantly involved in cost-benefits analyses. Under Posner's view, every human activity can be understood in terms of his version of law and economics. Even sexuality.

Posner attempted to apply the tenets of law and economics to sexuality, producing a book, *Sex and Reason*.[1] In the process, Posner purported to discuss lesbians, although always in a marginalized vein. In his supposedly monumental work on sexuality lesbianism is mentioned rarely, usually in a sentence or two, but always as a comparison to male homosexuality or heterosexuality. The one chapter on homosexuality is almost exclusively about male homosexuality; lesbianism is mentioned as a deviation from this "norm." Yet, through his marginalia in *Sex and Reason*, Posner sketches a portrait of lesbians. We are neither sexy nor reasonable. Posner's lesbians dress badly, are apt to be homely, and rarely engage in sexual activities. Posner does offer some consolation: estimates of these poorly dressed, homely, and undersexed creatures have been greatly exaggerated, and those who do exist tend to be creative.[2] In short, *Sex and Reason* is merely a rehearsal of the most superficial stereotypes of lesbians.

If I were to follow Posner's own methodology, I would assess the stereotypes that masquerade as facts for their accuracy, or at least their nonfalsifiability.[3] This effort would enable me to make conclusions about the viability of Posner's theory of lesbians within his theories of sex. It is tempting to accede to Posner's methodology. Engaging in factual refutation can be satisfying as well as fun. For example, Posner states:

> Then there is the common observation that homosexual men and heterosexual women are better dressed than either heterosexual men or homosexual women. Since men are sexually more aroused by visual cues than women are, we expect both men who are sexually interested in men and women who are sexually interested in men to dress better than either men who are sexually interested in women or women who are sexually interested in women.[4]

In refuting Posner's "fact" that lesbians dress badly I could meticulously footnote articles about lesbian chic—and even cite articles from the time Posner was writing *Sex and Reason* about the lesbian style wars, fashion features in lesbian/gay magazines like *Out!* and in issues of *Vogue* and *Mirabella*, as well as doing some interesting research about the historical appropriation of lesbian style in 1920s Parisian fashion. Yet succumbing to such a temptation trivializes the precarious state of lesbians within the legal system, even as such is demonstrated by lesbian apparel.

While Posner does not explicate what it means for anyone to be a "bad" dresser, one instance of this category is a woman whose dress does not reach sufficient levels of femininity. The gendered nature of valuations of dress can be dangerous for lesbians. There are cases, for example, in which gender nonconformity in dress is used as evidence not only to prove lesbianism but also murder.[5] Posner does not discuss such cases or any other ways in which lesbian dress might be constructed and valued in the social and legal realms. A book with the stated ambition to present a theory of sexuality that "explains the principal regularities in the practice of sex and in its social, including legal, regulation"[6] must do better than simply positing lesbians as bad dressers.

Unfortunately, the example of dress is characteristic rather than atypical of Posner's work. Posner never explores the social and legal meaning of the stereotypes he advances and never examines the assumptions upon which such stereotypes depend. Instead, Posner's theoretical grounding for sexual stereotypes is a compost of sociobiology and law and economics: bioeconomics. On such a theoretical ground, lesbians stand as neither sexy nor reasonable.

Lesbians are not very sexy because in terms of sociobiological theory we do not have to be. Optimal sexual strategies—the spreading of one's genes as many times as possible—result in a gendered divide. For men, promiscuity is the method of maximizing reproductive success. For women, the selection of an appropriate mate will maximize success ("Would he stick around after impregnating her? Had he the willingness to protect her and her offspring?"), but only if she is monogamous ("A man would be reluctant to extend protection to a woman who was likely to end up carrying other men's children").[7] I leave it to others to dispute Posner's sociobiological "facts" that women need men for protection and men are fixated on biological fatherhood. I am here interested in Posner's "natural" conclusion that men thus possess a strong sex drive, while women possess a weak one, and the consequences of that conclusion for lesbians. According to Posner, couple two women and their weak sex drives will dilute the possibilities for passion: "Lesbian couples have intercourse less frequently, on average, than heterosexual couples do, while male couples have intercourse more frequently than heterosexual couples do."[8]

Like many of Posner's "facts" about lesbians, this one is unsupported by a reference. Elsewhere in *Sex and Reason*, however, Posner does cite the notorious Blumstein and Schwartz study, *American Couples*, the usual authority for the proposition that lesbian couples are less sexual than other couples.[9] When Posner does cite the study, he notes that it "surprisingly" found that the "male homosexual cohabitations were more durable than the lesbian ones."[10] Posner is surprised because he would expect the lesbian couple, with their weaker sex drives, to be more faithful and content than a male couple: "Since there is less sexual strain in a lesbian union, the prospects for stable lesbian marriages are better."[11] Yet Posner does not bother to refute the study's finding about the relative instability of lesbian couples, even though this finding is inconsistent with his sociobiological theories. This lack of refutation must be contrasted with his effort to refute the study's finding that "male homosexual cohabitations are more stable than heterosexual cohabitations."[12]

Nevertheless, the "fact" that "lesbian couples have intercourse less frequently" than other couples merits some interrogation. I might even agree with it; I might even argue that lesbians never have intercourse. As usually understood, *intercourse* as a sexual term connotes penile penetration of a vagina. Posner himself, elsewhere in *Sex and Reason*, specifically limits *intercourse* to such a definition, although admitting of a "lesbian simulacra of intercourse such as the penetration of the vagina by an artificial penis."[13] Yet, whether lesbians are including a dildo within their particular sexual practices or not, in all my private and public conversations with countless lesbians, in all my listening to lesbians argue about sex and politics, in all my reading of lesbian theory, novels, stories, articles, letters, and poetry— and even in my own sexual encounters—I cannot remember ever having heard even a single lesbian ever describe a sexual relation with a woman as having "intercourse." Lesbians I have known simply do not use the word *intercourse* to describe sexual relations among themselves.

I am not simply suggesting that Posner is guilty of poor or inconsistent word choice. What I am suggesting is that intercourse—and even sex—may not be as neatly quantifiable a phenomenon as Posner assumes. For example, in a critique of the *American Couples* study, lesbian theorist Marilyn Frye ponders the violence done to lesbian sexual experience as lesbians attempted to answer survey questions about how frequently they "had sex":

> My guess is that different individuals figured it out differently. Some might have counted a two- or three-cycle evening as one "time" they "had sex"; some might have counted that as two or three "times." Some may have counted as "times" only the times both partners had orgasms; some may have counted as "times" those occasions on which at least one had an orgasm; those who do not have orgasms or have them far more rarely than they "have sex" may not have figured orgasms into the calculations; perhaps some counted as a "time" every episode in which both touched the other's vulva more than fleetingly and not for something like a health examination. For some, to count every reciprocal touch of the vulva would have made them count as "having sex" more than most people with a job or work would dream of having time for; how do we suppose those individuals counted "times"? Is there any good reason why they should *not* count all those as "times"? Does it depend upon how fulfilling it was? Was anybody else counting by occasions of fulfillment?[14]

Frye's posing of the question of fulfillment leads her to examine the methods by which heterosexual couples counted times they "had sex": "By orgasms? By *whose* orgasms?" Referring to another finding that 85 percent of long-term married heterosexual couples report it takes them eight minutes to "have sex," Frye speculates that "in a very large number" of those "times" the women did not experience orgasm. Frye further speculates that neither the woman's pleasure nor orgasms were pertinent in most of the heterosexuals' counting and reporting of the times they "had sex."[15]

Just as Frye's penultimate point is not that the *American Couples* study is incorrect, my point is not that Posner's "fact" that lesbian couples have "less intercourse" is inaccurate, or at least falsifiable.[16] The problem with

Posner is much more profound. Just as Frye posits that the *American Couples* study employs a simplistic male perspective on what it means to have sex, I am arguing that Posner's work reflects an overly simplistic and exclusively male perspective on what it means to have intercourse or sex. One consequence of such a perspective is that inaccurate facts might be adduced, but, more important, the perspective determines what facts will be adduced; I am not as worried about wrong answers as about erroneous questions. An inquiry that seeks to quantify lesbian sex and compare it to quantified heterosexual or gay male sex is misguided in its inception. As Marilyn Frye states, it "does violence" to lesbian existence.[17]

Further, this quantification of lesbian sexuality protrudes into other areas of inquiry. For example, the conclusion that lesbians are not very sexual forestalls any serious inquiry into the existence of laws prohibiting lesbianism or the prosecution of lesbians for sexual transgressions. Posner simply repeats the cliché that lesbianism was rarely, if ever, criminalized and lesbians were rarely, if ever, prosecuted.[18] As I have argued elsewhere, there is evidence of both criminal penalties and the imposition of those penalties, including executions. There is also evidence that lesbian sexuality may have been punished under other rubrics, such as vagrancy or prostitution, in a system of social and legal regulation of women's sexuality that punished all expressions of women's sexuality—including lesbianism—as generic deviancy.

The linking of all unacceptable sexual expression on the part of women, including lesbians, is not merely a historic link. If one takes seriously Posner's claim that much of the social hostility toward "homosexuals" presently encoded in legal regulation needs to be, at the very least, reconsidered, the "fact" of lesbians as not very sexual evolves into a mandate. Another sort of deviance is created, licensing legal regulation of sexual lesbians, not for their lesbianism but for their "excess" sexual expression. These excesses may or may not be quantifiable, but they exceed sexual limits. Such a legal regime imposing limits has the capacity not only to justify punishment but also to domesticate lesbian existence and sexuality by making us believe that the legalized version of lesbian sexuality is the correct, or only, one.

The complexity of lesbian lives, including lesbian sexualities, is lost in *Sex and Reason*. Our sexualities are obscured by a morass of sociobiological theory that prefers the simplistic to the complex. We emerge as stereotypes, crafted with a male perspective, when we emerge at all. It is no wonder that Posner's lesbians are not very sexy.

According to Posner, not only are lesbians not very sexy, we are not very reasonable. Lesbians are not very reasonable because in terms of law and economics theory we do not act rationally to maximize our benefits and reduce our costs.[19] Obviously, given the social and legal regulation of lesbian and gay male sexual expression, it does not maximize one's benefits and reduce one's costs to pursue "homosexuality." Posner shares his conclusion that "even in a tolerant society the life prospects of a homosexual—not in every case of course, but on average—are, especially for the male homosexual, grimmer than those of an otherwise identical heterosexual."[20] Grimness, like so many other qualitative and subjective judgments, is accorded an almost quantifiable precision. Yet the irrational unhappiness of homosexual choice leads Posner to the conclusion that society should not impose legal and social obstacles in the "path of the homosexual" but should "remove those obstacles in order to alleviate gratuitous suffering."[21] Posner's seemingly rational response to the irrational choice of homosexuals dissipates, however, in the subsequent passages. In order to convey Posner's cost-benefit rationalizations, I quote at length, although Posner's focus, as in so much of *Sex and Reason*, is exclusively male, in this case on male homosexuality:

> It becomes a reason for repression only if repression can change homosexual preference, incipient or settled, into heterosexual preference at acceptable cost and thereby make persons who would otherwise become or remain homosexuals happier. There is no reason to think that repression, psychotherapy, behavior modification, or any other technique of law or medicine can do so in a large enough number of cases to warrant the costs.
>
> Maybe we should just be patient; science, which has worked so many wonders, may someday, perhaps someday soon, discover a "cure" for homosexuality. I suspect, however, that most persons who are already homosexual will not want to be cured, not because they are oblivious to the advantages of being heterosexual but because being homosexual is part of their identity.[22] . . . But if the hypothetical cure for homosexuality were something that could be administered—costlessly, risklessly, without side effects—before a child had become aware of his homosexual propensity, you can be sure that the child's parents would administer it to him, believing, probably correctly, that he would be better off, not yet having assumed a homosexual identity.[23]

As this passage indicates, part of Posner's tolerance is predicated upon an essentialized and innate homosexual preference. Yet, as is made clear by the passage's continuation, Posner does not subscribe to an immutable preference. According to Posner, parents can prevent the "formation of homosexual preference" by "discouraging gender-nonconforming behavior *at its outset* (later is too late)," including not "condoning 'sissyish' behavior in infancy."[24] Supporting his advice to parents to discipline an infant for displaying "sissyish behavior" is Posner's underlying thesis—while a person's sexual preference is given, not chosen, the decision to engage in a particular act is a rational choice made in light of pertinent costs and benefits.[25]

Unlike their male counterparts, however, Posner's lesbians rarely possess any innate preference. This lack is explained by sociobiological theories of evolution (fewer lesbians survived because the women who did survive had male protectors), one empirical study of sexual preference concordance in twins (lesbianism is not a concordant quality based upon four sets of female twins), and a gendered congenital disparity ("Maybe the wires accidentally get crossed at birth in some more or less stable percentage of newborns, especially boys because of the greater complexity of the male reproductive system").[26] The minimal numbers of lesbians with a preference toward lesbianism maximizes the "search costs" of those lesbians: search costs, along with benefits, are the grounds of the relationship between sex and rationality from the law and economics perspective. As Posner hypothesizes (again equating homosexuality with male homosexuality), if "a village of one hundred persons contains a single homosexual," then "as long as he confines himself to the village, his search costs for a homosexual relationship will be infinite, unless other homosexuals visit the village. He can travel to other villages, but his search costs will still be high since they include the cost of travel."[27] Posner uses the centrality of search costs for sex to explain homosexual urbanization, but presumably urbanization is no remedy for lesbians given Posner's conclusion that only 1 percent—and not 10 percent as is widely accepted—of women are lesbians.[28] Lesbians are thus confined to a global village in which search costs approach the infinite and, thus, the irrational. Further, the benefits of any successful search are not high because Posner's lesbians are not very attractive, adding to the irrationality of the entire endeavor. Although "homely women should have relatively better lesbian than heterosexual opportunities because women tend to place less value on good looks in a sexual partner than men do," Posner sets the value of sex with an "attractive" person higher than the value of sex with an unattractive person.[29] Thus the benefit of sex with these "homely women" is relatively low, making the cost expended during the search not a very rational endeavor.

Yet lesbians may be the most rational women of all. According to

Posner, the fear that if "legal and social inhibitors of homosexual activity are relaxed, young men and women will succumb to the blandishments of homosexual sex and a homosexual style of life" is "misplaced" in the case of men, but is "a little more plausible with respect to women."[30] Women who dislike men may turn away from men and become practicing lesbians, "opportunistic" rather than "real" (innate) lesbians.[31] This deliberate commitment to lesbianism could—and perhaps, should—be subject to social and legal control. Thus, although Posner does not explicitly conclude, since lesbians are more rational than gay men, the law could rationally criminalize lesbianism as a rational deterrent, while not similarly criminalizing male homosexuality.

Posner, however, maintains throughout *Sex and Reason* that lesbianism, as well as other "deviant" sexual practices, should not be subject to rigorous legal and social control. For some conservatives this may be cause for Posner's censure; for some liberals this may be cause for Posner's acceptance. My own criterion for assessing any work that considers lesbianism within the context of law is whether such work contributes toward the survival of lesbians, both as individuals and as identity. Ultimately, Posner's work does neither.

While it may be soothing that Posner eschews the prosecution of lesbianism and proposes sex as a morally indifferent subject, his sociobiological grounding is disturbingly sexist and heterosexist. Posner's lesbians exist as aberrations in an evolutionary scheme that mandates attractive women serve strong men. The law and economics version of sexuality and law is a laissez-faire one; generally the law should not interfere, neither positively nor negatively, with lesbianism, although Posner does posit certain exceptions, notably the law's permissible deprivation of custody to any lesbian mother who believes lesbianism (or male homosexuality) would be a plausible option for her child. Posner's lesbians, as neither sexy nor rational, can be expected to price ourselves out of the sexual market—and out of existence.

Fortunately, Posner's lesbians are not the lesbians I have known, read about, or theorized. For an exposition of lesbian life and theory that is not simply formulaic, a reader would do well to consider other texts: ones that advance, challenge, and provoke our theorizing rather than one that invites us only to entertain or refute its insipid stereotypes. Texts that are inflected with the presence of real lesbians, most of whom are very sexy and quite reasonable.

12

To Market, to Market: Considering Class

Considering class in any context requires an interrogation of both status and relations. In the first instance, economic status is a social marker that engenders bias or privilege in ways similar to other identity categories. In other words, class operates to mark certain persons as classed, the usual inference being such persons are "lower-classed" in the same manner that marking someone as "racialized" means such persons are "nonwhite."

In the second and equally important instance, economic relations are the structures of participation in the market economy, including not only monetary exchanges for goods but also the "market for symbolic goods,"[1] which would include artistic and legal production. In the context of lesbian legal theories and reforms, both class status and market relations must be addressed in a specific and explicit manner.

Nevertheless, I continue to struggle with the degree of specificity and explicitness required because, despite an education that included Karl Marx, I (too often) assume that a lesbian politic includes a formal class analysis. This assumption prevails despite the fact that although there is often much discussion of equality, we rarely, if ever, articulate what this might mean in terms of its class content. In fact, we often act as if class is not a category important to equality.

One especially telling example occurred in the context of discussing discrimination in a feminist legal theory class. We were discussing a hypothetical that placed the students in the role of attorneys on a hiring committee with a legal services office. Today's role will be next year's reality for many of these students, assuming that legal services continues to exist. The hypothetical provided that the committee members conducted initial interviews in pairs, and the entire committee met to decide which applicants to call back for a second interview. On the interview notes for one applicant, the interviewer noted, "Dressed inappropriately." The issue to be discussed is, of course, whether an assessment of the appropriateness of dress constitutes "discrimination," in either a legal or ethical sense.

As in most law school classroom discussions, we freely revise the facts to uncover differences between analytic structures and results. If under a particular set of facts the applicant's dress can be interpreted as cultural, ethnic, or religious in some manner—a kente cloth, a yarmulke, a veil, a sari—the students have absolutely no problem concluding that the "Dressed inappropriately" notation is discrimination. If the applicant's dress can be construed within a gendered context—a man wearing a dress, a woman in a man's suit, hair too short or too long—the students discuss the situation for a longer time, but ultimately conclude that discrimination is occurring, although opinions differ concerning whether the discrimination is based upon sex/gender or sexual orientation. However, if the applicant's dress is attributable to a lower-class status—my favorite example is a woman wearing a dress made by her mother; it is pink and satiny and has rickrack stitched on its borders—the students are not troubled by the specter of discrimination. No matter how much I try to make my hypothetical applicant in the pink satiny dress sympathetic (describing how she had to save to buy her mother the material for the dress, describing how she picked out the pattern in a McCall's book), the students raise all the arguments that could have been raised in the ethnic and gender contexts but were not: arguments about the potential of her attire to be perceived negatively by judges and opposing counsel and clients. The word *professional* dominates this discussion.

It may be important that this feminist jurisprudence class is at the City University of New York (CUNY) School of Law, so that while the racial, religious, and gender identities of the students are diverse, their economic status is less variable. These students are themselves predominantly from working-class or impoverished backgrounds and will most likely devote their legal careers to representing working-class and impoverished persons; I think it would be difficult to locate a group of students who could be more sympathetic. Yet they roundly condemn this hypothetical applicant: "She should know better than to dress like that." They irrevocably link the *display* of class status to knowledge, yet another commodity. While they do not advocate legal redress, they do offer solutions: she should borrow a suit from a classmate; she should go to a thrift store; she should get Dress for Success from the library and pick another pattern and other material.

Interrogated as to the distinctions between a woman applicant wearing a veil or a man's suit or a rickrack-bordered dress, one student explains the differences not only in terms of knowledge but also in terms of choice. The veil is a viable cultural choice, the man's suit is a viable gendered or sexualized choice, but no one would *choose* to wear the attire of the lower classes, at least until such attire was appropriated and stylized by the higher classes. Further, many students consider appearing as a member of the lower classes as inconsistent with their vocation as public interest attorneys, specifically attorneys for impoverished populations. As cultural critic John Guillory expresses it:

> For while it is easy enough to conceive of a self-affirmative racial or sexual identity, it makes very little sense to posit an affirmative lower-class identity, as such an identity would have to be grounded in the experience of deprivation per se. Acknowledging the existence of admirable and even heroic elements of working class culture, the *affirmation* of lower-class identity is hardly compatible with a program for the abolition of want.[2]

Thus, it is not simply that lower class or poor is a rhetorical category or identity that allows prosperity to be normalized and other economic conditions to be pathologized, creating a group of others who are deviant.[3] The same process of categorization occurs in racial, ethnic, religious, and sexualized identities and may serve liberatory as well as repressive interests. However, although many identities that have been politicized may provoke debate over the relative merits of separatism and assimilation, such debates have little currency with regard to class. One explanation may be the inability to recognize class as an identity at all: "Classlessness is congruent with the basic tenet of the American creed, namely civic equality, and with the defining values of American society, notably equality of opportunity and individual success."[4] That this has long been recognized as inherently contradictory—"since if everybody is equal, there can be no superior positions to move into"[5]—does not seem to have abated its mythic status as truth.

A more powerful explanation, however, inheres in John Guillory's insight regarding the problematic nature of an affirmation of lower-class identity. While the condemnation of materialism, affluence, and consumerism is often part of progressive and humanist agendas, the maintenance of an insular and impoverished underclass is incompatible with the goal of economic justice. In other words, almost all of us—whether postmodern or liberal or even conservative—at least theoretically, advocate the abolition of poverty, the condition by which poor people are defined.[6]

After the discussion about inappropriate dress and the limits of discrimination, my office hours are especially busy. Students come to discuss the readings, to request recommendations, and, if they are female students, almost always manage to broach the subject of the interview outfit. They describe their outfits in detail. The unasked question hangs in the air: Is this outfit the equivalent of the pink satiny dress with the rickrack border from McCalls Pattern # 24457, although I am borrowing it from my roommate/bought it at a thrift shop/borrowed Dress for Success from the library? Even a blue suit is not automatically safe, because there is fabric and skirt length and blouse and shoes and "legs" to consider.

For lesbian students, sexual orientation issues complicate the discussion but do not change its fundamental nature. Because we are in New York and the students are applying to progressive legal employers, most students do not consider sexual orientation in and of itself to be a problem. The problem is not that one is a lesbian, as long as one is the "right kind" of lesbian. This "rightness" is expressed through appearance and style. As Danae Clark, in her excellent essay "Commodity Lesbianism,"[7] might phrase it, the students are not so much concerned with being "out" as with seeming "in." Seeming "in" requires both knowledge and money.

My role in this exchange is to impart knowledge. (Although I have also on occasion lent out clothes). In doing so, whether or not I believe I am being less than rigid, or even liberatory ("The most important thing is to be comfortable") or even subversive, I am ultimately agreeing to police them. I am agreeing that it is important to appear as if one belongs to the class of persons that one wishes to join. I am telling them what I did: how I learned to pass as a hippie student, as a member of the progressive bar, as a lesbian law professor, rather than as a poor kid in a homemade dress, perhaps not pink but definitely with rickrack.

I am saying, You can do it too.

I am implicitly telling them that they should.

Yet I am plagued by two political concerns. First, my advice to the students is an accommodation that I believe should be unnecessary. The applicant in the shiny pink homemade dress *should* have a cause of action for discrimination, just as surely as the applicant in the yarmulke and the female applicant in the man's suit should have causes of action. This does not mean that racial, religious, gendered, or sexual identities are commensurate with class identities or with each other: each is unique and has its own histories and manifestations. It also does not mean that the category of class should trump all other categories or become the exclusive category of analysis or the exclusive identity entitled to legal redress for discrimination.[8] Further, the inclusion of class as a protectable identity does not "dilute" other established protectable identities, such as racial and religious identities, or other seeking-to-become established identities, such as sexual minority status. Rather, I believe it is vitally important for the ultimate protection of all "minoritized" identities, be they racial, ethnic, religious, gendered, or sexual, that economic status be equally protectable. Otherwise, economics becomes the acceptable explanation for discrimination and other forms of legalized violence.

Second, I am increasingly troubled by the rift between class and sexuality. At one point I could comfortably express both class and sexuality concerns within the rubric of lesbianism, believing that a lesbian legal theory could address both class and sexual minority concerns. Theoretically, this should not have been possible given the disparate sociological groundings of economic class and sexual status. Nevertheless, a coincidence of interests seemed plausible. Such a coincidence of interests gradually dissipated, but the fracture is most revealed by the discovery/invention of lesbians as a "market" segment, an innovation with which lesbians and gay men have colluded. Obviously, lesbians have always been economic actors; not only do we routinely participate in the market economy, we have a long (and complicated) history as consumers and purveyors of specifically lesbian cultural items, from magazines to bars, from recordings to crafts. Yet the present situation is marked by a scale far surpassing women buying or selling handmade ceramic labryses at a lesbian festival as well as from the bars that operated at the edge of legality.[9]

Now, however, measured by capital's own rod—the dollar—the present lesbian and gay marketing phenomenon is a multimillion dollar enterprise involving multinational corporations, advertising campaigns, and orchestrated consumption.[10] While we gain a somewhat positive presence in the straight media as well as advertising dollars for our own media through such an invention, our place in the dominant market economy effectively commodifies lesbianism as a style (which can be purchased) rather than as a politic (which must be lived). As Clark expresses it, lesbians are invited "in as consumers" to be "part of the fashionable in crowd," while negating "an identity politics based on the act of coming out."[11] Thus, capitalism's notorious search for additional markets creates a rift between class and sexual identities by commodifying lesbian identity for the consumers who can afford to purchase it. While the creation of the lesbian "market" may have lagged behind that of the gay male market, recent sources proclaim its viability.[12]

The commodification of lesbian and gay identities is certainly not unique. For example, bell hooks writes of the problems caused by the "commodification of blackness": it "strips away" the potential of black identity to "subvert and undermine the status quo."[13] The commodification of blackness makes it possible for "white supremacist culture to be perpetuated and maintained even as it appears to become inclusive."[14] Similarly, the commodification of lesbianism makes it possible that heterosexist and sexist culture is perpetrated and maintained even as it appears inclusive.

Importantly, hooks's theorizing in this area includes a discussion of complicity, which she theorizes as rooted in the equation of "capitalism" with "self-determination":

> The contemporary commodification of blackness has become a dynamic part of that system of cultural repression. Opportunistic longings for fame, wealth, and power now lead many black critical thinkers, writers, academics and intellectuals to participate in the production and marketing of black culture in ways that are complicit with the existing oppressive structure. That complicity begins with the equation of black capitalism with black self-determination.[15]

Lesbian complicity is derived from these same roots. Or, as lesbian theorist Robyn Weigman expresses it, "products" are equated with "political progress."[16] Weigman's insight is especially important because she also notes the complicity in this equation:

> Music, clothing, vacation cruises, festivals, artwork, publishing—in all these areas, lesbian identity functions as the means for defining the specificities of both production and consumption. While this relation—of lesbian-made, -sold, and -owned materials—approximates in the 1990's a tamed separatism, it is more than disturbing that the commodification of the lesbian as a category of identity is often what passes, inside and outside the lesbian community, for evidence of political progress. At a recent women's music festival, for instance, the growth of the merchant area—in terms of both the number of products available and their diversity—was lauded by one performer as a sign of growing lesbian political power. . . .

Can we unproblematically herald the consolidation of the lesbian as a category of being when this being is increasingly signified by our saturation in commodity production, both countercultural and, to a limited but growing extent, "mainstream" as well? Must we, in other words, embrace a liberation contingent on production, marketing, and then vampiristically consuming "us"?[17]

Commodification may not just be the process by which products are merged with politics but may also include a specific rejection of politics: the present media images of how "cool it is to be a dyke" depend upon the retreat of the "boring old lesbians" who represent not only "unattractiveness" but "politics."[18] To collude with the denunciation of the stereotyped image of the outdated political lesbian is to reject the "radical political agenda of feminism, including its analyses of the social, cultural and economic."[19]

Nevertheless, it is difficult to resist the temptations and treats of being trendy, especially after one has been ignored or despised for so long. And it is even more difficult to believe one *should* resist. The participation (even if it is more negatively termed complicity or collusion) of other lesbians makes difficult any resistance to an enterprise on the basis that the enterprise is not truly "lesbian." Such a resistance would rest upon the positing of an authentic lesbian existence, a ground no longer available in a postmodern world. Yet the alternative—whatever a lesbian does must be good for lesbian survival—is at least as problematic. Indeed, it is the alternative that may be even more essentialist than the positing of authenticity, because the alternative fails to interrogate the differences—include economic—between lesbians. The alternative denies the reality that the ability to derive benefits from commodification presupposes a degree of class privilege.[20] Although it may be that none of us can escape participation in this commodification,[21] nevertheless, such participation has disparate rewards and disadvantages depending upon one's class status.

Not only does the dissipation of class analysis in lesbian and "queer" legal theorizing result in a lack of resistance to commodification and the maintenance of heterosexist structures, it has also resulted in our failure to adequately respond to those who advocate our demise. Relying on statistics derived from "marketing surveys" designed to convince advertisers that lesbians and gay men could be a profitable market, the New Right utilizes rhetoric with shocking similarities to pre-World-War-II anti-Semitism to portray us as economically privileged. The portrait of lesbians and gay men as economically privileged serves New Right rhetoric in at least two ways, however. First, the depiction taps into class resentments and anxieties. Second, economic advantage counters any claim that lesbians and gay men are discriminated against.[22] Yet our own rhetoric has often not effectively countered these falsehoods.[23] Instead, we have employed class-biased stereotypes to deride adherents of the New Right ranging from polite implications concerning a lack of education to more explicit insults like "trailer trash" and "shitkicker."

The dissipation of class analysis means not only that we cannot respond, but that our own positive legal reform movement is problematic because it fails to take into account both the economic disparities between lesbians and the market economy's operations upon lesbianism. The present emphasis on marriage is but one example. Marriage is widely touted as being an advantage that will provide economic benefits for lesbians and gay men, but this obscures the fact that it will not be an advantage for lesbians in all classes. The very availability of marriage could work to the economic disadvantage of lesbians receiving public entitlements because the state will impute the income of one "partner" to the other, who might otherwise be eligible for "welfare" benefits. Notwithstanding concrete harm to economically disadvantaged lesbians, marriage as an economic arrangement that supports the market economy is delegitimized, as if the feminist-marxist critiques of marriage are inapplicable to lesbians and gay men. Even more fundamentally, the very notion of the marital relation as a propertised one—including the theoretical basis of monogamy in private property—is considered irrelevant. What is considered relevant—although often expressed in a joking manner—is that couples who marry will get "lots of gifts" including silverware and toasters. For lesbian and gay attorneys, it has been often noted that we/they will profit economically if marriage and its corollary, divorce, are legalized: Our communities are converted into client bases; the professional status of some of us is secured.

I am suggesting that a serious consideration of economic structures might yield a very different emphasis in the lesbian and gay legal reform movement. But I am also suggesting that lesbian survival depends upon an agenda of economic empowerment and redistribution of wealth. Economic deprivation constricts choices, including the opportunity to create a life in which one's lesbianism can flourish. The historical work of gay and lesbian community historians and theorists demonstrates the link between economic conditions and the abilities of lesbians (and gay men) to survive as individuals and as communities. As John D'Emilio argues, by the beginning of the twentieth century,

Gay men and lesbians began to invent ways of meeting each other and sustaining a group life. . . . Lesbians formed literary societies and private social clubs. Some working-class women "passed" as men to obtain better-paying jobs and lived with other women—forming lesbian couples who appeared to the world as husband and wife. Among the faculties of women's colleges, in the settlement houses, and in the professional associations and clubs that women formed, one could find lifelong intimate relationships supported by a web of lesbian friends. By the 1920's and 1930's, large cities such as New York and Chicago contained lesbian bars. *These patterns of living could evolve because capitalism allowed individuals to live beyond the confines of the family.*[24]

As Jeffrey Escoffier—one of the few who have begun theorizing and historicizing the homo/economy—notes, "We have only the barest sense of the economic history of the lesbian and gay communities.[25] We need to apply the historical and economic insights to our own time and work toward realizing the conditions that promote lesbian existence.

It is not enough to have a policy—or even a statute—prohibiting discrimination on the basis of sexual orientation in a world in which so many lesbians cannot find any work at all, and so many more cannot find work that they find meaningful or rewarding, and so many must work so hard and so long for so little. It is not enough to have justice for only those lesbians who can afford to purchase it.

13

Lesbian Sex in a Law School Classroom

I have been writing and teaching about sex and sexuality for years, but I still find it excrutiatingly difficult. Talking about sex in a direct manner can seem impossible; most of us have been enculturated to shame, silences, or, at best, partial entitlement toward sex talk, particularly in nonintimate situations. Talking about lesbian sex can be especially difficult, not only because nonheterosexual sex is more imbued with shame than heterosexual sex but also because the very language in which we speak is rooted in the denial of lesbian desire.[1] Talking about lesbian sex in a classroom is complicated not only by the difficulties of sex talk and lesbian sex talk, but by the power and purposes inherent in the pedagogical pursuit. And talking about lesbian sex in a classroom as part of a curriculum devoted to turning students into attorneys can seem absolutely impossible, given the legal regime's prosecution and obfuscation of lesbian sexual desire and practices and the legal academy's devotion to its interpretation of the Socratic method.

These difficulties are manifest in my experience of developing and teaching a course entitled "Sexuality and the Law" at the City University of New York (CUNY) School of Law. Like many of my colleagues teaching similar courses, I have struggled to define the parameters of pedagogy and jurisprudence in a law school course on "sex." However, unlike many of my colleagues, I have not confined "Sexuality and the Law" to minority sexualities or devoted much attention to discrimination based upon sexual status. Instead, the course interrogates sex as a subject of legal regulation. Specifically, the course considers the legal treatment of various sexual practices such as reproduction, rape, pornography, prostitution, bestiality, and incest, as well as lesbianism, male homosexuality, bisexuality, heterosexuality, and transexuality/transgender, and resultant jurisprudential issues including consent, privacy, normalcy, and power. The varied list of sexual practices has an equalizing tendency, which forces students to articulate differences, if any, between various sexual practices. This process often leads to extended questionings of sex itself, and discussions about whether a specific practice is sex or not. Lesbianism is often the centrifugal force of the classroom conversations, perhaps because lesbianism is imbued with professorial authority.

Pedagogy and Boundary Problems

Whoever the professor and whatever the subject, pedagogical relations are often conceptualized as sexual. A psychoanalytic perspective stresses that "all pedagogy comes under the sign of the sexual" because "the ways in which we ordinarily model the relation of teacher and student—no matter how democratic—are always in the long run framed by familial terms" based upon sexual development models, primarily the oedipal.[2] One can analyze "modes of educative pleasure" based upon sexual acts, supported by Freud and Lacan, so that pedagogy can be phallic (Platonic pederasty in which a "greater" man penetrates a "lesser" with his penis/knowledge) or digital (Socratizing in which a finger penetrates the anal orifice).[3] Given that neither of these modes is intentionally lesbian, one might strive to conceptualize a model of pedagogy based upon lesbian sexuality. Although a few lesbian professors might welcome such a model, I remain rather suspicious of such a project. However, one need not adopt the psychoanalytic model to accept that pedagogical situations have a sexual component: "That the relation between teacher and student is 'erotic' is perhaps the least surprising statement one might make about it, nearly the oldest news in Western writing."[4]

Further, some pedagogical methodologies are more sexual than others. For example, a seminar that has a relatively small number of students and stresses class participation is more "intimate" than a large formal lecture class. In my own seminars I have perhaps heightened this intimacy by having class sessions once per week for three hours at the end of the day and by not scheduling a break that would dissipate group energy. This arrangement has caused some of the student smokers to joke about the best cigarette of the week being on Tuesday evenings after "Sex."

Such joking highlights the fact that not only are some pedagogical methodologies more sexual than others but some subjects are simply more sexual than others. Law school classes in tax, administrative law, civil procedure, or federal jurisdiction rarely suggest sexual analogies. By contrast, law school subjects such as civil rights and feminist jurisprudence are often considered more personal and thus more sexual. As women's studies professor Jane Gurko notes, the ultimate pedagogical and political goal of such courses can be easily interpreted as sexual.[5] When the course title contains *sex,* no translation is required.

The explicitly sexualized character of the course as well as my position as a lesbian law professor focuses my attention on three intersecting boundaries. I am often on patrol, checking the security of these boundaries, which I will call the professor boundary, the story boundary, and the rigor boundary. Of these three boundaries, which I will discuss in turn, the professor/student one is the most complicated and the most vital.

Almost all professors have multitudes of anecdotes about students arriving during office hours to "confess" their "true feelings" of love. For lesbian professors, these anecdotes are further embroidered with confessions of confused or newfound sexuality on the part of previously heterosexual female students or, once in a while, by stuttered explanations mixed with bravado on the part of male students. For me, the simplest problem posed by these events is their physical outcome: none. Of course, many teachers and many students do not agree with this position. For example, at the City University of New York School of Law, there is no bar to consensual sex between a professor and a student. A proposal to institute such a bar was opposed by many student groups, including the gay and lesbian group, as well as by a majority of the faculty. On the national law school level, proposals to bar professor/student sex are similarly stalled, and even where adopted such policies are attended by a great deal of controversy.

My support of a per-se ban of sexual relations between professors and students is complicated by my own histories within academic institutions as well as by my belief that any enacted ban would be subject to the forces of homophobia and sexism and thus applied in a discriminatory manner against lesbian professors and students. It also privileges the uniqueness of the academic enterprise, given my opinion that very different rules should apply outside academic institutions. And I often wonder whether being identified publicly with "sex" has had an effect on my adherence to the desirability of a per-se ban, despite all the complications and conflicts.

Teaching a course in which the explicit task is to address the sexual, I notice that the boundaries between professor and student often both intensify and blur in reaction to the hierarchal structure of the relationship.[6] Despite my framing of the syllabus as a series of questions[7] and the facilitation of classes by students as a part of the course requirements, my authority to create the syllabus as well as to give the grade in the course inaugurates me as an expert on the subject of sex. For some students, this power creates an aura of my general sexual competence and expertise, an aura I can find difficult to resist adopting. In reality, despite my greater scholarly knowledge of the subject, my experiential knowledge of many sexual practices discussed in the course is questionable at best. For some students, perceptions of my lack of particular experiences creates a space for them to attempt to install themselves as experts on particular aspects of sex.

Such student attempts to claim expertise are often accomplished through first-person narratives, implicating what I call the story boundary. In any three hour discussion, numerous digressions occur. But when the subject is sex, there seems to be an irrepressible urge to indulge in narration of experiences. This narration can be a method of violating the professor/student boundary: listening to students' sexual experiences makes it more difficult to maintain authority, and being questioned about my own sexual experiences makes it more difficult to maintain formality.

Yet the story boundary is also intimately connected to what I am calling the rigor boundary. This connection is experienced by many women's studies professors who seek to maintain a classroom atmosphere of academic analysis notwithstanding an underlying politics of consciousness-raising. While personal stories do have a place, I often find myself restricting students' personal revelations (sometimes to once a semester), lest the classroom discussion become a series of stories about students' own lives and their neighbors' lives, as well as the lives of TV talk show guests. Although some students seem to welcome this limit, many criticize it in political terms as repressive, conservative, and unfeminist. Yet I perceive the necessity for rigor in arguably political terms as well. Much of legal doctrine pertaining to sexuality is faulty precisely because it is limited by the sexual experience of those empowered to pronounce the doctrine. I do not want the class discussions merely to recapitulate and reposition these experiential limits: I want the class discussions to investigate limits and their consequences.

Pedagogical rigor is important not only in class discussions but also in every aspect of the course. Some of my attention to this boundary is admittedly caused by external pressures. While lesbian and gay studies have become somewhat respectable within the academy, their existence is still quite contested and controversial, especially in conservative institutions like law schools, and sex as a curriculum subject is hardly secure. Thus, part of the pedagogy is often an indirect attempt to forestall labels like *frivolity* and *perversity*. Such accusations can be mitigated by substituting *theorizing* for *talk*, *sexualities* for *sex*, adding a syllabus with appellate court cases and law review articles, and demanding a paper of publishable quality, preferably a law review casenote, as a course requirement. Nevertheless, many students state that they do not want the word *sex* on their law school transcript. While I refuse to rename the course, I strive for rigor. My response to concerns about having *sex* on a law school transcript is to tell students that *sex* will only be negative on the transcript if it is accompanied by a failing grade. And, yes, I have to tell them if they ask, there are students who have failed.

Legal Education, Diversity, and Lesbian Sex

Although I might be on pedagogical boundary patrols in any academic institution, pedagogy in the legal context possesses some important distinctions. Law school has heightened seriousness, preparing students for a standardized examination and entrance into a "profession" of power. Thus, even a *liberal* legal education (a rather rare animal) is fundamentally different from a liberal arts education. A liberal arts education strives to empower individual students, while a liberal legal education has as its ultimate goal the production of lawyers who will empower others through advocacy.

When the course content is sex, liberal legal pedagogy requires an interrogation not only of one's own sexual practices but also of the legal treatment of sexual practices of others. The necessity for such an interrogation is most apparent in the criminal context. Lofty discussions of whether or not some act constitutes sex and whether it should or should not constitute criminal sex are often grounded by elements of criminal statutes, case precedents, and theoretical perspectives on criminal justice, feminism, and liberalism. Lesbian s/m always provokes a good discussion in these instances, usually generated by a lesbian student.

The inclusion of lesbian students in the classroom is vital. A necessary aspect of the education of lawyers who will serve a range of disempowered persons is student and professor diversity. Most law schools give lip service to this requirement, but only a few have striven to realize it. Teaching at the City University of New York, a historically diverse institution, ensures that there will be actual variety in the classroom. Even in a self-selected elective such as "Sexuality and the Law," there will be students along various race, class, age, culture, dis/ability, gender, and sexuality axes as well as diversities in theoretical sophistication, academic performance, and life—including sexual—experiences. As a professor, I generally appreciate being in an institution with multiple constituencies, have advocated even more diversity within the institution, and have castigated other institutions for their lack of diversity. Nevertheless, diversity is problematic to me as a lesbian professor teaching about sex in a legal context.

The first problem is inherent in the phrase "as a lesbian professor." Theories about identity are played out, often inconsistently, by my students and by me. Within the classroom, identities struggle with reification: students may attempt to resist but habitually (and repeatedly) begin sentences with phrases such as "As a lesbian," "As a gay man," "As a straight woman," "As a regular guy," and "As an incest survivor." Interestingly, the next statement from students asserting an identity may intentionally undermine the validity of the asserted identity category. Such undermining can be an attempt to forestall accusations from fellow students, such as "That doesn't mean anything" or "You weren't always, according to what you said last week." Unlike the students in class—and unlike my approach here—I never categorize myself as a lesbian professor, although this fact is well-known to any student who has read the law school catalog. Within the classroom dynamic, my lesbianism is submerged into the identity of professor. It is perhaps the very diversity in the class that mandates the submergence necessary to facilitate among differing articulated standpoints. The lesbian students often experience this stance as betrayal, while the nonlesbian students seem to wait for me to put my professorial imprint on a specific lesbian perspective that will both settle the disputes among lesbian students and serve to neutralize the "authority" of my comments.

The second problem is that the classroom identity statements are relatively public acclamations that rest upon partial and privatized disclosures. Students will often confess certain aspects of their sexual lives during office appointments, sometimes as related to their interest in developing a casenote paper topic or in a more general conversation. For example, in any particular classroom I might know that a particular student is a "gay man" who sleeps with women, a previously heterosexual woman debating lesbianism, a former prostitute, a virgin, an s/m lesbian, a previously lesbian woman now married to a man. Of course, I do not know who else in the class knows what; I am only certain that students in the class know facts about each other's sexual histories that I do not. This situation often gives classroom discussions a subtext that bubbles to the surface, as when one student runs crying from the room or when a student lashes out at another student. It can also influence my choice of materials to assign.

The third and last problem is the most vexing one. Diversity becomes uncomfortable when the subject is lesbian sex. I often cannot help but feel that the same conversation among lesbians would be of a much higher quality. I censor my own comments and judgments not just as a professor but also as a lesbian; I assume that the other lesbians in the classroom censor their own comments as well. We do not disagree as much in this diverse setting as we would among ourselves. But this reluctance to disagree in "public" is not the major drawback of diversity. I am much more concerned with the political implications of any discussion of lesbian sex among nonlesbians. Even given this self-selected group at a progressive law school, I am nevertheless wary of exploitation and appropriation. Lesbian sexuality belongs to lesbians and should not be commodified for nonlesbians.[8] I often find myself, however, in the position of facilitating discussions about lesbian sex among nonlesbians, including men of various sexual identities. When such discussions are closely textual, based upon court cases, I am most comfortable. However, when the discussions contrast the court's language with other texts or experiences, I am most guarded. Unfortunately, given the scant case law sources that raise lesbian sexuality, the class discussions are most often centered on theoretical nonlegal texts or student-related experiences.

Jurisprudence as Hypothetical

Not only is legal doctrine, especially in the form of case law, meager in its treatment of lesbian sexuality but American jurisprudence is likewise sparse. Part of the struggle of theorizing lesbian sexuality within the law has been the predominance of lesbian imperceptibility, which often works to trivialize the perceptions of lesbianism that do occur. The opposite of trivializing also occurs: because there is so little legal material relating to lesbian sex, this material is taken to be typical or made representative. Thus, the relative rarity of appellate opinion concerning convictions for "deviate sex" based upon lesbianism can lead a student (or a scholar) to conclusions that lesbian sex is generally tolerated (because it rarely appears in appellate criminal cases) as well as to opinions that the "deviate sex" described—or not described—in the appellate opinions is typical lesbian sex.

Jurisprudence, the philosophy or theory of law, or, in more positivist terms, the science of law, is thus relatively ignorant of lesbian sexuality. Positivist conceptions of law require a "rule" to be articulated and then applied—in a scientific manner—to situations shaped as hypothetical. Lesbian sexuality is imperceptible within this positivist paradigm because the rules controlling lesbian sex are only partially articulated at best. Rules prohibiting "oral/anal contact," the "crime against nature," or "sexual contact between persons of the same gender" are imprecise from a legal positivist perspective because they cannot be "scientifically" applied to a hypothetical lesbian couple. For example, one woman stroking another woman's breasts is not oral/anal contact, but a court could interpret it to be a "crime against nature" or "sexual contact," if "sexual" is not confined to genital.

Pedagogically, I have struggled with materials to assign regarding lesbian sexual expression as regulated by the legal regime, changing the syllabus each year. There is scarce explicit theorizing about lesbian sexuality within the legal realm. While other professors have reported success using the piece I wrote applying the so-called sodomy statutes,[9] I have struggled with the idea of discussing my own work in class, especially when the material is sexually explicit. I have sometimes addressed this problem by assigning cases, but this is also problematic because discussions of legal doctrine and theory are often precluded by the poverty of the factual development within the cases.

My favorite example of a factually impoverished case is *People v. Livermore*, in which the crime seemed to consist of noises inside a tent overheard by state troopers standing outside for ten minutes, until the troopers unzipped the door, shining flashlights to reveal two women lying on a cot "partially covered by a blanket."[10] One needs a fair amount of lesbian imagination to provide sexual content, but whatever sexual content one supplies is conjecture. As one lesbian student asked, "So was she going down on her or were they finger fucking?"

"What differences would that make under the various statutes?" is my professorial query. By assigning this case in conjunction with various criminal statutes, I had hoped to prompt a discussion not only about vagueness but about vagaries of statutory drafting and judicial interpretation. But the class discussion is not so easily facilitated.

It seems like every pedagogical problem I have previously identified coalesces in the "finger fucking" class. Boundaries of professorial relations are implicated: should I explain what "finger fucking" means to a male student who looks quizzical and thus establish myself as an expert? What if I do not mean the same thing that the lesbian student means by it? What if the lesbian student made a sexual advance toward me last year and I interpret this remark as sexually aggressive? Boundaries of storytelling are threatened: a heterosexual student tells a story about being at camp as an adolescent; a former police officer tells a story about finding teenagers "necking" and not arresting them; a female student tells a story about being in the army. Boundaries of rigor start to dissolve: maybe there is too much laughter. Maybe a student will answer another student's casual inquiry about today's class by saying, "We just talked about finger fucking." Maybe finger fucking is not relevant to any student's paper or the bar examination or any future court case. Furthermore, the diversity of the class contributes to identity politics posturing: a lesbian, a gay man, a heterosexual woman, and even a former police officer reannounce their identities, as the other students solidify their own identities in opposition. My knowledge of partial disclosures by students forces me to attend to the psychological dimensions of the discussion. For example, the disclosure of an incest survivor prevented me from assigning another lesbian case that is more explicit but involves incest.[11] The disclosure of another student, who reported in confidence that he has had virtually no sexual experience, prevented me from simply assuming that every student knows what finger fucking means, that it does not mean something like one finger fucking another finger, as one student stated in a droll-enough-to-be-serious tone. And, finally, the very diversity of the class makes me pause as a male student struggles to articulate his understanding of lesbian sex and announces that women use their fingers like "little penises," and as a heterosexual woman disagrees and asks a lesbian for a real explanation of what lesbians do in their cots in tents while state troopers listen, and as a lesbian student starts to speak and is interrupted by another male student who says he does not want to hear the details, and he is interrupted by another male student who says he really wants to hear all this, and laughs, and turns to look at me.

I reconsider my strategy of never allowing the class to recess.

Instead, I pose another hypothetical. Using that favorite law professorial tactic of changing the facts, I attempt to shift from finger fucking to a consideration of rationales for the law's obfuscation of lesbian sexual practices. "Any ideas?" I ask.

One student volunteers, "It's because the courts don't want women finger fucking each other. And if everyone knows exactly what it means, they'll all go camping and try it out."

Everyone laughs. And I laugh with my students as if they are my friends. Someone tells a story. More laughter spills into the hall, and someone in the next classroom comes over and says his class cannot hear the tax lecture because of our laughter. And by the end of our class, we are no longer limited by our diversity but somehow enriched by it, even its problematic identities, partial disclosures, and risks of appropriation.

It is the kind of class that makes me feel that, despite the problems, combining pedagogy, jurisprudence, and lesbian sex is worthwhile. It is the type of day that makes me think somehow of Sappho; maybe she really should go to law school. Or maybe she has been here all along and I am just learning to recognize her, trailing her fragments in cases like *People v. Livermore*, singing a song about two women in a tent and their lovemaking, seducing with lyrics that might replace the Socratic method and transform law into a Lesbian poetry.

Notes

Introduction: The Appeal of Sappho

1. For excellent and intelligent recent discussions of Sappho, see Page duBois, *Sappho Is Burning* (Chicago: University of Chicago Press, 1995); and Margaret Williamson, *Sappho's Immortal Daughters* (Cambridge: Harvard University Press, 1995). For an important and original discussion of Sappho's lyrics as well as her lesbianism, see Jane McIntosh Snyder, *Lesbian Desire in the Lyrics of Sappho* (New York: Columbia University Press, 1997).

2. There are numerous translations of Sappho's work, including Josephine Ballmer, *Sappho: Poems and Fragments* (New York: Carol, 1993); Mary Barnard, *Sappho: A New Translation* (Berkeley: University of California Press, 1958); and Jim Powell, *Sappho: A Garland* (New York: Farrar, Straus and Giroux, 1993).

3. For further legends, see Joan DeJean, *Fictions of Sappho, 1546–1937* (Chicago: University of Chicago Press, 1989), a scholarly treatment of Sappho in the French tradition.

4. Monique Wittig and Sande Zeig, *Lesbian Peoples: Material for a Dictionary* (New York: Avon, 1979).

1. The Specter of a Lesbian Supreme Court Justice: Problems of Identity

1. "The Furies," in Nancy Myron and Charlotte Bunch, eds., *Lesbianism and the Women's Movement,* 15, 18 (Baltimore: Diana, 1975), reprinted from a 1972 statement.

2. Adrienne Rich, "Disloyal to Civilization: Feminism, Racism, Gynephobia,"

in *On Lies, Secrets, and Silence: Selected Prose, 1966–1978,* 275, 310 (New York: Norton, 1979).

3. Lillian Faderman, *Odd Girls and Twilight Lovers: A History of Lesbian Life in the Twentieth Century,* 230 (New York: Columbia University Press, 1991).

4. Bette Tallen, "How Inclusive is Feminist Political Theory: Questions for Lesbians," in Jeffner Allen, ed., *Lesbian Philosophies and Cultures,* 241, 254 (Albany: State University of New York Press, 1990).

5. As Margaret Burnham notes,

> Thomas was more vulnerable than any previous nominee—at least since Rehnquist—on civil rights matters, because, unlike the previous nominees, he had made his career as a civil rights basher. His record on civil rights was simple and unambiguous. But apparently intimidated by the Pin Point [Georgia, where Thomas spent his childhood] story, the senators barely asked Thomas about the policies he followed at the EEOC, where he had been Reagan's hatchet man. Thomas had led the ideological charge against affirmative action. But when he was questioned by senators about his views and his record, he silenced them by reminding them that "it should be clear from my biography that I understand that racism exists."

Margaret Burnham, "The Supreme Court Appointment Process and the Politics of Race and Sex," in Toni Morrison, ed., *Race-ing Justice, Engendering Power: Essays of Anita Hill, Clarence Thomas, and the Social Construction of Reality,* 290, 302 (New York: Pantheon, 1992).

6. Cornel West, "Black Leadership and the Pitfalls of Racial Reasoning," in Morrison, *Race-ing Justice,* 390, 393–94.

7. Maer Roshan, "Anne Radice and the Politics of Appeasement," *QW,* 23, 24 (June 7, 1992).

8. Act of October 23, 1989, P.L. 101–121, tit. III art. 304(a)- (c), 103 Stat. 744.

9. P.L. No. 101–512, 103(b), 104 Stat. 1915, 1963–66 (codified at 20 USC 954 (d) (1990).

For discussions of the controversy, including its first amendment ramifications, see Donald W. Hawthorne, "Subversive Subsidation: How NEA Art Funding Abridges Private Speech," 40 *Kansas Law Review* 437 (1992); Robert M. O'Neill, "Artists, Grants, and Rights: The NEA Controversy Revisited," 9 *New York Law School Journal of Human Rights* 85 (1991); Symposium, "Art, the First Amendment, and the NEA Controversy," 14 *Nova Law Review* 317 (1990); Nancy Ravitz, Comment, "A Proposal to Curb Congressional Interference with the National Endowment for the Arts," 9 *Cardozo Arts and Entertainment Law Journal* 475 (1991).

See also Bella Lewitzky Dance Foundation v. Frohnmayer, 754 F. Supp. 774 (C.D. Ca. 1991), holding that the NEA's requirement that grant recipients certify compliance with the policy against obscenity was unconstitutionally vague and chilling of protected speech. Cf. Fordyce v. Frohnmayer, 763 F. Supp. 664 (D.C.D.C. 1991), denying standing to a taxpayer protesting NEA's partial funding to the "anti-Christian" production *Tongues of Flame* on grounds that such funding violated the first amendment's establishment clause).

10. Tommi Aviolli Mecca, "A Lesbian Even Bush and Helms Could Love," *San Francisco Bay Times*, 4 (June 4, 1992).

11. "To some observers, the fact that a widely known lesbian was appointed to a position so mired in sexual politics seems to be much more than an accident. In fact, an interesting line of speculation gaining ground in more cynical corners of the art world is that Radice was appointed to her NEA post *because of—not despite*—her lesbianism." Roshan, "Anne Radice," 24; emphasis in original. The article quotes a "well-connected gay source at the NEA" as opining that "the administration realized that, as a lesbian, she'd be less susceptible to all the slak [*sic*] she would be getting about homophobia." Ibid., 24.

12. Fredric Jameson, "Postmodernism and Consumer Society," in Ann E. Kaplan, ed., *Postmodernism and Its Discontents: Theories, Practices*, 13, 17 (London and New York: Verso, 1988).

13. Allan C. Hutchinson, "Identity Crisis: The Politics of Interpretation," 26 *New England Law Review* 1173, 1194 (1992), critiquing Patricia Cain, "Feminist Jurisprudence: Grounding the Theories," 4 *Berkeley Women's Law Journal* 191 (1989).

14. Hutchinson, "Identity Crisis," 1196, citing Cain, "Feminist Jurisprudence," 192, n. 1.

15.

There is no question that the appearance in nineteenth-century psychiatry, jurisprudence, and literature of a whole series of discourses on the species and subspecies of homosexuality, inversion, pederasty, and "psychic hermaphrodism" made possible a strong advance of social controls into this area of "perversity"; but it also made possible the formation of a "reverse" discourse: homosexuality began to speak in its own behalf, to demand that its legitimacy or "naturality" be acknowledged, often in the same vocabulary, using the same categories by which it was medically disqualified.

Michel Foucault, trans. Robert Hurley, *The History of Sexuality*, 1:101 (New York: Vintage, 1978).

16. For example, discussing homosexuality in an interview, Foucault referred

to a recent biography of Proust in which the author demonstrated "how difficult it is to give meaning to the proposition 'Proust was a homosexual.' It seems to me that it is finally an inadequate category. Inadequate, that is, in that we can't really classify behavior on the one hand, and the term can't restore a type of experience on the other." Interview, "Sexual Choice, Sexual Act: Foucault and Homosexuality," in Lawrence D. Kritzman, ed., *Politics Philosophy Culture: Interviews and Other Writings, 1977–1984,* 286, 292 (New York: Routledge, 1988). Similarly, in a recent biography of Foucault an interchange in 1975 between "a young gay militant" and Foucault is described, in which the younger man asks Foucault his opinion about "gay liberation" and Foucault reportedly responded, "I believe the term 'gay' has become obsolete," and that people "are neither this nor that, gay nor straight." James Miller, *The Passion of Michel Foucault* 254 (New York: Simon and Schuster, 1993).

17. Miller, *The Passion of Michel Foucault*, 254–57.

18. Judith Butler, "Imitation and Gender Insubordination," in Diana Fuss, ed., *Inside/Out: Lesbian Theories, Gay Theories* 13, 14 (New York: Routledge, 1991).

19. Jacquelyn Zita, "Male Lesbians and the Postmodernist Body," in Claudia Card, ed., *Adventures in Lesbian Philosophy* 112 (Bloomington and Indianapolis: Indiana University Press, 1994).

20. See, e.g., Judith Butler, *Gender Trouble: Feminism and the Subversion of Identity* (New York: Routledge, 1990), a postmodernist critique of gender identity.

21. Monique Wittig, "The Straight Mind," in *The Straight Mind* (Boston: Beacon, 1992).

22. Butler, "Imitation and Gender Insubordination," 121; Diane Fuss, *Essentially Speaking: Feminism, Nature, and Difference,* 43 (New York: Routledge, 1989).

23. Sarah Hoagland, *Lesbian Ethics* 15 (Palo Alto: Institute of Lesbian Studies, 1988).

24. See, e.g., Julia Penelope, "Does It Take One to Know One?" in *Call Me Lesbian: Lesbian Lives, Lesbian Theory,* 17–38 (Freedom, Cal.: Crossing, 1992).

25. Jennifer Wicke, "Postmodern Identity and the Legal Subject," 62 *Colorado Law Review* 455, 467 (1991).

26. See chapter 8, this volume.

27. Mary Joe Frug, "Law and Postmodernism: The Politics of a Marriage," 62 *Colorado Law Review* 483, 487 (1991). Mary Joe Frug, a feminist law professor teaching at New England School of Law, was murdered in March 1991. Tributes to her life and work include, "In Memoriam: Mary Joe Frug," 62 *Colorado Law Review* 433 (1991); "In Memoriam, Mary Joe Frug, 1941–1991," 3 *Yale Journal of Law and Feminism* I (1991); "In Memoriam: Mary Joe Frug," 14 *Harvard Women's*

Law Journal I (1991); Carl Tobias, "Tribute to Mary Joe Frug," 24 *Connecticut Law Review* IX (1991); "Memorial Service for Mary Joe Frug," 26 *New England Law Review* 639 (1992). Her posthumously published work includes Mary Joe Frug, *Postmodern Legal Feminism* (New York: Routledge, 1992).

For an excellent engagement with Frug's work from a lesbian perspective, see Ruth Colker, "The Example of Lesbians: Posthumous Reply to Mary Joe Frug," 105 *Harvard Law Review* 1084 (1992).

28. Sexuality categories are not unique in this regard. For an especially provocative account of this phenomenon in a racial/ethnic context, see Michelle Cliff, *Claiming an Identity They Taught Me to Despise* (Watertown, Mass.: Persephone, 1980), in which a lesbian writer interrogates her own identity as a light-skinned Jamaican descendant of slaves from Africa. See also Judy Scales-Trent, *Notes of a White Black Woman: Race Color Community* (University Park, Penn.: Pennsylvania State University Press, 1995).

29. See chapter 6, this volume.

30. At the time of her nomination Shalala was the president of the University of Wisconsin at Madison, and the original piece was printed in the Madison, Wisconsin newspaper. "Gay Group Dogs Shalala with Phone Campaign," *Capital Times,* 10A, December 30, 1992. One example of the story's dissemination is "Shalala: Not Lesbian," *New York Newsday,* 16 (December 31, 1992).

31. "Gay Group Dogs Shalala."

32. Doug Ireland, "Press Clips: Flying to Reno," *Village Voice,* 8, February 23, 1993.

33. Butler, "Imitation and Gender Insubordination."

34. Ireland, "Press Clips."

35. Tracy Baim, "Clinton Top Picks Include No Open Gays/Lesbians," *Outlines* 15 (January 1993). The article predicted that Shalala's honesty on the issue of her sexual orientation would be considered during her Senate confirmation hearings. However, the sexual orientation issue is absent from the public records of the confirmation hearings. See 139 Cong. Rec. s93–01 (January 21, 1993).

36. See Michael Bailey, Richard Pillard, Michael Neale, and Yvonne Agyei, "Heritable Factors Influence Sexual Orientation in Women," 50 *Archives of General Psychiatry* 217 (March 1993). See also Natalie Angier, "Study Suggests Genes Sway Lesbians' Sexual Orientation," *New York Times,* A11, March 12, 1993.

37. See e.g., "Is This Child Gay? Born or Bred: The Origins of Homosexuality," *Newsweek* 46 (February 24, 1992); Chandler Burr, "Homosexuality and Biology," *Atlantic,* 47 (March 1993).

38. Steven Epstein, "Gay Politics, Ethnic Identity: The Limits of Social

Constructionism," *Socialist Review*, 9, May-Aug. 1987, reprinted in Edward Stein, ed., *Forms of Desire: Sexual Orientation and Social Constructionist Controversy*, 239, 241–42 (New York: Routledge: 1992).

39. Zita, "The Male Lesbian," 126.

40. Shane Phelan, *Identity Politics: Lesbian Feminism and the Limits of Community* 157, 170 (Philadelphia: Temple University Ress, 1989). Phelan argues that lesbian-feminism was too rigid and that, if we are to be "free, we must learn to embrace paradox and confusion."

41. Anzaldúa writes: "Identity is a river—a process. Contained within the river is its identity, and it needs to flow, to change to stay a river—if it stopped it would be a contained body of water such as a lake or a pond." Gloria Anzaldúa, "To(o) Queer the Writer—Loca, Escritora, y Chicana," in Betsey Warland, ed., *Inversions: Writings by Dykes, Queers, and Lesbians,* 249, 253 (Vancouver: Press Gang, 1991).

42. Valerie Janess, "Coming Out: Lesbian Identities and the Categorization Problem," in Ken Plummer, ed., *Modern Homosexualities* 65, 83 (London and New York: Routledge, 1992).

43. Lise Weil, "Conversation with Michelle Causse," 20 *Trivia: A Journal of Ideas* 90, 90–91 (1992).

44. Marilyn Frye, *The Politics of Reality* 160 (1983).

45. Sue-Ellen Case, *The Domain-Matrix: Performing Lesbian at the End of Print Culture*, 187 (Bloomington and Indianapolis: Indiana University Press, 1996).

2. Incendiary Categories: Lesbian/Violence/Law

1. Nicole Brossard, *The Aerial Letter,* trans. Marlene Wildeman, 121 (Toronto: Women's, 1988).

2. Judy Grahn, *Another Mother Tongue,* 235–48, 260–61 (Boston: Beacon, 1984).

3. Ibid., 239.

4. Mary Daly, *Pure Lust: Elemental Feminist Philosophy,* 197–314 (Boston: Beacon, 1984).

5. Ibid., 260. See also Mary Daly with Jane Caputi, *Websters' First New Intergalactic Wickedary of the English Language,* 157 (Boston: Beacon, 1987).

6. Monica Sjöö and Barbara Mor, *The Great Cosmic Mother,* 34–35 (New York: Harper and Row, 1987).

7. George Lakoff, *Women, Fire, and Dangerous Things: What Categories Reveal About the Mind,* 92–5 (Chicago: University of Chicago Press, 1987). In taking the title for his book on cognitive theory and linguistics from this example, Lakoff is relying on the work of other anthropological linguists, R. M. W. Dixon, *Where*

Have All the Adjectives Gone? (Berlin: Walter de Gruyter, 1982); Annette Schmidt, *Young People's Dyirbal: An Example of Language Death from Australia* (Cambridge: Cambridge University Press, 1985).

8. Lakoff, *Women, Fire, and Dangerous Things*, 99–100.

9. Ibid., 100–1, quoting Schmidt, *Young People's Dyirbal.* Lakoff does not rest his argument on the speaker of Dyirbal, however, as he believes that "native speakers of a language are only sometimes aware of the principles that structure their language." Ibid., 100. For Lakoff, the speaker's statement proves only that "for this speaker, there is a conceptual link between the presence of women in the category and the presence of fire and danger." Ibid., 101.

10. Stephen J. Pyne, *Burning Bush: A Fire History of Australia,* 136 (New York: Henry Holt, 1991). According to Pyne,

> Fire left no part of Australia untouched, and where Aborigines congregated, in seasonal gatherings or for more durable residence, free-burning fire proliferated. "It seems impossible," Eric Rolfes concluded, "to exaggerate the amount of burning in Aboriginal Australia." The coastal resources of Australia sustained an almost circumcontinental settlement; Aboriginal fires ringed the island continent. The most influential of European explorers, Captain James Cook, referred matter-of-factly to this "this continent of smoke." . . . That Aborigines burned, and burned extensively, cannot be disputed.

Ibid., 136–37.

11. "For the Aborigine, fire was a universal solvent of ecological existence, and the firestick, a universal implement." Ibid., 137.

12. Ibid., 106.

13. Ibid. Similarly, other writers on fire note the special status of fire: "Fire is a discontinuity, a chemophysical reaction that, for ancient man [*sic*], had no transitional phase. He could not have practiced with almost-fire. Moreover, his mastery of it is the more remarkable because, at the beginning, fire was very frightening to him. Almost all animals seem to be endowed with a profound fear of fire." Frank Rowsome, *A Bright and Glowing Place,* 41 (New York: Dutton, 1973). See also, Gaston Bachelard, *The Psychoanalysis of Fire* (Boston: Beacon, 1964); James Frazer, *Myths of the Origins of Fire* (New York: Hacker, 1974).

14. Lakoff, *Women, Fire, and Dangerous Things,* 6–8.

15. Ibid.

16. Ibid., 9.

17. As Robert Post recalls:

I vividly remember Robert Cover as a conference remarking on the question of why legal scholars pondered so carefully the words of then-Chief Justice Burger. It was not, said Cover, because the Chief Justice was so deep a thinker or so talented a writer, but because his judgments were enforced by the United States Army. His words were written, so to speak, in blood.

Robert Post, "Tradition, the Self, and Substantive Due Process: A Comment on Michael Sandel," 77 *California Law Review* 553, 559–60 (1989).

18. Robert M. Cover, "Violence and the Word," 95 *Yale Law Journal* 1601, 1605 (1986).

19. This is expressed in political theories variously dominated as "consent," "contract," or "obligation" theory. Such theories address the possibility of a foundation—other than violence or force—for the state's power. Classic theorists such as Hume, Locke, and Rousseau considered whether nation-states exercised legitimate authority based upon the consent of those against whom such authority was exercised. See generally, David Hume, *Political Essays* (Cambridge: Cambridge University Press, 1994); John Locke, *Two Treatises on Government* (Cambridge: Cambridge, 1994); Jean-Jacques Rousseau, *The Social Contract and Discourses* (Cambridge: Cambridge, 1977). Such ideas formed the theoretical underpinnings of American constitutionalism.

Feminist reconceptualizations of such theories stress their gendered nature. See, for example, Nancy Hirshmann, *Rethinking Obligation: A Feminist Method for Political Theory* (Ithaca: Cornell University Press, 1992); Carole Pateman, *The Disorder of Women: Democracy, Feminism, and Political Theory* (Stanford: Stanford University Press, 1989).

20. Jacques Derrida, "Force of Law: The 'Mystical Foundation of Authority,'" 11 *Cardozo Law Review* 920, 925 (1990).

21. Richard Posner, *Law and Literature: A Misunderstood Relation,* 249 (Cambridge: Harvard University Press, 1988).

22. Robert Cover, "Violence and the Word," 1601. Cover's use of gendered pronouns in this instance obscures the political and legal reality that it is more often than not male judges' understanding of texts that operate to deprive lesbians and other women of freedom, property, and children.

23. See Robert Leger, "Lesbianism Among Women Prisoners: Participants and Nonparticipants," 14:4 *Criminal Justice and Behavior* 448 (1987), a sociological study concluding that compared with heterosexual women, lesbians "had longer sentences, were arrested at an earlier age, were more likely to have been previously confined and had served more time."

24. Rosemary Coombe, " 'Same As It Ever Was': Rethinking the Politics of Legal Interpretation," 34 *Magill Law Journal* 603, 649 (1989). Coombe relies upon

the work on Pierre Bourdieu, whose theoretical framework enables one to "ana-lyze the ways in which symbolic practices exercise their own type of violence, a gentle invisible form of violence which is never recognized as such, or is recog-nized only by concealing the mechanisms upon which it depends." Ibid., 650, quoting Pierre Bourdieu, "Symbolic Power," in Denis Gleeson, ed., *Identity and Structure: Issues in the Sociology of Education* (Driffield, U.K.: Studies in Educa-tion, 1977).

25. P.L. 101–275, 104 Stat. 140 amending 28 U.S.C. 534. The complete text of the act is as follows:

That
(a) this Act may be cited as the 'Hate Crime Statistics Act.'
(b)(1) Under the authority of section 534 of title 28, United States Code [this section] the Attorney General shall acquire data, for the calendar year 1990 and each of the succeeding 4 calendar years, about crimes that manifest evi-dence of prejudice based on race, religion, sexual orientation, or ethnicity, including where appropriate the crimes of murder, non-negligent manslaughter; forcible rape; aggravated assault, simple assault, intimida-tion; arson; and destruction, damage or vandalism of property.
(2) The Attorney General shall establish guidelines for the collection of such data including the necessary evidence and criteria that must be present for a finding of manifest prejudice and procedures for carrying out the pur-poses of this section.
(3) Nothing in this section creates a cause of action or a right to bring an action, including an action based on discrimination due to sexual orienta-tion. As used in this section, the term "sexual orientation" means consensual homosexuality or heterosexuality. This subsection does not limit any exist-ing cause of action or right to bring an action, including any action under the Administrative Procedure Act or the All Writs Act.
(4) Data acquired under this section shall be used only for research or sta-tistical purposes and may not contain any information that may reveal the identity of an individual victim of a crime.
(5) The Attorney General shall publish an annual summary of the data acquired under this section.
c There are authorized to be appropriated such sums as may be necessary to carry out the provisions of this section through fiscal year 1994.
Sec. 2.
(a) Congress finds that—
(1) the American family life is the foundation of American Society,
(2) Federal policy should encourage the well-being, financial security, and health of the American family,
(3) schools should not de-emphasize the critical value of American family life.

(b) Nothing in this Act [this note] shall be construed, nor shall any funds appropriated to carry out the purpose of the Act [this note] be used, to promote or encourage homosexuality.

26. According to the National Gay and Lesbian Task Force (NGLTF) Policy Institute, which has issued annual reports on violence against lesbians and gay men for many years, this amendment was added as a means of preempting an amendment by Senator Jesse Helms. The Helms amendment provided that the Senate declare that

(1) the homosexual movement threatens the strength and survival of the American family as the basic unit of society;
(2) state laws prohibiting sodomy should be enforced;
(3) the federal government should not provide discrimination protections on the basis of "sexual orientation";
(4) school curricula should not condone homosexuality as an acceptable lifestyle in American society.

Anti-Gay/Lesbian Violence, Victimization, and Defamation, 21 (Washington, D.C.: NGLTF Policy Institute, 1989).

27. As early as 1984 activists were explaining that, like other women, lesbians are conditioned by their gender to accept violence so that when we are assaulted it does not even occur to us to question the basis for the attack.

Jill Tregor, program coordinator at CUAV, explained that of four hundred lesbians surveyed in the Bay Area in 1989 only 15 percent reported the crimes to anyone, because some lesbians who did not report

didn't see the incidents as important enough. And I have to emphasize here that these incidents ranged from verbal harassments to stabbings. I think as women, lesbians are conditioned to expect violence against them. Men are accustomed to believing that they have rights and that they deserve protection—and that's why they report antigay violence to authorities, while lesbians do not. Antigay violence is perceived as male by the media and by the community. Yet increasingly women are the victims.

Quoted in Victoria Brownworth, "An Unreported Crisis," *Advocate* 50, 52 (November 5, 1991).

28. Derrida, "Force of Law" 1015.

29. The phrase is from Cover, "Violence and the Word."

30. 479 N.W.2d, 891 (N.D. 1992).

31. 479 N.W.2d, 896, 897 (Henderson, concurring and dissenting). Ellipses and emphasis in original.

32. Ibid., 893.

33. 479 N.W.2d, 893–94.

34. M.A.B. v. R.B., 134 Misc. 2d 317, 510 N.Y.S.2d, 960 (N.Y. Sup. Ct. 1986).

35. 479 N.W.2d, 893–94. Compare with M.A.B. v. R.B., in which the court noted approvingly that "A. [the father's lover] and the father never embrace or touch in front of the children." 134 Misc. 2d, 328, 510 N.Y.S.2d, 966.

36. 479 N.W.2d, 894.

37. This assumption has marked the litigation and supporting social science evidence submitted on behalf of lesbian (and gay) parents. As noted by Nancy Polikoff in her discussion about the education of judges:

> Lawyers representing lesbian and gay parents often call witness to educate judges; these witnesses are primarily mental health professionals who testify that homosexuality is not a mental illness, that the children will not be harmed by living with a lesbian or gay parent, *that the children will not become lesbian or gay as a result of living with a lesbian or gay parent*, that lesbian and gay people do not have a propensity to molest children, and so on.

Nancy Polikoff, "Educating Judges About Lesbian and Gay Parenting: A Simulation," 1 *Law and Sexuality: A Review of Lesbian and Gay Legal Issues* 173, 175 (1991) (emphasis added). Polikoff also cites to an amicus curiae brief filed by Lambda Legal Defense and Education Fund on behalf of a gay man seeking adoption that includes a review of the psychological literature supporting the conclusion that "the father's sexual orientation would not affect the child's sexual orientation." Ibid., 175, n. 4. During the simulation the psychological expert witness on behalf of the lesbian mother testified that when asked whether she had a preference about the children's sexual orientation, the mother replied that "her choice was that both be heterosexual since it would be easier on them in their lives." Ibid., 217.

The future sexual orientation of the children as a component of their best interests may not always be explicitly stated. Standards such as whether the parent's sexuality "adversely effects" or "harms" a child often implicitly includes presumptions of adversity and harm from any sexuality other than heterosexuality.

38. Sarah Lucia Hoagland, *Lesbian Ethics* 8 (Palo Alto: Institute of Lesbian Studies, 1988).

39. Gloria Anzaldúa, "To(o) Queer the Writer—Loca, Escritora, y Chicana,"

in Betsey Warland, ed., *InVersion: Writings By Dykes, Queers, and Lesbians* 249, 249–50 (Vancouver: Press Gang, 1991).

40. Ruth Colker, "Feminism, Sexuality, and Self: A Preliminary Inquiry Into the Politics of Authenticity," 68 *Boston Law Review* 217 (1988); repr. and rev. in Martha Fineman and Nancy Thomadsen, eds., *At the Boundaries of the Law,* 135 (New York: Routledge, 1990).

41. Perhaps the most well documented case is that of Margaretha Linck, whose method of execution is unclear: the opinion devotes considerable energy to deciding whether burning or other methods are most appropriate but is inconclusive. See "A Lesbian Execution in Germany, 1721: The Trial Records," 6 *Journal of Homosexuality,* trans. Brigette Erickson, 27 (1980). For a discussion of other lesbian executions by burning, including a discussion of the relationships between lesbianism and the European witch burnings, see Ruthann Robson, *Lesbian (Out)Law,* 39–40 (Ithaca: Firebrand, 1992).

42. See generally Rene Girard, *The Scapegoat* (Baltimore: Johns Hopkins University Press, 1986); Rene Girard, *Violence and the Sacred* (Baltimore: Johns Hopkins University Press, 1978). See also Andrew McKenna, *Violence and Difference: Girard, Derrida, and Deconstruction* 135 (Urbana and Chicago: University of Illinois Press, 1992).

43. Richard Sherwin, "Law, Violence, and Illiberal Belief," 78 *Georgetown Law Journal* 1785, 1833 (1990).

44. Discourse, reason, and dialogic process are inextricably related and are opposed to irrationality and violence, especially in liberal conceptions of law:

> In the pursuit of the discourse ideal, liberalism affirms the right of each of us to voice interests or claims of entitlement in the face of other's, or the state's, power. This is a right not only to speak, but to be heard. For true dialogue can only proceed respectfully, with each party intent on both understanding and being understood by the other. Accordingly, persuasion (when it does not deceive) is the hallmark of the dialogic process.

Sherwin, "Law, Violence, and Illiberal Belief," 1791. This view of law as persuasion obviously conflicts with Richard Posner's view that while literature may persuade law operates through coercion. See Posner, *Law and Literature.*

Perhaps more interestingly, however, Sherman's conceptual opposition of persuasion and violence conflicts with the theorizing of lesbian philosopher Joyce Terblicot, who posits a "dyke method" of nonpersuasion based upon the violent coercion inherent in persuasion, even through dialogic processes or discourse. Joyce Treblicot, "Dyke Methods," in Jeffner Allen, ed., *Lesbian Philosophies and Cultures,* 17 (Albany: State University of New York Press, 1990).

45. See, for example, 18 U.S.C. 2385, federal sedition statute making it a crime to advocate overthrowing or destroying the government.

46. Drucilla Cornell, "Violence of the Masquerade," 11 *Cardozo Law Review* 1047, 1048 (1990).

47. This distinction is loosely based on Jacques Derrida's reading of Walter Benjamin's "Critique of Violence," in which Derrida distinguishes between the "founding violence" of law that Benjamin terms "mythic" and the violence that conserves, maintains, and enforces law that Benjamin terms "divine." Jacques Derrida, "Force of Law," 921, 981.

3. Convictions: Lesbians and Criminal Justice

1. The power of this perception was demonstrated to me by another gay/lesbian legal scholar who assumed that my presentation entitled "lesbians as criminals" concerned "lesbians and child custody."

2. In the legal literature, this argument was recently made in Robert Duncan, "Who Wants to Stop the Church: Homosexual Rights Legislation, Public Policy, and Religious Freedom," 69 *Notre Dame Law Review* 393, 407–11 (1994).

3. There are approximately 2,887 persons on death row—convicted of a capital crime and sentenced to death—in the United States. Of this number, 41 are women (approximately 1.4 percent); however, of the 41 women approximately 17 are "implicated" as lesbians (approximately 41 percent). See Victoria Brownworth, "Dykes on Death Row," *Advocate,* 62–64, June 15, 1992.

4. Assistant State Attorney Bob Johnson, quoted in *Gay Community News,* 1, September 17–23, 1989. The prosecutor also charged Annette Green with the highest degree of murder allowable under the applicable law, despite circumstances that comprise classic examples of lower degrees of murder, such as battering, mutual fighting, intimate relation, and diminished capacity (because of alcohol).

5. Telephone interview with William Lasley, November 13, 1989, defense counsel for Annette Green.

6. The feminist literature on female offenders is vast. Important works include Freda Alder, *Sisters in Crime: The Rise of the New Female Criminal* (New York: McGraw Hill, 1975); Susan S. M. Edwards, *Women On Trial* (Manchester: Manchester University Press, 1984); Coramae Richey Mann, *Female Crime and Delinquency* (Birmingham: University of Alabama Press, 1984); and Anne Worrall, *Offending Women: Female Lawbreakers and the Criminal Justice System* (London, New York: Routledge, 1990). A comprehensive anthology including women as offenders, victims, and workers is Barbara Raffel Price and Natalie J.

Sokoloff, *The Criminal Justice System and Women*, 2d ed. (New York: McGraw Hill, 1995). A useful overview of two decades of the literature occurs in Sally S. Simpson, "Feminist Theory, Crime, and Justice," 27:4 *Criminology* 605–31 (1989).

7. See, for example, Phyllis Crocker, "The Meaning of Equality for Battered Women Who Kill Men in Self-Defense," 8 *Harvard Women's Law Journal* 121 (1985); Elizabeth M. Schneider, "Describing and Changing: Women's Self-Defense Work and the Problem of Expert Testimony on Battering," 9 *Women's Right Law Reporter* 195, 207 (1986).

8. For a discussion of this conundrum in the context of "family," see Brenda Cossman, "Family Inside/Out," 44 *University of Toronto Law Journal* 1 (1994).

9. For a discussion of whether or not Aileen Wuornos fits any criteria of a serial killer, such as killing for pleasure, see Phyllis Chesler, "A Woman's Right to Self-Defense: The Case of Aileen Carol Wuornos," 66 *St. John's Law Review* 933, 946–8 (1993). Even if Wuornos does fit the criteria, she is certainly not the first woman to do so. Ibid., 946, citing Eric Hickey, *Serial Murderers and Their Victims,* 86 (Pacific Grove, Cal.: Brooks/Cole, 1987). Between 1800 and 1988 there was a total of thirty-four female serial killers. See also Ann Jones, *Women Who Kill,* esp. 129–39 (New York: Holt, Rhinehart and Winston, 1980), which discusses many cases, including Belle Paulson, a woman who lured a succession of men to her farm and murdered them for pecuniary gain.

10. See Chesler, "A Woman's Right to Self-Defense," 961–62. Chesler's most damaging observation is that because childhood acquaintances were offered payments for exclusive interviews with a producer, they may have interpreted the terms of these deals to include not cooperating with Wuornos's defense attorneys.

11. Neelley v. State, 1994 WL 248245 (Ala. June 10, 1994).

12. See Jane Caputi, *The Age of the Sex Crime* (Bowling Green, Ohio: Bowling Green University Press, 1987), who articulates this point with relation to male serial murderers whose victims are predominantly women.

13. Brownworth, "Dykes on Death Row."

14. Perez v. State, 491 S.W.2d 672, 673, 675 (Tex. Crim. App. 1973).

15. Robert Leger, "Lesbianism Among Women Prisoners: Participants and Nonparticipants," 14:4 *Criminal Justice and Behavior* 448 (1987).

16. See note 3 above.

17. Victor Streib, "Death Penalty for Lesbians," 1 *National Journal of Sexual Orientation Law* (1994), an electronic journal.

18. See generally, Pat Carlen, *Women, Crime, and Poverty* (Philadelphia: Open University Press, 1988); Coramae Mann Richey, "Minority and Female: A Criminal Justice Double Bind," 16:3 *Social Justice* 160–72.

19. Defense strategies have been less explicit because of the burden of the prosecution to prove its case and the complimentary lack of burden on the part of the defense.

20. This stereotyped construction is most operative in cases in which the "bad" lesbian is accused of murdering her lesbian partner.

21. See, for example, Marie Ashe, "The 'Bad Mother' in Law and Literature: A Problem of Representation," 43 *Hastings Law Journal* 1017 (1992); Dorothy E. Roberts, "Motherhood and Crime," 79 *Iowa Law Review* 95 (1993).

22. Editorial, *Miami Herald*, 26A, April 3, 1992.

23. People v. Martin, 4 Cal. Rptr.2d 660 (5th Dist. 1992).

4. Embodiment(s)

1. Andreas Huyssen, "Mapping the Postmodern," in Linda Nicholson, ed., *Feminism/Postmodernism,* 234, 239 (New York: Routledge, 1990).

2. Ibid., 271.

3. Jean-François Lyotard, *The Postmodern Condition: A Report on Knowledge,* trans. Geoff Bennington and Brian Massumi, 81 (Minneapolis: University of Minnesota Press, 1984).

4. Nicole Brossard, *The Aerial Letter,* trans. Marlene Wildeman, 122, 136 (Toronto: Women's Press, 1988).

5. Monique Wittig, *Les Guérillères,* trans. David Le Vay, 89 (New York: Avon, 1973).

6. Brossard, *The Aerial Letter,* 122.

7. As explained by Angla-Quebecois writer Gail Scott, referencing Brossard's work, fiction theory is "a reflexive doubling-back over the texture of the text" in which nothing, "not even 'theory' escapes the Poetry." Gail Scott, *Spaces Like Stairs,* 47 (Toronto: Women's Press, 1989). Feminism inheres in this postmodernist method because it breaks the "continuity of patriarchal mythologies" "into fragments in order to question syntax/context." Ibid. Scott continues that "fiction-theory, while it may be a method of exploring a space, a gap (never pretending to close it) between two or more ways of thinking, is the antithesis of a bridge."

8. Drucilla Cornell, "The Doubly-Prized World: Myth, Allegory, and the Feminine," 75 *Cornell Law Review* 644, 686 (1990).

9. Susan Bordo, "Feminism, Postmodernism, and Gender-Scepticism," in Nicholson, *Feminism/Postmodernism,* 133, 144.

10. Brossard, *The Aerial Letter,* 139.

11. Elizabeth Spelman, *Inessential Woman,* ix (Boston: Beacon, 1988).

12. Barbara Mehrhof and Pamela Kearon, "Rape: An Act of Terror," in Anne

Koedt, Ellen Levine, and Anita Rapone, eds., *Radical Feminism,* 230, 233 (New York: Quadrangle/New York Times, 1973).

13. Lucinda Cisler, "Unfinished Business: Birth Control and Women's Liberation," in Robin Morgan, ed., *Sisterhood is Powerful: An Anthology of Writings from the Women's Liberation Movement,* 245 (New York: Vintage, 1970).

14. Andrea Dworkin, *Woman Hating,* 174 (New York: Dutton, 1974). Michel Foucault published vol. 1 of *La Volente de Savoir* in France in 1976 (Paris: Editions Gallimard). The English translation, *The History of Sexuality,* vol. 1, trans. Robert Hurley (New York: Vintage), appeared in 1978 .

15. Diane Fuss, *Essentially Speaking: Feminism, Nature, and Difference,* 43 (New York: Routledge, 1989).

16. Wittig, *Les Guérillères,* 40, 45.

17. Monique Wittig, "The Mark of Gender," in Nancy K. Miller, ed., *The Poetics of Gender,* 63, 71 (New York: Columbia University Press, 1986).

18. Iris Young, "Impartiality and the Civic Public: Some Implications of Feminist Critique of Moral and Political Theory," in Seyla Benhabib and Dricilla Cornell, eds., *Feminism as Critique: On the Politics of Gender,* 56, 62 (Minneapolis: University of Minnesota Press, 1987).

19. Sue-Ellen Case, "Toward a Butch-Femme Aesthetic," in Lynda Hart, ed., *Making a Spectacle: Feminist Essays on Contemporary Women's Theater,* 283 (Ann Arbor: University of Michigan Press, 1989).

20. Leigh Megan Leonard, "A Missing Voice in Feminist Legal Theory: The Heterosexual Presumption," 12 *Women's Rights Law Reporter* 39, 43, 47 (1990).

21. Patricia Cain, "Feminist Jurisprudence: Grounding for Theories," 4 *Berkeley Women's Law Journal* 191, 195 (1989–90).

22. Ibid., 204–5.

23. Susan Bordo, "Feminism, Postmodernism, and Gender-Scepticism," in Nicholson, *Feminism/Postmodernism,* 151.

24. In fact, Flax advances the possibility that the motives of the privileged are an unconscious desire to halt the sharing of any "(revised) subjectivity with the 'others.' " Jane Flax, *Thinking Fragments: Psychoanalysis, Feminism, and Postmodernism in the Contemporary West,* 220 (Berkeley: University of California Press, 1990).

25. Barbara Christian, "The Race for Theory," in Gloria Anzaldúa, ed., *Making Face, Making Soul/Haciendo Caras: Creative and Critical Perspectives by Women of Color,* 335, 338 (San Francisco: Aunt Lute, 1990).

26. Frances Mascia-Lees, Patricia Sharpe, Colleen Cohen, "The Postmodernist Turn in Anthropology: Cautions from a Feminist Perspective," 15 *Signs* 7, 27 (Autumn, 1989).

27. Ibid., 14–15.

28. Bordo, "Feminism, Postmodernism, and Gender-Scepticism," 140.

29. Ibid.

30. Christian, "The Race for Theory," 339–40.

31. Katie King, "Producing Sex, Theory, and Culture: Gay/Straight Remappings in Contemporary Feminism," in Marianne Hirsch and Evelyn Fox Keller, eds., *Conflicts in Feminism,* 82, 91 (New York: Routledge, 1990).

32. Donna Haraway, "A Manifesto for Cyborgs: Science, Technology, and Socialist Feminism," in Nicholson, *Feminism/Postmodernism,* 223.

33. Ibid., 215. The relevance of the Jewish and lesbian identities of Adrienne Rich as author of the phrase "dream of a common language" remains unmentioned by Haraway.

34. Cherríe Moraga, "La Guerra," in Cherríe Moraga and Gloria Anzaldúa, eds., *This Bridge Called My Back: Writings by Radical Women of Color,* 27, 29 (New York: Kitchen Table, 1983).

35. Haraway, "A Manifesto for Cyborgs," 218.

36. Moraga, "La Guerra," 27, 34.

37. Paula Gunn Allen, *The Sacred Hoop,* 71 (Boston: Beacon, 1986).

38. Haraway, "A Manifesto for Cyborgs," 75.

39. Paula M. L. Moyo, "Postmodernism, 'Realism,' and the Politics of Identity: Cherríe Moraga and Chicana Feminism," in M. Jacqui Alexander and Chandra Talpade Mohanty, eds., *Feminist Genealogies, Colonial Legacies, Democratic Futures* (New York: Routledge, 1997).

40. Vivien Ng, "Race Matters," in Sally Munt and Andy Medhurst, eds., *Lesbian and Gay Studies: A Critical Reader* (London: Cassell, forthcoming).

41. Ibid.

42. See Audre Lorde, *Sister Outsider* (Trumansburg, N.Y.: Crossing, 1984).

43. Haraway, "A Manifesto for Cyborgs," 216.

44. Lorde, *Sister Outsider,* 68.

45. Christian, "The Race for Theory," 336.

46. Flax, *Thinking Fragments,* 230.

47. Catharine Stimpson, "Afterword: Lesbian Studies in the 1990s," in Karla Jay and Joanne Glasgow, eds., *Lesbian Texts and Contexts,* 377, 380–81 (New York: New York University Press, 1990).

48. Gayatri Chakravorty Spivak, *The Post-Colonial Critic: Interviews, Strategies, Dialogues,* Sarah Harasym, ed., 2 (New York: Routledge, 1990).

49. Lorde, *Sister Outsider,* 70.

50. See ALA. CODE 13–6–65 (a)(3) (1989); see also Commentary to 13A-6-63 and 13A-6-64 and Commentary to 13-6-65.

51. Ben Shalom v. Marsh, 881 F.2d 456, 457n.3 (7th Cir. 1989).

52. 491 S.W. 672, 673 (Tex. Crim. App. 1973).

53. 478 U.S. 186 (1986).

54. Ibid., 191.

55. Anna Marie Smith, "A Symptomology of an Authoritarian Discourse: The Parliamentary Debates on the Prohibition of the Promotion of Homosexuality," 10 *New Formations* 41, 48 (1990).

56. 569 So. 2d 1181, 1183 (Miss. 1990).

57. Spivak, *The Post-Colonial Critic*, 51. Perhaps Spivak gained this perspective from her translation of the ultimate postmodernist, Jacques Derrida, who writes about writing thusly: "If 'writing' signifies inscription and especially the durable institution of a sign (and that is the only irreducible kernel in the concept of writing), writing in general covers the entire field of linguistic signs." Derrida, 44. Derrida's "unreducible kernel" is essentialist:

> the appeal to an "irreducible kernel" of meaning in any term is surely inconsistent with the further course of Derrida's ideas on language and meaning. . . . Derrida, given where he wants to go next, is not in a position to advance an argument that appeals to an essential kernel of *anything*. He will soon rule out the possibility of any central, essential meaning for a word.

John M. Ellis, *Against Deconstruction,* 24 (Princeton: Princeton University Press, 1989).

58. Spivak, *The Post-Colonialist Critic,* 205.

59. Fuss, *Essentially Speaking*, 32.

60. Adrienne Rich, "Notes Toward a Politics of Location," in Adrienne Rich, *Blood, Bread, and Poetry: Selected Prose, 1979–1985* (New York: Norton, 1986).

61. Jonathan Culler, *Framing the Sign: Criticism and Its Institutions,* 148 (Norman, Okla.: University of Oklahoma Press, 1987).

62. The Legal Services Act, 42 U.S.C. 2996e governs legal services offices which receive funding from the federal Legal Services Corporation, and places limitations on the practice of law by attorneys working in legal services offices. Subsection (d)(5) of the Act provides "No class action suit, class action appeal, or amicus curiae class action may be undertaken, directly or through others, by a staff attorney, except with the express approval of a project director of a recipient in accordance with policies established by the governing body of such recipient." The regulations are more explicit: "Recipients are prohibited from initiating or participating in any class action." 45 C.F.R. 1617.3.

63. Wright, Miller, and Kane, 7a *Federal Practice and Procedure* 1751 (St. Paul: West, 1986).

64. 39 F.R.D. 69, 213 (1966).

65. FED. R. CIV. P. 23(b) provides:

An action may be maintained as a class action if the prerequisites of subdivision (a) are satisfied, and in addition:

(1) the prosecution of separate actions by or against individual members of the class would create a risk of

(A) inconsistent or varying adjudications with respect to individual members of the class which would establish incompatible standards of conduct for the party opposing the class, or

(B) adjudications with respect to individual members of the class which would as a practical matter be dispositive of the interests of the other members not parties to the adjudications or substantially impair or impede their ability to protect their interests; or

(2) the party opposing the class has acted or refused to act on grounds generally applicable to the class, thereby making final injunctive relief or corresponding declaratory relief with respect to the class as a whole; or

(3) the court finds that the questions of law or fact common to the members of the class predominate over any questions affecting only individual members, and that a class action is superior to the other available methods for the fair and efficient adjudication of the controversy. The matters pertinent to the findings include: (A) the interest of members of the class individually controlling the prosecution or defense of separate actions; (B) the extent and nature of any litigation concerning the controversy already commenced by or against members of the class; (C) the desirability or undesirability of concentrating the litigation of the claims in the particular forum; (D) the difficulties likely to be encountered in the management of a class action.

66. General Telephone Company of the Southwest v. Falcon, 457 U.S. 147, 157n.13 (1982).

67. Stephen C. Yeazell, *From Medieval Group Litigation to the Modern Class Action,* 1 (New Haven: Yale University Press, 1987).

68. Harris v. General Dev. Corp., 127 F.R.D. 655, 659 (N.D.Ill. 1989).

69. Ragsdale v. Turnock, 625 F.Supp. 1212, 1221 (N.D.Ill. 1986).

70. FED. R. CIV. P. 19.

71. Patrykus v. Gomilla, 121 F.R.D. 357, 361 (N.D. Ill. 1988): "There is an unusual factor in this case that must be considered: the potential social prejudice against homosexuals, or against persons who associate with homosexuals, that may deter class members from suing in their own names."

72. Herbert Newberg, *Newberg on Class Actions,* 3 3.10, 3-47 (Colorado Springs: Shepard's/McGraw-Hill, 1985).

73. Patrykus, 121 F.R.D., 362.

74. Ragsdale, 625 F.Supp., 1221–22.

75. See Friendship Medical Center, Ltd. v. Chicago Board of Health, 505 F.2d 1141, 1145–48 (7th Cir. 1974).

76. Newberg, *Newberg on Class Actions,* 2.01, 2-1.

77. FED. R. CIV. P. 23(c)(4)(B).

78. Ragsdale, 625 F.Supp., 1219.

79. Marvin Frankel, "Some Preliminary Observations Concerning Civil Rule 23, 43 F.R.D. 39 (1967). Remarks of United States District Judge Frankel at the Eighth Circuit's judicial conference.

80. Nicole Brossard, *Picture Theory,* 165–188 (New York: Roof, 1990), the chapter entitled "Hologram"; Nicole Brossard, "Memory: Hologram of Desire," 13 *Trivia* 42 (1988).

81. Michele Causse, "Interview with Michele Causse: Catherine Gonnard in Lesbia," trans. Lise Weill, 14 *Trivia* 59, 64–65 (1989).

82. Joan Nestle, "Desire Perfected: Sex After Forty," in Barbara Sang, Joyce Warshow, and Adrienne J. Smith, eds., *Lesbians at Midlife: The Creative Transition,* 180, 182 (San Francisco: Spinsters, 1991).

83. Causse, "Interview with Michele Causse," 64–65.

5. Reflections and Taxonomies: The Feminist Jurisprudence Question

1. 478 U.S. 186 (1986).

2. Although by its terms Amendment 2 did not include transgendered persons and the Court does not consider any transgender issues, it is possible that the case could be important in litigating for furthering the rights of transgendered persons.

3. ___U.S. ___, 116 S.Ct. 1620 (1996).

4. Nancy Polikoff, "We Will Get What We Ask For: Why Legalizing Gay and Lesbian Marriage Will Not 'Dismantle the Legal Structure of Gender in Every Marriage,' " 79 *Virginia Law Review* 1535, 1546 (1993).

5. Evan Wolfson, "Crossing the Threshold: Equal Marriage Rights for Lesbians and Gay Men and the Intra-Community Critique," 21 *New York University Review of Law and Social Change* 567 (1994).

6. Diana Majury, "Refashioning the Unfashionable: Claiming Lesbian Identities in the Legal Context," 7 *Canadian Journal of Women and the Law/Revue Femmes et Droit* 286 (1994).

7. Ibid., 313.

8. 852 P.2d 44 (1993).

9. Ibid., 52 n. 11.

10. Francisco Valdes, "Queers, Sissies, Dykes, and Tomboys: Deconstructing the Conflation of 'Sex,' 'Gender,' and 'Sexual Orientation' in Euro-American Law and Society," 83 *California Law Review* 1, 207 (1995).

11. Mary Anne Case, "Disaggregating Gender from Sex and Sexual Orientation: The Effeminate Man in the Law and Feminist Jurisprudence," 105 *Yale Law Journal* 1 (1995).

12. Carl Stychin, "Exploring the Limits: Feminism and the Regulation of Gay Male Pornography," 16 *Vermont Law Review* 857 (1992).

13. Tamara Packard and Melissa Schraibman, "Lesbian Pornography: Escaping Our Bonds of Sexual Stereotypes and Strengthening Our Ties to One Another," 4 *UCLA Women's Law Journal* 299 (1994).

14. Ann Scales, "Avoiding Constitutional Depression: Bad Attitudes and the Fate of Butler," 7 *Canadian Journal of Women and the Law/Revue Femmes et Droit* 349 (1994). For a more doctrinal explanation of the Canadian Supreme Court's decision in Butler, helpfully targeted at American legal scholars, see Note, Jodi Aileen Kleinick, "Suppressing Violent and Degrading Pornography to 'Prevent Harm' in Canada: Butler v. Her Majesty the Queen," 19 *Brooklyn Journal of International Law* 627 (1993).

15. Ruth Colker, "A Bisexual Jurisprudence," 3 *Law and Sexuality* 127, 136 (1993).

16. While several articles encompass transgender issues, a specifically transgendered jurisprudence has not yet been articulated as a possibility.

17. Kellye Teste, "An Unlikely Resurrection," 90 *Northwestern Law Review* 219 (1995).

18. Didi Herman, "A Jurisprudence of One's Own? Ruthann Robson's Lesbian Legal Theory," 7 *Canadian Journal of Women and the Law/Revue Femmes et Droit* 509, 521 (1994).

19. Majury, "Refashioning the Unfashionable," 313.

6. Beginning from (My) Experience: The Paradoxes of Narrative

1. Muriel Rukeyser, "Käthe Kollwitz," in *The Collected Poems of Muriel Rukeyser,* 479–84 (New York: McGraw Hill, 1978). The poem was originally published in *The Speed of Darkness* (New York: Random House, 1968).

2. Florence Howe and Ellen Bass, eds., *No More Masks! An Anthology of Poems by Women* (New York: Doubleday, 1973).

3. Martha Kearns, *Käthe Kollwitz: Woman and Artist* (Old Westbury, N.Y.: Feminist Press, 1976).

4. Plato, *Republic,* book 7, in Edith Hamilton and Huntington Cairns, eds., *Plato: The Collected Dialogues* 575, 747 (Princeton: Princeton University Press, 1961). Plato, circa 428 B.C.–347 B.C., is the reputed author of thirty-five dialogues that feature the learned Socrates and are structured dialectically. The allegory of the cave, appearing in the extended dialogue *Republic*, which mostly concerns theories of justice, is a rejection of empiricism. In the allegory of the cave Socrates describes persons chained in a cave, unable to view each other, and able only to see a series of shadows on the wall of the cave. These shadows are considered "real." When one individual escapes, he realizes that the shadows are in fact shadows and are made by a series of statues of objects.

5. G. W. F. Hegel, *The Phenomenology of Mind,* trans. J. B. Baille, 142 (New York: Harper Torchbooks/HarperCollins, 1967).

6. See Joan Scott, "Experience," in Judith Butler and Joan W. Scott, eds., *Feminists Theorize the Political,* 27 (New York: Routledge, 1992), who discuss only the sense of experience as used by Anglo-American historians—and not the sense of experience as perception—and note that "experience is something people have."

7. Karl Marx and Frederick Engels, *The German Ideology,* ed. C. J. Arthur, 47 (New York: International, 1974).

8. Judith Grant, *Fundamental Feminism: Contesting the Core Concepts of Feminist Theory,* 4 (New York: Routledge, 1993); she argues that "much of the richness" as well as "a good portion" of the problems of feminist theory are traceable to the three "core concepts" of feminism, which are "woman," experience, and personal politics.

9. "Consciousness Raising," in Anna Koedt, Ellen Levine, and Anita Rapone, eds., *Radical Feminism,* 280 (New York: Quadrangle/New York Times, 1973). The unsigned piece also includes a list of topics that could be discussed by a group.

10. Catharine A. MacKinnon, *Toward a Feminist Theory of the State,* 95 (Cambridge: Harvard University Press, 1989).

11. Carol Williams Payne, "Consciousness Raising: A Dead End?" in *Radical Feminism,* 282. The article has a 1971 copyright.

12. See Joreen, "The Tyranny of Structurelessness," in Koedt, Levine, and Rapone, *Radical Feminism*, 285, 293: "Unstructured groups may be very effective in getting women to talk about their lives; they aren't very good for getting things done."

13. The term *false consciousness* is derived from Marx, although apparently Marx himself never utilized the phrase. Nevertheless, the concept is fundamental to the Marxist concept of ideology, especially given the postulate that the ruling class is able to control the means of intellectual as well as material production. See

Michèle Barrett, *The Politics of Truth: From Marx to Foucault,* 7–10 (Stanford: Stanford University Press, 1991). The feminist adoption of the term may or may not have been influenced by Marxism; see Grant, *Fundamental Feminism,* 32, which argues that although some early radical feminists may have believed it was so derived, it merely followed from feminism's emphasis on experience.

14. Judith Roof, *Come As You Are: Sexuality and Narrative,* 104 (New York: Columbia University Press, 1996).

15. Bonnie Zimmerman, *The Safe Sea of Women: Lesbian Fiction 1969–1989* (Boston: Beacon, 1990).

16. See Mary Dunlap, "Foundering on the Seas of Hopelessness: A Review of Gays/Justice," 87 *Michigan Law Review* 1366, 1368, n. 7 (1989); Mary Dunlap, "Sexual Speech and the State: Putting Pornography in Its Place," 17 *Golden Gate University Law Review* 359, 378, n. 10 (1987).

17. Kenneth Plummer, *Telling Sexual Stories: Power, Change, and Social Worlds,* 87, 168 (London, New York: Routledge, 1995).

18. As Aristotle notes, a narrative (mythos in Greek) must have a beginning, a middle, and an end. Aristotle, *Poetics,* trans. Leon Golden, 2d ed., chapter 7, 14 (Tallahassee: Florida State University Press, 1981). Aristotle's definitions of these terms endure. A beginning is that which itself is not by necessity after anything else but after which something naturally develops. An end is the opposite: "that which is naturally after something else, either necessarily or customarily, but after which there is nothing else." Ibid.

19. Peter Brooks, *Reading for the Plot: Design and Intention in Narrative,* 37 (Cambridge: Harvard University Press, 1982).

20. Teresa de Lauretis, *Alice Doesn't: Feminism, Semiotics, Cinema,* 140 (Bloomington and Indianapolis: Indiana University Press, 1984).

21. Roland Barthes, *The Pleasure of the Text,* trans. Richard Miller (New York: Farrar, Straus and Giroux 1975).

22. Robert Weisberg, "Proclaiming Trials as Narratives: Premises and Pretenses," in Peter Brooks and Paul Gewirtz, eds., *Law's Stories: Narrative and Rhetoric in Law,* 61, 64 (New Haven: Yale University Press, 1996).

23. See generally, Austin Sarat, "Narrative Strategy and Death Penalty Advocacy," 31 *Harvard Civil Rights-Civil Liberties Law Review* 353 (1996); Christopher Meade, Note, "Regarding Death Sentences: The Narrative Construction of Capital Punishment," 71 *New York University Law Review* 732 (1996).

24. Robert Chang, "Toward an Asian American Legal Scholarship: Critical Race Theory, Post-Structuralism, and Narrative Space," 81 *California Law Review* 1241, 1269, n. 127 (1993); repr. in 1 *Asian Law Journal* 1, 29, n. 127 (1994).

25. Marc Fajer, "Can Two Real Men Eat Quiche Together? Storytelling,

Gender-Role Stereotypes, and Legal Protection for Lesbians and Gay Men," 46 *Miami Law Review* 511 (1992).

26. William Eskridge, "Gaylegal Narratives," 46 *Stanford Law Review* 607 (1994).

27. Larry Cata Backer, "Constructing a 'Homosexual' for Constitutional Theory: Sodomy Narrative, Jurisprudence, and Antipathy in United States and British Courts," 71 *Tulsa Law Review* 529 (1996).

28. Mari Matsuda is generally believed to have coined the term *outsider jurisprudence*. Mari J. Matsuda, "Public Response to Racist Speech: Considering the Victim's Story," 87 *Michigan Law Review* 2320, 2323 and n. 15 (1989). Others have used the term *outsider scholarship, see,* for example, Mary Coombs, "Outsider Scholarship: The Law Review Stories," 63 *University of Colorado Law Review* 683 (1992), or *outsider narratives,* see, for example, Jerome Culp, "Telling a Black Legal Story: Privilege, Authenticity, 'Blunders,' and Transformation in Outsider Narratives," 82 *Virginia Law Review* 69 (1996). This is not to suggest, however, that personal revelation is coextensive with outsider jurisprudence.

29. Fajer, "Can Two Real Men Eat Quiche," 515.

30. Backer, "Constructing a 'Homosexual.' "

31. See, for example, Anne Coughlin, "Regulating the Self: Autobiographical Performances in Outsider Scholarship," 81 *Virginia Law Review* 1229 (1995); Daniel Farber and Suzanna Sherry, "Telling Stories Out of School: An Essay on Legal Narratives," 45 *Stanford Law Review* 807 (1993); Mark Tushnet, "The Degradation of Constitutional Discourse," 81 *Georgia Law Journal* 251 (1992).

32. Compare Tushnet, "The Degradation of Constitutional Discourse," with Coughlin, "Regulating the Self," and Farber and Sherry, "Telling Stories Out of School."

In his critique of narrative, Tushnet discusses the work of Catharine MacKinnon, who does not provide autobiographical narratives, the work of conservative Stephen Carter, author of *Reflections of an Affirmative Action Baby* (New York: Basic, 1991), and the Clarence Thomas confirmation hearings, as well as the work of Patricia Williams. In contrast, Farber and Sherry choose as their focus "feminist and critical race theorists" and Coughlin is interested solely in criticizing the autobiographical moves of those deemed "outsiders."

33. See, for example, Jane Baron, "Resistance to Stories," 67 *Southern California Law Review* 255 (1994); Richard Delgado, "On Telling Stories in School: A Reply to Farber and Sherry," 46 *Vanderbilt Law Review* 665 (1993); Richard Delgado, "Coughlin's Complaint: How to Disparage Outsider Writing, One Year Later," 82 *Virginia Law Review* 95 (1996); Fajer, "Can Two Real Men Eat Quiche"; Alex Johnson, "Defending the Use of Narrative and Giving Content to the Voice of

Color: Rejecting the Imposition of Process Theory in Legal Scholarship," 79 *Iowa Law Review* 803 (1994).

34. For example, in the exciting and important work of Asian-American scholars utilizing narrative, the methodology is not only explicated but defended. See, for example, Chang, "Toward an Asian American Legal Scholarship"; Margaret Chon, "On the Need for Asian-American Narratives in Law: Ethnic Specimens, Native Informants, Storytelling, and Silences," 3 *Asian-Pacific Law Journal* 4 (1995).

35. Similarly, Eskridge, "Gaylegal Narratives," 609, expresses surprise at the virtual absence of references to "gay" narratives in the original Farber and Sherry piece.

As Fajer notes, Farber and Sherry only refer to his previous article, Fajer, "Can Two Real Men Eat Quiche," in a footnote that grudgingly, it seems to me, accords some validity to lesbian/queer narratives because the "phenomenon of 'closeting' " has made "information about the lives of gay men and lesbians" "unavailable to scholars." Marc Fajer, "Authority, Credibility, and Pre-Understanding: A Defense of Outsider Narratives in Legal Scholarship," 82 *Georgia Law Journal* 1845, 1847 (1994), quoting and citing Farber and Sherry, "Telling Stories Out of School," 829, n. 119.

In their piece, Daniel Farber and Suzanna Sherry, "The 200,000 Cards of Dimitri Yurasov: Further Reflections on Scholarship and Truth," 46 *Stanford Law Review* 647 (1994), responding to Eskridge (in the same issue of the pertinent law journal), Farber and Sherry do discuss sexual minority issues.

36. Farber and Sherry, "Telling Stories Out of School," 834.

37. Daniel Farber and Suzanna Sherry, "Legal Story Telling and Constitutional Law: The Medium and the Message," in Brooks and Gewirtz, *Law's Stories*, 37, 37–38.

38. Farber and Sherry, "Telling Stories Out of School," 835–36.

39. Kathryn Abrams, "Hearing the Call of Stories," 79 *California Law Review* 971, 979 (1991).

40. Fajer, "Authority, Credibility, and Pre-Understanding," 1864.

41. Abrams, "Hearing the Call of Stories," 1028, who states the existence of such criticism rather than advancing it.

42. Farber and Sherry, "Telling Stories Out of School," 839.

43. Chang, "Toward an Asian American Legal Scholarship," 1274.

44. Fajer, "Authority, Credibility, and Pre-Understanding," 1853.

45. Delgado, "On Telling Stories in School," 669.

46. Johnson, "Defending the Use of Narrative," 832–33.

47. Baron, "Resistance to Stories," 266.

48. Farber and Sherry, "Telling Stories Out of School," 836.

49. Coughlin, "Regulating the Self," 1281. As Coughlin asserts,

Personal stories tend to pre-empt responses other than sympathy or silence, precisely because any critical commentary or desire for clarification may be dismissed as ad hominem—and any criticism necessarily is ad hominem, since the material available for criticism or clarification is the scholar's personal experience. Ironically, therefore, the power of the autobiographical exchange to inspire readers' sympathy turns out to be a significant shortcoming within the context of an academy whose participants, even when sympathetic to an idea, are committed to immediate, often face-to-face, critical inquiry and debate. By rejecting any critical reaction as a treacherous failure of sympathy for the author's pain, if not as the product of prejudiced ignorance, and dismissing criticism as a personal attack on the author's character, autobiographical rhetoric is no less coercive of readers than the legal rhetoric that the outsiders desire to supersede.

Ibid., 1281–82 (footnotes omitted).

50. Fajer, "Authority, Credibility, and Pre-Understanding," 1857.

51. Farber and Sherry, "The 200,000 Cards," 655.

52. Arthur Austin, "Evaluating Storytelling as a Type of Nontraditional Scholarship," 74 *Nebraska Law Review* 479 (1995).

53. Ibid., 515–23.

54. Ibid., 527–28.

55. Farber and Sherry, "Telling Stories Out of School," 809, 819, 824.

56. Delgado, "On Telling Stories in School," 673–74.

57. De Lauretis, *Alice Doesn't.*

58. Roof, *Come As You Are,* xxiii.

59. Ibid.

60. Fredric Jameson, "Reification and Utopia in Mass Culture," in *Signatures of the Visible,* 9, 13 (London and New York: Routledge, 1992).

61. Jameson describes the adventure tale in which the denouement is a reifying structure that "reaches down into the very page-by-page detail of the book's composition" so that each chapter, and even each paragraph, is a sub-plot (presumably complete with its own beginning, middle, and end), thus transforming the "transparent flow of language as much as possible into material images and objects we can consume." Jameson, "Reification and Utopia," 13. Later, Jameson also discusses more sophisticated genres in literature as well as cinema and music.

62. Roof, *Come As You Are,* 39.

63. Roland Barthes, "Introduction to the Structural Analysis of Narratives" in

Image, Music, Text, ed. and trans. Stephen Heath, 79 (New York: Farrar, Straus and Giroux 1977).

64. Hayden White, "The Value of Narrativity in the Representation of Reality," in W. J. T. Mitchell, ed., *On Narrative,* 1–2 (Chicago: University of Chicago Press, 1990).

65. Roof, *Come As You Are,* xxxi.

66. Walter Kaufman, *Hegel: A Reinterpretation,* 250 (New York: Doubleday, 1966). Kaufman states that this idea is "at the heart" of Hegel's philosophy of history and that all else receives blood from it. Ibid.

67. Robert Weisberg, "Proclaiming Trials as Narratives," 77–78.

68. Hayden White, "Storytelling: Historical and Ideological," in Robert Newman, ed., *Centuries' Ends, Narrative Means,* 58, 69 (Stanford: Stanford University Press, 1996).

69. Roof, *Come As You Are,* 187.

70. Michael Roemer, *Telling Stories: Postmodernism and the Invalidation of Traditional Narrative,* 3 (London and Lanham, Md.: Rowman and Littlefield, 1995).

71. See, generally, Lynne N. Henderson, "Legality and Empathy," 85 *Michigan Law Review* 1574 (1987).

72. Charles Baxter, "Counterpointed Characterization," in *Burning Down the House: Essays on Fiction,* 109, 112 (Saint Paul, Minn.: Graywolf, 1997). The reference is to Leo Tolstoy's classic story "The Death of Ivan Illych," which writer and critic Vladimir Nabokov calls "Tolstoy's most artistic, most perfect, and most sophisticated achievement." Vladimir Nabokov, *Lectures on Russian Literature,* ed. Fredson Bowers, 238 (New York: Harcourt Brace Jovanovich, 1981). As the story opens, Ivan Illych is dead, but the "unfeeling vulgarity of the bureaucratic middle-class city life in which so recently Ivan had participated" continues and "his civil service colleagues are thinking of how his death will affect their careers" and what promotions it might occasion. Ibid., 239.

73. Lucie E. White, "Seeking ' . . . The Faces of Otherness . . . ': A Response to Professors Sarat, Felstiner, and Cahn," 77 *Cornell Law Review* 1499, 1508–9 (1992).

74. Roger C. Schank, *Tell Me A Story: Narrative and Intelligence,* 57 (Evanston: Northwestern University Press, 1990).

75. Plummer, *Telling Sexual Stories*, 173.

76. Celia Kitzinger and Rachel Perkins, *Changing Our Minds: Lesbian Feminism and Psychology,* 73 (New York: New York University Press, 1993), citing J. B. Bradford and C. C. Ryan, *National Lesbian Health Care Survey: Mental Health Implications* (Richmond Va.: Survey Research Laboratory, Virginia Commonwealth University, 1987).

77. Kitzinger and Perkins, *Changing Our Minds,* 78.

78. Ibid., 186.

79. Ibid., 184.

80. See, for example, Gloria Steinem, *Revolution from Within* (New York: Little, Brown, 1992).

81. Kitzinger and Perkins note that the replacement of *oppression* with the term *homophobia* is part of the domination of psychology over politics. Kitzinger and Perkins, *Changing Our Minds,* 186.

82. The Report, *The Gay Agenda* (Video, 1992).

83. Didi Herman, *The Antigay Agenda: Orthodox Vision and the Christian Right,* 78 (1997). Rather than using the generic term *conservative,* Herman defines what she calls the "Christian Right," but part of the value of her book is that she focuses upon what might be termed the mainstream Christian Right rather than its more radical elements. Herman also makes clear that the rhetoric of disease and seduction, as well as most of the Christian Right's attention, is aimed at gay men. Her insightful treatment of the Christian Right's strategy regarding lesbians, in a chapter called "No Lesbians, Gay Lesbians, Feminist Lesbians," argues that lesbians are generally made invisible, or made an extension of gay men, or made an extension of feminism. Ibid., 92–110.

84. Richard Duncan, "Wigstock and Kulturkampf: Supreme Court Story-telling, the Culture War, and *Romer v. Evans,*" 72 *Notre Dame Law Review* 345 (1997).

85. The case Duncan cursorily relates is Smith v. Fair Employment and Housing Comm'n 12 Cal. 4th 1143, 913 P.2d 909, 51 Cal. Rptr. 2d 700 (1996), in which a landlord argued that she could engage in marital status discrimination because her religious beliefs included the idea that unmarried cohabitation was sinful. The California Supreme Court, reversing the court of appeals, decided the landlord's religious beliefs could not prevail over the interest in nondiscrimination. Duncan simply relates the facts but does not discuss the legal issues.

See also Swanner v. Anchorage Equal Rights Comm'n, 874 P.2d 274 (Alaska) (per curiam), cert. denied, 115 S. Ct. 460 (1994) (same); Attorney General v. Desilets, 636 N.E.2d 233 (Mass. 1994), holding in favor of landlord; State by Cooper v. French, 460 N.W.2d 2 (Minn. 1990), holding in favor of landlord.

For discussions of some of the cases and doctrinal explication of the conflict between prohibiting discrimination on the basis of marital status and the free exercise of religion, see David Kushner, Note, "Free Exercise, Fair Housing, and Marital Status—Alaskan Style, 12 *Alaska Law Review* 335 (1995); Malgorzata (Margo) K. Laskowska, Comment, "No Sinners Under My Roof": Can California Landlords Refuse to Rent to Unmarried Couples by Claiming a Religious

Freedom of Exercise Exemption from a Statute Which Prohibits Marital Status Discrimination?" 36 *Santa Clara Law Review* 219 (1995).

86. Thus, Duncan echoes Justice Scalia's dissenting opinion in Romer v. Evans, 116 S.Ct. 1620, 1631 (Scalia, J., dissenting).

87. Duncan, "Wigstock and Kulturkampf," 347. Duncan states that "if one searches for sophisticated legal reasoning in the Court's decision in Romer he [*sic*] will be disappointed because 'there is no there there,' " footnoting to "Gertrude Stein's famous description of Oakland" in Gertrude Stein, *Everybody's Autobiography* (1937), ibid., 347, n. 12.

88. Ibid., 362.

89. Fajer, "Authority, Credibility, and Pre-Understanding," 529.

90. Teresa Bruce, "Doing the Nasty: An Argument for Bringing Same-Sex Erotic Conduct Back into the Courtroom," 81 *Cornell Law Review* 1135, 1172 (1996).

91. While Larry Cata Backer attempts to be optimistic that change is possible through exposing the courts to many narratives, his work supports his conclusion that the outlook is "bleak." See Backer, "Constructing a 'Homosexual,' " 595.

92. Julie Shapiro, "Custody and Conduct: How the Law Fails Lesbian and Gay Parents and Their Children," 71 *Indiana Law Journal* 623, 647–48 (1996).

93. For example, William Eskridge, in his article "Gaylegal Narratives," cites some of my work as exemplifying "work in which gaylesbian narratives are central to the argument presented." Ibid, 609, n. 12, citing Ruthann Robson, *Lesbian (Out)Law: Survival Under the Rule of Law* (Ithaca: Firebrand, 1992), Ruthann Robson, "Lavender Bruises: Intra-Lesbian Violence, Law, and Lesbian Legal Theory," 20 *Golden Gate Law Review* 567 (1990). Yet it does not seem to me that narratives were central. In the almost two hundred pages of *Lesbian (Out)Law*, for example, there are perhaps three "personal" narratives, one section in which sexual episodes from a novel are used as "facts" upon which the "law" of statutes regulating lesbian sexuality are applied, and the standard factual recitations in discussions of important or illustrative cases.

94. Sue-Ellen Case, *The Domain-Matrix: Performing Lesbian at the End of Print Culture,* 27 (Bloomington and Indianapolis: Indiana University Press, 1996).

95. Ibid., 33.

96. George Landow, *Hypertext: The Convergence of Contemporary Critical Theory and Technology,* 3 (Baltimore: Johns Hopkins University Press, 1992). As more fully elaborated by another critic,

"Hypertext" is not a system but a generic term, coined a quarter of a century ago by a computer populist named Ted Nelson to describe the writing done in the nonlinear or nonsequential space made possible by the computer. Moreover, unlike print text, hypertext provides multiple paths between text segments, now often called "lexias" in a borrowing from the pre-hypertextual but prescient Roland Barthes. With its webs of linked lexias, its networks of alternate routes (as opposed to print's fixed unidirectional page-turning) hypertext presents a radically divergent technology, interactive and polyvocal, favoring a plurality of discourses over definitive utterance and freeing the reader from domination by the author.

Robert Coover, "The End of Books," *New York Times Book Review*, June 21, 1992.

97. Landow, *Hypertext*, 101.

98. Ibid., 101–2. For Aristotle, the proper magnitude of a narrative is "one that can easily be taken in by the memory." Aristotle, *Poetics,* 15 (chapter 7, l. 30).

99. As Robert Coover phrases it,

And what of narrative flow? There is still movement, but in hyperspace's dimensionless infinity, it is more like endless *expansion*; it runs the risk of being so distended and slackly driven as to lose its centripetal force, to give way to a kind of static low-charged lyricism—that dreamy gravityless lost-in-space feeling of the early sci-fi films. How does one resolve the conflict between the reader's desire for coherence and closure and the text's desire for continuance, its fear of death? Indeed, what is closure in such an environment? If everything is middle, how do you know when you are done, either as reader or writer?

Coover, "The End of Books."

100. White, "The Value of Narrativity in the Representation of Reality."

101. See, for example, Neil Postman, *Technopoly: The Surrender of Culture to Technology,* 179 (1992).

102. Sven Birkerts, *The Gutenberg Elegies: The Fate of Reading in an Electronic Age* (New York: Faber and Faber, 1994).

103. Ibid., 164.

104.

If men learn this [writing], it will implant forgetfulness in their souls; they will cease to exercise memory because they rely on that which is written, calling things to remembrance no longer from within themselves, but by means of external marks. What you have discovered is a recipe not for memory, but for reminder. And it is no true wisdom that you offer your disciples, but only its semblance, for by telling them of many things without teaching them you will make them seem to know much, while for the most

part they know nothing, and as men filled, not with wisdom, but with the
conceit of wisdom, they will be a burden to their fellows.

Plato, *Phaedrus,* in *Plato, The Collected Dialogues,* 520 (ll. 274d–75b). Socrates'
position at the end of the dialogue is predictably more nuanced. Socrates does not
per se condemn the form of writing but seeks to make a distinction between writing that has been done "with a knowledge of the truth," and whose author can
defend it orally, with writing that is simply composed of phrases that the writer
has twisted, pasted, and pulled. Ibid., 524 (l. 278c–d).

105. David Abrams, *The Spell of the Sensuous: Perception and Language in a
More-Than-Human World,* 100–39 (New York: Pantheon, 1996). Throughout this
excellent book Abrams argues that we have replaced our ability to "read" nature
with the ability to read inked marks upon flat pages.

106. Interestingly, Coover implies that hypertext is more respectful of nature
than print, because of the "forest-harvesting, paper-wasting" required to produce
print media. Coover, "The End of Books."

107. George Landow, *Hypertext,* 101–19, chapter 4, entitled "Reconfiguring
Narrative."

7. The Codification of Lesbian Relationships: Examples from Law and Literature

1. This general process has been explored in detail by numerous legal theorists
from various schools of jurisprudential thought. For an excellent overview and
incisive analysis, see Margaret Davies, *Asking the Law Question* (Sydney: Sweet
and Maxwell, 1994.)

2. The one caveat I might add would be in the literary field, in which an
increasing number of "lesbian" novels are childhood memoirs in which any les-
bian relationships barely exist, and, in fact, there is little explicit recognition of any
possibility of lesbianism. See, for example, Dorothy Allison, *Bastard Out of
Carolina* (New York: Dutton, 1992); Blanche McCrary Boyd, *The Revolution of
Little Girls* (New York: Knopf, 1991); Karin Cook, *What Girls Learn* (New York:
Pantheon, 1997); Jacqueline Woodson, *Autobiography of a Family Photo* (New
York: Dutton, 1995).

3.

[Lesbian] Writers as politically diverse as Barbara Deming, Joan Nestle,
and Audre Lorde have told dismayed tales of being ostracized because they
thought the wrong things, wanted sex the wrong way, or had a child of the
wrong gender. To this day, arguments rage over whether leather dykes and

toddling male children should be allowed at lesbian music festivals. . . .

At the Michigan Womyn's Music Festival in 1989, a white performer who sang about being cradled as a child in "ebony arms" was publicly condemned for condoning racism. A few summers ago, Brooklyn Women's Martial Arts boycotted the annual women's training camp objecting to— among other things—an instructor who worked for her local police department. In both cases, a critique could well be made, but suppressing deviation and closing down discussion do not advance the cause. And more and more lesbian activists are convinced that the motivation for these strictures is fear—of ideological contamination by patriarchy.

Alisa Solomon, "Dykotomies: Scents and Sensibility," in Arlene Stein, ed., *Sisters, Sexperts, Queers: Beyond the Lesbian Nation,* 210, 214 (New York: Plume/Penguin, 1993).

4. Stanley Fish, *Is There a Text in This Class? The Authority of Interpretative Communities* (Cambridge: Harvard University Press, 1980).

5. In the United States the predominant legal organization is the Lambda Legal Defense and Education Fund. The major lesbian organization is the National Center for Lesbian Rights (NCLR). Additionally, the American Civil Liberties Union (ACLU) has projects devoted to sexual orientation issues. Other gay, lesbian, bisexual and transgender organizations such as National Gay and Lesbian Task Force (NGLTF) and Gay and Lesbian Alliance Against Defamation (GLAAD) do not engage in litigation, although they do lobby for legislative change.

6. See, generally, Mark Crispin Miller, "The Crushing Power of Big Publishing," *Nation* 11, March 17, 1997.

7. See Victoria Brownworth, "Who Will Publish Our Books?" 5 *Lambda Book Report* 10, May 1997, which interviewed numerous lesbian and feminist publishers in the United States and concluded "there can be no question" that independent publishers, as well as bookstores, are in serious trouble; see also Thomas Goetz, "War for Independents: Can Small Presses Survive Megapublishing?" *Village Voice* 52, March 25, 1997.

8. Both Victoria Brownworth, "Who Will Publish Our Books?" and Thomas Goetz, "War for Independents," make the point about celebrity books. Frank Rich makes a more extensive argument in *Star of the Month Club,* an op-ed piece in the *New York Times,* Sunday, March 23, 1997, arguing that there has been a "Hollywoodization" of publishing that seeks books by celebrities as well as attempting to portray authors as "Calvin Klein models."

9. The collusion between chain book stores and publishers has not been limited to lesbian/gay or other minority interest books. The American Booksellers Association, which represents forty-five hundred U.S. bookstores, sued several

major publishers in June 1994 alleging violations of the Sherman Anti-Trust Act due to discriminatory pricing policies. Most of the defendants have entered into settlement agreements that promise standard criteria for pricing and promotions, but the largest publisher of trade books in the United States, Random House, has refused to settle and has boycotted the annual ABA convention. *New York Times,* August 12, 1996, D7.

10. Braschi v. Stahl Associates, 74 N.Y.2d 201, 543 N.E.2d 49, 544 N.Y.S.2d 784 (1989).

11. See, generally, Raymond O'Brien, "Domestic Partnership: Recognition and Responsibility" 32 *San Diego Law Review* 163 (1995); Alice Rickel, "Extending Employee Benefits to Domestic Partners," 16 *Whittier Law Review* 737 (1995).

12. See Ellen Neuborne, "One in Ten Firms Extends Benefits to Life Partners," *USA Today,* January 24, 1997, in reference to a study by Society for Human Resource Management.

13. Berkeley, California was the first municipality in the United States to pass a domestic partner ordinance. Many other major cities such as Seattle and New York City followed suit within the next decade. See O'Brien, "Domestic Partnership," 181.

To date, the most expansive domestic partner policy in the United States is in the City of San Francisco. Ordinance 481–96, the Non-Discrimination in City Contracts and Benefits Ordinance, which went into effect June 1, 1997, requires all entities having contracts with the city to extend domestic partnership benefits to their employees on the same terms that benefits are extended to married couples. The ordinance has caused some consternation on the part of the Catholic Church; Catholic Charities receives over five million U.S. dollars from the city per year to provide various services to residents, including services for persons with AIDS. While the archbishop of San Francisco and the mayor, Willie Brown, originally appeared to be headed for litigation, there has been an agreement about the terms by which the Catholic Church will comply with the ordinance. See, generally, Victoria Slind-Flor, "San Francisco's Domestic Partnership Law Causes Big Stir," *National Law Journal* A6, col. 1 (February 17, 1997).

14. This is usually accomplished in the states through the governor's executive order or through orders or policies of chief executive orders relating to their departments. With the election or appointment of new officials, these orders can be rescinded. Further, these orders can often conflict across agencies or with other policies within the agency. For example, the situation in the state of New York is especially noteworthy:

State Attorney General Dennis Vacco says his little-noticed action extending health benefits to the domestic partners of his staff, including homosexuals, proves he is not the bigot critics have made him out to be. Just weeks after he took office in January, he drew fire for rescinding an order that forbade discrimination against job applicants in his office on the basis of sexual orientation; state law has no such provision, he noted. At almost the same time, he extended health benefits to live-in lovers, giving to non-unionized workers the same benefits as unionized staff. "If I were such a narrow-minded bigot, I would have said, 'They can't have health benefits either,' " he told the Associated Press.

Update, *New York Law Journal* 1, col. 1 (July 26, 1995).

15. See, generally, O'Brien, "Domestic Partnership."

16. In the United States most states have a residency requirement and most require at least a declaration that the marriage is "irretrievably broken." All such legal proceedings at a minimum require service of process on the partner and a court appearance. In some localities judges routinely order the parties to attempt reconciliation or attend mediation.

17. While many states allow so-called no fault divorce, in most states one party must demonstrate that the marriage is "irretrievably broken." One of the easiest methods of demonstrating that fact would be for the party to represent that she had "fallen in love with someone else." In those states, such as New York, that still have rather conservative laws, adultery remains one of the available grounds for divorce.

18. Although adultery prosecutions are rare, they do occur. For example, in Commonwealth v. Stowell, 449 N.E.2d 357 (Ma. 1983), the Massachusetts Supreme Court declined to declare the state adultery statute unconstitutional as an infringement of privacy. Ms. Stowell had challenged the statute after being charged with adultery based upon police officers looking in the window of a van parked off a wooded road and seeing the adult occupants engaged in sex. Responding to the officers, the occupants of the van told the police officers they were married but not to each other. Both were arrested for adultery.

19. Bonnie Zimmerman, *The Safe Sea of Women: Lesbian Fiction 1969–1989,* 34–48 (Boston: Beacon, 1990).

20. Zimmerman noted that most of the lesbian writers in her study, which ended in 1989, seemed to believe in an essential self or core identity. Ibid., 51. Zimmerman then analyzed the derivation of this core identity as either innate or chosen, arguing that in literature these "two models of identity do not necessarily oppose each other." Ibid., 52.

21. Ibid., 77.

22. Ibid.

23. Ann Barr Snitow, "Mass Market Romance: Pornography for Women Is Different," in Ann Snitow, Christine Stansell, and Sharon Thompson, eds., *Powers of Desire: The Politics of Sexuality* (New York: Monthly Review Press, 1983).

24. Zimmerman, *The Safe Sea of Women,* 110.

25. Ibid., 133.

26. *Les Guérillères* was originally published in France in 1969 (Paris: Les Editions de Minuit); the first English translation appeared in the United States in 1971 (New York: Viking Press), with the first mass-market paperback in 1973 (New York: Avon), and subsequent popular versions in 1980 and 1985.

27. Sally Gearheart's *The Wanderground* was originally published by Persephone Press (Watertown, Mass.) in 1978 and, after that press's demise, was reprinted by Alyson Books (Boston) in 1984. Donna Young's *Retreat* was published in 1979 (Tallahassee, Fla.: Naiad). Camarin Grae's *Paz* was published in 1984. She is better known for her subsequent books such as *The Secret in the Bird* (Tallahassee, Fla.: Naiad, 1988) and *Edgewise* (Tallahassee, Fla.: Naiad, 1989).

28. Snitow, "Mass Market Romance," 250–52.

29. Robyn Wiegman, "Introduction: Mapping the Lesbian Postmodern," in Laura Doan, ed., *The Lesbian Postmodern,* 1, 3 (New York: Columbia University Press, 1994).

30. Sue O'Sullivan, "Girls Who Kiss Girls and Who Cares?" in Diane Hamer and Belinda Budge, eds., *The Good, the Bad, and the Gorgeous: Popular Culture's Romance with Lesbianism,* 78, 90 (London, San Francisco: Pandora/HarperCollins, 1994), reprinted in Sue O'Sullivan, *I Used to Be Nice,* 115 (London: Cassell, 1996).

31. Alisa Solomon, "Dykotomies: Scents and Sensibility," in Arlene Stein, ed., *Sisters, Sexperts, Queers: Beyond the Lesbian Nation,* 210, 214 (New York: Plume/Penguin, 1993).

32. Ibid., 91. Sullivan notes, however, that just as the strident lesbian politico is a stereotype, so too is the lesbian who is young and "provocatively attractive and fashionable." "Both images are fantastical; neither image corresponds any more to the multilayered realities of lesbians' lives than any other media caricatures of women do." Ibid., 92.

33. See generally, Karen Thompson and Julie Andrezejewski, *Why Can't Sharon Kowalski Come Home?* (San Francisco: Spinsters/Aunt Lute, 1988).

34. In re Kowalski, 478 N.W.2d 790, 795 (Minn. App. 1991), which discusses unreported trial court's opinion and disagrees.

35. The best interest standard governs awards of child custody and visitation in all United States jurisdictions, although it is interpreted with great variety.

36. Julie Shapiro, "Custody and Conduct: How the Law Fails Lesbian and Gay

Parents and Their Children," 71 *Indiana Law Journal* 623, 647–48 (1996), footnotes omitted.

37. S.E.G. v. R.A.G., 735 S.W.2d 164 (Mo. App. 1987).

38. See also McKay v. Johnson, 1996 WL 12658 (Minn.App. 1996), in which the mother agreed never again to allow children to accompany her lover to a gay and lesbian pride parade; in Hertzler v. Hertzler, 908 P.2d 946 (Wy. 1995), the appellate court reconsidered trial court's finding that a political event harmed the child, stating, "When the judge asked Jimmie about the gay and lesbian pride parade, there was no indication that Jimmie was upset by the parade. In fact, he stated that he did not know what type of parade it was and that the people wore colorful shirts."

39. See, generally, Samuel A. Marcosson, "Symposium: 'Don't Ask Don't Tell.' A Price Too High: Enforcing the Ban on Gays and Lesbians in the Military and the Inevitability of Intrusiveness," 64 *University of Missouri-Kansas City Law Review* 59 (1995); Diane Mazury, "The Unknown Soldier: A Critique of 'Gays in the Military' Scholarship and Litigation," 29 *University of California-Davis Law Review* 223 (1996); C. Dixon Osburn, "Symposium: 'Don't Ask Don't Tell.' A Policy in Desperate Search of a Rationale: The Military's Policy on Lesbians, Gays, and Bisexuals," 64 *University of Missouri-Kansas City Law Review* 199 (1995).

40. S. Rep. No. 112, 103d Cong., 1st Sess. 292 (1993).

41. Kenneth L. Karst, "The Pursuit of Manhood and the Desegregation of the Armed Forces," 38 *University of California-Los Angeles Law Review* 499, 561 (1991).

42. As lesbian theorist Marilyn Frye has noted, "politically correct" has come to be a "term of negative valuation signifying a praxis of righteous bullying combined with superficial and faddish political thought or program." Yet, as Frye argues, this usage is a reversal of its original intent. Frye also argues that the term is worth reclaiming, for being political is valuable, as is being correct. Marilyn Frye, "Getting It Right," 17 *Signs* 781 (1992), reprinted in Marilyn Frye, *Willful Virgin: Essays in Feminism,* 13 (Freedom, Cal.: Crossing, 1993).

43. Heather Conrad, *NEWS,* 238–44 (Racine, Wisc.: Mother Courage, 1987).

44. Despite too many of these lapses, *NEWS* is an engaging novel about ordinary women throughout the world, many of whom are employed as clerical workers, who "take over the world" through their access to corporate and government computers in order to prevent war, famine, and bring economic justice.

45. Interview with Sarah Schulman by Michael Bronksi, *Gay Community News* 16, 20, Spring 1997.

46. Shapiro, "Custody and Conduct."

47. In re Doustou, No. CH93JA0517–00 (Cir. Ct. Of Cty. Of Hendrico, Va. Sept. 7, 1993), on file with author. Doustou is the child Tyler's last name.

48. Bottoms v. Bottoms, 457 S.E.2d 102 (Va. 1995) reversing Bottoms v. Bottoms, 444 S.E.2d 276 (Va. Ct. App. 1994).

49. See chapter 9, this volume.

50. See, for example, New Jersey Rev. Stat. 2c:14–4, criminalizing public lewdness; Vermont Stat. title 13 2601.

51. See, for example, McGuire v. State, 489 So.2d 729 (Fl. 1986), which upheld conviction for indecent exposure of a female jogger who did not wear a top on a public beach; State v. Turner, 382 N.W.2d 252 (Minn. Ct. App. 1986), which upheld conviction for violation of a city ordinance that prohibited topless sunbathing for females; Borough of Belmar v. Buckley, 453 A.2d 910 (N.J. App. Div. 1982), which upheld conviction of a borough ordinance that prohibited indecent exposure for a sunbathing topless female.

52. In In re Williams, 464 S.E.2d 816 (Ga. 1996), the Georgia Supreme Court accepted an attorney's argument in an attorney disciplinary proceeding (which could result in suspension of the attorney's license to practice law) that the attorney's conviction for public indecency was not a crime of moral turpitude and did not bear on his fitness to practice law. Interestingly, the court describes the attorney's crime thusly: "Williams was convicted for conduct which took place in his own apartment, not directly relating to any third persons, other than the two state's witnesses, neighbors in Williams' apartment complex, who had observed Williams while they were on the grounds outside Williams' apartment." Ibid., 818, n. 5.

53. See, for example, State v. Whitaker, 793 P.2d 116 (Ar. App. 1990), which upheld a conviction of "public" lewdness that occurred in the livingroom of a man's house when the man exposed his genitals to members of his family; Greene v. State, 381 S.E.2d 310 (Ga. App.1989), which upheld a conviction for public indecency based on the defendant's appearing nude in the presence of a teenage female babysitter in the bedroom and bathroom of his own home; McGee v. State, 299 S.E.2d 573 (Ga. App. 1983), which allowed the conviction for masturbation of a man in a woman's apartment.

54. In Young v. State, 849 P.2d 336 (Nev. 1993), the court described the lavatory as follows:

The restroom in which the offenses occurred is approximately ten feet wide and fifteen feet long, with a door at the entry which is "locked open" with a deadbolt. Upon entering in an easterly direction, there are two wash basins and two urinals on the south wall. A metal partition separates the basin-urinal area from two commodes. The commodes are on the south wall facing north and are further separated by a partition. Although both stalls are doorless, one cannot see into the stalls from the entrance or the basin/urinal area. The partitions are partial, estimated to be approximately two feet off the ground and extending upward about six feet. The partial partitions allow anyone entering the restroom to see under the partition to determine whether the stalls are occupied.

Thus, although the detectives suspected illegal homosexual activity, their efforts to apprehend the perpetrators were frustrated because "they could be seen and heard approaching the stalls, thus enabling the individuals to discontinue their activities and elude detection." The detectives therefore sought an order authorizing surreptitious surveillance. It was through a strategically placed camera that the state gained the evidence of "public" sex. The court rejected the argument that "public" required being observed by someone other than a person viewing through surreptitious surveillance, as well as constitutional attacks to the surveillance, and sustained the convictions.

55. The legal scholarship on privacy as a source of lesbian and gay rights is vast in the United States, Australia, and Canada. For an overview of these arguments, see Didi Herman, *Rights of Passage: Struggles for Lesbian and Gay Legal Equality* (Toronto: University of Toronto Press, 1994); Victor Samar, *The Right To Privacy: Gay Men, Lesbians, and the Constitution* (Philadelphia: Temple University Press, 1992); Gail Mason, "(Out)Laws: Acts of Proscription in the Sexual Order," in Margaret Thorton, ed., *Public and Private: Feminist Legal Debates,* 66 (Melbourne: Oxford University Press, 1995).

56. See, for example, Thorton, *Public and Private.*

57. See, for example, Mason, "(Out)Laws."

58. Teresa Bruce, "Doing the Nasty: An Argument for Bringing Same-Sex Erotic Conduct Back Into the Courtroom," 81 *Cornell Law Review* 1135 (1996).

59. 478 U.S. 186 (1986).

60. Bruce, "Doing the Nasty," 1171. The argument quoted by Bruce is cited to Marc Fajer, "Can Two Real Men Eat Quiche Together? Storytelling, Gender-Role Stereotypes, and Legal Protection for Lesbians and Gay Men," 46 *University of Miami Law Review* 511, 545–50 (1992).

61. Bruce, "Doing the Nasty," 1171.

62. Several states in the United States have statutes that prohibit discrimination based upon sexual orientations, including Wisconsin (the first state in 1982), Massachusetts, Hawai'i, Connecticut, California, Massachusetts, and New Jersey. Additionally, there are more than one hundred municipal ordinances.

63. The admissibility of such evidence is subject to a state's rape shield statute, which would generally prohibit testimony about a victim's prior sexual history. Compare People v. Kemblowski, 559 N.E.2d 247 (Ill. App. 1990), in which the court reversed admission of victim's testimony that she was a lesbian based upon

the rape shield statute, with State v. Williams, 487 N.E.2d 560 (Oh. 1986), in which the court allowed the defendant to produce evidence of the victim's reputation in the community as a prostitute because she testified on direct examination that she never consented to sex with men because she was a lesbian.

64. See, generally, Shapiro, "Custody and Conduct."

65. See, generally, Evan Wolfson, "Crossing the Threshold: Equal Marriage Rights for Lesbians and Gay Men and the Intra-Community Critique," 21 *New York University Review of Law and Social Change* 567 (1994).

66. While most of the antigay rhetoric and representation is devoted to gay male sexuality, lesbian sexuality is easily assimilated into the model of "disease, anarchy, excess, deceit" and satanism. See Didi Herman, *The Anti-Gay Agenda: Orthodox Vision and the Christian Right,* 108–9 (Chicago: University of Chicago Press, 1997).

67. See generally, Lillian Faderman, *Surpassing the Love of Men* (New York: Morrow, 1980), a historical analysis of the toleration of women's "romantic" friendships and the demise of that toleration with the sexualization of women's relationships.

68. See, generally, Didi Herman, *Rights of Passage*; Ruthann Robson, *Lesbian (Out)Law: Survival Under the Rule of Law* (Ithaca: Firebrand, 1992); Susan Boyd, "Expanding the 'Family' in Family Law: Recent Ontario Proposals on Same Sex Relationships," 7 *Canadian Journal of Women and the Law/Revue Femmes et Droit* 545 (1994); Brenda Cossman, "Family Inside/Out," 44 *University of Toronto Law Journal* 1 (1994); Paula Ettlebrick, "Wedlock Alert: A Comment on Lesbian and Gay Family Recognition," 5 *Journal of Law and Policy* 107 (1996); Steven K. Homer, Note, "Against Marriage," 29 *Harvard Civil Rights–Civil Liberties Law Review* 505 (1994); Robert Morris Kap (ā'ihiahilina), "Configuring the Bo(u)nds of Marriage: The Implications of Hawaiian Culture and Values for the Debate About Homogamy," 8 *Yale Journal of Law and Humanities* 105 (1996); Ann Robinson, "Lesbiennes, marriage et famille," 7 *Canadian Journal of Women and Law* 393 (1994); Ruthann Robson, "Resisting the Family: Repositioning Lesbians in Feminist Legal Theory," 19 *Signs* 975 (1994); Wolfson, "Crossing the Threshold."

69. The genesis of such statutes against marital status discrimination, however, is not based upon preferences given to married persons, although married men were routinely awarded higher wages in the United States under the so-called family wage custom. Instead, marital status discrimination was necessitated by the routine and widespread discrimination against married women. See, generally, Deborah Rhode, *Justice and Gender,* 24–8 (Cambridge: Harvard University Press, 1989); Reva B. Siegel, "The Modernization of Marital Status Law:

Adjudicating Wives' Rights to Earnings, 1860–1930," 82 *Georgetown Law Journal* 2127 (1994).

70. As reported by the *San Francisco Chronicle,* A15, April 15, 1997, at the weekly supervisors' meeting the day before board of supervisor Leslie Katz introduced "measures updating the city's human rights ordinance to add anti-discrimination language against people based on their marital status and their domestic partner status. The proposal also would ban discrimination based on the perception of someone's status."

71. This example is derived from litigation in the United States concerning marital status discrimination against unmarried heterosexual cohabitants by a landlord who raises a religious exemption. See Swanner v. Anchorage Equal Rights Comm'n, 874 P.2d 274 (Alaska) (per curiam), cert. denied, 115 S. Ct. 460 (1994); Smith v. Fair Employment and Hous. Comm'n, 30 Cal. Rptr. 2d 395 (Ct. App.), review granted and opinion superseded by 880 P.2d 111 (Cal. 1994); Donahue v. Fair Employment and Hous. Comm'n, 2 Cal. Rptr. 2d 32 (Ct. App. 1991), review granted and opinion superseded by 825 P.2d 766 (Cal. 1992), review dismissed, 859 P.2d 671 (Cal. 1993); Attorney General v. Desilets, 636 N.E.2d 233 (Mass. 1994); State by Cooper v. French, 460 N.W.2d 2 (Minn. 1990).

For discussions of the cases and doctrinal explication of the conflict between prohibiting discrimination on the basis of marital status and the free exercise of religion, see David Kushner, Note, "Free Exercise, Fair Housing, and Marital Status— Alaskan Style," 12 *Alaska Law Review* 335 (1995); Malgorzata (Margo) K. Laskowska, Comment, " 'No Sinners Under My Roof': Can California Landlords Refuse to Rent to Unmarried Couples by Claiming a Religious Freedom of Exercise Exemption from a Statute Which Prohibits Marital Status Discrimination?" 36 *Santa Clara Law Review* 219 (1995).

72. Zimmerman, *The Safe Sea of Women*.

73. Jeanette Winterson, *Art Objects: Essays on Ecstasy and Effrontery,* 191 (New York: Vintage, 1995).

8. States of Marriage

1. Bowers v. Hardwick, 478 U.S. 186 (1986).

2. Generally, such laws employ one or more of these three distinct strategies to criminalize lesbian and gay sexual expression: the natural strategy, the anatomically specific strategy, and the gender-specific strategy. The natural strategy relies upon understandings of "naturalized" sexuality as including only a certain traditional type of heterosexuality. The anatomically specific strategy prohibits certain body parts of one person from coming into contact with certain body parts of

another person. The gender-specific strategy, a rather recent development, prohibits sexual contact between persons of the same sex and might even prohibit a person kissing another person of the same gender.

3. Criminal Code (Tas) ss 122 and 123 is presently being considered by the High Court in *Toonen*. For discussions of the controversy, see Rodney Croome, "Sexual (Mis)Conduct: The High Court and Gay Law Reform in Tasmania" (1995) 20 *Alternative Law Journal* 282; Myke Dobber, "Sex Crime" (1995) 20 *Alternative Law Journal* 285.

4. For example, as recently as 1996 many men were prosecuted for solicitation of sodomy pursuant to a municipal ordinance in Topeka, Kansas, T.C.C. section 54–133. The definition of sodomy is based upon KS ST 21–3505, which provides that criminal sodomy is "sodomy between persons who are 16 or more years of age and members of the same sex or between a person and an animal" and sodomy is defined as " oral contact or oral penetration of the female genitalia or oral contact of the male genitalia; anal penetration, however slight, of a male or female by any body part or object; or oral or anal copulation or sexual intercourse between a person and an animal." Such men typically became the targets of criminal prosecution when approached by undercover law enforcement officers while sitting in their cars in the lot of a public park; an officer would engage in casual conversation and obtain a vague promise for a sexual relationship to occur in a private residence. See City of Topeka v. Movsovitz, Case No. 95-MC-00021 (in the District Court of Shawnee County, Kansas). I am grateful to Professor Charlene Smith of Washburn University College of Law, Topeka, Kansas, for information regarding this case and the opportunity to meet Max Movsovitz, the defendant who is challenging the constitutionality of the ordinance.

5. For example, in Bottoms v. Bottoms, 457 S.E. 2d 102 (Va. 1995), the Virginia Supreme Court upheld a trial court that expressed this view.

6. The so-called nexus test for custody requires that there be a showing of harm caused by the parent's sexual behavior. However, even courts employing this "liberal" test (as compared to the per se disqualification test), often resort to rhetoric concerning the example set by a nonlaw-abiding citizen.

7. Sex in such an instance has been interpreted to mean only gender and not sexual orientation or transgenderism. For discussions of the doctrinal intricacies that have developed because of this approach, see Mary Ann Case, "Disaggregating Gender from Sex and Sexual Orientation: The Effeminate Man in the Law and Feminist Jurisprudence," 105 *Yale Law Journal* 1 (1995); Katherine Franke, "The Central Mistake of Sex Discrimination Law: The Disaggregation of Sex from Gender," 144 *University Pennsylvania Law Review* 1 (1995).

8. At present in the United States these laws are limited to those passed by

municipalities and a handful of states, including Wisconsin (the first in 1982), Massachusetts, Hawai'i, Connecticut, California, Minnesota, and New Jersey. A recent vote on the Employment Discrimination Act of 1995, Senate Bill 2056, that would have prohibited discrimination on the basis of sexual orientation in employment (exempting, however, the military and religious organizations) was defeated by a single vote in the United States Senate on September 10, 1996.

9. The Hate Crime Statistics Act, 28 U.S.C. s 534, mandates the collection of data concerning crimes evincing prejudice on the basis of "race, religion, sexual orientation, or ethnicity." Interestingly, the Act does not include gender as a category. While the federal statute only relates to the collection of statistics, a few states have enhanced penalties for criminal acts that evince bias, including bias on the basis of sexuality; see, for example, New Hampshire Revised Statutes ss 651.6.

10. Romer v. Evans, ___ U.S. ____, 116 S.Ct. 1620 (1996).

11. 483 U.S. 522 (1987).

12. Hurley v. Irish-American Gay, Lesbian and Bisexual Group of Boston, 515 U.S. 557 (1995).

13. Advocates in *Hurley,* however, also argued that the parade itself was an affair of state, given the tremendous support—in terms of state services and resources—that the City of Boston lent to the parade.

14. The text of the amendment entitled "No Protected Status Based on Homosexual, Lesbian, or Bisexual Orientation" provides:

> Neither the State of Colorado, through any of its branches or departments, nor any of its agencies, political subdivisions, municipalities or school districts, shall enact, adopt or enforce any statute, regulation, ordinance or policy whereby homosexual, lesbian or bisexual orientation, conduct, practices or relationships shall constitute or otherwise be the basis of or entitle any person or class of persons to have or claim any minority status, quota preferences, protected status or claim of discrimination. This Section of the Constitution shall be in all respects self-executing.

15. As the Court stated, "We must conclude that Amendment 2 classifies homosexuals not to further a proper legislative end but to make them unequal to everyone else. This Colorado cannot do. A State cannot so deem a class of persons a stranger to its laws."

16. Romer v. Evans, ___ U.S. at ___, 116 S.Ct. at 1629 (Scalia dissenting).

17. See Singer v. Hara, 522 P.2d 1187 (Wa. 1974).

18. 852 P.d. 44 (Haw. 1993).

19. Article 1, section 5 of the Hawai'i constitution provides: "No person shall be deprived of life, liberty or property without due process of law, nor be denied

the equal protection of the laws, nor be denied the enjoyment of the person's civil rights or be discriminated against in the exercise thereof because of race, religion, sex or ancestry." Haw. Const. art. I, s 5 (1978).

In addition to the equal protection claim on which they prevailed, plaintiffs also argued that the denials of marriage licenses to same sex couples was a denial of the right to due process under Article 1, section 5, and a denial of the right to privacy under Article I, section 6 of the Hawai'i constitution, which explicitly provides that "the right of the people to privacy is recognized and shall not be infringed without the showing of a compelling state interest." The court, however, rejected both the due process and privacy claims, concluding that it did not believe that "a right to same-sex marriage is so rooted in the traditions and collective conscience of our people that failure to recognize it would violate the fundamental principles of liberty and justice that lie at the base of all our civil and political institutions" or "that a right to same-sex marriage is implicit in the concept of ordered liberty, such that neither liberty nor justice would exist if it were sacrificed." 852 P.d. at 556–57.

20. Baehr v. Miike, 65 USLW 2399, 1996 W.L. 694235 (Circ. Ct. Haw. (December 3, 1996). Lawrence Miike is the director of the Department of Health, substituted for the previous director, Lewin.

21. PL 104–199, 110 Stat. 2419 to be codified at 28 U.S.C. 1738C.

22. The statute provides:

No State, territory, or possession of the United States, or Indian tribe, shall be required to give effect to any public act, record, or judicial proceeding of any other State, territory, possession or tribe respecting a relationship between persons of the same sex that is treated as a marriage under the laws of such other State, territory, possession, or tribe, or a right or claim arising from such relationship.

23. [1996] NZFLR 481. The six plaintiffs were three female couples who had applied to the Registrar General for marriage licenses and been denied.

24. Ibid., 505.

25. M. V. H., (1996), 27 O.R. (3d) 593, 132 D.L.R. (4th) 538 (Ont. Ct. (Gen. Div.)).

26. Canada (Attorney General) v. Mossop, (1993), 17 C.H.R.R. D/349 (S.C.C.).

27. Egan v. Canada, (1995), 2 S.C.R. 513, 124 D.L.R. (4th) 609.

28. See, for example, Susan Boyd, "Expanding the 'Family' in Family Law: Recent Ontario Proposals on Same-Sex Relationships," 7 *Canadian Journal of Women and the Law/Revue Femmes et Droit* 545 (1994), which discusses Ontario; Ann Robinson, "Lesbiennes, marriage et famille," 7 *Canandian Journal of Women and Law* 393 (1994), which discusses Quebec.

29. For an intelligent and comprehensive discussion of the Canadian context, see Didi Herman, *Rights of Passage: Struggles for Lesbian and Gay Legal Equality* (Toronto: University of Toronto Press, 1994).

30. W. v. G. (Supreme Court of NSW, Equity Division, Hodgson J, 2 February 1996, Ref No 4607 of 1994).

31. Quilter, [1996] NZFLR 505.

32. Section 4, New Zealand Bill of Rights.

33. M. V. H., 134 D.L.R. 4th at 560(x).

34. Importantly, however, while the Canadian Charter is constitutional, it does not include a specific provision on sexual orientation, unlike the New Zealand Bill of Rights. However, Canada does not contain a section similar to section 4 of the Bill of Rights.

35. M. v. H. 134 D.L.R. 4th at 560. Quoting Speech of Chief Justice Lamer to the Empire Club of Canada, April 1995.

36. See Honorable Mr. Justice W. M. C. Gummow, "Full Faith and Credit in Three Federations," 46 *South Carolina Law Review* 979 (1995), which discusses the United States, Canada and Australia.

37. U.S. Const. Art IV 1.

38. See, for example, Robert L. Cordell II, "Same-Sex Marriage: the Fundamental Right of Marriage and an Examination of Conflict of Laws and the Full Faith and Credit Clause," 26 *Columbia Human Rights Law Review* 247 (1994); Barbara J. Cox, "Same-Sex Marriage and Choice-of-Law: If We Marry in Hawaii, Are We Still Married When We Return Home?" 1994 *Wisconsin Law Review* 1033; Deborah M. Henson, "Will Same-Sex Marriages Be Recognized in Sister States? Full Faith and Credit and Due Process Limitations on States' Choice of Law Regarding the Status and Incidents of Homosexual Marriages Following Hawaii's *Baehr v. Lewin,*" 32 *University of Louisville Journal of Family Law* 551 (1993–94); Thomas M. Keane, "Aloha Marriage? Constitutional and Choice of Law Arguments for Recognition of Same Sex Marriages," 47 *Stanford Law Review* 499 (1995).

39. Although the availability of legalized marriage does not necessarily mean that a group is considered equal, as is the situation with the granting of previously withheld legalized marriage to former slaves in the American South. See Laura F. Edwards, " 'The Marriage Covenant Is at the Foundation of All Our Rights': The Politics of Slave Marriages in North Carolina After Emancipation," 14 *Law and History Review* 81 (1996).

40. Human Rights Act 21 (m).

41. While some may consider this view rather harsh, it nevertheless seems to me that once the court recognizes that discrimination on the basis of sexual orientation is occurring, then all else is tangential.

42. Quilter, [1996] NZFLR, 486.

43. Quilter, [1996] NZFLR, 489. The statutes the Court considered included the Family Protection Act of 1955; the Administration Act 1969, as amended 1987; the Joint Family Homes Act 1964; the Judicature Act 1908; the Legal Services Act 1991; the Matrimonial Property Act 1976; the Family Proceedings Act 1980; the Parental Leave in Employment Protection Act 1987; the Rates Rebate Act 1973; Social Security Act 1964; the Status of Children Amendment Act 1987; the Accident Rehabilitation and Compensation Insurance Act 1993; the Adoption Act 1955; the Government Superannuation Fund 1956; and the Holidays Act 1981. The Court reasoned that because the words *husband* or *wife* appear in the statutes, this would mean that if same-sex marriage were allowed, these statutes would not be applicable to such marriages.

44. House Report No. 104–664 (July 9, 1996). 104th Cong., 2nd Sess. 1996.

45. The House Report attempts to deflect the obvious objections to its articulation of procreation as the purpose of marriage by resorting to *ipse dixit* reasoning:

> There are two standard attacks for this rationale for opposing a redefinition of marriage to include homosexual unions. First, it is noted that society permits heterosexual couples to marry regardless of whether they intend or are even able to have children. But this is not a serious argument. Surely no one would propose requiring couples intending to marry to submit to a medical examination to determine whether they can reproduce or to sign a pledge indicating that they intended to do so. Such steps would be both offensive and unworkable. Rather, society has made the eminently sensible judgment to permit heterosexuals to marry, notwithstanding the fact that some couples cannot or simply choose not to have children.
>
> Second, it will be objected that there are greater threats to marriage and families than the one posed by same-sex "marriage," the most prominent of which is divorce. There is great force in this argument. . . . But the fact that marriage is embattled is surely no argument for opening a new front in the war.

Ibid.

46. 852 P.2d at 57.

47. As the court stated:

> "Homosexual" and "same-sex" marriages are not synonymous; by the same token, a "heterosexual" same-sex marriage is, in theory, not oxymoronic. A "homosexual" person is defined as "[o]ne sexually attracted to another of the same sex." Taber's Cyclopedic Medical Dictionary 839 (16th ed. 1989). "Homosexuality" is "sexual desire or behavior directed toward a person or

persons of one's own sex." Webster's Encyclopedic Unabridged Dictionary of the English Language 680 (1989). Conversely, "heterosexuality" is "[s]exual attraction for one of the opposite sex," Taber's Cyclopedic Medical Dictionary at 827, or "sexual feeling or behavior directed toward a person or persons of the opposite sex." Webster's Encyclopedic Unabridged Dictionary of the English Language at 667. Parties to "a union between a man and a woman" may or may not be homosexuals. Parties to a same-sex marriage could theoretically be either homosexuals or heterosexuals.

Ibid. 52, n. 11.

48. Ibid., 52, n. 12.

49. See Singer v. Hara, 522 P.2d 1187 (Wash. App. 1974), which relies on Article 31 of the Washington constitution, providing "equality of rights and responsibilities shall not be denied or abridged on account of sex."

50. Quilter, [1996] NZFLR, 486.

51. Ibid.

52. 355 A.2d 204 (N.J. App. 1976).

53. Ibid., 209.

54. For a brilliant and comprehensive discussion of the range of theoretical approaches that might apply, see Margaret Davies, *Asking the Law Question* (Sydney: Sweet and Maxwell, 1994).

55. For a cogent examination of what she calls the We Are Family/We Are Not Family debate, see Brenda Cossman, "Family Inside/Out," 44 *University of Toronto Law Journal* 1 (1994). For a response to intracommunity criticism that gay/lesbian marriage may be problematic, see Evan Wolfson, "Crossing the Threshold: Equal Marriage Rights for Lesbians and Gay Men and the Intra-Community Critique," 21 *New York University Review of Law and Social Change* 567 (1994).

56. For a detailed discussion of the circumstances surrounding the litigation, see Karen Thompson and Julie Andrzejewski, *Why Can't Sharon Kowalski Come Home?* (San Francisco: Spinsters/Aunt Lute, 1988).

57. Ibid.

58. *In re Kowalski*, 478 N.W.2d 790 (Minn. App. 1991).

59. Ibid., 797.

60. Hilary Astor, "Mediation of Intra-Lesbian Disputes," 20 *Melbourne University Law Review* 953 (1996).

61. W. v. G. (Supreme Court of NSW, Equity Division, Hodgson J, 2 February 1996, Ref No 4607 of 1994).

62. Ibid., 40.

63. For an overview of Australian law, see Gail Mason, "(Out)Laws: Acts of

Proscription in the Sexual Order," in Margaret Thorton, ed., *Public and Private: Feminist Legal Debates,* 66, 72–76 (Melbourne: Oxford University Press, 1995); Sylvia Winters, "Gay and Lesbian Relationships and the Law of New South Wales," 1 *Australian Gay and Lesbian Law Journal* 72–80 (1992).

64. The notion of equality is itself problematic. For example, in seeking equality to heterosexuals, gay men and lesbians make heterosexuality the norm by which other sexualities are measured. This then provokes other issues, such as whether other sexualities are entitled to formal equality or comparable equality, as evidenced by the so-called sameness/difference debates of feminist legal theory.

65. The Ford Pinto was a subcompact car manufactured by the Ford Motor Company of the United States with a fuel tank positioned behind (rather than above) the rear axle, a series of bolts located near the fuel tank that could pierce the tank, a fuel filler tank prone to disconnect, causing gasoline to spill, and an economic bumper. These specifications contributed to the Pinto's propensity to burst into flames when the car was involved in a rear-end collision. The Ford Pinto situation became especially notorious because there is evidence that the corporation had knowledge of the design defects that could cause death but performed a cost-benefit analysis (valuing each life at $200,000), determining that the costs of remedying the problems by a safety device, which would have cost Ford $137,000,000, did not outweigh the benefit of the lives saved, which would have cost Ford only $36,000,000. See Grimsahw v. Ford Motor Company, 119 Cal. App. 757, 174 Cal. Rptr. 348 (1981); Gary T. Schwartz, "The Myth of the Ford Pinto Case," 43 *Rutgers Law Review* 1013 (1991).

66. Although not so radical that other legal scholars do not agree. See, generally, Martha Fineman, *The Neutered Mother* (New York: Routledge, 1996); Wayne Morgan, "Love is a Battlefield," presentation at ALTA, 1996. See also Steven K. Homer, Student Note, "Against Marriage," 29 *Harvard Civil Rights-Civil Liberties Law Review* 505 (1994).

67. Robert Morris (Kap ā'ihiahilina), "Configuring the Bo(u)nds of Marriage: The Implications of Hawaiian Culture and Values for the Debate About Homogamy," 8 *Yale Journal of Law and Humanities* 105 (1996).

68. See chapter 9.

69. Jane Kelsey, *The New Zealand Experiment: A World Model for Structural Adjustment?* (Auckland: Aukland University Press, 1995) 332–34.

70. Ibid., 224.

71. See Anna Yeatman, "Justice and the Sovereign Self," in Margaret Wilson and Anna Yeatman, eds., *Justice and Identity: Antipodean Practices,* 195 (1995). See also Margaret Thorton, "Embodying the Citizen," in Thorton, *Public and Private,* 198.

9. Resisting the Family: Repositioning Lesbians in Legal Theory

1. Michael Grossberg, *Governing the Hearth* (Chapel Hill: University of North Carolina Press, 1985).

2. See Celia Kitzinger and Rachel Perkins, *Changing Our Minds: Lesbian Feminism and Psychology* (New York: New York University Press, 1993); Caryatis Cardea, "Lesbian Revolution and the Fifty-Minute Hour: A Working Class Look at Therapy and the Movement," in Jeffner Allen, ed., *Lesbian Philosophies and Cultures* (Albany: State University of New York Press, 1990).

3. Martha Burnham, "An Impossible Marriage: Slave Law and Family Law," 5 *Journal of Law and Inequality* 198 (1987).

4. Jane Collier, Michele Rosaldo, and Sylvia Yanagisako, "Is There a Family? New Anthropological Views," in Barrie Thorne and Marilyn Yalom, eds., *Rethinking the Family: Some Feminist Questions,* 2d ed., 31 (Boston: Northeastern University Press, 1992).

5. Kath Weston, *Families We Choose: Lesbians, Gays, Kinship,* 99 (New York: Columbia University Press, 1991).

6. I am appreciative of the research conducted by Lisa Sbrana for these citations. When I asked her to complete this assignment and put it on my desk, I did not expect to find a neatly organized but nonetheless overflowing carton of computer printouts. This mass is a tangible testament to the mass of references to the family in only a few of the many jurisdictions.

7. See chapter 2, this volume.

8. Braschi v. Stahl Associates, 74 N.E.2d 201, 543 N.E.2d 49, 544 N.Y.S.2d 784 (1989).

9. In re Kowalski, 478 N.W.2d 790 (Minn. App. 1991).

10. Alison D. v. Virginia M., 77 N.Y.2d 651, 572 N.E.2d 27, 569 N.Y.S.2d 586 (1991).

11. For an extended discussion of the situation, see Karen Thompson and Julie Andrzejewski, *Why Can't Sharon Kowalski Come Home?* (San Francisco: Spinsters/Aunt Lute, 1988).

12. 478 N.W.2d at 795, 796.

13. Kaye suggested that it "should be required that the relationship with the child came into being with the consent of the biological or legal parent" and that the person seeking visitation "at least have had joint custody of the child for a significant period of time." She also noted that other factors should likely be added, but did not specify what such factors might be.

14. In footnote 3 of its opinion, the court notes that its definition of the family in *Braschi* is "completely unrelated to the concept of the 'functional family' as that term has developed" in the zoning cases which "have absolutely no bearing" on

the scope of the noneviction protections at issue in *Braschi*. The adamancy of the court's disclaimer is rather disingenuous: both *Braschi* and the zoning cases involve the right to occupy property and constructions of the family that will be enforced through state power.

15. See Deborah Anna Luepnitz, *The Family Interpreted: Psychoanalysis, Feminism, and Family Therapy* (New York: Basic, 1988), arguing against family psychologists who have naturalized and universalized family functions, especially as such functions are gendered; Collier, Rosaldo, and Yanagisako, "Is There a Family?" 31 , which critiques Malinowski's functionalist approach to family and his conclusion of the universality of the family.

16. Catharine MacKinnon, *A Feminist Theory of the State* (Cambridge: Harvard University Press, 1989).

17. Martha Fineman, *The Neutered Mother* (New York: Routledge, 1996).

18. Martha Minow, "Redefining Families: Who's In and Who's Out?" 62 *University of Colorado Law Review* 269 (1991).

19. Joan Nestle, *A Restricted Country,* 123 (New York: Firebrand, 1989).

20. Andrew Sullivan, "Here Comes the Groom: A (Conservative) Case for Gay Marriage," *New Republic,* 20, August 28, 1989.

21. Weston, *Families We Choose,* 202–5.

22. The example is from Deborah Rhode, *Justice and Gender* (Cambridge: Harvard University Press, 1989).

23. As expressed by Foucault, there is a

plurality of resistances, each of them a special case: resistances that are possible, necessary, improbable; others that are spontaneous, savage, solitary, concerted, rampant, or violent; still others that are quick to compromise, interested, or sacrificial; by definition, they can only exist in the strategic field of power relations. But this does not mean that they are only a reaction or rebound, forming with respect to the basic domination an underside that is in the end always passive, doomed to perpetual defeat.

Michel Foucault, *The History of Sexuality: An Introduction,* trans. Robert Hurley, 96 (New York: Vintage, 1978).

24. Ibid.

25. Michele Barrett and Mary McIntosh, *The Anti-Social Family,* 159 (London: Verso, 1982).

26. Sarah Lucia Hoagland, *Lesbian Ethics* 63 (Palo Alto: Institute for Lesbian Studies, 1988).

27. See Mary Coombs, "Agency and Partnership: A Study of Breach of Promise Plaintiffs," 2 *Yale Journal of Law and Feminism* 1 (1989).

28. Urusla LeGuin, "She Unnames Them," in Irene Zahava, ed., *Hear the Silence: Stories by Women of Myth, Magic, and Renewal* (Trumansburg, N.Y.: Crossing, 1986).

10. The Third Sex, Third Parties, and Child Custody

1. David F. Greenburg, *The Construction of Homosexuality*, 406 (Chicago: University of Chicago Press, 1988).

2. Congressional Record, 49th Congress, 1st Session, March 26, 1886, p. 2786.

3. See, generally, Lillian Faderman, *Odd Girls and Twilight Lovers: A History of Lesbian Life in Twentieth-Century America*, 35–61 (New York: Columbia University Press, 1991); Lillian Faderman, *Surpassing the Love of Men: Romantic Friendship and Love Between Women from the Renaissance to the Present*, 239–53 (New York: Morrow, 1981); Greenburg, *The Construction of Homosexuality*, 397–433; George Chauncey, Jr., "From Sexual Inversion to Homosexuality: Medicine and the Changing Conceptualization of Female Deviance," 58–59 *Salmagundi* 114 (1982–1983).

4. Faderman, *Surpassing the Love of Men*, 240.

5. Karl Friedrich Otto Westphal, "Die Kontrare Sexualempfindung: Symptom eines neuropathologischen (psycopathischen) Zustandes," 2 *Archiv fur Psychiatrie und Nervenkrankheiten* 73–108 (1869), cited in Faderman, *Odd Girls*, 316.

6. Havelock Ellis, *Studies in the Psychology of Sex: Sexual Inversion* (Philadelphia: Temple University Press, 1901 [1897]).

7. Richard von Krafft-Ebing, *Psychopathia Sexualis: A Medico-Forensic Study*, trans. Harry Wedeck (New York: Putnam, 1965 [1886]).

8. For a general history of the American sexologists, see Janice M. Irvine, *Disorders of Desire: Sex and Gender in Modern American Sexology* (Philadelphia: Temple University Press, 1990).

9. Ellis, *Studies in the Psychology of Sex*, 195.

10. Ibid., 200–2.

11. As George Chauncey notes, Havelock Ellis considered that his theories, specifically the congenital basis of homosexuality, had "politically progressive implications, since it might remove homosexual behavior from the purview of the law." Chauncey, "From Sexual Inversion to Homosexuality," 136.

12. See Erwin J. Haeberle, "Swastika, Pink Triangle, and Yellow Star: The Destruction of Sexology and the Persecution of Homosexuals in Nazi Germany," in Martin Duberman, Martha Vicinus, George Chauncey, Jr., eds., *Hidden from History: Reclaiming the Gay and Lesbian Past*, 365 (New York: New American Library/Penguin, 1989).

13. Jonathan Katz, *Gay American History: Lesbians and Gay Men in the U.S.A.,* 129–207 (New York: Cromwell, 1976).

14. Ibid., 129.

15. Ellis, Studies in the Psychology of Sex, 253.

16. Ibid., 254.

17. Ibid., 255.

18. Faderman, *Odd Girls,* 41.

19. J. D'Emilio and Estelle Freedman, *Intimate Matters: A History of Sexuality in America,* 57 (New York: Harper and Row, 1988).

20. As George Chauncey points out, "Most of the early accounts of sexual inversion discussed only the invert, leaving her sexual partner anonymous and undefined. . . . Many accounts simply treated [these sexual partners] as normal wives, playing their proper feminine roles, as if it did not matter that their 'husbands' were biologically female." Chauncey, "From Sexual Inversion to Homosexuality," 125. Although Chauncey notes that subsequent sexologists began to take more interest in the so-called passive homosexual woman (ibid., 128–29), there was a continuing argument that the nonmasculine lesbian remains essentially untheorized—and perhaps untheorizable—in the medical model of homosexuality that is based upon a heterosexual matrix. See, for example, Esther Newton, "The Mythic Mannish Lesbian: Radclyffe Hall and the New Woman," in Duberman, *Hidden from History,* 281, 292, who refers to the nonmasculinized lesbian lover Mary in Radclyffe Hall's famous lesbian novel, asserting that "Mary's real story has yet to be told."

21. Ellis, *Studies in the Psychology of Sex,* 256.

22. Faderman, *Odd Girls,* 40.

23. Ellis, *Studies in the Psychology of Sex,* 262.

24. Carol Smith-Rosenberg, "Discourses of Sexuality and Subjectivity: The New Woman, 1870–1936," in Duberman, Vicinus, Chauncey, *Hidden from History,* 264, 271.

25. Chauncey persuasively supports his conclusion of "the organic relationship between the women's movement and inversion" with this passage from an article published in 1900:

> The female possessed of masculine ideas of independence; the viragint who would sit in the public highway and lift up her pseudo-virile voice, proclaiming her sole right to decide questions of war or religion, or the value of celibacy and the curse of women's impurity, and that disgusting antisocial being, the female sexual pervert, are simply different degrees of the same class—degenerates.

Chauncey, "From Sexual Inversion to Homosexuality," 141, quoting William Lee Howard, "Effeminate Men and Masculine Women," 71 *New York Medical Journal* 686, 687 (1900).

26. In his diagnosis of a "case of homosexuality in a woman," Freud disagrees with the notion of a third sex, instead concluding that there is a "continual mingling and blending" of inherited and acquired factors," which undergirds the importance of Freud's finding that his young female patient was "in fact a feminist." Sigmund Freud, "The Psychogenesis of a Case of Homosexuality in a Woman" (1920), in Sigmund Freud, *The Standard Edition of the Complete Psychological Works of Sigmund Freud,* 18:146–72, ed. James Strachey (in collaboration with Anna Freud), 24 vols. (London: Hogarth, 1955). Of course, this patient also exhibited a strong attachment to her mother and an envy of her brother's penis, ibid., 000–00, although Freud's earlier work describes such characteristics as universally female, see Sigmund Freud, "Femininity," *Standard Edition,* 22:112–35 (1956).

27. Cf. Sheila Kitzinger, *The Social Construction of Lesbianism,* 42 (London: Sage, 1987), which argues that the "effect of the new science of sexology was to scare women back into marriage and conformity" and states that "one reason" historians "cited for the demise of the first wave of feminism was the success of the sexologists' diagnosis of feminists as suffering from the newly invented disease" of lesbianism.

28. See Radicalesbians, "The Woman Identified Woman," in Anne Koedt, Ellen Levine, and Anita Rapone, eds., *Radical Feminism,* 240, 242 (New York: Quadrangle/New York Times, 1973): "Lesbian is the word, the label, the condition that holds women in line"; Anne Koedt, "Lesbianism and Feminism," ibid., 246, 246–48, which discusses "lesbian baiting."

29. Psychoanalysis is linked with sexology and sexual theory, and Freud's work is undoubtedly indebted to the work of many sexologists. As the scholar Jeffrey Weeks notes, in Freud's influential "Three Essays on the Theory of Sexuality," *Standard Edition,* 7:125–243 (1953), published in 1905, he acknowledges the contributions of sexologists Krafft-Ebing and Havelock Ellis, as well as others. Jeffrey Weeks, *Sexuality and Its Discontents: Meanings, Myths, and Modern Sexualities,* 67–68 (London and New York: Routledge, 1985).

30. The most obvious example is Radclyffe Hall's *The Well of Loneliness* (Garden City, N.Y.: Blue Ribbon Books, 1928), the first edition of which contained an introduction by none other than the famous sexologist Havelock Ellis. It was banned in Great Britian for its explicit defense of lesbianism and, for several decades, was considered to be the foremost lesbian novel. See Jeanette Foster, *Sex Variant Women in Literature,* 279–80 (Tallahassee, Fla.: Naiad, 1985 [1956]), which describes the publication of *The Well,* its reception, as well as a plot synopsis and

critical evaluation; Bonnie Zimmerman, *The Safe Sea of Women: Lesbian Fiction 1969–1980,* 7 (Boston: Beacon, 1990): "For over forty years, *The Well of Loneliness* and Stephen Gordon [the main character] virtually defined lesbianism"; and Newton, "The Mythic Mannish Lesbian," 282, which discusses the implications of the fact that "*The Well*, at least until 1970, was *the* lesbian novel."

31. According to Weeks, *Sexuality and Its Discontents*, 73, "Sexology did not appear spontaneously at the end of the nineteenth century. It was constructed upon a host of pre-existing writings and social endeavors."

32. Michael Warner, "Introduction," in Michael Warner, ed., *Fear of a Queer Planet: Queer Politics and Social Theory,* vii, xxi–xxii (Minneapolis: University of Minnesota Press, 1993).

33. Of course, the entire biological foundations of parenthood are presently contested. The legal consequences of such contests have provoked much commentary. See, for example, Lori Andrews and Lisa Douglas, "Alternative Reproduction," 65 *Southern California Law Review* 623 (1991); Janet Dolgin, "Just a Gene: Judicial Assumptions About Parenthood," 40 *University of California-Los Angeles Law Review* 637 (1993).

34. Meyer v. Nebraska, 262 U.S. 390 (1923).

35. Pierce v. Society of Sisters, 268 U.S. 510 (1925).

36. 262 U.S., 399.

37. 268 U.S., 534–35.

38. Ibid., 535–36.

39. The *Lochner* era is generally dated from Allgeyer v. Louisiana, 165 U.S. 578 (1897) until Nebbia v. New York, 291 U.S. 502 (1934). The era takes its name from its most notorious case, Lochner v. New York, 198 U.S. 45 (1905), in which the Court declared unconstitutional a state statute limiting work hours in bakeries to sixty hours per week and ten hours per day because it interfered with "liberty of contract" protected by the due process clause of the fourteenth amendment. According to one scholar, *Lochner* is "one of the most condemned cases in United States history and has been used to symbolize judicial dereliction and abuse." Bernard Siegan, *Economic Liberties and the Constitution,* 23 (Chicago: University of Chicago Press, 1980). Other commentators agree. See, generally, Baker, "Property and Its Relation to Constitutionally Protected Liberty," 134 *University of Pennsylvania Law Review* 741 (1986); Robert McCloskey, "Economic Due Process and the Supreme Court," in Philip Kurland, ed., *Supreme Court Review: 1962,* 34–62 (Chicago: University of Chicago Press, 1962); Cass Sunstein, "Lochner's *Legacy*," 87 *Columbia Law Review* 873 (1987).

40. This choice is an individual right to make the decision, but, importantly, it is also a right of access to information about the decision. Thus in *Griswold,*

involving arrests for providing "information, instruction and medical advice" concerning the use of contraception, Justice Douglas relied upon the educational—rather than the parenting—aspects of *Meyer* and *Pierce* to declare that the state may not "contract the spectrum of available knowledge." Griswold v. Connecticut, 381 U.S. 479, 482 (1965).

41. Planned Parenthood of Southeastern Pennsylvania v. Casey, 510 U.S. 1309 (1992).

42. Lassiter v. Department of Social Services, 452 U.S. 18 (1981). Writing for a bare majority of the Court, Stewart accorded some weight to the state's contention that termination proceedings are not as complicated as criminal proceedings but also noted that termination proceedings could contain confusing expert evidence. He therefore reasoned that trial court discretion should generally govern the appointment of counsel.

43. Santosky v. Kramer, 455 U.S. 745 (1982). Like *Lassiter, Santosky* was decided by a bare majority of the Court, only this time the Court's opinion was written by Justice Blackmun, author of the compelling dissent in *Lassiter*.

44. See, for example, Michael H. v. Gerald D., 491 U.S. 110 (1989); Lehr v. Roberston, 463 U.S. 248 (1983); Caban v. Mohammed, 441 U.S. 380 (1979); Quillon v. Walcott, 434 U.S. 246 (1978); Stanley v. Illinois, 405 U.S. 645 (1972).

45. This view is articulated by Justice Stewart, dissenting in *Caban*, and subsequently approvingly affirmed by the Court in *Lehr,* 463 U.S., at 266, n. 25.

46. Justice Blackmun makes this clear in *Santosky*, 455 U.S., 766, although in Santosky the Court is not applying the compelling state interest test but the less stringent test of Matthews v. Eldridge, 424 U.S. 319, 335 (1976), which requires balancing the three distinct factors of the private interests affected by the proceeding, the risk of error created by the state's chosen procedure, and the countervailing governmental interest supporting the use of the procedure.

47. See, for example, Ohio v. Akron Center for Reproductive Health, U.S. 497 U.S. 1309 (1990); City of Akron v. Akron Center for Reproductive Health, 462 U.S. 416 (1983); Planned Parenthood Ass'n v. Ashcroft, 462 U.S. 476 (1983); H.L. v. Matheson, 450 U.S. 398 (1981); Bellotti v. Baird, 443 U.S. 622 (1979); Planned Parenthood Ass'n. v. Danforth, 428 U.S. 52 (1976). Compare In Re T.W., 551 So. 2d 1186, 1195 (Fla. 1989), which held that under the Florida constitution's explicit privacy provision, minors' constitutional rights are not properly balanced against the relaxed "significant" state interest of federal constitutional law, but can only be overcome by a "compelling" state interest similar to adults.

48. Suzette M. Haynie, Comment, "Biological Parents v. Third Parties: Whose Right to Child Custody is Constitutionally Protected?" 20 *Georgia Law Review* 705 (1986).

49. See Bennett v. Jeffreys, 40, N.Y. 2d 543, 356 N.E. 2d 277, 387 N.Y.S. 2d 821 (1976).

50. Although the student commentator reported that "ten states currently apply a best interests standard to third-party custody disputes," and listed six jurisdictions as explicitly doing so, 20 *Georgia Law Review* 721, the number is now significantly less. For example, the commentator included Connecticut as one of the six jurisdictions that have clearly adopted the best interest standard, ibid., 721, n. 58, citing McGaffin v. Roberts, 193 Conn. 393, 479 A.2d 176 (1984). However, the Connecticut courts have subsequently rejected *McGaffin* in light of the Connecticut statute enacted in 1985 and amended in 1986, which explicitly provides that "in any dispute as to the custody of a minor child involving a parent and a nonparent, there shall be a presumption that it is in the best interest of the child to be in the custody of the parent," Conn. Gen. Stat. 46(b)-56(b). Perez v. Perez, 561 A.2d 907 (Conn. 1989).

51. Comment, "Third Party Custody and Visitation: How Many Ways Should We Slice the Pie?" 1 *Detroit College Law Review* 162 (1989).

52. Isabel Marcus, "Locked In and Locked Out: Reflections on the History of Divorce Law Reform in New York State," 37 *Buffalo Law Review* 375, 386–89 (1988–1989).

53. See, for example, Ellen Lewin, *Lesbian Mothers: Accounts of Gender in American Culture* (Ithaca: Cornell University Press, 1993), an anthropological and sociological study of American lesbian mothers begun in 1977; Del Martin and Phyllis Lyon, *Lesbian/Woman,* 131–63 (San Francisco: Glide, 1972), the chapter entitled "Lesbians Are Mothers Too"; Audre Lorde, "Turning the Beat Around: Lesbian Parenting 1986," in *A Burst of Light,* 39 (Ithaca: Firebrand, 1988), which discusses parenting by lesbians of color; Matile Rothschild, "Life as Improvisation" in Barbara Sang, Joyce Warshaw, and Adrienne J. Smith, eds., *Lesbians at Midlife: The Creative Transition,* 91 (San Francisco: Spinsters, 1991): "There had always been lesbian mothers" but not until the early 1970s did they begin to organize.

See also Sandra Pollack and Jeanne Vaughn, eds., *Politics of the Heart: A Lesbian Parenting Anthology* (Ithaca: Firebrand, 1987); Harriet Alpert, ed., *We Are Everywhere: Writings by and About Lesbian Parents* (Freedom, Cal.: Crossing, 1988).

54. The important published legal works include Paula Ettlebrick, "Who Is a Parent? The Need to Develop a Lesbian Conscious Family Law," 10 *New York Law School Journal of Human Rights* 513 (1993); Nancy Polikoff, "This Child Does Have Two Mothers: Redefining Parenthood to Meet the Needs of Children in Lesbian-Mother and Other Nontraditional Families," 78 *Georgetown Law Journal*

459 (1990); Carmel B. Sella, "When a Mother Is a Legal Stranger to Her Child: The Law's Challenge to the Lesbian Nonbiological Mother," 1 *University of California–Los Angeles Women's Law Journal* 135 (1991).

Much legal work also occurs through litigation, lobbying, education, and support by organizations such as the National Center for Lesbian Rights, Lambda Legal Defense and Education Fund, many local defense committees, ad-hoc committees, and advocacy groups, and countless individual legal workers and lesbians.

55. See, for example, Katharine Bartlett, "Re-Expressing Parenthood," 98 *Yale Law Journal* 293 (1988), which suggests a redirection of the law toward parental status based upon "responsibility and connection"; Janet Dolgin, "Just a Gene: Judicial Assumptions About Parenthood," 40 *UCLA Law Review* 637 (1993), which examines and critiques the underlying biological assumptions in unwed father and surrogate mother cases; John Lawrence Hill, "What Does It Mean to Be a 'Parent'? The Claims of Biology as the Basis for Parental Rights," 66 *New York University Law Review* 353 (1991), which argues for "intention" to replace biology as determinative of parental status.

56. Alison D. v. Virginia M., 572 N.E.2d 27 (N.Y. 1991).

57. For extended discussions of *Alison D.*, see Ettlebrick, "Who Is a Parent?"; and Kimberly Carr, Comment, "Alison D. v. Virginia M.: Neglecting the Best Interests of the Child in a Nontraditional Family," 58 *Brooklyn Law Review* 1021 (1992).

58. In an unreported opinion, the trial court dismissed the petition. The appellate division affirmed, 155 A.D.2d 11, 552 N.Y.S.2d 321 (1990).

59. 572 N.E.2d 29.

60. 572 N.E.2d 30.

61. 471 N.W.2d 202 (Wis. 1991).

62. 471 N.W.2d 204.

63. Ibid., 205–6.

64. Ibid., 206–9.

65. As the court noted, under the Wisconsin statute the ability to bring an action for custody is conferred on a broader basis than the ability to bring an action for visitation.

66. Ibid., 213–14 (Abrahamson dissenting). The other dissenting justice relied solely on the principle that the best interest of the child demands accommodations to a child's rights in a nontraditional relationship. Ibid., 214–15 (Bablitch dissenting).

67. 472 N.W.2d 175 (Minn. App. 1991).

68. Ibid., 177.

69. Ibid., 178.

70. Minn. Stat. 257.022 (2b) (Supp. 1989).

71. 829 P.2d 660 (N.M. Ct. App. 1992).

72. The court also noted that sexual orientation alone is not determinative.

73. Ibid., 665. 533 N.W. 2d 678 (Wis. 1995).

74. Nancy S. v. Michelle G., 228 Cal. App. 3d 831, 279 Cal. Rptr. 212 (Ct. App. 1991).

75. 279 Cal. Rptr. 214.

76. Ibid., 216.

77. Ibid.

78. Ibid., 218, citing Brenda J. Runner, "Protecting a Husband's Parental Rights When His Wife Disputes the Presumption of Legitimacy," 28 *Journal Family Law* 115 (1989–90).

79. Ibid.

80. The court relied upon Polikoff, "This Child Does Have Two Mothers," 464, for its formulation of functional parenthood as including "anyone who maintains a functional parental relationship with a child when a legally recognized parent created that relationship with the intent that the relationship be parental in nature." 279 Cal. Rptr. 219.

81. The court stated that adopting the functional parenthood relationship would necessitate "years of unraveling the complex practical, social and constitutional ramifications of this expansion of the definition of parent." 279 Cal. Rptr. 219.

82. Although the court in *Nancy S.* does not explicitly refer to constitutional doctrine, the court notes that the "critical importance in California of the right to parent has been affirmed and reaffirmed." 279 Cal. Rptr. 217, quoting In re Jenkins, 116 Cal. App. 3d 767, 774 (1981).

83. Z.J.H., 471 N.W.2d 207.

84. Holtzmann v. Knott, 533 N.W.2d 419 (Wis. 1995).

85. In re Angel Lace M., 516 N.W.2d 678 (Wis. 1994).

86. See, for example, Emily C. Patt, "Second Parent Adoption: When Crossing the Marital Barrier Is in a Child's Best Interest," 3 *Berkeley Women's Law Journal* 96 (1987–88); Elizabeth Zuckerman, Comment, "Second Parent Adoption for Lesbian-Parented Families: Legal Recognition of the Other Mother," 19 *U.C. Davis Law Review* (1986).

87. Reported at 17 Fam. L. Rptr. 1523 (D.C. Super. Ct. Fam. Div. August 30, 1991), In re T. & M., considered dual petitions for adoption: one lesbian adopted her lover's biological child conceived through artificial insemination, while the other lesbian adopted her lover's previously adopted child.

88. D.C. Code 16–312(a) (1989).

89. 17 Fam. L. Rptr. 1524. The court stated:

At bottom adoption cases are decided by the application of the best interests of the child standard, and whenever possible other conflicting considerations give way to that standard.

   Here the court concludes that the "cut-off" language need not be read in such a way as to thwart the best interests of these children. This is so because neither of the original legislative purposes underlying the provision has application to this specific factual situation.

Ibid.

90. In re Adoption of Evan, 583 N.Y.S.2d 997 (Surr. Ct. 1992).

91. Matter of Caitlin and Emily, *New York Law Journal* 28 (Monroe Cty Fam. Ct. January 25, 1994).

92. In re Adoption of J.M.G., 632 A.2d 550 (N.J. Super. Ct. 1993).

93. 628 A.2d 1271 (Vt. 1993).

94. Adoption of Tammy, 619 N.E.2d 315 (Mass. 1993). For a brief discussion, see Recent Case, 107 *Harvard Law Review* 751 (1994).

95. Despite variances in the statutes and opinions, the cases are remarkably similar. The most distinguishable case is Tammy, 619 N.E.2d 315, in which the lesbian partners filed a joint petition for adoption under the Massachusetts statute. The Massachusetts Supreme Court allowed the adoption of Tammy by both petitioners: Susan (Tammy's biological mother) and Helen (Tammy's nonlegal mother).

96. For example, in Matter of Dana, *New York Law Journal* (Putnam Cty. Fam. Ct. January 26, 1994), the court stated that although there was no question that the adoption was in the best interest of the child, the "issue can only be reached once the legal predicate is established, i.e., that the party has a legal basis in law to be an adoptive parent." Ibid. The court concluded that the New York legislature's clear intent was "to deny a single person the right to adopt another's child while the natural parent, a single person, retains parental rights." Ibid. The court opined that it was the role of the legislature to change the law, while also noting that "by this decision, the Appellate Courts of this state will have the opportunity to decide whether that avenue is the one." Ibid.

   Additionally, the Supreme Court of Vermont's decision in B.L.V.B. & E.L.V.B., 628 A.2d 1271, reversed a trial court's denial of an adoption.

97. For example, a second-parent adoption would not have been a solution in *Kulla v. McNulty*, 472 N.W.2d 175, in which the lesbian legal mother later married the child's biological father.

98. The court in Nancy S. specifically mentions adoption as a method to prevent the "tragic situation." 279 Cal. Rptr. 219, and n. 8.

99. The trial judges in *Evan* and *J.M.G.* are most affirmative in their antidiscrimination rationale. As the judge stated in *Evan*, the "fact that petitioners maintain an openly lesbian relationship is not a reason to deny adoption," supporting his conclusion with a lengthy footnote considering the social science, psychological, and legal literature. 583 N.Y.S.2d, 1001, n. 1. The judge thereafter considers the law of New York that "a child's best interest is not predicated or controlled by parental sexual orientation," and the adoption statute's explicit rejection of homosexuality as excluding prospective parents. Ibid., 1001–2. Similarly, the judge in *J.M.G.* expansively states that New Jersey law "has recognized that the rights of parents cannot be denied, limited or abridged on the basis of sexual orientation." 632 A.2d, 553.

100. The New Jersey trial court expressed the compelling quality of the analogy, first taking note of a precedent that did not foreclose the possibility that a stepparent could apply to a person who lived with but was not married to the legal parent, 632 A.2d, 553, and n. 3, and then concluding that it

> feels constrained by the state of the law from proclaiming J.M.G. an actual "stepparent," given the fact that same-sex marriages are not legal in this state. However, I am convinced that in this adoption, J.M.G. should be treated as a stepparent as a matter of common sense, and in order to protect the child's interests in maintaining her relationship with her biological mother.

Ibid., 553.

101. Evan, 583 N.Y.S.2d, 998.

102. Caitlin and Emily, *New York Law Journal* 28.

103. J.M.G., 632 A.2d 551.

104. B.L.V.B. & E.L.V.B., 628 A.2d 1272.

105. Tammy, 619 N.E.2d 316.

106. Evan, 583 N.Y.S.2d 998.

107. J.M.G., 632 A.2d 551.

108. Tammy, 619 N.E.2d 316.

109. Caitlin and Emily, *New York Law Journal*, 28.

110. B.L.V.B. & E.L.V.B., 628 A.2d, 1271.

111. 619 N.E.2d 317. In considering the best interests of the child determination required for adoption, the court referred to the practical consequences of the adoption, which "will entitle Tammy to inherit from Helen's family trusts and from Helen and her family." Ibid., 320.

112. This preference is based upon the continuation of the lesbian's desire to parent the child as much as the continuation of both lesbians' desire to co-parent the child, as well as the child's desire to have the lesbians as parents.

113. For example, the Model Uniform Parentage Act, 5(2) applies to married women when the artificial insemination is performed by a licensed physician. For states adopting the act, see 9B Uniform Laws Annotated 287 (Minneapolis: West, 1987). However, more recently, two other related uniform laws have been proposed that change the emphasis on marriage, although these have not been as widely adopted. See The Uniform Status of Children of Assisted Conception, 9B U.L.A. 50–1 (Supp. 1989) and Uniform Putative and Unknown Fathers Act, 9B U.L.A. 16 (Supp. 1989).

For scholarly treatments of the "unmarried" woman's constitutional rights with reference to alternative insemination, including her right to obtain it despite licensed physicians' disinclination to inseminate unmarried women, see Donovan, "The Uniform Parentage Act and Unmarried Motherhood by Choice," 11 *New York University Review of Law and Social Change* 193 (1982–83); Patricia Kern and Kathleen Ridolfi, "The Fourteenth Amendment's Protection of a Woman's Right to Be a Single Parent Through Artificial Insemination by Donor," 7 *Women's Rights Reporter* 251 (1982); Karen Morrisey, "Artificial Insemination by Donor: Practical and Legal Issues Involved in Single Motherhood," 1 *Wisconsin Women's Law Journal* 97 (1985); see also Denise Kaiser, Note, "Artificial Insemination: Donor Rights in Situations Involving Unmarried Recepients," 26 *Journal of Family Law* 793 (1987–1988).

114. C.M. v. C.C., 377 A.2d 821 (N.J. Juv. & Dom. Rel. Ct., 1977). C.C. was apparently not a lesbian. As described by the court, C.M. testified that he and C.C. had been "seeing each other for some time. She wanted a child and wanted him to be the father, but did not want to have intercourse with him before their marriage." Ibid., 821.

115. Ibid., 824–25.

116. For example, in McIntyre v. Couch, 780 P.2d 239 (Or. App. 1989), the court rejected the sperm donor's argument that the state statute should not apply because the statutory requirements of physician intercession and marital status were unsatisfied. The court construed the physician and marital language as not mandatory, remanding the case for determination of the existence of any agreement that the sperm donor assume parental status.

117. 224 Cal. Rptr. 530 (Ct. App. 1986).

118. Ibid., 532.

119. The court justified its deference to the physician requirement of the Uniform Parentage Act as enacted by the California state legislature with refer-

ence to the health reasons and the need for the presence of a "professional third party such as a physician" to "create a formal, documented structure for the donor-recepient relationship." Ibid., 534–35. The court rejected the legal mother's argument that the marital distinction in another statute not explicitly requiring a physician in cases of the artificial insemination of married women violated her constitutional right to equal protection as guaranteed by the fourteenth amendment to the United States Constitution because a married woman and an unmarried woman are not similarly situated for equal protection purposes because the "marital relationship invokes a long-recognized social policy of preserving the integrity of marriage." Ibid., 536.

120. Ibid.

121. Ibid.

122. 599 N.Y.S.2d 377 (Fam. Ct. 1993).

123. Perhaps the best illustration of this attention and dissension are the letters written as a response to the description of the case, entitled "Judge Denies Parental Status to Gay Sperm Donor," which appeared in *Lesbian/Gay Law Notes* 33 (May 1993). Although *Lesbian/Gay Law Notes* does not regularly feature letters, the next issue contained thirteen letters from members of the lesbian and gay legal community, including the attorney for Thomas S., expressing with various viewpoints.

In another forum, the spring 1994 Feminism and Legal Theory Conference on parenting included two papers devoted substantially to the case, Susan Boyd, "Familial Disputes? Sperm Donors, Lesbian Mothers, and Child Custody Law"; and Nancy Polikoff, "Adjudicating Paternity Claims in the Context of Alternative Families."

The case is also discussed in Victoria Brownworth, "Family in Crisis: When AI Donors Claim Fatherhood," 4 *DENUEVE: The Lesbian Magazine* 44 (April 1994).

124. 599 NYS2d 378–9.

125. The court notes that both Thomas S. and Sandra R., the nonlegal mother, are attorneys. Ibid., 378.

126. Ibid., 380.

127. Ibid., 382.

128. *Lesbian/Gay Law Notes* 33 (May 1993).

129. Letter from Lesley Yulkowski, *Lesbian/Gay Law Notes* 2 (June 1993).

130. Letter from Ann Philbin, ibid., 4.

131. Letter from Emily Olshansky, ibid., 3.

132. As Professor Arthur Leonard stated in his reply to the letters criticizing his digest of the opinion in *Lesbian/Gay Law Notes* (June 1993), "I recently wrote a book for which I immersed myself in scores of court opinions on lesbian and gay

issues. On the basis of that experience, I hesitate to accept the official findings of 'fact' in court opinions as conclusive of reality. . . . We should view court 'findings' in gay cases with some skepticism." Ibid., 4. My own experience in researching lesbian and gay judicial decisions mirrors Leonard's, and thus I agree wholeheartedly. However, I would not limit my skepticism of "facts" as "conclusive of reality" to the legal realm or confine it to discernable biases such as homphobia, which often operate in judicial opinions, given the tremendous power and popularization of recent theory disputing such a correlation. Thus, I depart from any proferred model of "intentionality" based upon "conduct" rooted in factual conclusions to determine parenthood.

133. Victoria Brownworth reports on a decision in a similar case in California in which the trial court granted the sperm donor joint custody. Brownworth, "Family in Crisis," 45.

134. See, for example, Phyllis Chesler, *Mothers on Trial,* 66–94 (New York: McGraw-Hill, 1986), which estimates that 70 percent of women lose custody if seriously challenged by men.

135. For a discussion of some of the similarities and differences between lesbians and gay men in custody decisions pursuant to marital relations, see Jenni Millbank, "Lesbian Mothers, Gay Fathers: Sameness and Difference," 2 *Australian Gay and Lesbian Law Journal* 21 (1992).

136. 599 NYS2d 381. This contention is legally incorrect under New York Law. While adjudication of paternity may have some effects under other statutory schemes such as intestate sucession, only Thomas S.'s marriage to the biological mother, Robin Y., would render the child "legitimate" under the definition of legitimatcy contained in New York Domestic Relations Law 24.

137. As Susan Boyd observed, this argument is an invocation of the entire patriarchal history of relationships with children. Susan Boyd, "Familial Disputes?" 130. Even the United States Supreme Court has implicitly rejected such notions by according state statutory classifications based upon legitimacy a more than rational basis scrutiny under the equal protection clause of the fourteenth amendment, see Lalli v. Lalli, 439 U.S. 259 (1978); Trimble v. Gordon, 430 U.S. 762 (1977).

138. See, for example, B. Drummond Ayres, Jr., "Judge's Decision in Custody Case Raises Concerns," *New York Times,* Sept. 9, 1993, A16; Elizabeth Kastor, "The Battle for the Boy in the Middle: Little Tyler's Mom Is a Lesbian, So Grandma Got to Take Him Away," *Washington Post,* October 1, 1993; Bill Hewitt, "Fighting for Tyler," *People,* September 27, 1993, 71.

139. Transcript of Hearing, 9–10, In re: Kenneth Tyler Doustou, Pamela Kay Bottoms v. Sharon Lynne Bottoms (Circuit Court of County of Henrico,

Virginia) (No. CH93JA0517–00). On file on with the author; hereafter Bottoms Transcript.

140. Bottoms Transcript, 195–96.

141. Ibid., 196.

142. Ibid.

143. Ibid., 197.

144. See, Opening Brief for Appellant, In re: Kenneth Tyler Doustou, Pamela Kay Bottoms v. Sharon Lynne Bottoms (Court of Appeals of Virginia) (Record No. 1930–93–2). On file on with the author. See also, Brief of Amicus Curiae National Center for Lesbian Rights, et al., In re: Kenneth Tyler Doustou, Pamela Kay Bottoms v. Sharon Lynne Bottoms (Court of Appeals of Virginia) (Record No. 1930–93–2). On file with the author.

145. Roe v. Roe, 324 S.E.2d 691 (Va. 1985).

For a discussion of the different standards relating to lesbianism as applied in custody cases between parents, see Ruthann Robson, *Lesbian (Out)Law: Survival Under the Rule of Law* (Ithaca: Firebrand, 1992), 130–34.

146. Mason v. Moon, 385 S.E.2d 242 Va. App. 1989), cited in Bottoms Transcript, 196. The trial judge in Bottoms refers to the "extraordinary" nature required by "the Mason case," but does not discuss the facts of the case.

147. Mason, 385 S.E.2d 246.

148. 569 So.2d 1181 (Miss. 1990).

149. Ibid., 1183.

150. Ibid., 1184.

151. Ibid.

152. 569 So.2d 1185 (Roberston, dissenting). As the court's opinion states, the legal mother last worked in a convenience store; she lived with her children and her lover in a trailer; she testified that "she sometimes slept until 11 A.M.," and there was conflicting testimony about "the children being outdoors during cold weather with inadequate clothing." 569 So.2d, 1182, 1183. The legal mother also testified that conditions at the trailer "were a lot better" now than when her husband, the grandparents' son, had lived there. Ibid., 1183.

153. Both the majority and dissenting justices agree that the standard in Mississippi is a presumption in favor of the legal parent that third parties can overcome only upon a clear showing that the parent has abandoned the child; or that the conduct of the parent is so immoral as to be a detriment to the child; or that the parent is unfit mentally or otherwise to have custody of the child. 569 So.2d, 1184, citing Rodgers v. Rodgers, 274 So.2d, 671, 673 (Miss. 1973); Milam v. Milam, 509 So.2d 864, 866 (Miss. 1987); 569 So.2d, 1186 (Robertson dissenting), citing Luttrell v. Kneisley, 427 So.2d, 1384, 1387 (Miss. 1983).

154. Such an approach would certainly be consistent with the testimony of Pamela Bottoms. When asked by her attorney to tell the court why she believed she should have custody of the child rather than her daughter, she stated, "Tyler is a bundle of joy. You have to know him. He shouldn't be raised by two lesbians. He is being taught to call Sharon's lover 'Da Da.' I can do more for Tyler financially. He is going to be mentally . . . " Testimony of Pamela Kay Bottoms, Bottoms Transcript, 53.

155. Testimony of Kay Bottoms, Bottoms Transcript, 57. The trial judge's oral ruling contains a reference to this "cursing" and "standing in the corner" as "other evidence" of the child being afflicted. Bottoms Transcript, 197.

156. Testimony of Sharon Bottoms, Bottoms Transcript, 17.

157. The trial judge stated, "The mother's conduct is illegal. It is a class 6 felony in the Commonwealth of Virginia." Bottoms Transcript, 196.

158. The paternal grandparents agreed that the children's father "should not have custody due to his financial situation and his drinking problem." 569 So.2d, 1183. As the dissenting justice declares,

> It is important that An's estranged husband makes no claim to custody. His closet is filled with as many skeletons as hers, if not more. David White is a career drunk who, after An threw him out, took up with a live-in girlfriend of his own. His financial neglect of his children has been massive. Indeed, most of An's neglect is attributable to the employment she has been forced to pursue because of David's irresponsibility.

Ibid., 1186 (Robertson dissenting).

159. In this instance this may have been beneficial. Sharon Bottoms testified that she had been sexually abused by her mother's male partner from the time she was about twelve years old until she left home at seventeen or eighteen. She further testified that this man lived with Kay Bottoms for sixteen years, leaving only "about two weeks" before the first custody hearing regarding Sharon Bottoms's child. Testimony of Sharon Bottoms, Bottoms Transcript, 20–25. Interestingly, when Sharon Bottoms told her mother, Kay Bottoms, about the sexual abuse by the male partner, it seems that Kay Bottoms did not initially believe her daughter. Ibid., 23–24. However, Pamela Bottoms excluded her male partner from the house on the advice of the attorney she consulted after Sharon had refused to allow the child to visit while the male partner was present; Pamela Bottoms also decided to petition for custody. Testimony of Pamela Bottoms, Bottoms Transcript, 62.

160. For example, in Gerald D. & Margaret D. v. Peggy R., 1980 WL 20452 (Del. Fam. Ct. 1980), although the court noted that the legal mother had been liv-

ing with her parents and the grandparents participated in all aspects of the child's life, it applied the standard in disputes between a parent and a third party (which the court articulated as "best interest determination but any third party seeking such custody bears a heavy burden of persuasion") to award custody to the lesbian legal mother.

In another case the Massachusetts Supreme Court reversed a trial judge's denial of the lesbian mother's petition to remove guardianship from an unrelated third party, holding that the mother's actions did not consititute abandonment and that her lesbianism did not render her unfit. Bezio v. Patenaude, 410 N.E.2d 1207 (Mass. 1980).

161. The state as third party, notably as a party in abuse, neglect, dependency, delinquency, or deprivation cases, in which the state assumes custody of the child or awards custody to another person, is beyond the scope of this article. However, it is important to note that lesbianism does occur as an issue in such proceedings. See In re Breisch, 434 A.2d 815 (Pa. Super Ct. 1981); see also In re J.A. & L.A., 601 A.2d 69 (D.C. 1991). Further, a grandmother reportedly contacted state authorities and charged her daughter and her daughter's lover with abusing the daughter's child, although the mother later posted bail for her daughter. See Ingrid Ricks, "A Family Affair," 653 *Advocate* 49, April 19, 1994.

11. Neither Sexy Nor Reasonable

1. Richard A. Posner, *Sex and Reason* (Cambridge: Harvard University Press, 1992).

2. Ibid., 91, 99, 106, 123, 294, 304–5.

3. Ibid., 5–7.

4. Ibid., 106.

5. See Perez v. State, 491 S.W. 672 (Tex. Crim. App. 1973).

6. Posner, *Sex and Reason,* 2–3.

7. Ibid., 91.

8. Ibid.

9. Philip Blumstein and Pepper Schwartz, *American Couples: Money, Work, Sex* (New York: William Morrow, 1983).

10. Posner, *Sex and Reason,* 306, n. 41.

11. Ibid., 306.

12. Ibid., 307.

13. Ibid., 21. Posner also writes: "Vaginal intercourse is a close substitute for sodomy, but one available only to heterosexuals." Ibid., 291.

14. Marilyn Frye, "Lesbian 'Sex,' " in Jeffner Allen, ed., *Lesbian Philosophies*

and Cultures, 305, 307–8 (Albany: State University of New York Press, 1990). This essay originally appeared in 35 *Sinister Wisdom* (1988) and is reprinted in Marilyn Frye, *Willful Virgin,* 109 (Freedom, Cal.: Crossing, 1992).

15. Frye, "Lesbian Sex."

16. As stated, I do not adopt Posner's methodology of attempting to falsify Posner's factual conclusions and thereby discredit Posner's theories of lesbians within his theories of sex.

17. Frye, "Lesbian 'Sex,' " 307.

18. Posner, *Sex and Reason,* 70, 300.

19. Although Posner explicitly states that the law and economics portion of his theory is not dependent on an acceptance of sociobiological theories, ibid., 110, much of his evaluation of benefits and costs are linked to "facts" supported by sociobiological rationales.

20. Ibid., 305.

21. Ibid., 308.

22. A portion of the omitted text is a parenthetical referencing of Foucault's well-known formulation of homosexuality as identity being formulated in the nineteenth century, citing *History of Sexuality,* 1:43, 101 (New York: Viking, 1978). Another portion of the omitted text attempts an analogy between Jewish identity and "homosexual" identity, accomplishing only an offensive digression:

> Jews are conscious of the advantages of converting, changing their name, and otherwise obliterating as far as possible the traces of their ancestry; and many Jews might if asked say that they would rather have been born into another group. But most of them do not convert, because (I conjecture) their being Jewish is part of their identity, so conversion would have a taste of death to it—like replacing one's body with another, albeit handsomer, one.

Posner, *Sex and Reason,* 308.

23. Ibid.

24. Ibid., 308–9.

25. Ibid., 87.

26. Ibid., 99, 101–2.

27. Ibid., 126.

28. Ibid., 128, 294–95.

29. Ibid., 123.

30. Ibid., 299.

31. Ibid., 179.

12. To Market, to Market: Considering Class

1. Pierre Bourdieu, "The Market for Symbolic Goods," 14 *Poetics* 13 (1985).

2. John Guillory, *Cultural Capital: The Problem of Literary Canon Formation,* 13 (Chicago: University of Chicago Press, 1993).

3. See, for example, Thomas Ross, "The Rhetoric of Poverty: Their Immorality, Our Helplessness," 79 *Georgetown Law Journal* 1499 (1991), which notes that the creation of the abstract category of the poor is a rhetorical device employed by the courts to abnormalize the poor.

4. Stephen Edgell, *Class* 121 (New York: Routledge, 1993).

5. Ibid.

6. The commitment to the eradication of poverty, however, is obviously a different matter. As Professor Thomas Ross points out, Americans commonly hold ideas that poverty is inherent, irremedial, eternal ("There have always been poor people"), the result of abstract forces (the "politics of distribution"), or a demonstration of moral weakness on the part of those people who are poor, yet "all that has ever been required to eliminate poverty is a redistribution of wealth." Ross, "The Rhetoric of Poverty," 1509–10.

7. Danae Clark, "Commodity Lesbianism," 25:6 *Camera Obscura* 181 (1991).

8. For example, one suggestion has been to eliminate affirmative action based upon minority racial status and replace it with affirmative action based upon economic disadvantage. Richard Kahlenberg, "Class, Not Race," *New Republic* 21, April 3, 1995. Such suggestions impose a divisive either/or model of access as well as promoting false notions of scarcity.

9. For a discussion of the ways in which the law operated on "gay bars" in the 1950s, see Joan Howarth, "First and Last Chance: Looking for Lesbians in Fifties Bar Cases," 5 *Southern California Journal of Law and Women's Studies* 153 (1995).

10. See generally, Grant Luckenbill, *Untold Millions: Gay and Lesbian Markets in America* (New York: Harper Business/HarperCollins, 1995).

11. Clark, "Commodity Lesbianism," 193.

12. See, for example, Jeff Barge, "Moving Out and Upward: Lesbians Attract Marketers," *Crains Small Business* 9, February 1995.

13. bell hooks, "Spending Culture: Marketing the Black Underclass," in *Outlaw Culture: Resisting Representations,* 145, 149 (New York: Routledge, 1994).

14. Ibid., 150.

15. Ibid., 148.

16. Robyn Wiegman, "Introduction: Mapping the Lesbian Postmodern," in Laura Doan, ed., *The Lesbian Postmodern,* 1, 3 (New York: Columbia University Press, 1994).

17. Ibid., 3–4.

18. Sue O'Sullivan, "Girls Who Kiss Girls and Who Cares?" in Diane Hamer and Belinda Budge, eds., *The Good, the Bad, and the Gorgeous: Popular Culture's Romance with Lesbianism,* 78, 90 (San Francisco, London: Pandora/HarperCollins, 1994). Reprinted in Sue O'Sullivan, *I Used to Be Nice* (London: Cassell, 1996).

19. Ibid., 91. Sullivan notes, however, that just as the strident lesbian politico is a stereotype, so too is the lesbian who is young and "provocatively attractive and fashionable." "Both images are fantastical; neither image corresponds any more to the multilayered realities of lesbians' lives than any other media caricatures of women do." Ibid., 92.

20. As bell hooks writes, "When the chips are down it is usually the black folks who already have some degree of class privilege who are most able to exploit for individual gain the market in blackness as a commodity." hooks, "Spending Culture," 147.

21. According to Robyn Wiegman, "We have little alternative action but to participate." The "commodification of the lesbian" is "not a check we deposit by choosing to sign our name on the back. *That* signature will always precede us." Wiegman, "Introduction," 4–5.

22. As Suzanne Goldberg notes,

Take Back Cincinnati, a group organized to promote a voter initiative to amend Cincinnati's charter to exclude lesbians, gay men, and bisexuals from protection against discrimination, explained in its literature that a "group wanting true minority rights must show that it is discriminated against to the point that its members cannot earn average income, get an adequate education or enjoy a fulfilling cultural life."

Suzanne Goldberg, "Lessons from the Cultural Wars: Lesbians and the Religious Right," unpublished ms.

23. M. V. Lee Badgett's work demonstrates that gay or lesbian status (defined by sexual behavior) results in a negative economic impact at a rate of 11 percent to 27 percent for men and 11 percent to 14 percent for women. M. V. Lee Bagett, "Economic Evidence of Sexual Orientation Discrimination," in Amy Gluckman and Besty Reed, eds., *Homo/Economics: Capitalism, Community, and Lesbian and Gay Life in the United States* (New York: Routledge, 1995).

The Lesbian/Gay/Bisexual Policy Network (c/o Professor Badgett, School of Public Affairs, University of Maryland, College Park, MD 20742) is one of the few groups attempting to research and disseminate accurate economic information about sexual minorities in the United States.

24. John D'Emilio, "Capitalism and Gay Identity," in *Making Trouble: Essays*

on *Gay History, Politics, and the University,* 8 (New York: Routledge, 1992); emphasis added.

Other important works that discuss the relationship between economics and the formation of lesbian or gay identities and communities include Allan Berubé, *Coming Out Under Fire: The History of Gay Men and Women in World War Two* (New York: Free Press, 1990); Lillian Faderman, *Odd Girls and Twilight Lovers: A History of Lesbian Life in Twentieth-Century America* (New York: Columbia University Press, 1991); Elizabeth Lapovsky Kennedy and Madeline Davis, *Boots of Leather, Slippers of Gold: The History of a Lesbian Community* (New York: Routledge, 1993); Esther Newton, *Cherry Grove, Fire Island: Sixty Years in America's First Gay and Lesbian Community* (Boston: Beacon, 1993).

25. Jeffrey Escoffier, "The Political Economy of the Closet: Notes Toward an Economic History of Gay and Lesbian Life Before Stonewall," in Gluckman and Reed, *Homo/Economics*.

13. Lesbian Sex in a Law School Classroom

1. Marilyn Frye, "Lesbian 'Sex,' " in *Willful Virgin,* 109–19 (Freedom, Cal.: Crossing, 1992).

2. Juliet Flower MacCannell, "Resistance to Sexual Theory," in Donald Morton and Mas'ud Zavarzadeh, eds., *Theory/Pedagogy/Politics,* 66–67 (Urbana and Chicago: University of Illinois Press, 1991).

3. Ibid., quoting Jane Gallop, "The Immoral Teachers," 63 *Yale French Studies* 117–28 (1982).

4. John Guillory, *Cultural Capital,* 182 (Chicago: University of Chicago Press, 1993).

5. Jane Gurko, "Sexual Energy in the Classroom," in Margaret Cruikshank, ed., *Lesbian Studies: Present and Future,* 25, 29 (Old Westbury, N.Y.: Feminist Press, 1982).

6. As expressed by Jane Gurko:

The problem lies in the fact that any noncoercive power imbalance tends to trigger romantic fantasies on both sides of an unequal relationship, regardless of the sexes involved. It's almost automatic in the classroom: the teacher becomes an object of hero worship, and conversely as "hero," indulges in ego-inflating fantasies of power over her "worshipper."

Gurko, "Sexual Energy in the Classroom," 27.

7. Each weekly unit is presented as a question: "Does 'gender' equal 'sex'?" "Is consent limited to adults?" "Should the law regulate sexual representation

(pornography)?" "Does the law adequately distinguish between disease and sex?" "Are sexual minorities 'minorities'?" "Should the law regulate sexual commerce (prostitution)?" "How important are the legal distinctions between sexuality and reproduction?"

8. This problem is not unique to pedagogical situations. For example, the poet Chrystos addresses the problem of publishing lesbian erotic poetry in Chrystos, *In Her I Am* (Vancouver: Press Gang Publishers, 1993).

9. Ruthann Robson, "Crimes of Lesbian Sex," in Ruthann Robson, *Lesbian (Out)Law: Survival Under the Rule of Law* (Ithaca: Firebrand, 1992). The chapter also appears in an anthology, William Rubenstein, ed., *Lesbians, Gay Men, and the Law* (New York: Free Press, 1993; Minneapolis: West, 1995).

10. People v. Livermore, 9 Mich. App. 47, 155 N.W. 2d 711 (1968).

11. While the class does contain a segment on incest, my concern in this segment was not incest. I therefore thought that interjecting incest through the facts of a case and then stating that the incest was irrelevant to the class segment was problematic. The case, however, raises the interesting issue of whether or not penetration is required in convictions for lesbian sex. Salyers v. State, 755 P.2d 97 (Cr. Ct. App. Okl. 1988).

Index

Sally Munt, editor, *New Lesbian Criticism: Literary and Cultural Readings*

Timothy F. Murphy and Suzanne Poirier, editors, *Writing AIDS: Gay Literature, Language, and Analysis*

Noreen O'Connor and Joanna Ryan, *Wild Desires and Mistaken Identities: Lesbianism and Psychoanalysis*

Don Paulson with Roger Simpson, *An Evening in the Garden of Allah: A Gay Cabaret in Seattle*

Judith Roof, *Come As You Are: Sexuality and Narrative*

Judith Roof, *A Lure of Knowledge: Lesbian Sexuality and Theory*

Claudia Schoppmann, *Days of Masquerade: Life Stories of Lesbians During the Third Reich*

Alan Sinfield, *The Wilde Century: Effeminacy, Oscar Wilde, and the Queer Moment*

Jane McIntosh Snyder, Lesbian Desire in the Lyrics of Sappho

Chris Straayer, *Deviant Eyes, Deviant Bodies: Sexual Re-Orientations in Film and Video*

Dwayne C. Turner, *Risky Sex: Gay Men and HIV Prevention*

Thomas Waugh, *Hard to Imagine: Gay Male Eroticism in Photography and Film from Their Beginnings to Stonewall*

Kath Weston, *Families We Choose: Lesbians, Gays, Kinship*

Kath Weston, *Render Me, Gender Me: Lesbians Talk Sex, Class, Color, Nation, Studmuffins . . .*

Carter Wilson, *Hidden in the Blood: A Personal Investigation of AIDS in the Yucatán*